Can Latin America Compete?

Can Latin America Compete?
Confronting the Challenges of Globalization

Edited by
Jerry Haar and John Price

palgrave
macmillan

First published in 2008 by
PALGRAVE MACMILLAN™
175 Fifth Avenue, New York, N.Y. 10010 and
Houndmills, Basingstoke, Hampshire, England RG21 6XS.
Companies and representatives throughout the world.

PALGRAVE MACMILLAN is the global academic imprint of the Palgrave Macmillan
division of St. Martin's Press, LLC and of Palgrave Macmillan Ltd. Macmillan® is
a registered trademark in the United States, United Kingdom and other countries.
Palgrave is a registered trademark in the European Union and other countries.

ISBN-13: 978-1-4039-7543-0
ISBN-10: 1-4039-7543-4

Library of Congress Cataloging-in-Publication Data

Can Latin America compete?: confronting the challenges of globalization / Jerry Haar
and John Price, eds.
     p. cm.
   Includes bibliographical references and index.
   ISBN 1-4039-7543-4 (alk. paper)
   1. Latin America—Economic policy. 2. Latin America—Economic conditions—1982–
3. Competition—Latin America. 4. Globalization—Economic aspects—Latin America.
I. Haar, Jerry, 1947– II. Price, John, 1966 Nov. 29–

   HC125.C3125 2007
   382'.1—dc22

                                                                           2007009455

A catalogue record for this book is available from the British Library.

Design by Macmillan India Ltd.

First edition: February 2008

10 9 8 7 6 5 4 3 2

Printed in the United States of America.

This book is dedicated to the industrious and creative entrepreneurs across Latin America whose intense work ethic, strength of purpose, and perseverance enable them and the economies that they lead to succeed in spite of the obstacles strewn in their path by government and society.

Contents

List of Figures and Tables

Figures

Tables

Foreword

The World Economic Forum's latest assessment of Latin America's competitiveness provides a mixed picture: good growth and improvements in many of the pillars of competitiveness, but not good enough when compared to other leading emerging markets. And this is what *competitiveness* is all about: a global contest where progress is not enough if one falls behind the pack. Winning the competitiveness race brings huge rewards: the attention and investment of the world's leading companies as well as the migration of innovative brainpower. Where finite and mobile human and financial capital meet, growth and jobs are created.

There are numerous reasons for the incomplete and uneven performance record of the Americas during the last two decades. By the counting of coeditors Jerry Haar and John Price in this book, there are more than a dozen reasons to be precise. To tackle them all comprehensively, a total of 21 expert authors contributed to this rich and compelling volume. Each of 14 competitiveness drivers were analyzed to understand how and why they shape economies, document successes and failures in the region, and provide tangible solutions for government and business going forward. The key competitiveness factors analyzed in this book include education and training; infrastructure and logistics; capital markets and consumer credit; technology and innovation; tax, labor, and regulatory reform; the rule of law; and public safety.

Wisely, Haar and Price place great emphasis on innovation as well as the technology gap confronting the Americas, a gap that separates countries within the region and even regions within each country. Apart from portions of the Brazilian economy, no Latin American country can yet call itself an innovation economy, when measured by global standards. Business and government are waking up to the extreme disadvantage of economies such as those in Latin America with low R&D investment and few patents awarded. Latin America has traditionally competed on the basis of its abundance of natural resources but the volatility and lack of depth inherent in a commodity-driven economy leave the region vulnerable. The road out of that trap must be led by innovation.

Companies such as Merck believe that the innovation imperative is the only way to compete efficiently and effectively in a global marketplace and improve the standard of living of the population. However, the region must focus on the *prerequisites* of innovation and competitiveness if it is to succeed; and that would include enabling conditions such as education, health, and the rule of law. An educated and healthy workforce is indispensable to growth, development, and competitiveness. In fact, as many scholars and development experts have pointed out, health should be viewed as an *input* or *driver* of economic growth rather than just the result of improved economic conditions.

Over a century of pan-regional health initiatives by governments have helped Latin America to improve its health. Continued progress requires a legal environment that enables the genius locked within the region to leverage ideas and develop new health solutions that are best suited to Latin America. A commitment to open markets is essential to the transfer of technology and ideas to the region and investment by global health sector firms. Expanding consumer credit across the region enables much of the population to access private sector–supplied health solutions that formerly were out of reach. These are the building blocks of a healthy society, a key contributor to competitiveness.

Health, education, and the rule of law comprise a universal prescription of competitiveness that is hardly unique to Latin America. Some of the world's best examples of progress are found outside of the region, providing both enviable and instructive best practices. Singapore, Slovenia, South Korea, Chile, and Ireland are all shining examples of improved competitiveness. The many benefits of their progress include healthier and more productive societies.

Can Latin America Compete? is a timely, relevant, and engaging work that provides a report card on how the region is confronting the competitive challenges of globalization and the choices before Latin America to achieve progress in the lives of its citizens.

Tadeu Alves
President Latin America Human Health
Merck & Co. Inc.

Preface

Latin America today is a paradox. On the one hand, foreign investors and portfolio managers are gravitating rapidly toward Asia, treating the Americas like a jilted lover. Over half a million manufacturing jobs from Mexico and Central America have followed suit. Authoritarian rule and nationalizations, widespread poverty, income inequality, and gang violence, and poor infrastructure coupled with low educational achievement and technology diffusion paint a grim picture of the region. On the other hand, stable fiscal and monetary policies, unrelenting growth of exports—both traditional and nontraditional—along with healthy consumer spending and the global reach of *multilatinas* such as Odebrecht (Brazil), América Móvil (Mexico), and Carvajal (Colombia), and steady progress toward institutional reforms provide solid reasons for optimism.

The picture is mixed but the question remains: Can Latin America compete?

In Latin America, competitiveness is more than just a political buzzword. It is the primary concern of business, labor, government, and citizens at large. The traditional political paradigm in Latin America has been defined by how far a country embraces or rejects the economic model vigorously promoted by the United States and its interlocutors, the IMF, World Bank, and IDB. More evolved political thinking in Latin America is now concerned with competitiveness, specifically how the one region of the world most exposed to globalization will compete with Chinese, Indian, and Eastern European labor; Russian, African, Canadian, and Australian resources; and American capital.

Electronics assemblers in Nogales, Mexico, today fear Chinese labor much more than any economic threat from the United States. Guatemalan textile plants are closing as their Korean owners move production to Indonesia. Colombian flower exporters are losing U.S. contracts to African cultivators. Bolivian natural gas competes for investment with Australia. In none of these scenarios is the U.S. bogeyman in sight. Latin American political leaders must now focus on competing, not because Washington tells them to but because their own businesses, labor unions, and voters compel them to do so. More than at any time in its history, Latin America is on its own. This realization is equally alarming and exciting.

The Latin American commodity-led boom that began suddenly in 2003 lifted the region out of a deep economic hole and provided an unexpected windfall to business and government. This boost of fortune provides a welcome opportunity to better prepare Latin America for global competition. The region's rising currency rates brought on by the export surge turns competitiveness from a theoretical discussion into a life-and-death issue for dozens of marginal industries such as textiles, electronics, and auto parts. In 2006, Latin America conducted 11 presidential elections. Three of them were won with old-school anti-American rhetoric. The other eight elections, representing 94 percent of the voting economies, chose a leader who promised to improve the competitiveness of their country by untying the noose of inefficient government, investing in education and infrastructure, and cleaning up corrupt legal systems.

Latin America is engaged in a full-scale debate on how to improve its competitiveness. The discussion is self-initiated and vigorously argued by voters and congress democratically empowered as never before. Like in all political debates, it comes as laden with wild rhetoric as it does with reasoned logic. Latin Americans can take solace in the knowledge that their dilemma is shared by most of the world and that simple solutions there are not. Likewise, the worldwide race to compete offers a global array of solutions. Tax reform in Poland, customs efficiency in Taiwan, IT technical training in India, and infrastructure investment in China are all best practice examples that emerged from markets that are or were more economically challenged than Latin America.

When the concept for this book first took root in 2005 and was shared by some early collaborators, it became painfully obvious that the issue of competitiveness was growing in importance and would outlive any media buzz that the *politicos* wanted to thrust upon it. Competitiveness is an issue with endless authors in North America, Europe, and Japan, but its arrival in Latin America is more recent and still evolving. It is the hope and ambition of all of this work's authors that *Can Latin America Compete?* will contribute in some small way to addressing the region's new challenge and will spawn more debate inside the region.

The book is written for all those concerned with Latin American competitiveness, starting with businesses that compete in the region, invest in the region, and trade to and from the region. The health and welfare of Latin American business will determine the region's future more than any political idea or leader. Private businesses in Latin America bear the tax bill, provide almost all new employment, lead all sources of investment, and more than in any other emerging market provide basic services from telephony to electricity.

The contributing authors of this book together form a rich mosaic of backgrounds and experience and include entrepreneurs, academics, policymakers, advisers, and journalists. Every one of them dedicates their professional career in one form or another to Latin America. Their desire to write this book stems not only from their credentials but also from their passion to witness the creation of a modern, competitive, and democratic Latin America, strong enough to fend for itself and define its own destiny.

Gratitude

Writing and coediting a book like this that tackles a broad and controversial subject is akin to marshaling troops across a mud field. As near as the target appears, getting there is far more work than one could ever plan for, and at the same time, concluding the journey is that much more gratifying. We are deeply appreciative, first of all, to one another for the commitment, determination, collegiality, and support that this arduous project required. We would also like to thank our authors, who, as leading experts in their respective fields, could have spent their time on more lucrative ventures but whose belief in this project compelled them to be so generous with their time.

John owes a debt of gratitude to his colleagues at InfoAmericas, Jan Smith and Tricia Juhn, who actually believed him when he told them that writing a chapter would neither cut into their day jobs nor affect their sleeping patterns. In the field of Latin American crime and security, John would like to mention the invaluable investigative reporting of Sam Logan who lives and breathes the subject each day from his office in Rio de Janeiro. In the area of banking reform, he owes much thanks for the pinch-hitting effort of Christopher Humphrey, a talented writer and analyst, and an old friend. Last, but certainly not least, he wishes to thank his loving wife, Ulli, and son, Samuel, who lived too many mornings and evenings without his presence—theirs is an immeasurable sacrifice.

Jerry is very grateful to Dean Joyce Elam of the College of Business Administration at Florida International University (FIU) and Edward Glab, director of the Knight-Ridder Center for Excellence in Management in the college, for their support. Albert Fishlow and Thomas Trebat of Columbia University's Institute for Latin American Studies, and Leslie Bethell, director of the Centre for Brazilian Studies at the University of Oxford, provided a "home" for two summers and an invaluable infrastructure for research and writing. He thanks his family, especially his wife, Barbara, for her understanding and patience—and great soup—during the arduous tasks of researching and writing.

Both of us are extraordinarily thankful to Merck, Inc., especially Clemens Caicedo, Tadeu Alves, and Grey Warner, for their generous financial and moral support without which this opus may not have seen the light of day. Deanna Salpietra of the Knight-Ridder Center for Excellence in Management in FIU's College of Business Administration provided invaluable research and editing assistance; this book could never have seen the light of day without her energy and dedication. We are very grateful to Professor Timothy M. Shaw of the University of London and editor of the Palgrave Macmillan Series in International Political Economy for approving the book project and to Kate Ankofski and Smitha Manoj and the staff of Macmillan India Ltd who were very responsive and helpful throughout the process of manuscript submission through final acceptance.

Notes on Contributors

Isabel Bortagaray is a doctoral candidate at the School of Public Policy, Georgia Institute of Technology. Her research interest is science and technology policy, with a particular focus on economic and social development. Her PhD dissertation is titled "The Building of Agricultural Biotechnology Capabilities in Small Countries: The Cases of Costa Rica, New Zealand and Uruguay." She studied sociology at the undergraduate level and worked for five years in the area of science and technology and development before embarking on her doctoral studies. Her published work includes numerous articles and technical reports.

Mauricio Carrizosa is sector manager for economic policy operations in the Latin America and the Caribbean Regional Office of the World Bank. He obtained his BA degree from the University of the Andes in Bogota and his MA degree in economics from the University of Chicago in 1974. He formerly held positions in academia, research institutions, and government in Colombia. He has authored several articles, primarily on fiscal and monetary policy, and one book on capital market development. His recent work at the bank has focused on macroeconomics, fiscal policy, and trade.

Tamara Ortega Goodspeed is an associate with the education program of the Partnership for Educational Revitalization in the Americas (PREAL), and coordinates PREAL's national and regional report card efforts. She holds a master's degree in public affairs with a focus on international development from Princeton University and an undergraduate degree in political science from Yale University. Prior to working at PREAL, she served as a Peace Corps volunteer, English teacher in Equatorial Guinea, and as a family educator for a local literacy project in Nebraska.

José Luis Guasch is currently senior regional adviser for the Latin America and Caribbean region at the World Bank in Washington, D.C. He has also been professor of economics at the University of California, San Diego, since 1980. He has written extensively for leading economic and finance journals and is the author of several books about Latin America and the Caribbean. Some of his most recent publications are *Labor Markets: The Unfinished Reform in Latin America and the Caribbean* (Washington, D.C.: World Bank, 1999), and *Closing the Gap in Education and Technology in Latin America* (Washington, D.C.: World Bank, 2003), of which he is a coauthor. He holds a PhD in economics from Stanford University.

Jerry Haar is a professor of management and international business and associate dean Management in the College of Business Administration at Florida International University. He was formerly associated with the North-South Center, University of Miami, and has held visiting appointments at Harvard, Wharton, Oxford, Stanford, and the American Enterprise Institute. He was also a research associate at Columbia University and a Fulbright Scholar at the Fundação Getúlio Vargas in Brazil. A former director of the Washington Office of the Council of the Americas, he has written 12 books, including *Winning Strategies for the New Latin Markets* (Upper Saddle River, NJ: Financial Times/Prentice Hall, 2003) with Fernando Robles and Françoise Simon, and numerous articles. He has consulted for firms such as ExxonMobil, Shell, IBM, Microsoft, ING, Merrill Lynch, Ford, Olympus, Wendy's, KPMG, Disney, Heineken, and YPF. He holds a PhD from Columbia University.

Linn Hammergren is currently a senior public sector management specialist in the World Bank's Latin America Regional Department. She has a doctorate in political science, and prior to joining the bank taught at Vanderbilt University, managed judicial reform projects for USAID throughout Latin America, and worked with USAID/Washington as a Democracy Fellowship. Her publications include four manuals for judicial reform practitioners, three books (*The Politics of Justice and Justice Reform in Latin American: Peru in Comparative Perspective* [Boulder: Westview Press, 1998]; *Development, the Politics of Administrative Reform: Lessons from the Latin American Experience* [Boulder: Westview Press, 1983]; and *Envisioning Reform: Practical and Conceptual Obstacles to Improving Judicial Performance in Latin America* [University Park: Pennsylvania State University Press, 2007]), and several articles and monographs on the politics of judicial reform.

Benjamin Herzberg is a senior private sector development specialist in the SME Department of the World Bank Group, which he joined in 2003. He provides advisory services on investment climate reform, public-private dialogue mechanisms, monitoring and evaluation, and competitiveness. Previously, as senior business development adviser at the Office of the High Representative in Bosnia-Herzegovina, he headed the "Bulldozer Initiative" aimed at eliminating regulatory obstacles to business competitiveness. He earlier worked on stimulating investment in the SME sector for the OSCE in Bosnia and held positions in the private sector in France, Israel, and the United States. Herzberg holds a postgraduate degree from the Université des Sciences et Techniques, Lille, and a summa cum laude master's degree from the Université de la Sorbonne, Paris, France.

Christopher Humphrey is a consultant on development economics at the World Bank, focusing on the Andean region in Latin America. His work involves both lending operations as well as policy research. Previous to his work with the World Bank, he worked as an investigative journalist in Mexico City, writing stories on business, finance, economic policy, energy, and politics. He holds a BA in political science from Reed College and an MA in international economics from the Johns Hopkins School of Advanced International Studies. He has written numerous reports on different issues for the World Bank, including a 2003 study on the economic impact of narcotics production in southern Mexico and a 2006 analysis of long-term growth and poverty reduction in Peru. He closely followed the aftermath of the Tequila Crisis and its impacts on the Mexican banking sector.

Tricia Juhn is the codirector of the Financial Services Practice at InfoAmericas, lending expertise in the key areas of remittances, credit cards, and retail banking. Before joining InfoAmericas, she consulted for the World Bank. Prior to that assignment, she was director of research at Violy, Byorum & Partners, a Latin American M&A advisory firm, in New York City. From 1997 to 1999, she was a consultant at FIND/SVP, developing the company's new Latin American practice. She is the author of *Negotiating Peace in El Salvador* (Macmillan/St Martins, New York, 1998), and has written several articles about Latin America.

Peter T. Knight is coordinator of the e-Brasil Project (www.e-brasilproject.net), president of Telemática e Desenvolvimento Ltda. (www.tedbr.com), partner of Telematics for Education and Development (www.knight-moore.com), and board member of the *Journal of E-Government*. He led the World Bank's Electronic Media Center (1994–1997), was a division chief in the bank's Economic Development Institute, and lead economist for Brazil. He has held positions at Cornell University, the Ford Foundation, and the Brookings Institution. He received his PhD in economics from Stanford University and degrees from Dartmouth College and Oxford University. He has been published extensively in various languages; his latest books are *Rumo ao e-Brasil* (Rio de Janeiro: Garamond, 2006) and *e-Brasi: Um programa para acelerar o desenvolvimento socioeconômico aproveitando a convergência digital* (São Caetano do Sul, SP: Yendis, 2006).

Claudio M. Loser is a senior fellow at the Washington-based Inter-American Dialogue, working on economic, trade, and financial issues. He is also president of Centennial Latin-America, a consulting firm. A native of Argentina, he worked for 30 years at the International Monetary Fund, and for 8 years served as director of its Western Hemisphere Department. He has published in numerous journals, most recently on China-Latin American relations and on the macroeconomic effects of foreign worker remittances. In 2004, he developed the book *Enemigos,* on Argentina's relations with the IMF, together with the journalist Ernesto Tenembaum. He holds a PhD from the University of Chicago.

Rosane A. Marques is an industrial economist with experience in consulting, teaching, and research on technology capacity building, supply chain relationships, and innovation policies in developing countries. She presently works as an internal consultant at the Brazilian Agency for Industrial Development on the innovation policies in the aeronautics and nanotechnology sectors. Previously she worked in policy and project development for the state governments of Bahia and Rio Grande do Sul and for the industrial association in the latter state. She is also a doctoral candidate in business administration at the Federal University of Bahia (Brazil) where her dissertation research centers on innovation capabilities accumulation in the aeronautics sector.

John Price is the president and cofounder of InfoAmericas, a Latin American market intelligence firm with offices in Miami, Mexico City, and Sao Paulo. Since 1993, he has overseen three separate industry practices. In consumer goods and logistics, he has guided dozens of multinationals facing business strategy challenges in Latin America. In the field of trade promotion and competitiveness, he has advised the governments of Peru, Colombia, Chile, Guatemala, El Salvador, Paraguay, the Dominican Republic, and Mexico inside the region as well as Canadian and American governments regarding their Latin American interests. As a leading contributor to *Tendencias*, InfoAmericas' online newsletter, he has written more than 100 articles on Latin American business issues. He has taught international trade and international marketing at the Universidad de Guanajuato, the Universidad de las Americas in Mexico City, and FIU in Miami. In 1988, he received a BCOMM graduate from Queen's University in Canada.

Jeffrey M. Puryear is vice president for social policy at the Dialogue. He directs the Dialogue's education program, PREAL. He previously served as head of the Ford Foundation's regional office for the Andes and the Southern Cone, and as a research scholar at New York University. He received his PhD in comparative education from the University of Chicago. He has authored numerous articles on inter-American affairs. He has published one book, *Thinking Politics: Intellectuals and Democracy in Chile, 1973–1988* (Baltimore: Johns Hopkins University Press, 1994).

Christopher Sabatini is senior director of policy at the Council of the Americas. Previously, he worked as the senior program officer for Latin America and the Caribbean at the National Endowment for Democracy. From 1995 to 1997, he was a Diplomacy Fellow with the American Association for the Advancement of Science and worked at the U.S. Agency for International Development's Center for Democracy and Governance. He has published numerous articles and book chapters on a wide range of themes concerning Latin America, democratization, security and defense, political parties, and the effectiveness of international programs to support democratic development. He holds a doctorate in government from the University of Virginia.

P. Clayton Schaefer is an analyst, Spanish linguist, and researcher specializing in Latin America. He holds a degree in international relations from Pomona College where he was senior editor of the political magazine, *The Undecided*. He did fieldwork in Cuba looking at land tenure and property rights issues, and a major research and analysis project on the current political state in Venezuela. His present work has to do with real estate and credit market reform in the Caribbean.

Peter F. Schaefer is a writer, researcher, and businessman with 37 years of experience in developing nations. Much of his work has been focused on property rights as a key component in national economic development. In 1974 he developed a national plan for the Minister of Finance of South Vietnam, the key component of which was stability and security through secure property rights. He has worked with governments, businesses (agriculture, mining, and housing), and the U.S. government (senior adviser to the administrator of USAID and currently advising the Pentagon on Iraq reconstruction and stabilization). He completed his BA at the Maxwell School, Syracuse University, and MA from Georgetown University.

Jan Smith is the cofounder of InfoAmericas and codirector of the firm's Financial Services Practice. His experience in financial services ranges from market entry validation to competitive intelligence services, and includes work in remittances, card products, wealth management, and export financing. An adviser to many of the leading banks and credit providers in Latin America, he is considered one of the region's leading experts on consumer and small business credit. Prior to founding the firm's Financial Services Practice, he launched the InfoAmericas' Brazil office, which he directed from 1997 to 2002. He holds a business administration degree from the University of the Americas in Mexico City and a masters in philosophy from the Pontifical Catholic University in São Paulo, Brazil. He has lived in seven countries, and speaks English, Spanish, Portuguese, and Arabic.

Lee M. Tablewski is a political economist and director of training and of "Project Mexico" at the Institute of the Americas, an independent, nonprofit research center on the campus of the University of California, San Diego. Since joining the institute in 1989, Tablewski has developed its programs on Latin American energy, water sector reform, health care and social security, philanthropy and civil society, capital markets, science journalism, and equity and free trade. Previously he was with the North-South Center at the University of Miami where he focused on innovation and development. He earned his undergraduate and graduate degrees at Columbia University, New York.

Scott Tiffin is currently director of knowledge management and international relations for the business school at the Universidad Adolfo Ibáñez in Chile. His research focuses on technological innovation and entrepreneurship in natural resource–based business, how innovation clusters form and can be built, and the transformation of universities into globalizing, knowledge-based enterprises. He recently edited *Entrepreneurship in Latin America* (Westport, CT: Praeger, 2004), the first book on this topic. He has taught at Babson College in Boston and has also been the president of a decision-support software startup company. He has a PhD from the Université de Montreal in technology management. In this field, he has undertaken many consulting projects around the world over the past two decades for business and governments.

John H. Welch is senior vice president, Sovereign Strategy, at Lehman Brothers. Prior to that he was chief economist for Latin America and Head of Latin American Fixed Income Research, West LB. He has also worked with Barclays Capital, BNP Paribas, and the Federal Reserve Bank of Dallas. He has been an assistant professor at University of Texas, Austin, and University of North Texas. Welch earned his AB in economics from Columbia University and PhD in economics at the University of Illinois.

Introduction: Can Latin America Compete?

John Price and Jerry Haar

A decline in foreign direct investment and reinvestment in the Americas, in tandem with a sharp rise in Asia; the resurgence of antiliberal populism (for example, in Venezuela, Bolivia); widening income inequality; excessive business regulation; barriers to financial access; lackluster educational performance; paltry expenditures in R&D; and deteriorating infrastructure lead one to seriously question: Can Latin America compete? On the other hand, macroeconomic stability, low inflation, privatization, trade liberalization, increasing technology adoption and dissemination, and the ongoing boom in the demand and prices of commodities serve as significant counterweights to the negative indicators cited. The growth and expansion, regionally and globally, of Latin American *multilatinas* such as Embraer, Carvajal, América Móvil, Falabella, Odebrecht, and Techint are testimony that selected Latin American *firms*—if not entire nations—can, indeed, compete.[1]

The commodity-led boom in Latin America has reignited a debate regarding the region's place in the world economy and its ability to compete. From 2003 to 2005, Latin American economies, when measured in dollars, expanded by an astonishing 53 percent[2] but their productivity over the three years grew less than 4 percent. The region's modest economic growth during the last two decades, owing to the low rate of accumulation of productive factors and owing to poor productivity performance, is borne out in comparisons of growth competitiveness with other regions of the world (figure 0.1).

Total factor productivity actually declined by 0.6 percent annually in the 1990s, with only a handful of countries registering gains—most notably Argentina, Chile, and Uruguay (figure 0.2).

The positive external shock to the region, owing to the growth in demand and prices of commodities, is just that—an external shot in the arm providing temporary relief to Latin American consumers and domestic businesses. It is not an inoculation against the cyclical and long-term impacts of economic volatility.

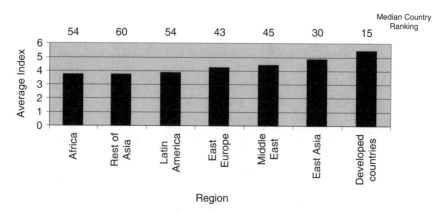

Figure 0.1 Growth competitiveness index by region

Source: Inter-American Development Bank, *Competitiveness—The Business of Growth, 2001 Report* (Washington, D.C.: Inter-American Development Bank, 2001).

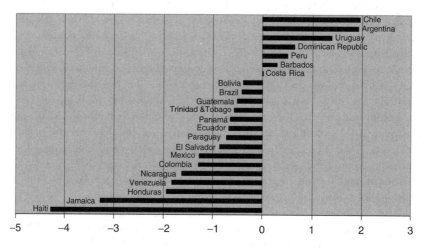

Figure 0.2 Total factor productivity average growth rate in the 1990s (in percent)

Source: Inter-American Development Bank, *Competitiveness—The Business of Growth, 2001 Report* (Washington, D.C.: Inter-American Development Bank, 2001).

Sustainable wealth creation in Latin America will be a reality only once the region improves its global competitiveness by enacting the painful and long-term reforms that it has so far evaded.

Often overlooked is the fact that the global commodity boom has not benefited all sectors within commodity-oriented economies. The noncommodity exporters in South America's resource-rich countries were the first group in this economic boom cycle to cry foul on the issue of competitiveness. As skyrocketing mineral prices have boosted Brazilian, Chilean, and Peruvian currencies, for example, less competitive export sectors, such as textiles in Peru, wineries in Chile, or auto parts in Brazil, have all lost ground in international markets. The immediate reaction of these beleaguered sectors is to lobby their governments to weaken their currencies or throw up protective barriers.[3] However, when one considers the success of textiles in Italy, wineries in Australia, and auto parts in Canada, all rich nations, the question arises, why can't Latin America compete while sustaining strong currencies? When Latin American currencies tumbled in 2001–2002, Latin American global competitiveness standings rose, albeit slightly; and sure enough they have fallen again since 2003 as commodity prices have risen. In 2005, Chile's coveted position as the 19th most competitive country in the world the year before dropped five positions to 24th.[4]

Over the short to medium term Latin America will enjoy rosy economic prospects thanks to its enviable supplier position in many commodity markets.[5] Copper, soy, iron ore, petroleum, timber, gold, silver, meat, coffee, sugar and ethanol, and cotton comprise the region's leading commodity exports. Economically, Latin America is better positioned now than it has been in a quarter century to begin tackling two of the long-term competitiveness driver issues: education and infrastructure, and hopefully will invest heavily and intelligently in both over the next few years. However, the region's ability to compete will remain hampered until it takes on the politically sensitive battles of reforming its labor, taxation, pension, customs, legal, and judicial policies and codes.[6] Economic boom times in any society rarely lead to tough political decision making. Venezuela is a prime example where no government during the last three and a half decades took any action to lessen the nation's dependence on petroleum as a percentage of exports (always above 80 percent) and export earnings, irrespective of the price of that commodity.[7] (The price in 1970 was $1.80 per barrel.) With commodity prices forecasted to remain strong through the end of the decade, most analysts do not expect Latin America's ranking in global competitiveness measurements to improve and its relative position vis-à-vis its emerging competitors in Asia and Eastern Europe is expected to drop.

Latin America's new political leadership faces historic decisions in the next few years that will dictate whether the region remains trapped in its commodity price–driven boom-bust cycle or whether it can reform itself and, by doing so, improve its long-term competitiveness and economic wealth. The choice can be crudely simplified as one between creating an Argentina versus an Australia. Both countries are endowed with abundant natural resources and have historically attracted capital and immigrants—the three ingredients of capitalist success: land, labor, and capital. Yet their performance could not be more dissimilar. In 2005, Australia ranked 10th (out of 117) in the World Economic Forum's competitiveness index and enjoyed a per capita income of over $32,000, while Argentina ranked 72nd and its average citizen earned $13,000 per annum.[8]

Globalization's New Face

And yet, hope springs eternal—even in Latin America—that competitiveness will be addressed with more than just lip service by the new cadre of political leadership taking over. Ironically, it is globalization—that highly charged, politicized metaphor, process, and trend—that today is making pragmatists of even the most populist politicians. The political backlash in Latin America that has ushered in the left on the heels of a widespread rejection of the Washington Consensus—the recipe of ten major reforms that were adopted in the name of modernization[9]— is now kept in check by the world's future economic powerhouses, China and India. As over one-third of the world's population and labor force, located in these two countries, enthusiastically rejoins the world's economic system after a 50-year hiatus, downward pressure is being placed on wages and product prices around the world, forcing competitors such as Latin America to slash waste, boost efficiency, and radically reform their policies to embrace open markets. Globalization has been a blessing overall for both China and India, generating massive investment and wage growth, pulling millions out of poverty, converting the two into cheerleaders of global free trade.[10] Though the two giants differ dramatically, in both countries one finds a popular rejection of excessive government intervention and enthusiasm for globalization.

Equally enthralled by laissez-faire economics are the emerging tigers in Eastern Europe. Since the demise of communism a decade and a half ago, they have transformed themselves from state-planned economies into some of the most liberal markets in the world, promoting flat tax policies, open borders, and a pro-business environment. Latin American leftists, opportunists, and naysayers can no longer discredit globalization as a proxy of American hegemony. Globalization is now the inspiration and economic catalyst of the world's two most populous countries,[11] as also of a growing list of small and mid-size countries in Asia, Europe, and parts of the Middle East that have embraced reform and led the charge at World Trade Organization (WTO) free trade talks.

Latin America's Competitiveness Gap: How Much Does It Cost the Region?

The *Global Competitiveness Report* published by the World Economic Forum and the *World Competitiveness Yearbook* produced by IMD Business School, both organizations located in Switzerland, have become the annual business environment scorecards for nations around the world. Their importance cannot be overstated. Global capital, in all its forms, follows these rankings closely and tends to rush disproportionately into the world's most competitive countries, particularly those blessed with capital markets capable of absorbing investment. The world's most competitive markets enjoy much lower costs of capital than do less-competitive nations.[12] In today's climate of rising interest rates and shrinking liquidity, that translates into a huge advantage. It is capital, technology, and knowledge-intensive industries that most countries wish to foster for they pay the highest wages. Table 0.1 lists the ranking of Latin American and Caribbean countries according to the *Global Competitiveness Report*.

Equally important as the global race to attract capital is the ability to recruit and retain the world's most innovative and entrepreneurial minds. Recent economic history teaches us that entire industries can migrate from one country to another in a few short years, if not months. Ship building in the United States and Europe,

Table 0.1 Growth competitiveness index rankings, 2005

Country	2005 rank
Chile	23
Uruguay	54
Mexico	55
El Salvador	56
Colombia	57
Trinidad and Tobago	60
Costa Rica	64
Brazil	65
Peru	68
Jamaica	70
Argentina	72
Panama	73
Venezuela	89
Honduras	93
Guatemala	97
Nicaragua	99
Bolivia	101
Dominican Republic	102
Ecuador	103
Paraguay	113
Guyana	115

Source: Augusto Lopez-Claros, *Global Competitiveness Report* (Geneva, Switzerland: World Economic Forum, 2005).

despite government subsidies, took less than a decade to migrate to South Korea. Mexican textile and electronics assembly operations fled the country in less than two years when oil prices drove Mexico's currency skyward in 2000. Value-added, asset-light industries such as R&D and software programming can move even faster. No education system in place today can respond to the quickness of capital so it is imperative for nations to roll out the welcome mat to highly skilled engineers, scientists, inventors, entrepreneurs, and managers who determine the start-up success of a new enterprise or industry. The world's more nimble and often higher-paying industries such as software, research, design, robotics, and pharmaceuticals follow the footsteps of the people and capital that drive them.

In Latin America, governments pay careful attention to the level of foreign direct investment (FDI) that they attract and proudly publish the annual tally. However, scant attention is paid to the capital and brainpower that migrate from the region each year. Since the early 1990s, when currency controls were done away with across Latin America, close to $600 billion[13] of net foreign investment has been captured in Latin America. However, in the same period of time, more than $200 billion of capital has flown the coop.[14] A fact worth taking into account is that most FDI captured in the last decade in Latin America was used to purchase assets and companies already built rather than create companies (and jobs) or even expand existing assets.[15] On the other hand, the overwhelming majority of capital flight is in the form of cash, used to purchase foreign bonds and stocks, seed capital for growth in other countries, and real estate (second homes, commercial

Table 0.2 Knowledge indicators for most recent year

Country	Innovation	Education	Information infrastructure	Aggregate indicator
Argentina	6.15	7.49	5.53	6.09
Brazil	5.02	5.75	5.50	5.42
Chile	5.51	6.13	6.59	6.08
Mexico	4.67	4.43	5.51	4.87
Latin America	3.30	4.50	4.73	4.18
Singapore	7.82	5.50	9.01	7.82
Korea	8.32	7.86	9.00	8.32
Taiwan	8.30	6.98	8.93	8.30
Malaysia	5.46	4.48	7.02	5.46
South Africa	5.00	4.47	5.26	5.00
Hungary	7.00	7.33	6.66	7.00
Poland	6.98	8.22	6.59	6.98

Source: World Development Indicators, 2005 (Washington, D.C.: World Bank).

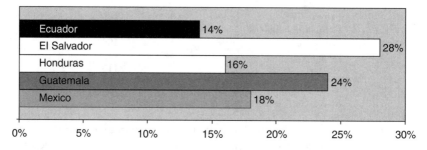

Figure 0.3 Percentage of adults receiving remittances
Source: National Survey of Latinos (Washington, D.C.: Pew Hispanic Center, 2003).

real estate). Capital flight, combined with inadequate funding—public and private—of science, education, and technology, clearly puts Latin America at a disadvantage vis-à-vis other regions in the world.

The region's brain drain is even more revealing of a lack of competitiveness see Table 0.2. Approximately eight million Latin Americans left the region during the 1990s.[16] The majority of these migrants comprise rural and urban poor, relatively uneducated, though often skilled. They leave via land to the United States to work on farms and in the service sector of the largest cities. Some argue that the migration of these people provides a political safety valve in Central America and Mexico, alleviating these countries of excess unemployment. The same thinking points to the estimated $30 billion (of a total of $55 billion) of remittances that these uneducated migrants send home to Latin America as additional export income for these countries.[17] Figure 0.3 illustrates the percentages of adults receiving remittances by country.

However, the $1,900[18] per annum sent home each year by the average working-class Mexican remittance sender in the United States is a fraction of what they earn while working in the United States and arguably a fraction of the economic contribution that the person could make if they were living in Mexico where the per capita average income in 2006 was $7,500 and where the average worker earned $12,500.[19]

Less debate surrounds the other half of the migration issue—the flight of educated people from Latin America to North America, Europe, even Asia.[20] From 1990 to 2005, an estimated 1.5 million college-educated Latin Americans fled the region,[21] staying at least five years, if not permanently, abroad. A significant portion of college-educated migrants leave to do postgraduate studies, only to remain abroad and work. Many others are entrepreneurs fleeing the targeting of kidnappers in places such as Mexico City or gang-led crime in São Paulo in search of a safer haven for their families. Others are upper-middle-class professionals whose life savings were destroyed by devaluation and gave up on their own economies. In the last decade these include the Dominican Republic, Venezuela, Argentina, Brazil, and Mexico. Though the United States has partially closed its doors by decreasing H1-B visa quotas by 80 percent, other countries such as Canada, Great Britain, Ireland, and Italy are aggressively wooing skilled immigrants from Latin America and other regions.

The cost to Latin America of its lack of competitiveness over the last 15 years, when measured by net flight of capital and brainpower is estimated at $1.2 trillion dollars[22] and continues to cost the region $160 billion per year, equal to 7 percent of regional GDP. Latin America is forgoing $35 billion per year[23] in tax revenue that is earned by those who fled abroad and the wealthy whose offshore income is near impossible to tax. As the global economy moves forward into a period of less-benevolent conditions with rising interest rates in the United States and Europe and a leveling of commodity prices, Latin America's competitiveness gap will cost even more as liquidity dries up, pulling investors out of emerging markets and sending more capital fleeing from the region's wealthy classes. This bodes ill not only for the region but, in the long term, for the receiving countries in industrialized nations.[24]

Modern Economic History and Struggle with Reform

The last time that Latin America rode a commodity-driven economic wave was in the 1970s when the U.S. economic machine marched to 5+ percent growth, Western Europe was still expanding, and Japan enjoyed double-digit growth. Russia remained outside of the global market as a commodity supplier, leaving Latin America in an enviable position to supply Western markets with minerals, oil, and foodstuffs. Latin America's natural resources had enjoyed a favorable climate since World War II, raising its currencies but rendering its nascent manufacturing industries as uncompetitive. The economic thinking of the day[25] combined with the lobbying power of domestic tycoons led to a regionwide policy of import substitution that raised massive barriers to imported manufactured goods. As a result, the region was highly vulnerable to any sudden downturn in commodity prices.

That vulnerability grew more acute with the dismantlement of the Bretton Woods economic system in 1971 that had rigidly controlled global currencies and international capital flows. Latin America's favorable economic standing proved a compelling magnet to the upstart world of international banking that reemerged as an economic force post–Bretton Woods. Latin American governments removed their own monetary controls allowing capital to flow into and out of their markets. Foreign debt then tripled between 1975 and 1982, rising from $75 billion to $314 billion, or 50 percent of the region's GDP. Unlike the institutional funding sources such as the IMF and World Bank that offered long-term, fixed low-interest funding, the new money arriving from abroad was short-term and variably priced, though also low interest bearing at the date of issue. International banks did not demand of their clients the kind of bureaucratic oversight and transparency that World Bank funds did. This made the funding far more attractive to Latin American governments that, in the best cases, wanted autonomy over the funds without an auditor breathing down their necks and in the worst cases had less than honorable plans for the borrowed monies.

The oil shock of 1979 proved favorable to Mexico, which was exporting more than $10 billion per year in petroleum, and further spiked its currency. By 1980, Mexico's non-oil exporters were in quick retreat as national production costs made them noncompetitive, spurring a current account deficit of $11.5 billion, which in turn was financed by short-term variable foreign debt. In 1981, Mexico's private sector predicted calamity and moved $20 billion offshore, further weakening the country's current-account deficit. The final straw was the oil price collapse in 1982, when the peaked prices finally burst the balloon on economic growth and oil demand in many industrialized markets. Mexico's debt default in August 1982 triggered a rapid and massive retreat by international bankers from Latin America as they all rushed to recall their short-term paper. Thus was born the region's lost decade of economic growth and development.

The 1980s were not only a decade of economic misery for Latin America but also one of civil wars, as parts of the region became front and center in the globalized Cold War between the United States and the Soviet Union. Keeping the region supportive of Washington's foreign policies meant tolerating enormous levels of corruption and incompetence in many of Latin America's governments. The United States influenced development banks and the U.S. government itself provided much of the region's funding in the 1980s.

The age of politically motivated funding quickly ended in the late 1980s after the demise of the Soviet Union and, as a result, the cessation of Russian influence in the region. A declining threat south of the Rio Grande shifted U.S. foreign policy and monies elsewhere and Latin American governments suddenly had to reinvent themselves in order to appeal to the new well of foreign funding—Wall Street. What Wall Street demanded of Latin American governments was economic reform—open borders to trade and investment, tradable and stable currencies, privatization, slashed budgets, and lower taxes. Latin American political leaders responded and began to deliver on most of the economic reforms. In return, the region received record foreign capital inflows in the form of debt and equity investments. Privatizations ushered in massive FDI, with Latin America capturing over 60 percent of all emerging market FDI in 1999.[26]

The Washington Consensus—"Mission (Un)Completed"

The economic reforms of the 1990s had mixed success in some markets and were an outright failure in others. Debate still rages about where and what went wrong. By the late 1990s, there was widespread popular angst against the Washington Consensus. The return of populism to politics in Venezuela, Ecuador, Bolivia, Peru, and Mexico is partly explained by the wide-scale rejection of neoliberal reforms, and undoubtedly includes also a healthy dose of anti-Americanism caused by that country's unpopular war in Iraq and the renewed neglect of Latin America.

There is, however, an emerging counterargument, one that demonstrates that the failure of the Washington Consensus lies not in the reforms it espoused but in the reforms that were carried out partly or not at all or implemented poorly.[27] Of the ten areas of reform outlined in the Washington Consensus, only two were properly executed in Latin America, another four were mismanaged, and the four most difficult reforms were never touched. Across the region, Latin America's technocrat-led governments did dismantle many of their import barriers and open key sectors to foreign direct investment, successfully completing two of the ten reforms. Privatization of state assets was pursued vigorously but too often nepotism or outright corruption muddied the bidding process, causing assets to be sold below market value and failing to deliver value to its citizens.

The Washington Consensus called for establishing competitive exchange rates but most governments refused to float their currencies until crisis forced them to do so. Carlos Salinas's government in Mexico spent $30 billion defending an over-valued currency in the hope that he would emerge as the first non-devaluation president in years and win the vote for presidency of the newly formed WTO. Not to be outdone, Brazil's Fernando Cardoso spent $40 billion defending the real so that he could be reelected. Overvalued currencies in both markets led to the capture of short-term international finances and negative real-interest rates, thereby breaking another of the ten commandments of the Washington Consensus. Argentina's currency board formula failed to work in a strong dollar world.[28] Runaway government spending at the federal and provincial levels forced infla-tion above competitive rates, damaging the peso's competitiveness. The desper-ate adoption of floating currencies and devaluation by all three countries brought sudden and deep misery to the working classes, bringing scorn for neoliberal policies.

The Washington Consensus called for the redirection of privatization monies to investments in education, health, and infrastructure. Instead, spending dropped in all three areas as leaders wasted their excess cash, foolishly defending overpriced currencies, or worse, siphoning off billions into their own pockets and those of their cronies. The mismanaged privatization schemes of the 1990s could be con-sidered the greatest plundering of Latin America since the days of the Spanish empire. Ironically, Latin American leaders today, along with the World Bank, are all calling for more investment in education and infrastructure citing the lack of investment during the neoliberal 1990s.

The Washington Consensus called for another three levels of modernization that strike at the heart of competitiveness and to this day remain untouched by the region's reformers. The first is tax reform. The consensus called for flatter and simpler taxes, a wider tax base, and much stricter tax code enforcement. With the exception of Chile, nowhere has this been achieved. In most markets, a large segment of the population is not obliged to pay income tax and pays limited value-added taxes that are not levied on basics such as food, clothing and medicine. Not surprisingly, tax collection rates are low—Mexico's rate of 11 percent of GDP is the lowest of any OECD (Organisation of Economic Co-operation and Development) country. At the same time, the wealthy avoid large portions of their income tax obligations and almost none of their estimated $80 billion in annual offshore income is taxed at home. Cutting the tax system at both ends leaves a very narrow base, insufficient to build modern education or infrastructure systems, let alone guarantee basic health services for all. Instead, extra pain is brought to bear on the struggling professional middle class, who become fed up and leave, taking their desperately needed skills with them. A narrow tax base keeps rates uncompetitively high, driving large swaths of the economy underground, as much as 50 percent in some countries. While in most markets, the tax base is narrow, if not relatively simple, in Brazil, the tax system acts like a spider web, trapping growth with its complexity and omnipotence. Federal, state, and municipal governments all fight for a portion of the wallets of business and consumer alike. Taxes are invented at a dizzying rate, creating a booming industry for Brazilian lawyers and accountants alike but at the same time strangling business competitiveness by creating additional compliance costs.

Another Washington Consensus tenet that has gone unheeded is that of deregulation and building a level playing field that allows all companies to compete head on. With few exceptions, Latin American industry regulators still lack the authority, if not good intentions, to correct the anticompetitive practices of powerful industrialists. A noted example is the battle waged between Telmex and foreign long-distance carriers who claimed that Mexico's local phone company held a monopoly position and, therefore, could and did charge outlandishly high (and unfair) connection rates for out-of-country calls. In March 2004, the WTO ruled that Mexico's international telecommunications regime violates that nation's WTO commitments. U.S. carriers estimated that Mexico's artificially high interconnection fees—the fee to complete calls from the United States to Mexico—had cost U.S. companies and consumers well over $1 billion since 2000.[29]

The ability of select companies to operate above the law prevents competitors, homegrown or foreign, from entering the market. The lack of competition keeps pricing artificially high, acting like a tax on the entire market. The costs to society are even greater when competition is weak in industries such as telecommunications, transportation, education, or banking—all vital services whose output ripple affect the performance of many segments of the economy. The lack of competition also provides a disincentive for modernization, limiting sector performance in the home market and jeopardizing its exportability.

Even more perilous is the lack of fairness and oversight of Latin America's legal system. No institution in Latin America has evaded reform more effectively than the judiciary. At best it acts as a cozy club protecting the well-connected in government and business from the rule of law. At worst, Latin America's judicial system is boldly corrupt, handing out legal decisions to the highest bidder, often riding roughshod over the very laws it is designed to enforce. In business, the losing side of contractual disputes is more often or not the foreign investor or small business plaintiff who courageously, if naively, pursues repayment of losses. The impacts are palpable. Latin America fails to attract the foreign direct investment that its economies merit, especially minority investors and joint-venture investments that would be more beneficial to the region than the 100 percent corporate asset sales that are the norm. The lack of justice for small and medium-size enterprises (SMEs) limits competition in many sectors, allowing quasi monopolies to overprice, taxing the economy as a whole. The biggest losers—as always—are the consumers.

The fourth untouched reform was that of protecting property rights, both intellectual property (IP) and real estate. In Latin America, the protection of IP is distortedly viewed as a means of providing favorable terms to global pharmaceutical firms, driving up the costs of medicine for all. Yet, the enforcement of IP is fundamental to the funding and management of innovation. Risk capital, the fuel that feeds innovative industries such as software, biotechnology, agronomy, even design and music, will not park itself in legal jurisdictions where intellectual property rights or their enforcement are questioned.[30] Latin America is home to inventive talent in multiple fields and many an innovator gets his start with angel funding from family and friends, but if his ideas are to reach a competitive scale, they will need risk capital financing. Too often in Latin America, good ideas die en route to market or are forced to go abroad for financing, never to return.

Latin America has resisted enforcement of IP laws for a number of reasons. First and foremost is a lack of funding to police what is a widespread problem. It is estimated that software piracy averages 57 percent across the region, costing the industry $864 million in lost sales and the region close to $40 billion in unrealized GDP.[31] Latin American governments have only begun to fund special police who are trained to conduct software compliance audits on companies and crack down on black market sales of pirated software, music, and branded consumer goods.

In several Latin American markets, populist-flavored laws have been designed to protect home owners from seizure of property by lenders when mortgages are defaulted. Other laws protect renters from expulsion when they fail to meet rental obligations. In some jurisdictions, squatters are granted title of property if they can prove they have "lived" there for long enough. All of these laws have the perverse effect of driving up the cost of mortgage lending due to the additional risk borne by the lender. Legitimate renters are forced to pay larger deposits than they might otherwise pay without the laws in place by frightened property owners. As a result, Latin America has very low home-ownership rates, depriving the working poor of the most powerful wealth creation tool in economic history and helping to reinforce the region's abysmal wealth distribution.[32]

Moving beyond the Washington Consensus

The Washington Consensus, though a good starting point, is not enough to make Latin America competitive. There are other drivers of competitiveness that need to be addressed if Latin America is to even hold its position in the global economy, let alone move upward.

Logistics costs in Latin America are among the highest in the world, averaging 10 to 30 percent of the cost of goods sold on imported products and 5 to 15 percent of cost of goods sold (COGS) on exported goods compared with 5 percent on shipments in and out of the United States and even less in Europe. The recent export boom has drawn attention to the miserable condition of Latin America's transport infrastructure, particularly its road and rail links, but also its sea and air cargo ports. Only 14 percent of Latin American roads are paved, usually linking the largest cities but leaving huge tracts of hinterland provinces in the economic dark ages. Extending paved road links, especially into less-developed regions, will rely entirely on public investment because they simply cannot be structured as profitable investments. Private investment has, and will likely continue, to be directed at export-inducing infrastructure such as ports and air cargo ports because of the low country risk associated with their dollar-generating business models. However, the viability of that investment is threatened by the bottleneck created by inefficient customs. Clearing inbound air shipments in Latin America takes anywhere from 48 hours to one week. In Taipei, it takes on average 18 minutes from the time the plane touches down. With so many manufacturing companies in Latin America reliant upon imported components, import customs clogs have a direct impact on the region's export competitiveness.[33]

Beyond infrastructure, Latin America's transportation service industry is riddled with protective laws that add costs and stifle investment. The most glaring example may be the taxes levied on trucking shipments that cross state borders in Brazil. With so much of Brazil's industrial base centered in the state of São Paulo, competitor states have levied taxes on inbound truckloads in an effort to motivate manufacturers to move out of São Paulo and into their areas. Repeated across multiple state borders, the practice has the effect of diminishing any economy of scale advantages that a huge trucking market like Brazil's ought to have. The resulting fragmented trucking market lacks the necessary profitability to fund it own modernization, adding time and costs to Brazilian logistics.

Latin America's capital markets shrank considerably in the 1990s as domestic companies chose to list American Depository Receipts (ADRs) in the U.S. market rather than capture low price/earnings (P/E) multiples in their own markets. The recent revival of Latin equity market listings has more to do with the additional burdens thrust upon new listings in the United States since the passage of the Sarbanes-Oxley Act in 2002 than major improvements in how their own markets are run. With the notable exception of the São Paulo–based Novo Mercado, Latin American capital markets still lack the necessary regulations to uphold reporting transparency and corporate governance to international standards, not to mention their enforcement, that are needed to attract large volumes of retail investors and corporate listings.[34] As a result, their P/E ratios under perform, driving listings elsewhere. With narrow bases, listing fees are expensive, keeping everybody save the largest national companies away from equity markets altogether. Latin America once had insufficient investors to support its equity markets. After a decade of building successful pension systems in the major markets combined with record export income, investment monies now far outweigh the publicly traded asset base in the region, unnecessarily forcing national savings abroad.

Small and mid-size businesses in Latin America have long been denied competitive sources of funding. Capital flight keeps the region's lending system dependent upon foreign capital, driving up costs and creating volatility that makes long-term lending cost prohibitive. The historical fiscal imprudence of governments that created huge debt loads (Brazilian public debt = 50 percent of GDP), obliges them to crowd the narrow debt markets even further. Which Brazilian bank will lend to a small company at 25 percent when it can lend risk free to the federal government at 14 percent? Without a thriving SME sector, wealth will remain concentrated in the hands of a few industrialists. SME viability is also vital to the competitiveness of large exporting companies for they provide the non-core outsourced services and manufacture inputs that make up so much of an exporter's cost base. If SMEs can't compete, then the large exporters can't compete either.[35]

Another great hindrance to the success of small enterprise is the tremendous administrative costs that they bear in their efforts to comply with the plethora of laws and regulations. Administrative reform crosses many territories of government including company registration, tax laws and procedures, labor laws, as well as safety, health, and environment. All too often, regulations are built one on top of another as a band-aid solution to problems that arise over time, eventually ballooning into a labyrinth of rules that no small company has the time or finances to tackle. Manufacturing start-ups in Mexico still average 58 days versus 3 days in the United States. In Brazil, the number averages over 100 days. Table 0.3 illustrates the kind of administrative burdens businesses face in Latin America.

Remarkably, these numbers represent an improvement over the past. Latin America desperately needs to follow the footsteps of its Eastern European competitors and throw out many of its laws and procedures and start again, building a far simplified set of rules. Without a radical remake of many of its administrative rules, Latin America will never foster the kind of business-friendly environment that its small and mid-size businesses need to compete in a global economy.

Public safety is rarely looked at as a competitiveness issue. However, undisputedly, the rising crime rate and surging gang violence in parts of the Americas are negatively impacting the consolidation of democracy and economic development. The Inter-American Development Bank estimates that per capita GDP would be 25 percent higher if the region's crime rate was equal to the world average.[36] There are 27.5 homicides per 100,000 people in Latin America, compared with 22 in Africa, 15 in Eastern Europe, and 1 in Western Europe's wealthiest countries. In the past decade, homicide rates have risen by 380 percent in Peru, 330 percent in Colombia, and 300 percent in Argentina.[37] Business associations

Table 0.3 Brazil: Ease of doing business

BRAZIL		Latin America & Caribbean		GNI per capita (US$)	
Ease of doing business (rank)	119	Lower middle income		Population (m)	
Starting a business		**Registering property**		**Trading across borders**	
Procedures (number)	17	Procedures (number)	15	Documents for export	
Time (days)	152	Time (days)	47	(number)	
Cost (% of income per capita)	10.1	Cost (% of property		Signatures for export	
Minimum capital (% of		value)	4.0	(number)	
income per capita)	0.0			Time for export (days)	
		Getting credit		Documents for import	
Dealing with licenses		Strength of legal rights		(number)	
Procedures (number)	19	index (0–10)	2	Signatures for import	
Time (days)	460	Depth of credit		(number)	
Cost (% of income		information index (0–6)	5	Time for import (days)	
per capita)	184.4	Public registry coverage			
		(% of adults)	9.6	**Enforcing contracts**	
Hiring and firing workers		Private bureau coverage		Procedures (number)	
Difficulty of hiring		(% of adults)	53.6	Time (days)	
index (0–100)	67			Cost (% of debt)	
Rigidity of hours		**Protecting investors**			
index (0–100)	80	Extent of disclosure		**Closing a business**	
Difficulty of firing		index (0–10)	5	Time (years)	
index (0–100)	20	Extent of director		Cost (% of estate)	
Rigidity of employment		liability index (0–10)	7	Recovery rate (cents on	
index (0–100)	56	Ease of shareholder		the dollar)	
Hiring cost (% of salary)	27	suits index (0–10)	4		
Firing cost (weeks of salary)	165	Strength of investor			
		protection index (0–10)	5.3		
		Paying taxes			
		Payments (number)	23		
		Time (hours per year)	2600		
		Total tax payable			
		(% of gross profit)	147.9		

Source: National Survey of Latinos (Washington, D.C.: Pew Hispanic Center, 2003).

in Latin America rank crime as the number one issue negatively affecting trade and investment. The notorious Salvadoran gang Mara Salvatrucha, known as MS-13, and other gangs, have an estimated presence of 100,000 in Central America and Mexico. Brazil's infamous drug names, Comando Vermelho ("Red Command") in Rio de Janeiro and the PCC ("First Command of the National Capital") in São Paulo have brutalized police and ordinary citizens alike;[38] and Hugo Chávez's Venezuela has achieved the dubious honor of its capital, Caracas, being called the most violent city on the continent, with the highest murder rate in the world—one that tripled between 1998 and 2005.[39]

The economic impacts of crime on economic development cannot be under-stated. Direct and indirect costs impact foregone foreign investment; reduce tourism; increase insurance costs for firms; decrease worker productivity; and reduce commercial transactions in neighborhoods regarded as unsafe.[40] No other factor better explains the exodus of the region's best and brightest as well as Latin America's underperformance in tourism, even foreign direct investment.[41] Latin American destinations such as Brazil, Colombia, Peru, and Venezuela, all rich with natural and cultural assets, attract less than $80 per capita in foreign tourist receipts. Aruba, just off the coast of Venezuela, brings in more than $7,000 per capita in foreign tourism. Even Cuba, with little access to the U.S. market, attracts over $200 per capita in tourism monies. The differences lie in the actual and perceived levels of public safety, which keep people away from arguably more exotic and compelling attractions in South America.

Public insecurity in Latin America's largest cities, as previously discussed, is the principal driver of the region's recent brain drain. It is Latin America's upper-middle classes that suffer the brunt of kidnappings and robberies. Wealthy enough to attract attention but unable to afford bodyguards, armored cars, and other expensive safety precautions, the professional classes are the preferred target of Latin American thieves. The exodus of the professional classes, even at a steady trickle, costs the region billions of dollars in lost productivity and wealth each year.

With weak rules of law and limited economic opportunity, the outlook on improved public safety in the Americas is not a promising one. A major exception is Colombia where large city mayors and, especially, President Alvaro Uribe have implemented strong and just law-and-order initiatives that have reduced crime and increased feelings of citizen approval of their governmental bodies.

Can Latin America Compete?

Can the region compete in the global economy? The truth is that Latin America has no choice but to compete. Globalization is no longer a simple political choice. Technology makes it impossible for countries to survive as economic islands. If a Brazilian manufacturer finds it difficult to hire a competitively priced product designer at home, then he can reach out and hire a Polish freelancer to do the job. Increasingly, businesses can outsource services abroad through electronic commerce without ever alerting their governments.[42]

When Latin American governments have tried to stem the flow of capital with currency controls, they have always been thwarted by the genius of their own people. When the Chavez administration tried to impose currency controls, people bought ADR listings of CANTV and sold them for dollars, suffering a minor commission fee in the process. Caracas today is littered with places where one can buy dollars on the black market, at a 10 to 12 percent premium. An estimated 1.5 to 2 million[43] Latin American individuals and businesses hold bank accounts abroad; most companies engaged in international commerce can do so without bothering to convert into their own currency by keeping their working capital offshore.

With its competitive future in the near term tied to the export of commodities, Latin America needs global market access to place its products. Historically, this has been easily managed for the sale of minerals and oil, often in tight global supply, with consumer nations unwilling to levy tariffs on their import. However, Latin America aspires to be the world's leading food basket as a highly competitive supplier of grains, beef, vegetables and fruit, and processed agricultural goods. To do so, it must break down trade and commercial barriers in the United States, Europe, Japan, Korea, and even India. As the Doha round of WTO negotiations has clearly shown, protective powers are still very much alive in those markets and will force Latin America to keep its own borders open if the region wishes to sell its agriculture goods internationally. Expanding agrifood sales abroad is more than an economic opportunity for Latin America. It may be the best chance to bring wealth to the least-developed regions and peoples on the continent, a vital ingredient of long-term stability. Firms such as Sadia, Perdigão, Arcor, Bimbo, and Anderson, Clayton & Company are expanding their reach in global as well as regional markets.[44]

Latin America still relies on international suppliers for much of its capital. Breaking the cycle of capital flight in Latin America requires convincing cynical domestic investors to believe in their countries as safe investment havens. That reality, though not an impossible one, still remains a few decades away. Until then, healthy investment levels will require international capital. As a result, Latin America is fully engaged in the global economy and will remain so in spite of political rhetoric to the contrary. Perhaps with the sole exception of Venezuela whose oil windfalls for now offset capital flight, and Bolivia, no other country in Latin America can avoid globalization. That leaves the region little choice but to compete. How, where, when, and under what conditions will be examined closely in this book.

Overview of the Chapters

Claudio M. Loser's overview of Latin America's recent macroeconomic history identifies the forces and factors that have shaped the environment for competitiveness. He notes that the region has gone a long way in improving the management of its macroeconomic policies—a far cry from the period prior to the 1990s when weak revenues, limited external reserves, balance of payments problems, money-losing public enterprises, and high and volatile inflation rates undermined innovation and productive investment. With the adoption of prudent fiscal and monetary policies and other economic reform measures, Latin America enhanced its competitive environment. Still, Loser acknowledges that macro conditions alone, although necessary, are insufficient for the region to achieve sustainable results in the global marketplace. He cites improved technologies; better education; an effective business climate; access to financing; and legal, regulatory, judicial, and infrastructure reforms (both physical and social) as critical ingredients for achieving competitiveness.

As Loser correctly discerns, education is a key determinant of Latin America's ability to compete. Jeffrey Puryear and Tamara Ortega Goodspeed validate this point with their comprehensive assessment of education in the region, arguing that the quality of the labor force, which depends on the quality of schools, must receive far more attention that it has in the past. The authors assert that Latin America neglects its education systems at its peril, since companies can find cheap labor elsewhere; improving enrollment without improving learning will have only a limited impact on productivity; and educational inequalities worsen existing income inequalities—underutilizing large segments of the potential labor force and heightening social tensions. Puryear and Goodspeed spell out "education fundamentals" for competitiveness—ones that policymakers should urgently address. These include establishing clear learning standards, requiring a second language; measuring how much students learn; and making schools accountable to citizens. Puryear and Goodspeed also call for countries to regularly participate in at least one global test of student achievement.

The emerging paradoxes of Latin America's legal and judicial reform movement are discussed by Linn Hammergren. She notes that beginning in the early 1980s, Latin American nations embarked upon a process of legal and judicial reform that continues through the present time. The reforms were accompanied by other complementary developments including re-democratization, financial and technical support offered by the donor community, renewed global interest in judicial reform, and rapid and widespread communication. Hammergren tallies and explains the accomplishments of reform and specifically discusses judicial workloads, operation of the courts, access to the judicial system among lower income groups, and issues such as abuse of power and legal enforcement.

Of the many impediments retarding Latin America's competitiveness, one is the lack of credible commercial laws, especially concerning property, according to Peter and Clayton Schaefer. Politically and technically the region has been unable to reform itself, despite decades of work and trillions of dollars, they argue. Echoing a number of the principles found in Hernando de Soto's groundbreaking *The Other Path,* the writers pinpoint imperfect or repressive legal systems and the accompanying lack of recognition and protection of property rights as detrimental to growth and competitiveness and that condemn the poor to live in "zero sum societies." As they explain:

> Government complicity, in one form or another, highlights the important point that the lack of both IPR and real property rights are evidence of failed property law systems, failure that profoundly inhibits investment, innovation, commerce, and, thus, growth in Latin America. A country may have low taxes, tariffs, and duties, a good location and low labor costs but if potential investors cannot protect their capital, their technology and their products, they will not invest.

José Luis Guasch and Benjamin Herzberg provide a comprehensive view of competitiveness within the context of regulatory and investment climate issues, using Mexico as a case study. Drawing heavily upon the findings of the World Bank's *Doing Business Database,* they assert that developing countries are rapidly realizing that they must examine (and reform) regulations, the investment regime, and administrative procedures that keep prices inefficiently high, deter entry, and increase transaction costs. They emphasize that investment climate reform, designed to unleash the private sector as an engine of economic growth, is a key component of poverty reduction and economic reform strategies. This entails providing a sound legal and regulatory framework that encourages investment and business development, and strengthening the capacity of government to respond efficiently to enterprise needs. Guasch and Herzberg's critical assessment of the Mexican Federal Regulatory Improvement Commission (COFEMER) provides lessons for improving this entity and guidance as to how other Latin American countries should proceed with their own institutional reform initiatives.

Taxes are unquestionably a major determinant of competitiveness, ranking second after "policy uncertainty," among major obstacles identified by the World Bank's Investment Climate Assessments survey of business firms worldwide. Mauricio Carrizosa evaluates the Latin American tax policy experience and prospects from the competitiveness perspective, with special attention to the causal relationship between taxation and public expenditures. He assesses the key tax and public expenditure competitiveness factors affecting growth: the adverse effect of the fiscal burden, the possibly positive growth impact of public investment and public expenditure quality, and the growth effects of different aspects of the tax structure. Carrizosa subsequently reviews the tax policy experience and prospects of Chile, Mexico, Ecuador, Nicaragua, and Guyana.

Christopher Sabatini analyzes Latin America's labor situation in the present times—a situation he regards as clearly dysfunctional. The region remains one of the most inflexible labor markets in the world. The costs of hiring new employees and firing unnecessary ones erode private sector productivity and discourage new investment. Sabatini reviews employment trends after the economic reforms of the 1990s and then looks deeper at the current state of labor laws in the region, focusing specifically on examples in Argentina, Peru, and Chile. He then delves into the reasons for the lack of reform and its cost in terms of competitiveness; the relationship between labor laws and the growth of the informal economy; and suggests policy actions to improve competitiveness and labor conditions in the hemisphere.

Without healthy and vibrant capital markets, Latin American countries are restrained from accumulating the investment, venture capital, and borrowing necessary to fuel growth, development, and competitiveness. John H. Welch examines the case of Brazil to illustrate progress in the modernization of capital markets. He notes that things have changed dramatically in that country but only since 1990, and mainly in the areas of money markets and governments bonds. Foreign capital markets have remained the main provider of long-term capital to both the public and private sector until very recently. Welch highlights the recovery of credit markets and the boom in Brazilian equities since the mid-1990s.

Banking and credit are presented in a chapter by Jan Smith, Tricia Juhn, and Christopher Humphrey. They assert that development of a formal banking system is the sine qua non of competing in an interdependent world. In their view, exclusionary banking systems, like the ones that have developed throughout Latin America, are correlated with poverty, chronic underperformance, and volatility.

Even in Brazil, Latin America's most sophisticated financial market, over two-thirds of households have no access to financial services at all; and only 15 percent have some type of a formal bank account. In Mexico City, one of the more densely banked urban areas in the region, 75 percent of households have no access at all to formal financial services. For Latin America as a whole, approximately 85 percent of the population is unbanked, compared to less than 10 percent in the United States. The authors discuss the structure, importance, and dynamics of banking in Latin America, the various products (for example, credit cards), and present an outlook for banking in the region vis-à-vis the issue of competitiveness.

Recognizably, a solid foundation of educational achievement will allow a nation to broaden and deepen its technological base—indispensable in a rapidly digitizing world. Scott Tiffin and Isabel Bortagaray assert that continuous innovation of new products, processes, and services creates competitiveness, new enterprises, profits, employment, and socioeconomic development. They go on to claim that the interest in competitiveness and innovation may be greater and more widely held by stakeholders at local, urban levels in Latin America than at national and regional levels. For these researchers, the problem is not that Latin American business is not innovative, but that innovation focuses on new market creation and new business models rather than on new product invention and design with significant scientific and technological value added. In examining local innovation systems in seven metropolitan areas, Tiffin and Bortagaray develop a model for "cluster" (industrial enclave) innovation and then develop contributory elements, such as knowledge inputs, financing, and support systems that must be assessed in evaluating technological innovation in urban clusters.

Closing the technology gap in the Americas is a critical challenge addressed by Peter T. Knight and Rosane A. Marques. In evaluating whether Latin American countries can close the technology gap, which separates them from the world's technological leaders, the writers highlight three key aspects of technological change: innovative behavior and the accumulation and evolution of technological capabilities of the firm; the management and generation of innovation, including interaction with other firms; and government policies that regulate and coordinate the quantity and quality of technological development. Using Brazil as a case example, Knight and Marques assess in detail how this nation, the largest and highest ranking among Latin nations in technology standing, is seeking to reduce the gap that separates it from the advanced countries.

Formalization by providing property rights is the only way to create a rising economic tide in the Americas that would benefit everyone. Without well-developed infrastructure, industries—let alone entire nations—cannot compete in the global economy. Unfortunately, the Americas is not faring well in this regard. Lee M. Tablewski finds that total investments to expand and maintain public and private infrastructure amounted to $47 billion in Latin America and the Caribbean. This sum is equivalent to about 2 percent of the regional GDP, while investment rates in China and other Asian and East European countries are three times higher than those in Latin America. Using water as a case study, Tablewski vividly illustrates the problems involved in reforming and expanding coverage of this critically important resource. He finds that that investment in the water sector is falling below 2 percent of GDP, and foreign private firms are leaving Latin America in what can be described as a rout. However, he highlights and benchmarks Chile as a nation that has met performance and profitability expectations, demonstrating the success of political support for economic policy and aggressive but balanced regulation in Chile.

Closely related in infrastructure is transportation and logistics. John Price highlights the region's grave deficiencies in road, rail, and port assets and zeros in on the need for an efficient transportation system and the active participation of modern logistics companies. He argues that Latin America has been unable to create its own large-scale competitive transportation service firms and has had mixed success in attracting the investment and technology transfer of international logistics service companies. While the rest of the world has reduced logistics costs since 1980, they have risen in most of Latin America. He draws upon examples from Brazil and Colombia to illustrate the dysfunction of the former in transportation and logistics and the exemplary practices in the latter, including the Colombian government's $11 billion infrastructure investment through 2010 and that nation's ability to complete projects under budget and ahead of schedule.

Often overlooked in the competitiveness debate is the issue of public safety, considered a "quality of life indicator." John Price argues that if a nation's competitiveness is tied to its ability to attract and retain talented people and investment capital, then violence is an extremely important competitiveness factor. In Latin America, homicide rates are among the highest in the world, although there is great variation in crime levels from country to country and between cities and rural areas. While Costa Rica, Colombia, and Peru have improved public safety and security in recent years, far more countries such as Brazil, Mexico, Argentina, Venezuela, Jamaica, Guatemala, and El Salvador have witnessed increases in violent crimes such as homicides. Price calculates and reports the direct economic costs of crime; estimates the indirect costs, as well; and discusses the origins, dynamics, and dimensions of Latin America's public safety problems.

Notes

1. Alonso Martínez, Ivan de Souza, and Francis Liu, "Multinationals vs. Multilatinas: Latin America's Great Race," *Strategy + Business,* Fall 2003, 1–12; Fernando Robles, Françoise Simon, and Jerry Haar, *Winning Strategies for the New Latin Markets* (Upper Saddle River, NJ: Financial Times/Prentice Hall, 2003); Jon I. Martínez, José Paulo Esperança, and José de la Torre, "Organizational Change among Emerging Latin American Firms: From 'Multilatinas' to Multinationals," *Management Research* 3, no. 3 (Fall 2005): 175–188.
2. *Market Indicators,* Economist Intelligence Unit.
3. Sylvia Maxfield and Ben Ross Schneider, eds., *Business and the State in Developing Countries* (Ithaca: Cornell University Press, 1997); Ben Ross Schneider, *Business Politics and the State in Twentieth-Century Latin America* (Cambridge: Cambridge University Press, 2004); Kenneth Shadlen, "Neoliberalism, Corporatism, and Small Business Political Activism in Contemporary Mexico," *Latin American Research Review* 35, no. 2 (2000): 73–106.

4. IMD, *Global Competitiveness Yearbook* (Lausanne: IMD, 2005).

5. Organization for Economic Cooperation and Development and the Food and Agricultural Organization, *OECD-FAO Agricultural Outlook—2006-2015* (Paris and Rome: OECD and FAO, 2006); Deutsche Bank, *China's Commodity Hunger: Implications for Africa and Latin America* (Deutsche Bank Research, June 13, 2006).

6. World Bank, *Doing Business in 2006* (Washington, D.C.: World Bank Group, 2006).

7. Moisés Naim, "The Real Story behind Venezuela's Woes," *Journal of Democracy* 12, no. 2 (April 2001); Michael Enright and Scott Saavedra, *Venezuela: The Challenge of Competitiveness* (London and New York: Palgrave Macmillan, 1996); Moisés Naim, *Paper Tigers and Minotaurs: The Politics of Venezuelan Economic Reform* (Washington, D.C.: Carnegie Endowment for International Peace, 1993); Asdrúbal Baptista and Bernard Mommer, *El Petroleo en el Pensamiento Económico Venezolano* (Caracas: IESA, 1987).

8. Central Intelligence Agency, *The World Factbook* (Dulles, VA: Potomac Books, 2006).

9. John Williamson, *The Progress of Policy Reform in Latin America* (Washington, D.C.: Institute for International Economics, 1990).

10. Nevertheless, there is a downside to globalization for China—namely, the inability of the economy to generate enough jobs for its population, especially those citizens who continue to flock to the cities in large numbers. Although the United States and other industrialized nations lament, and in many cases condemn, the outsourcing of jobs to China, that nation is actually *losing* manufacturing jobs. See Caroline Baum, "So Who's Stealing China's Manufacturing Jobs? www.bloomberg.com (accessed October 14, 2003); Daniel W. Drezner, "The Outsourcing Bogeyman," *Foreign Affairs,* May/June 2004.

11. "China and India: What you Need to Know Now," *Business Week,* August 22–29, 2005; William H. Overholt, *China and Globalization* (Santa Monica, CA: RAND Corporation, 2005); Jagdish Bhagwati, *In Defense of Globalization* (New York: Oxford University Press, 2004).

12. That includes commercial bank financing, venture capital, and debt/equity financing. For empirical studies on comparative cost of capital see Alan Auerbach, "The Cost of Capital and Investment in Developing Countries," *Policy Research Working Paper Series # 410* (Washington, D.C.:World Bank, 1990); L. Booth, V. Aivazian, A. Demirguc-Kunt, and V. Maksimovic, "Capital Structures in Developing Countries," *The Journal of Finance* 56, no. 1 (February 2001): 87–130; and Peter Henry, "Capital-Account Liberalization, the Cost of Capital, and Economic Growth," *American Economic Review* 93, no. 2 (May 2003): 91–96.

13. *Market Indicators,* Economist Intelligence Unit.

14. Ibid.

15. For further information and studies on privatization in Latin America see Alberto Chong and Florencio López-de-Silanes, eds., *Privatization in Latin America: Myths and Reality* (Washington, D.C.: World Bank 2005); Melissa Birch and Jerry Haar, eds., *The Impact of Privatization in Latin America* (Coral Gables: University of Miami Press, 2000); Armando Castelear Pinheiro and Ben Ross Schneider, "The Fiscal Impact of Privatization in Latin America," *Quarterly Review of Economics and Finance* 34 (1994): 9–42; Sunita Kukiri, *Privatization: The Lessons of Experience* (Washington, D.C.: World Bank 1992); Kathryn L. Dewenter and Paul H. Malatesta, "Public Offerings of State-Owned and Privately-Owned Enterprises: An International Comparison," *Journal of Finance* 52, no. 4 (September 1997): 1659–1679; Neil Roger, "Recent Trends in Privatization of Infrastructure," *Public Policy for the Private Sector,* no. 196 (September 1999).

16. "2000 Census," US Department of Immigration and Naturalization Services, 2001.
17. Migrant workers from Latin America and the Caribbean sent home almost $54 billion in 2005, a jump of 17 percent over the previous year, according to a report issued by the Inter-American Development Bank in March. This amount surpassed international aid and came close to matching the $61.5 billion in foreign direct investment in 2005. Jane Bussey, "Banking on the Unbanked," *Miami Herald,* April 17, 2006. The literature on remittances is extensive. Most notable are the following: Manuel Orozco, *Worker Remittances in International Scope* (working paper, Multilateral Investment Fund and Inter-American Dialogue, Washington, D.C., March 2003); Manuel Orozco, "Globalization and Migration: Impact of Family Remittances in Latin America," *Latin American Politics and Society* 44, no. 2 (2002): 41–66; SELA (Latin American Economic System), *CurrentTtrends in Migrants' Remittances in Latin America and the Caribbean: An Evaluation of Their Social and Economic Importance,* report prepared for the regional seminar Migrants' Remittances: An Alternative for Latin America and the Caribbean?" July 26–27, 2004, Caracas, Venezuela, www.sela.org. Both the Pew Hispanic Center and Inter-American Development Bank maintain websites with a broad range of studies, reports, and policy papers on remittances.
18. "Latin America Remittance Market," *Tendencias,* March 2006.
19. Additionally, there is the socioeconomic "dysfunctionality" factor, as remittance recipients may no longer feel the need to work and choose instead to merely live off these foreign welfare payments and spend the money on consumer goods rather than on necessities or activities to improve economic mobility (for example, vocational training courses).
20. The health services field provides a prime example where, for decades, hospital staff, from physicians to orderlies, have streamed in from India, Nigeria, Taiwan, the Philippines, Jamaica, and other foreign lands. See Lowell, B. Lindsay, and Allan Findlay, *Migration of Highly Skilled Persons from Developing Countries: Impact and Policy Responses,* Project Report for the International Labor Office and the United Kingdom's Department for International Development, Geneva, 2002; Fitzhugh Mullan, "The Metrics of the Physician Brain Drain," *New England Journal of Medicine* 353, no. 17 (October 2005): 1810–1818; and Çaglar Özden, *Brain Drain in Latin America* (Mexico City: Population Division, Department of Economic and Social Affairs, UN Secretariat, February 2006).
21. Çaglar Özden, "Educated Migrants: Is There Brain Waste?" Chapter 7, International Migration, Remittances and the Brain Drain (Washington, D.C.: World Bank, October 24, 2005).
22. The $200 billion of capital flight over the last 15 years has a present value of $389 billion, given 10 percent annual returns. The estimated 1.3 million college-educated Latin Americans who fled the region earned $682 billion abroad over 15 years and would have earned 1/3 that level or $227 billion if they had stayed home. The 12 million less- than-college-educated Latin Americans living abroad earned $1.8 trillion over 15 years and would have earned $616 billion, if they stayed home. $389 billion + $227 billion + $616 billion = c. $1.2 trillion.
23. The present value of capital flight measures $389 billion and generates capital gains of $38.9 billion per year (10 percent return). Average top end tax brackets in Latin America are 35 percent. Since offshore tax revenue is almost never collected in Latin America, this represents $13.6 billion in untaxed income. Highly educated migrants' untaxed income that would have been taxed locally = $32.5 billion income x 25 percent

tax bracket = $8.1billion. Less-educated migrants' untaxed income that would have been taxed locally = $88 bn x 15 percent tax bracket = $13.2 billion $13.6 bn + 8.1 bn + $13.2 bn = c. $35 bn.

24. The depletion or exodus of capital—physical and human—from the region robs Latin America of the inputs necessary to broaden and deepen consumer, industrial, and export markets and achieve productivity and innovation in both manufacturing and services—either as a direct producer or an outsourcing locale.

25. In the post–World War II period, the influential Argentine economist Raúl Prebisch widely promoted an economic model of import substitution industrialization (ISI). ISI is a trade and economic policy that advocates the substitution of imported products—mainly finished goods—with locally produced substitutes. Economically and practically unsound, this economic model, with its high tariff rates and massive government spending on state-owned enterprises, produced waste, inefficiency, high public debt, and uncompetitive industries. See Robert Packenham, *The Dependency Movement* (Cambridge, MA: Harvard University Press, 1992). For the evolution of Latin American economic policy from statist to neoliberal see Jeffry A. Frieden, Manuel Pastor, and Michael Tomz, eds., *Modern Political Economy and Latin America: Theory and Policy* (Boulder, CO: Westview Press, 2000); Sebastian Edwards, *Crisis and Reform in Latin America: From Despair to Hope* (Washington, D.C.: World Bank, 1995).

26. *Latin America Regional Overview,* Economist Intelligence Unit, 2006.

27. For a detailed review and critique of the "Washington Consensus" and associated studies on economic and social reform in the Americas see Carlos Santiso, "The Contentious Washingtron Consensus: Reforming the Reforms in Emerging Markets," *Review of International Political Economy* 11, no. 4 (October 2004): 828–844.

28. For more on currency boards—pro and con—see John Williamson, *What Role for Currency Boards?* (Washington, D.C.: Institute for International Economics, 1995); Atish R. Ghosh, Anne-Marie Gulde, and Holger C. Wolf, "Currency Boards: More Than a Quick Fix?" *Economic Policy* (2000): 269–335; Steven H. Hanke, "The Disregard for Currency Board Realities," *Cato Journal* 20, no. 1 (Spring/Summer 2000): 49–59; Nouriel Roubini, *The Case against Currency Boards: Debunking 10 Myths about the Benefits of Currency Boards,* (New York: Stern University Press, 1988), www.stern.nyu.edu/~nroubini/asia.

29. "U.S. Wins WTO Telecommunications Case against Mexico," Press Release, U.S. Department of State, March 12, 2004. For details of the origin, development, resolution, and final ruling on the issue see http://www.cuts-international.org/pdf/Telmex-1-2006.pdf.

30. Kamal Saggi, "Trade, Foreign Direct Investment, and International Technology Transfer: A Survey," *The World Bank Research Observer* 17, no. 2 (2002): 191–235; Keith E. Maskus and Guifang Yang, "Intellectual Property Rights, Licensing, and Innovation," Policy Research Working Paper Series, #2973, World Bank, February 2003; Isabel Bortagaray and Scott Tiffin, "Innovation Clusters in Latin America," paper presented at the 4th International Conference on Technology Policy and Innovation, Curitiba, Brazil, August 28–31, 2000.

31. "7th Annual BSA Global Software Piracy Study," *Business Software Association,* June 2002.

32. Hernando de Soto, *The Mystery of Capital* (New York: Basic Books, 2003). Mexico provides a bright spot in the Latin American constellation due to a number of reform measures that have led to a proliferation of home mortgage lending. "Piggybanks Full of Pesos," *Business Week,* March 13, 2006; John Christy, "Make Room for Mexico in Your Portfolio," Forbes.com (accessed July 12, 2006).

33. A critical obstacle to facilitating trade in the Latin America region is the glacial rate at which goods clear customs. It is estimated that only 10 percent of the region's customs operations are automated, which helps explain why, for the average shipment, delays and bottlenecks in customs account for 20 percent of transit time and 25 percent of overall transit costs. Governments are realizing that outdated customs procedures are putting them at a competitive disadvantage and are therefore taking measures to streamline processes. In Febuary 2006, for example, UPS signed a groundbreaking agreement with the government of El Salvador to expedite the shipment of most goods crossing the country's borders. Under the terms of the pact: (a) courier companies are able to withdraw merchandise from customs at El Salvador International Airport within 48 hours from when goods arrive, assuming they meet requirements; (b) shipments whose Free on Board value is lower than $200 can be removed upon presenting the corresponding air bill and invoice; and (c) if the Free on Board value is between $200 and $3,000, the removal of goods will be authorized upon presenting the merchandise declaration.

34. Incisive analyses and assessments of capital market infrastructure and dynamics in the Americas may be found in Guillermo A. Calvo, *Emerging Capital Markets in Turmoil: Bad Luck or Bad Policy?* (Cambridge, MA: MIT Press, 2005); Augusto de la Torre and Sergio Schmukler, *Whither Latin American Capital Markets?* (Washington, D.C.: World Bank, October 2004); and Kenroy Dowers, Felipe Gomez-Acebo, and Pietro Masci, "Developing a Strategy for Reforming Capital Markets in Latin America and the Caribbean," in *Focus on Capital: New Approaches to Developing Latin American Capital Markets,* ed. Kenroy Dowers and Pietro Masci (Washington, D.C.: Inter-American Development Bank, 2003).

35. The importance of Latin American SMEs (small and medium size enterprises) to competitiveness and supply chain linkages is well documented. See Jane W. Lu and Paul W. Beamish, "The Internationalization and Performance of SMEs," *Strategic Management Journal* 22, nos 6–7 (2001): 565–586; Roberto Alvarez and Gustavo Crespi, "La Importancia Relativa de las Pequeñas y Medianas Empresas: Un Análisis de sus Determinantes en la Indústria Manufacturera, *Cuadernos de Economía* 38, no. 115 (2001): 347–365; Zoltan J. Acs and Lee Preston, "Small and Medium-Sized Enterprises, Technology, and Globalization: Introduction to a Special Issue on Small and Medium-Sized Enterprises in the Global Economy," *Small Business Economics,* 9, no. 1 (February 1997): 1–6; Carlo Pietrobelli and Roberta Rabellotti, *Upgrading in Clusters and Value Chains in Latin America: The Role of Policies* (Washington, D.C.: Inter-American Development Bank, 2004); Jörg Meyer-Stamer and Tilman Altenburg, "How to Promote Clusters: Policy Experiences from Latin America," *World Development* 27, no. 9 (1999): 1693–1713; World Bank, *Enabling SMEs to Enter the International Supply Chain* (Washington, D.C.: Global Facilitation Partnership for Transportation and Trade, June 2005); Rainer A. Sommer, "Small and Medium Sized Enterprises: No Longer Just Coping with the Supply Chain," *International Journal of Management and Enterprise Development* 1, no.1 (2003): 4–10; Bob Ritchie and Clare Brindley, "Disintermediation, Disintegration and Risk in the SME Global Supply Chain, International Journal of Management and Enterprise Development," *Management Decision* 38, no. 8 (2000): 575–583; Richard J. Arend, "SME-Supplier Alliance Activity in Manufacturing: Contingent Benefits and Perceptions," *Strategic Management Journal* 27, no. 8 (2006): 741–763.

36. Testimony of Adolfo A. Franco, assistant administrator, Bureau for Latin America and the Caribbean, U.S. Agency for International Development, before the House

Committee on International Relations Subcommittee on the Western Hemisphere, April 20, 2005.

37. Andres Oppenheimer, "Latin Economies Hurt by Crime," *Miami Herald,* April 24, 2004.

38. Jens Glüsing, "The Mafia's Shadow Kingdom,*" Spiegel Online,* May 22, 2006. In mid-May the PCC carried out 293 attacks, murdering 41 policemen and security officers, burning 83 buses, and firing gunshots at subway stations and fire departments.

39. Ibid.

40. William C. Prillaman, "Crime, Democracy, and Development in Latin America," *Policy Papers on the Americas,* vol. 14 (Washington, D.C.:Center for Strategic and International Studies, June 2003).

41. Marcelo S. Bergman, "Crime and Citizen Security in Latin America," *Latin American Research Review* 41, no.2 (June 2006): 213–322.

42. Brian R. Hook, "Latin America: Outsourcing's New Hot Spot," Ecommercetimes.com, (accessed June 21, 2005); Datamonitor plc, *Call Center Outsourcing in Latin America and the Caribbean* (New York: Datamonitor, May 10, 2004); Dale Pinto, *E-Commerce and Source-Based Income Taxation* (San Francisco: IBFD, 2003). For a comprehensive source of information on offshore e-commerce issues and tax and regulatory aspects see www.offshore-e-com.com.

43. Jan Smith Ramos, "Advising the Wealthy in Latin America", *InfoAmericas Tendencias Report,* May 29, 2003.

44. John Dyslin, "Prospering across the Border—Latin American Food Companies: The Leading 150, *Prepared Foods,* July 1993.

CHAPTER 1

The Macroeconomic Environment of Competitiveness[1]

Claudio M. Loser

Looking back at the economic history of Latin America in the last quarter century, it is possible to identify a number of troublesome features: low average economic growth; high inflation relative to other parts of the world; high volatility regarding terms of trade, capital flows, and economic performance; fluctuating exchange rates; balance of payments crises; high unemployment; and widespread poverty and income inequality. If these were all that characterized the performance of the region, there would be little hope for it. But the picture is different as the interested observer looks at more recent years and at more detailed numbers. Inflation has been declining; exchange rates in real terms have stabilized; macroeconomic indicators have improved with regard to the fiscal accounts and monetary policy; international trade has boomed; poverty has been on the decline; and the external accounts are much stronger than they have been in many years. Is this attributable to good luck, favorable world conditions, or hard work? The answer, typically, is a combination of the three. And to avoid simplistic generalizations, not all countries have done equally well, or have acted in a similarly prudent fashion. This chapter seeks to fulfill a complex task. Under the basic premise that macroeconomic stability is a precondition for competitiveness, it will review some of the key principles that determine the basis for good macroeconomic performance, the recent experience of the region in this regard, and some lessons for the future.

Macroeconomic Management and the Impact on Competitiveness

In most debates, competitiveness is associated with the real exchange rate, namely, the movement in the exchange rate between a country and its trading partners, in comparison with the relative price developments. A depreciation of the currency makes exports more attractive and imports less so. However, this narrow view disregards the broader aspects of competitiveness, measured in terms of increased productivity, an increasing traded-goods sector, and a stronger balance of payments. Actually, the exchange rate may be responding to external or domestic developments. When a country experiences falling terms of trade, the exchange rate will likely depreciate. The same can be said about a domestic crisis, which can result in or be caused by massive capital outflows. In other instances the exchange rate may actually appreciate due to favorable external or domestic conditions, sometimes even resulting in an "overshooting" of the currency.[2]

An equally important aspect that is frequently overlooked in discussions about the exchange rate is that, for a given set of technologies and capital investment, the real exchange rate is the counterpart of real wages in the economy. Thus, a marked depreciation of the currency is most likely accompanied by a decline in real wages as the main mechanism to increase competition. The opposite is true regarding an appreciation of the currency, which is frequently accompanied by higher wages, even though they may not be sustainable. Thus, it is important to see that the main motors of sustained growth are developments in productivity, and in human capital embodied in the labor force, rather than movements in the exchange rate alone. The exchange rate will provide the room for an improved competitive environment, but without new investment, broadly defined, such competitiveness will not allow for sustained growth.

The experience of Latin America is full of examples of such movements, frequently associated with serious domestic and external events. The macroeconomic response to these events has been central to how the economy has reacted to these events, and how this has affected the medium-term prospects of the economy.

The episodes of increased competitiveness in the region have tended to be associated with a decline in average wage. However, other factors may have resulted in deviations, as was the case in 1994, when the Mexican peso depreciated sharply late in the year, but wage developments only reflected the shock subsequently, in 1995.

The "high" exchange rate/low wage outcome cannot be considered a sustainable solution for the countries in the region, if the main economic policy objective is to increase the well-being of the population at large. An adequate balance between these variables is a necessary condition but by far cannot be seen as the best outcome from a welfare point of view. However, it has been a characteristic of Latin America at least for the last quarter century, as the next sections will show.

Economic Growth Performance in Latin America

Overall Trends

The Latin American region has been characterized by high volatility and limited overall growth, at least since the debt crisis began in the early 1980s. After a period of rapid growth based on high commodity prices (mainly for oil) and heavy borrowing, economic growth came to a halt. Commodity prices collapsed

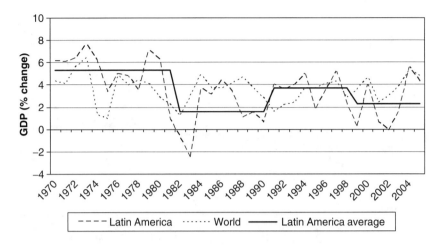

Figure 1.1 Latin America: GDP growth, 1970–2005

and interest rates rose as advanced economies, particularly the United States and Europe, started to correct inflationary pressures. As capital flows dried up, Latin America was confronted with the need to redress its structural imbalances. The 1980s was a period of democratic consolidation and of major reforms, as also of economic upheaval, and became commonly known as the *Década Perdida* (Lost Decade), at least economically. After 1980, Latin America grew at a slower pace than the world at large, with the exception of the period of reform and opening that took place in the early 1990s (figure 1.1). Even that most recent period was followed by several years when the region suffered a sharp decline in the rate of growth, as Brazil, Argentina, and Uruguay had major problems following the Mexican and Asian crises. Meanwhile, other regions, particularly China and other countries in Asia, recovered from their own crises. It has to be noted, however that the pace of economic growth declined worldwide, and not only in Latin America.

A related and dramatic picture emerges when cumulative per-capita growth is compared in Latin America and other regions. Although Latin America had a per capita income of about US$4,500 in 2005, the per capita income of the advanced economies is about four times that of Latin America in purchasing power terms.

While the region remains ahead of others in per capita levels, it has fallen well behind in terms of cumulative growth. Figure 1.2 presents the per capita income for Latin America and other regions, with a common central point (1990 = 100). Not only did developing Asia move much faster but the advanced economies also grew faster than Latin America. Such performance does not bode well for the establishment of an environment conducive to enhancing competitiveness.

The remainder of the chapter will analyze the different aspects of macroeconomic performance and policy. These generally suggest, surprisingly, a more prosperous future for the region.

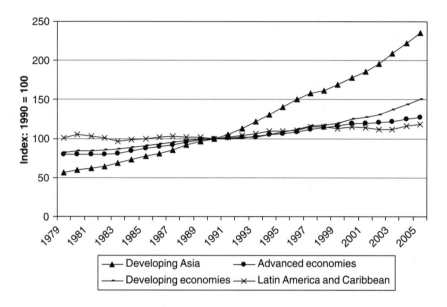

Figure 1.2 Latin America and other regions: GDP per capita

Performance by Country

A first observation is that the region cannot be seen as a single entity. Performance among the different countries in the region has been divergent, with some countries performing very well and others doing poorly. Table 1.1 provides information on the average economic growth rate for the countries in Latin America and the Caribbean over a 15-year period. Not surprisingly, Chile, the stellar performer of Latin America, comes first, although not for the subperiod 2001–2005. Trinidad and Tobago (a major oil and gas producer) and Belize come a close second. They are followed by most Central American countries, the Dominican Republic, Peru, Argentina, and Mexico among the larger countries. However, Argentina has fallen below average in the past five years on account of the serious crisis it suffered in 2001–2002. A clear conclusion is that it is extremely difficult to come up with a general statement on economic performance in the region, except that the larger countries, apart from Chile and Peru, have done relatively poorly during the period, while some of the smaller countries have done well on account of an array of serious reforms introduced during the period as well as favorable circumstances in some cases.

Poverty and Income Distribution

Latin America is characterized not only by a wide disparity in economic growth, but also by serious issues regarding poverty and income distribution. While the two issues cannot be seen as being equivalent from a conceptual point of view, they are closely interrelated. Latin America does not have by any means the

Table 1.1 Latin America and the Caribbean: Average rate of growth, 1990–2005

Country	Av. 1990–2005	Av. 2000–2005
Chile	5.6	5.2
Trinidad and Tobago	5.3	9.2
Belize	5.3	7.7
Panama	5.2	4.6
Costa Rica	4.7	4.1
Dominican Republic	4.5	4.5
El Salvador	3.8	2.4
Bolivia	3.6	3.4
Guatemala	3.5	3.2
Peru	3.5	4.7
Argentina	3.4	2.2
Honduras	3.2	4.7
Nicaragua	3.2	3.9
Mexico	3.1	3.2
Colombia	3.1	4.0
Guyana	3.0	0.0
Ecuador	2.9	4.8
Latin America	**2.9**	**2.3**
East Caribbean countries	2.8	2.3
Venezuela	2.7	3.5
Uruguay	2.3	0.9
Paraguay	2.1	1.9
Brazil	2.1	3.1
Suriname	2.0	5.1
Bahamas, The	1.9	2.5
Barbados	1.2	2.2
Jamaica	1.1	1.8
Haiti	0.0	−0.5

Source: International Monetary Fund, *World Economic Outlook Database,* April 2006.

highest levels of poverty in the world. Moreover there has been a steady, albeit slow, progress in this area in recent years, as conditions have tended to improve over time. Total poverty has declined by almost 16 percent in the last 15 years, and indigence, or extreme poverty, by 25 percent. However, this decline has not been steady, mainly on account of the crises experienced by Argentina, Uruguay, and Venezuela in 2001–2002, which resulted in a sharp increase in poverty in those countries at the time, and which has been reversed only recently. Of equal importance is the fact that poverty rates are only now declining to the levels prevailing just before the oil crisis of the 1980s, when the region was expanding at a very rapid, though unsustainable, rate.

Poverty has been accompanied by a highly concentrated distribution of income in many countries in the region. Indices such as the GINI coefficient, which measures inequality in income distribution within a country, show a fairly unequal distribution. While indicators have improved in recent years, significant portions of the population are excluded from education (about 10 percent of the population is illiterate), good health (10 percent of the population is undernourished,

11 percent has inadequate water supplies, and 25 percent has no sewage), and work opportunities (10 percent urban unemployment).[3]

The Curse of Inflation

Before the 1990s the Latin American region had long been the worst performer with regard to inflation. A poor appreciation of ongoing monetary developments and policies, significant fiscal imbalances, and a stop-and-go approach to prudent macroeconomic policies resulted frequently in major inflation shocks. Since the end of World War II, Latin America had taken a policy approach that mixed highly protectionist industrial policies with a narrow interpretation of the Keynesian policies so much in vogue after the Great Depression. In practice, governments acted on the assumption that an expansionary fiscal and monetary policy could promote economic growth in the longer run, without any consideration for domestic and external constraints. These domestic policies, compounded by a high volatility of external conditions, resulted in a sharp increase in prices, to almost 500 percent in 1990. The performance of individual countries varied, from very low rates in fully dollarized countries such as Panama or strictly pegged ones like those in the English Caribbean, to a peak rate of some 25,000 annual percent in Bolivia in 1984.

Over time, Latin America learned to cope with inflation, although it was not able to tame it for long. Indexing schemes, freezes, and predetermined exchange rate depreciation schedules resulted in a short-term slowdown in inflation, but most attempts had failed by the early 1990s.

The costs of inflation ended up being very significant. Inflation, recognized as the most regressive tax as it affects the poor the most, contributed to the low-growth track record of the region, until efforts started in earnest to reduce it. The efforts in Brazil were arguably the most interesting as the government pursued a policy of de-indexation by introducing in 1994 a new currency, the *real*, which was intended to adjust for the previous indexation. The results were initially spectacular; however, in the end, Brazil fell into the same trap that many countries had experienced before (Argentina, Chile, and Uruguay in the 1970s) and would experience after (Mexico and Argentina in the 1990s). It focused its attention on the stability of the exchange rate, without paying sufficient attention to other macroeconomic variables such as monetary and fiscal policy. Eventually, with mounting debt, increasing public sector deficits, and intractable external imbalances, the Brazilians had to modify their exchange rate policy and started to adjust public finances.

In any event, the efforts to reduce inflation succeeded in the region and inflation converged quickly, although not fully, with existing rates of inflation in the rest of the world. The decline in inflation is arguably one of the main gains observed in the region in the last decade, together with the opening up to international trade. Possibly reflecting the requirements of structural and social policy changes, the rate of inflation for the region remains above that of the rest of the world.

Another important development is that inflation in different countries has tended to converge, most notably for Brazil, Chile, and Mexico. While the specter of hyperinflation seems to have disappeared from the region, several countries have seen high rates of inflation, by regional standards. Venezuela has regularly exceeded the average for the region, while Argentina has seen its rate of inflation increase to the two-digit range.

Several countries have implemented inflation targeting as their main policy mechanism, most notably Chile, Colombia, Peru, and Brazil. Mexico has not introduced inflation targeting as an explicit monetary policy, but follows that approach in practice.[4] All these countries have been successful in reducing inflation from the high levels observed in the 1980s and in the early 1990s.

The Links to the External Sector

Latin America has witnessed a struggle almost since independence between the wish to be autarkic and the wish to have strong links with the outside world. The autarkic forces reached their maximum importance during the Import Substitution Industrialization efforts of the post–World War II period.[5] In turn, the periods of close relationship with the external world extended from the mid-nineteenth century to the time of the Great Depression. The most recent period of globalization that became evident in the 1990s was not unlike the previous period of British-promoted free trade.

Trade Flows in Latin America

Throughout the period of import substitution and integration, Latin American foreign trade has remained dependent on primary commodities, even as its productive base has become diversified, with the possible exception of Mexico in recent years.[6] Figure 1.3 illustrates these results, with particular emphasis on

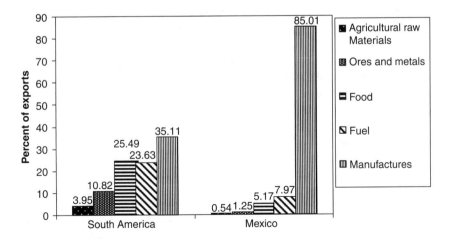

Figure 1.3 Export structure in South America and Mexico

South America and Mexico. Such dependence is subject to debate,[7] which is beyond the scope of this chapter, although there is no definitive proof that the dominance of industrial exports compared with other classes of exports increases welfare. What is clear is that the high dependence on primary commodities has resulted in major fluctuations, and generally in a secular decline, in the region's terms of trade.

The region has seen large fluctuations in its terms of trade, while at the same time it has been affected by fluctuations in demand for its industrial products. The Latin American countries have had the largest variability in exports of any large developing country, and certainly much higher than that of industrial countries.[8] As a consequence, the rate of economic growth of exports for the region has been highly dependent on the behavior of the world economy, either through changes in volumes or in terms of trade, which have tended to decline as well over the medium term. In turn, this has had a significant impact on the behavior of GDP in Latin America and the Caribbean. The terms of trade variability have been accompanied by a large volatility in income. In fact, the ratio of the standard deviation to the average rate of growth for the region is the highest, together with sub-Saharan Africa, among developing countries. This situation has generated a difficult environment for policymaking in the region, resulting in stop-and-go cycles; these cycles have precluded stable conditions that could help enhance competitiveness.

In itself, volatility in terms of trade should not be a source of lower income. Under normal conditions, countries could adjust their policies to account for the volatility of their external income through countercyclical policies, that is, policies that would help absorb resources during times of bonanza and free them when the favorable conditions reverse. However, this policy has been pursued only to a limited extent in Latin America. Expansionary polices have been carried out at times of expansion, with no accumulation of reserves or reductions in debt that could have helped at the times of recession. Accordingly, the effect of external volatility has not been mitigated in times of slowdown, and often declines terms of trade have ended in serious crises. In recent years, only Chile and, to a lesser extent, Venezuela, Mexico, and Trinidad and Tobago have followed countercyclical policies.

An additional observation about the trade pattern of the region is that in recent years the importance of trade has increased significantly for Latin America and the Caribbean. However, after the efforts at trade integration resulted in an increase in intraregional trade, the share of regional trade has remained broadly unchanged.

The increase in trade has been associated with a sharp decline in the trade restrictiveness that characterized the region previously. Figure 1.4 shows the changes in trade restrictiveness,[9] and also the ratio of exports and imports to GDP. Contrary to the fears that a decline in protection to domestic industries would result in a flood of imports and no incentives to exports, both magnitudes have increased significantly over the last 15 years. This behavior suggests strongly that the opening of trade in the region had a major impact on increasing the integration of Latin America with the world economy, and provided an effective

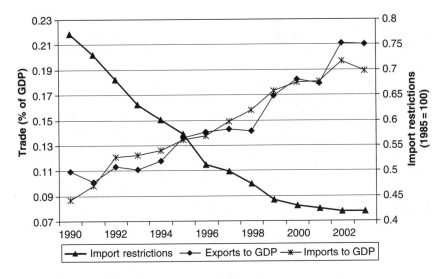

Figure 1.4 Latin America: Import restrictions and external trade

increase in competitiveness. The external current account was dependent on other factors, including the availability of financing, the exchange rate, and the macroeconomic policies that the countries in the region followed during the period.

While the increase in trade reflected in part the process of integration in the region, this has been only a small contributing factor. For example, trade within Latin America and the Caribbean rose from 17 percent of the total trade in 1990–1991 to 19 percent in 1997–1998, and was at about the same level in 2004–2005. Over the same period trade with the United States was the highest of any region, with 41 percent in 1990–1991, 47.5 percent in 1997–1998, and about the same level in 2004–2005. Over the same period trade with China rose sharply, but by 2004–2005 it constituted only some 4.5 percent of the total. In the end the reduction in restrictions has been more important than the efforts to integrate the region.

Capital Flows and the Balance of Payments

One of the most dramatic findings with regard to the behavior of the Latin American economy was the region's high dependence on private capital flows, in the form of both foreign direct investment and portfolio flows. An initial observation about the nature of these capital inflows was that they have tended to increase in times of economic bonanza and high liquidity and to reverse subsequently as conditions changed, at least until the early part of the first decade of the twenty-first century.[10] This was the case in the period ahead of the debt crisis of 1982, the opening of the Latin American economies in the early 1990s, and the period through the peak of Plan Real in Brazil in 1998. The availability of financing and a favorable climate for investment resulted in a large expansion of the public sector expenditure as well as private sector investment.

As conditions reversed, for example at the time of the financial tightening of 1981–1982, or in the mid-1980s, when oil prices plummeted, borrowing countries in the region were seen as a high risk by foreign investors. High public sector deficits and growing debt burdens appreciated exchange rates, and, at times, overexposure by the private sector on account of this appreciation resulted in a major reversal of capital flows, with the consequent need to adjust the current account. While in these circumstances the public sources of financing, particularly the IMF and other international financial organizations, such as the World Bank and the Inter-American Development Bank (IDB), were expected to provide countercyclical funds, their ability or their willingness to lend were far lower than the decline in private financing. Accordingly, the countries had to correct to a large extent their previous imbalances in order to reduce their debt burden and have access to the more limited official resources.[11]

It is only in recent years, after the Brazilian (1998–1999) and Argentine (2001–2003) crises, that a different pattern has emerged. As countries started pursuing stronger macroeconomic policies, increasing terms of trade, improving external account balances, and accumulating reserves, the result was reduced dependence on foreign financing and greater financial stability. Thus the region has been able to experience more rapid growth, and generally a lower rate of inflation, aided by the resurgence of foreign financing and the growing presence of foreign remittances by local émigrés, particularly in Mexico, Central America, Ecuador, and the Caribbean.

Remittances

In 2005, remittances to Latin America from different sources (mainly, the United States, Europe, and Japan) amounted to about US$50 billion (more than 2 percent of the region's GDP), or about the same as the amount of foreign direct investment to the region, providing significant support to the economies of the receiving countries.[12] While it is difficult with current information to determine the exact amount of remittances that is consumed and saved at home, it is clear that savings from remittances have acquired more importance and have replaced foreign funds in financing investment. This trend has not eliminated the typical volatility characterizing external conditions in Latin America that was noted before, but has reduced its magnitude, thus helping the region to attain more sustainable economic growth.

The benefits of remittances to the countries in the region are clear. However, some issues may affect competitiveness. Remittances provide a network of protection to the remitters' families, who usually form the poorer segments of the population. These resources are used for basic necessities, education, and health—the main contributors to human capital in the receiving countries—as well as for other types of investments, including housing and the creation of microenterprises. Nevertheless, the emigrants are frequently among the most enterprising and productive members of their communities. In those circumstances, the question, which will remain largely unanswered here, is whether the loss of income at home is larger than the income generated by the emigrants abroad. The tentative answer is that the productivity will be higher abroad, insofar as there is no complementary capital in the Latin American environment that could help increase the productivity of emigrants had they stayed at home.

A second issue is the effect of remittances on the overall state of the economy. The presence of large flows into the economy is likely to result in a real appreciation of the currency of the receiving country, as illustrated in figure 1.5. The key issue then is whether the appreciation will have an adverse effect on the growth prospects of the economy. In practice, the effect of remittances is the same as that of finding new exports (Dutch disease[13]) or of a change in terms of trade. The effect will be an appreciation of the currency but it will not be detrimental to the well-being of the population at large, as income (including remittances) has increased. In the end, even if there are clear negative effects from remittances, they need to be accepted as part of the process of globalization, which will in practice entail not only movements of goods but of labor and capital. In this regard, the policy issue confronting the national authorities is to create the conditions for increased domestic and foreign investment that enhance the prospects for growth in the countries now facing a major emigration, such as those in the Andes, Central America, the Caribbean, and Mexico.

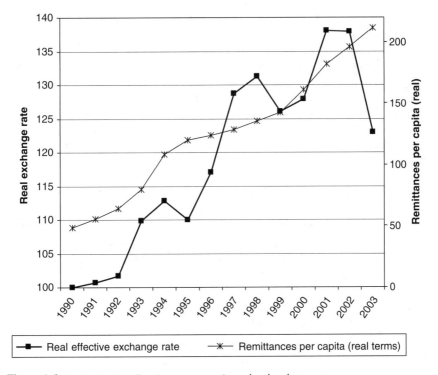

Figure 1.5   Latin America: Remittances per capita and real exchange rates

Macroeconomic Policies in Latin America

Over the last quarter century macroeconomic policies were reactive to changes in the conditions in the world economy, and as a consequence they were eminently procyclical in nature. Accordingly, at times of high capital inflows, the current account of the balance of payments deteriorated, reflecting either an appreciation of the exchange rate that accommodated these flows, or a fiscal expansion financed by such capital flows and resulting in a deterioration of the fiscal balance and thus of the external current account. Eventually, as external debt mounted and capital flows reversed, or the terms of trade deteriorated, the external current account conditions could not be sustained, and the authorities were forced to implement tighter fiscal and monetary policies, while the exchange rate adjusted to deal with the gap. This was the general scenario in Latin American countries because their international reserves were very low and their ability to borrow from the official sector (IMF, World Bank, and other multilateral and bilateral creditors) was very limited. During the past two decades, the volatility of capital flows and the procyclical economic policies have had a seriously adverse effect on investment, savings, and economic growth, and eventually on the exchange rate.

The stop-and-go fiscal policy process that was so typical of the region through the mid-1990s had an adverse effect on the conditions for investment and growth. This was further compounded by an accommodating monetary policy that resulted in high and variable rates of inflation. For many decades and until several years ago, this vulnerability of the economy generated a very adverse environment for competitiveness. Clearly, the variability of the real exchange rate, wages, and real interest rates made it extremely difficult for the private sector to invest in long-term projects. Only very high-yielding or short-term private projects were implemented, while creating incentives to stop capital flight. The high rate of return did not mean that only financially sound projects were incorporated. Frequently, the existence of trade or tax preferences made certain undertakings particularly appealing. However, there was a discrepancy between private returns and social rates of return. These projects (import-substituting industries, non-traditional exports, and utilities) entailed high costs to the society at large. The direct participation of the public sector in certain economic activities (utilities, transport, extractive industry, and so on) further complicated the profitability and competitiveness of the economy, as normally profitable activities (frequently in the export sector) were heavily taxed, or had to make use of expensive inputs. Moreover, the stop-and-go policies, and the corresponding changes in private flows, ended up having significantly negative impacts on investment, which was highly dependent on these flows.

Developments in Macro Policies in Recent Years

In the 1990s many Latin American countries became engaged in what later became known as the "Washington Consensus," another term for market-friendly reforms, including those relating to taxation, public finances, financial sector reform, trade, privatization, and labor reform.[14] The impact of these policies on the region's performance was favorable, dramatic, even though certain countries went through major crises, as was the case in Argentina, Brazil, and Mexico. Perhaps the most favorable development was that inflation declined to levels well in line with the rest of the world, as monetary policy became more effective, the financial system was liberalized, and fiscal imbalances were reduced.

The decline in fiscal imbalances has been particularly steep in recent years as the larger countries in Latin America—Argentina, Brazil, Chile, Colombia, Mexico, and Peru—adjusted their finances. There has been a marked improvement in the fiscal primary balances (the fiscal account excluding interest payments and the key indicators of fiscal policy effort). The effect on the overall fiscal balance of the region has been notable, and should be seen as the main contributor to the break from the past when the regional economies were particularly vulnerable to external shocks.

Expenditures have been rationalized without reducing significantly the resources devoted to social consolidation. Taxes have tended to be streamlined, and revenues have increased, partly on account of higher export revenues associated with a favorable environment. Moreover, public enterprises, either through their privatization or through an improvement in their management, have stopped being a drain on the public finances.

Public debt has declined markedly, from 32 percent of GDP in 2003, when it reached the highest point in recent years, to 22 percent in 2005, as many countries, including Brazil, Chile, and Mexico, reduced their deficits.[15] These efforts have been supplemented by a notable improvement in monetary policy, the development of a generally more solid financial system, and a deepening of financial intermediation. The reduction in the levels of debt and a general decline in interest rates and spreads for the region have helped improve the conditions for a more sustainable path for economic growth.

In the more recent past the economy's performance has also been supported by a sharp improvement in the terms of trade. In this regard Latin American governments may have become confident that the changes are of a permanent nature, and may be tempted to adjust policies accordingly. However, the turbulence that has become evident during the past two years suggests again that this is not a sustainable situation, as commodity prices are characteristically cyclical and may decline in the near future, with adverse effects on the public finances and the balance of payments.

The Bottom Line

Latin America has come a long way in the management of its macroeconomic policies. The external environment has not been benign, as the economies of the region were highly dependent on the behavior of their terms of trade and the volatility in the availability of private financing. Over a period that extended through the 1980s, the countries in the region were not able to ameliorate the effects of these unpredictable conditions. Weak revenues and money-losing public enterprises made the control of the public finances very difficult. With limited external reserves and cyclical availability of foreign financing, the Latin American countries made use of domestic credit financing, resulting in high and volatile rates of inflation.

This macroeconomic environment was detrimental to innovation and productive investment, and may explain the extremely poor performance of the Latin American economy during the period. Furthermore, the attempts to stabilize the economies through exchange rate anchoring plans resulted in episodes of real appreciation, supported by heavy borrowing. These bids eventually failed, resulting in deep balance of payments crises and sharp exchange rate adjustments. These fluctuations further affected competitiveness.

Only in the last 15 years or so have these conditions changed, although not in all countries and not at all times. External conditions remain volatile. However, in response to the experience of the 1980s and 1990s, countries in the region have made a determined effort to reign in their macroeconomic policies. Monetary policies have helped tame inflation and fiscal policies have become much more effective in dealing with previous domestic policy shortcomings and external volatility. Exchange rate conditions, helped by flexible regimes, have provided a more stable environment and are creating the conditions for enhanced competitiveness. It is likely that a new era has begun, where the macroeconomic conditions for trade-related growth are more predictable and stable.

All this progress does not mean that the conditions for enhanced competitiveness have been established for good, that the macro conditions will remain favorable, or that other structural policies are being pursued appropriately. Competitiveness remains fundamentally dependent on improved technologies; better education; an improved business climate; a stronger legal, regulatory, and judicial framework; a better physical and social infrastructure; and access to financing in a competitive environment. However, it means that for the first time in many years, macroeconomic policies stand on a more rational basis and bode well for a favorable future for the region.

Notes

1. This chapter has benefited enormously from the author's association with the following institutions: Centennial Group—Latin America, the Inter-American Dialogue, George Washington University, and the International Monetary Fund, particularly Inter-American Dialogue. Extremely useful comments were provided by different colleagues, particularly P. R. Narvekar and Graciana del Castillo, colleagues at the Centennial Group.

2. The term "overshooting of a currency" refers to a movement of the currency beyond what is predicted to be the longer-term equilibrium value of the currency. This tends to occur at the outset of a currency crisis, or at times of a positive confidence shock which may reflect a short-term overinvestment in the particular currency.

3. CEPAL, *Social Panorama of Latin America,* 2005, provides a detailed description of current social conditions in the region.

4. *Inflation targeting* is the common term for a monetary policy whereby the monetary authorities define a target rate or range for domestic inflation. On the basis of the divergences between the target rates of inflation and the actual rates, the monetary authorities adjust the interest policies to attain the targeted rate of inflation. This policy approach assumes (with considerable reason) that the relationship between monetary aggregates and inflation cannot be predicted accurately in the short run, but that inflation will react to a change in the policy stance in a predictable fashion. This approach, followed by the UK, New Zealand, and countries in Latin America, was developed in response to the more traditional approach, which targets monetary aggregates on the assumption of a well-known and stable relationship between these aggregates and the rate of price increase. The difference between the approaches is less significant than proponents of each approach may suggest as they both emphasize the use of the same monetary instruments as a way to control inflation, although the money supply or credit approach emphasizes the use of an intermediate objective, domestic credit, as a means to control prices.

5. See V. Bulmer-Thomas, *The Economic History of Latin America since Independence* (Cambridge, MA: University Press, 2003) and Corporación Andina de Fomento (CAF), "Recovering Growth in Latin America: Trade Productivity and Social Inclusion" (Caracas, *Reporte de Economía y Desarrollo*, 2005).

6. The integration of Mexico with its North American neighbors (the United States and Canada) under NAFTA resulted in a sharp increase in trade among the three member countries. Mexico increased its manufacturing exports significantly, but to a large extent these exports entailed a relatively low value added based on assembly activities or *maquilas*. Accordingly the high percentage of manufacturing exports needs to be viewed with caution.

7. CAF, "Recovering Growth in Latin America."

8. The standard deviation of the annual percentage change in terms of trade for Latin America and the Caribbean was close to 4.4 percent, compared to 1.65 for developing Asia, and 1 percent for advanced economies.

9. The index of trade restrictiveness includes information on tariff and nontariff barriers to trade. It has been built as a simple weighted average of the index of tariffs and an index of quantitative restrictions, based on World Bank information.

10. Capital inflows and outflows have been volatile for most countries in the region, notwithstanding the presence of direct control on inflows (Brazil, Chile, and Colombia), or the strict prudential regulations, at least in the banking system (Argentina).

11. The International Monetary Fund (IMF) was created and has operated as a lender of last resort in times of financial crisis. However, according to its articles of agreement and its practices, it is not been expected to provide a full compensation for the loss of resources from the private sector. On the contrary, the principle has been to provide resources in support of policies that would make the countries less dependent on financial shocks as those observed in Latin America.

12. Remittances have become a decisive element in the determination of the balance of payments, poverty alleviation, and economic growth for the countries of origin of emigrants to the United States, the European Union, Japan, and other countries (including those within Latin America). The significance of these flows for the Latin American economy cannot be underestimated for those countries that are major recipients of these flows, such as Mexico, most Central American and Caribbean countries, as well as Bolivia, Colombia, Ecuador, and Peru. The behavior of remitters

has been well covered by the literature within and outside the region, with significant contributions by the Inter-American Dialogue, the IDB, and a number of other academic and international organizations. Among the different conclusions about how individuals act regarding these remittances, one of great policy significance is that these are voluntary transfers among individuals, and thus are better left alone, without official intervention to channel these flows to alternative uses.

13. The term "Dutch Disease" originated from the effect that gas findings in the North Sea had on the Dutch economy. It was found that the increase in the supply of exports would lead to an appreciation of the local currency, with an adverse effect on other exports or on import-competing items. The term is now used as a description of the same or equivalent (higher prices for commodities) effects in other economies.

14. The "Washington Consensus," a term coined by John Williamson of the Institute for International Economics, was the alleged common view of the US government, the IMF, World Bank, and the Inter-American Development Bank to incorporate market reforms. Actually it was a movement that started in Chile in the 1970s and Mexico in the 1980s. Because of guilt by association with serious financial crises in the region, the "Washington Consensus" has now been declared a failure by many, as described in Birdsall's Washington contentious. In fact it was the lack of sufficient reform, accompanied by a limited emphasis on social policies, as well as institutional buildup that generated the problems that parts of the region are facing today.

15. Argentina constitutes a special case. After it suffered its worst economic crisis in recent history, in 2001 the authorities announced a default on its external debt. Following several years of tough negotiations, the public debt was subject to significant restructuring and its face value and net present value cut. As of the time of writing this issue has not been settled fully because a significant number of creditors did not accept the deal.

References

Birdsall, N., and A. de la Torre. 2001. *Washington Contentious*. Washington, D.C.: Center for Global Development and Inter-American Dialogue. www.thedialogue.org/publications.

Bulmer-Thomas, V. 2003. *The Economic History of Latin America since Independence*. Cambridge, MA: Cambridge University Press.

Cardoso, F. H. 2006. *The Accidental President of Brazil, a Memoir*. Washington, D.C.: Public Affairs.

Collyns, C., and G. R. Kinkaid, eds. 2003. "Managing Financial Crises: Recent Experience and Lessons for Latin America." *IMF Occasional Papers* # 217. Washington, D. C.: International Monetary Fund.

Corporación Andina de Fomento. 2005. "Recovering Growth in Latin America: Trade Productivity and Social Inclusion." Caracas, *Reporte de Economía y Desarrollo*.

CEPAL. 2005. *Social Panorama of Latin America*. Santiago de Chile: CEPAL.

———. 2005. *Statistical Yearbook*. Santiago de Chile: CEPAL.

Edwards, S. 1995. *Crisis and Reform in Latin America: From Despair to Hope*. Washington, D.C.: World Bank Group and Oxford University Press.

Franko, P. 2003. *The Puzzle of Latin American Economic Development*. Lanham, MD: Rowman and Littlefield.

Inter-American Development Bank. 2006. "The Politics of Policies: Economic and Social Progress in Latin America." *Annual Report*. Washington, D.C.: Inter-American Development Bank.

Inter-American Dialogue. 2004. *All in the Family, Latin America's Most Important International Financial Flows.* Washington, D.C.: Inter-American Dialogue.

International Monetary Fund. 2003–06. *Global Financial Stability Report—Market Development and Issues.* Washington, D.C.: International Monetary Fund.

International Monetary Fund. 2004–2006. *World Economic Outlook.* Washington, D.C.: International Monetary Fund.

Kuczynski, P., and J. Williamson, eds. 2003. *After the Washington Consensus.* Washington, D.C.: Institute of International Economics.

Loser, C. 2003. "External Debt Sustainability Guidelines for Low- and Middle-Income Countries." G24 Technical Papers. http://www.g24.org.

———. 2004. "A Counter-Cyclical Financing Mechanism for Developing Countries: Wishful Thinking or Policy Requirement?" G-24 Technical Papers. http://www.g24.org.

Perry, G. et al. 2006. *Poverty Reduction and Growth: Virtuous and Vicious Circles.* Washington, D.C.: World Bank.

Singh, A. et al. 2005. "Stabilization and Reform in Latin America: A Macroeconomic Perspective on the Experience since the Early 1990s." *IMF Occasional Papers # 238.* Washington, D.C: International Monetary Fund.

World Bank. 2001. *Inequality in Latin America and the Caribbean: Breaking with History?* wbln0018.worldbank.org/LAC.

———. 2005–2006. *World Development Indicators.* Washington, D.C.: World Bank.

CHAPTER 2

Coveting Human Capital: Is Latin American Education Competitive?

Jeffrey M. Puryear and Tamara Ortega Goodspeed[1]

> A country's ability to absorb new technologies, to produce goods and services that can reach standards of quality and performance acceptable in international markets, [and] to engage with the rest of the world in ways that are value-creating, is intimately linked to the quality of its schools.
>
> A. Lopez-Claros, M. Porter, and K. Schwab,
> *Global Competitiveness Report 2005–2006*, p. xxi

Latin America's ability to compete successfully in global markets depends significantly on the quality of its labor force, which in turn depends on the quality of its schools. Good education improves workers' skills; promotes growth; reduces poverty; and provides an important foundation for building the institutions, transparency, and good governance that enable production to happen.

It is no coincidence that two of the nine "pillars" critical to national competitiveness and productivity in the World Economic Forum's Global Competitiveness Index deal directly with primary education and higher education and training. A third pillar—innovation—is powerfully linked to strong research institutions, the availability of high quality scientists and engineers, and effective university–private sector collaboration in order to create new knowledge/products. But Latin America lags in all of these areas. Without substantial improvements to its education systems, the region will clearly be at a disadvantage as it seeks to position itself in the global knowledge economy.

Latin America neglects its education systems at its peril. Why?

- Companies can find cheap labor elsewhere. Latin America's success increasingly depends on developing a large pool of highly skilled labor, both because the global economy is becoming more knowledge intensive and because huge numbers of lower-wage, unskilled Chinese and Indian workers drive down demand for low-skill workers elsewhere (Birdsall et al., 2007, forthcoming). Indeed, surveys indicate that nearly 60 percent of firms that do business in Latin America cite the lack of skilled personnel as an important constraint to productivity in the region (De Ferranti et al., 2003, p. 118).

- Improving enrollment without improving learning will have only a limited impact on productivity. Recent studies have found that investments in quality (particularly as measured by student achievement in mathematics and science) matter as much, if not more, for growth than getting kids in school and keeping them there longer (Hanushek, 2005). Unless Latin America can produce top-quality graduates capable of taking on more complex tasks and adapting to changing environments, the most competitive firms and workers (and the benefits these accrue for a country's economy) will continue to go elsewhere.
- Educational inequalities exacerbate the region's income inequalities—underutilizing large portions of the potential labor force and adding to social tension. Latin America is notorious for the large and growing income inequalities between its rich and poor citizens. Education both contributes to these inequalities (through its effects on earnings) and is affected by them (because poverty constrains people's access to learning). The result is that while an elite few capture substantial wage premia for completing secondary and tertiary education (Birdsall et al., 2007, forthcoming), the vast majority of Latin America's current and future workforce fails to live up to its potential. This in turn has a negative impact on growth and social stability.

Education in Latin America: Steady Expansion

Latin American countries are working hard to improve schools, with some success. Not only are more children in school, they stay longer, leading to an increasingly educated labor force. Most governments recognize the importance of making quality education for all a driving force in economic development and social equity, and are investing more to make that happen. Throughout the region, countries have also taken important steps to establish national standards, create and consolidate national testing systems, and place more authority and responsibility in the hands of municipal governments and schools—critical components in making schools better. Leaders from business, politics, churches, the media, and civil society are also joining the effort. However, despite these significant achievements, student learning remains low and inadequate for the needs of modern societies.

Levels of Education Are Rising, but Remain behind Competitors

The numbers related to education in Latin America are growing steadily. Enrollments are rising at every level, and more children are completing more

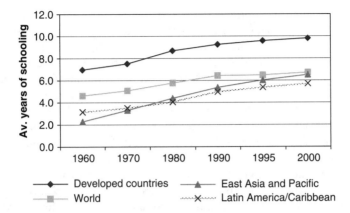

Figure 2.1 Average years of schooling of the labor force, by region, 1960–2000

Source: Barro and Lee, 2001.

Note: "Labor force" is defined as those aged 25 and over.

years of schooling than ever before. Progress, however, still lags behind many parts of the world, including East Asia and Eastern Europe.

Years of Schooling

Over the past several decades, the region has seen a steady increase in average years of schooling of its labor force rising from around three years in 1960 to nearly double that in 2000. Nonetheless, the average worker still attains far less than a complete high school education. A workforce with so little education makes it hard for countries to move beyond industries focused on primary materials and manual labor to those based on advanced production processes and higher value-added products (Lopez-Claros et al., 2005).

Moreover, workers in Latin America have less education than their counterparts in East Asia and Eastern Europe, and the gap with East Asia may be growing (figure 2.1). Indeed, recent World Bank analysis shows that Latin American workers have almost one and a half years less schooling than do workers in countries with similar incomes, while workers in the East Asian Tigers have almost one year more (De Ferranti et al., 2003, p. 45).

Basic Education

More Latin American children enter school today than ever before and most of them complete primary school. Preschool enrollment rates are above the world average, and most countries are close to getting every child (except the poorest and most isolated) to enter primary school.

Even so, four of every ten children still do not enroll in preschool—a disturbing figure given the importance of early instruction in providing children, and particularly poor children, with the foundation for future learning. One in ten still do not complete primary school, and less than half of young people in rural Brazil, Guatemala, and Nicaragua do so (ECLAC, 2005a, 2005b).

The most noteworthy problem, however, comes at the secondary level, where enrollment and completion rates in most countries are still below those of countries with similar levels of income—and particularly below the East Asian Tigers. Around two-thirds of secondary-aged youths are enrolled in secondary school, far fewer than in OECD (Organisation for Economic Co-operation and Development) countries, Korea, Ireland, or Hong Kong. According to one recent estimate, secondary enrollment rates in Latin America are almost 19 percentage points *behind* what would be expected given countries' incomes, while rates in the East Asian Tigers are nearly 18 percentage points *higher* than would be expected (De Ferranti et al., 2003, p. 28).

Few Latin American countries regularly report secondary completion rates, but among those that do around 60 percent or less of the secondary-aged population graduates. Argentina, Paraguay, and Mexico have rates below those in Malaysia, the Philippines, and Thailand, where gross domestic product (GDP) per capita is similar or lower.

Tertiary

Around a quarter (26 percent) of university-age youths are enrolled in higher education in Latin America, well above the rate of 16 percent in 1985 (World Bank 2006a; Winkler, 1990). This is similar to the world average (24 percent) and is well above the average for East Asia and the Pacific (17 percent).

However, enrollments are still less than half the average for high-income countries (67 percent) and well below rates in more successful economies, such as the United States and Korea. Recent estimates suggest that Latin American tertiary enrollments are around 10 percentage points lower than one would expect for its income, while East Asian Tigers have a surplus of about 5 percentage points (De Ferranti et al., 2003). And enrollments at this level appear to be growing more slowly in Latin America than in East Asia and high-income countries, probably due at least partially to bottlenecks at the secondary level in Latin American countries.

Moreover, most Latin American university students never complete their studies. Forty percent of Argentine university students drop out in the first year, and only a quarter of those admitted goes on to graduate. Only a third of those admitted in Chile and half of those admitted in Colombia graduate (Holm-Nielsen et al., 2005, p. 46). The situation is similar in Mexico, where only 30 percent of those who enter in any given year graduate (Oppenheimer, 2005, p. 318). This has tremendous ramifications both in terms of overall skill levels and for education finance, where large sums of public monies support a small cadre of college students who seldom complete their degrees, at the expense of large numbers of students who never reach the tertiary level.

At the graduate level, available evidence suggests that Latin America is also at a disadvantage. While OECD countries produce one new PhD per 5,000 people, in Brazil the ratio is 1 per 70,000; in Chile, 1 per 140,000, and in Colombia 1 per 700,000 (Holm-Nielsen et al., 2005, p. 41). The region's limited number of scientists and advanced degree recipients weakens the region's competitiveness by limiting the countries' ability to use and generate knowledge, and to carry out research.

Investment in Education Is Increasing, but Remains Inadequate, Inefficient, and Inequitable

Almost all governments are devoting more money to education, both as a percentage of GDP and in per pupil terms. Public spending increased from 2.7 percent of GDP in 1990 to 4.3 percent in 2004. This is about the same as the world average (4.4 percent), although lower than the 5.6 percent that high-income countries spend (World Bank, 2006).

However, even after adjusting for differences in the cost of living, spending per primary school student varies widely, ranging from around US$190 in Nicaragua to around US$1,450 in Chile, and remains well below that of developed countries, where spending averages around US$4,200 per student. Although there is no magic number for optimal spending, it is unlikely that Nicaragua is getting the same quality education for its students as the Chileans, who spend almost ten times more. Nor are the Chileans likely to be getting the same globally competitive quality education as OECD countries that invest three times as much. Moreover, current spending levels are almost certainly insufficient to meet the additional needs common among children from disadvantaged families.

Spending is also inefficient. Primary and secondary repetition (that costs the region over U.S.$11 billion a year, according to UNESCO estimates), spending on absent or poorly performing teachers, and a lack of information on which policy interventions are most effective keep countries from getting the best returns from their investment. Furthermore, Latin American governments still spend on average more than three times as much per student at the university level than at the primary level, and in Nicaragua and Brazil the ratio is much higher (figure 2.2).[2] Because much of government expenditure on tertiary education goes to subsidize the tuition of the rich (who would pay university tuition were subsidies not available) at the expense of the poor (who seldom finish secondary school), one can argue that such high ratios soak up public funds that might be better spent improving primary and secondary education for the poor.

Perhaps not surprisingly, each of the five Latin American countries that participated in the 2000 Program for International Student Assessment (PISA) examination had learning scores below what would be expected given their level of per student investment (figure 2.3).

Principal Challenges

Latin America faces four major barriers to making education a more effective tool in improving competitiveness—quality, equity, science and technology, and teachers.

Quality: More Education Has Not Led to More Learning

Despite progress in increasing enrollments and spending, the quality of education that most children receive is strikingly low. Latin American students perform poorly on national and international tests, evidence that is disheartening, especially given the importance of education quality for growth.[3]

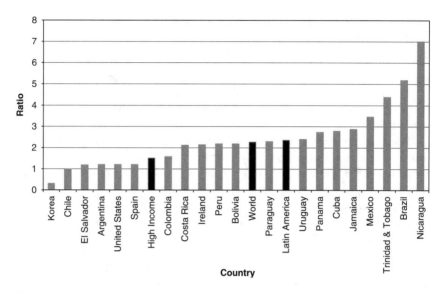

Figure 2.2 Ratio of spending per pupil: Higher vs. primary education, 2004

Source: PREAL calculations based on data from *World Development Indicators 2006,* and World Bank EdStats online database, http://devdata.worldbank.org/edstats/cd5.asp (accessed June 2006). Brazil, Nicaragua, Trinidad & Tobago from *World Development Indicators 2005* (Washington, D.C.: World Bank).

Note: All data most recent year within two years of date listed.

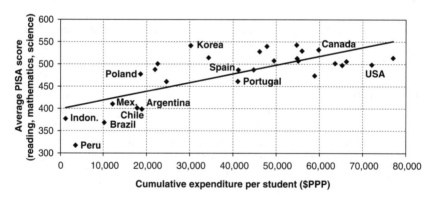

Figure 2.3 Student performance on PISA and spending per student, 2000

Source: OECD/UNESCO, *Literacy Skills for the World of Tomorrow* (Paris: OECD/UNESCO, 2003), adapted from figure 3.7b, p. 113.

Note: Scores reflect average student performance across the three assessment areas. Expenditure is expressed in US dollars using purchasing power parities ($PPP).

Basic Education

Since 1995, only eight Latin American countries have participated in a major global achievement test. In every case they have scored well below the international average and near the bottom among participating countries. The results are striking for a number of reasons.

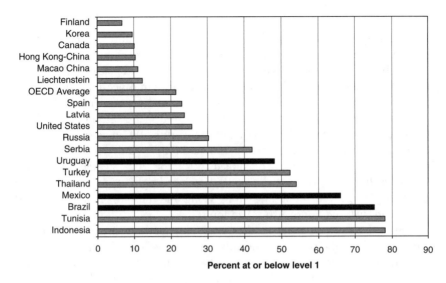

Figure 2.4 Percentage of students performing at or below the most basic level on the PISA mathematics test, selected countries, 2003

Source: Based on data from OECD, 2004, table 2.5a, p. 354.

Note: Data shows student performing at or below level 1 on the combined mathematics scale and includes all participating non-OECD countries, United States, Canada, Mexico, Spain, and top two OECD scorers.

First, they show that Latin American students have serious deficiencies in the basic mathematics and reading skills needed in today's world. For example, in the 2003 PISA exam, roughly half the 15-year-olds in the three participating Latin American countries (Brazil, Mexico, and Uruguay) had serious difficulties in using reading as a tool for further learning, analyzing problems, or building new skills. A majority (three-fourths in Brazil, two-thirds in Mexico, and nearly half in Uruguay) could not consistently apply basic mathematical skills to understand an everyday situation (figure 2.4). Indeed, when business executives in 117 countries were asked to rate whether education in their country meets the needs of a competitive economy, only one Latin American country (Costa Rica, ranked 39th) scored above average, and ten ranked outside the top 100 (Lopez-Claros et al., 2005).

Second, even the most affluent Latin American students tested scored at or below the OECD average, and well below the top students in other regions (IDB, 2006, pp. 17–18). Likewise, the best Chilean students scored below the *average* for students in such top performers as Singapore and Korea on the most recent Trends in International Mathematics and Science Study (TIMSS).

Third, Latin American students do poorly, even when compared with countries similar GDP per capita. For example, only the top 25 percent of Chilean eighth graders scored at the *average* level for countries with similar levels of development (e.g., Russia, Latvia, Malaysia) on the 2003 TIMSS test.

Tertiary

Unfortunately, there is little hard data available on the quality of tertiary education in Latin America. Universities are generally independent and accountable to no one. Two of the region's largest universities, Universidad Nacional Autónoma (UNAM) in Mexico and Universidad de Buenos Aires in Argentina refuse to seek national accreditation or submit to external evaluation (Oppenheimer, 2005).

Existing evidence suggests that the region's universities are not of globally competitive quality. In a 2005 ranking of the world's 500 universities, no Latin American university ranked in the top 100, and only 2 (University of São Paulo in Brazil and UNAM in Mexico) ranked in the top 202 (Shanghai Jiao Tong University, 2005).[4] By comparison, South Korea had eight universities in the top 500, China had seven (excluding Hong Kong and Taiwan), Hong Kong and Taiwan had five, and South Africa had four.

Many university professors in the region do not have masters or doctoral degrees, and the majority work at the university only part-time.[5] On average, fewer than one in ten Latin American professors have a PhD. In Colombia and Mexico less than 4 percent do. Brazil, where 30 percent of professors hold doctorates, does much better, but is still below the average for more advanced economies.

In addition, issues of overcrowding, deteriorating physical facilities, lack of equipment, obsolete instruction material, outdated curricula, and the need to provide remedial instruction to compensate for poor quality primary and secondary instruction, undermine universities' ability to provide high quality education (Holm-Nielsen et al., 2004). Links between universities and the private sector are weak, undermining national research and development capacities.

Equity: Poor and Minority Children Learn Less and Leave School Earlier than Their Better-off Peers

Latin America is the most unequal region in the world. Its combination of high inequality and poverty seriously inhibits economic growth. Since education is the most important productive asset that most people will ever own, the region's unequal distribution of quality education is a major constraint on the region's competitiveness. Rampant inequality leaves many poor, rural, and indigenous individuals without the tools they need to be successful economically, socially, and as citizens—underutilizing large portions of the potential labor force and adding to social tension.

A greater percentage of the poor are starting primary school than ever before, particularly in Brazil, Costa Rica, Ecuador, El Salvador, and Venezuela. However, children from poor families routinely score much lower on tests and leave school sooner than those from better-off families.

With the exception of Jamaica, the wealthiest fifth of 21- to 30-year-olds gets five to seven more years of schooling than the poorest fifth. In most countries, the gap has either remained the same or gotten worse.

Indigenous and Afro-Latin children are also at a disadvantage. They are less likely than their peers to complete primary school or to enroll in secondary school.

For example, in Paraguay enrollment rates for Guarani-only speakers fall from 93 percent for primary school-aged students to 47 percent for those in the secondary-age group, a decline of 46 points. For Spanish speakers the fall is less than half that amount (19 percentage points) (IDB, 2006). The indigenous and Afro-Latin children also tend to score below their white peers in achievement tests. However, racial/ethnic gaps, at least in terms of literacy and primary enrollment, do seem to be lessening (Winkler and Cueto, 2004).

Skills in Technology, Mathematics, Science, and English All Lag Behind

Latin American schools do a poor job of providing the more specific skills necessary to be competitive. Even those who achieve basic competency in reading and mathematics are unlikely to acquire the advanced mathematics, science, technology, and English skills that allow countries to innovate and attract foreign investment.

Science and Technology

Evidence suggests that Latin American children, and especially poor children, lag behind in acquiring computer and other technology skills. Among the poor the rate of those never having used a computer is 29 percent in Mexico and 10 percent in Uruguay. Only around six in ten Mexican students and seven in ten Uruguayan students report that they can create/edit a document or move files from one place to another on a computer without help. This is less than the average for OECD countries, Latvia, and Russia (whose GDP per capita are similar to Latin America), although higher than in Thailand.[6]

In addition, international test scores suggest that very few secondary students in Latin America have a strong foundation in mathematics and science. Few students participating in the PISA 2003 mathematics test performed at internationally competitive levels (IDB, 2006).[7] Only 1 percent of students from Uruguay, the region's best performer, scored at the highest level in mathematics, compared with 7 to 8 percent in Korea and Finland and 11 percent in Hong Kong (OECD, 2004). In science, average scores for Latin American students were also below those of countries with similar levels of income, and well below the OECD mean (figure 2.5).

Business leaders in the region also give the quality of mathematics and science education in their countries low marks when asked to rate whether it lags far behind most other countries (a score of 1) or is among best in world (a score of 7). Costa Rica, with a score of 4, was the highest-ranked Latin American country (66th of 117 participating countries). Fifteen countries scored below 3.5. The Dominican Republic, Guatemala, and Honduras ranked in the last three spots, with a score of 2.3.

At the tertiary level, the region produces very few science or engineering graduates. The bulk of university graduates study social science, law, or business. In most countries, less than a quarter receive science or engineering degrees. By contrast, nearly 40 percent of all Korean university graduates, and nearly 30 percent of all Irish and Finnish graduates are trained in science or engineering. In Latin America,

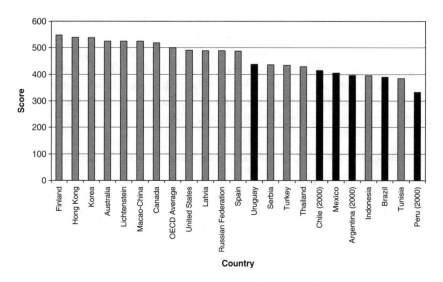

Figure 2.5 Average PISA science scores, by country, 2003

Source: OECD, 2004, and OECD/UNESCO, *Literacy Skills for the World of Tomorrow* (Paris: OECD/UNESCO, 2003).

Note: Detailed proficiency levels for science will not be available until the 2006 test. However a score close to 400 indicates that students can generally recall only simple factual knowledge and use it to draw conclusions. Test scores for Chile, Argentina, and Peru are from the 2000 PISA science examination.

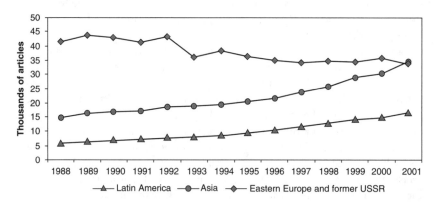

Figure 2.6 Scientific and engineering article output of emerging and developing countries by region, 1988–2001

Source: IDB, 2006, graph B.3.2.b.

only Mexico has similar rates. Not surprisingly, when business executives in 117 countries were asked to rank the availability of scientists and engineers in their country, no Latin American country scored in the top 50, and only five scored above the mean (Argentina, Costa Rica, Chile, and Venezuela) (Lopez-Claros et al., 2005). Latin America's scientific output is also low compared to other regions, both in terms of scientific and engineering articles and patents granted (figure 2.6).

English Language Skills

For good or ill, fluency in English is an important asset for competitiveness. It is the primary language of international business, Web content, and cutting-edge research publication. And for Latin America, it is the language of operation of a major trading partner and neighbor. English language call centers, tourism, and other services have the potential to provide a significant source of income and employment. Not surprisingly, more countries are placing English (or at least some second language) on the list of fundamental skills students should develop.

But few studies track how many people speak English in any given country or their level of proficiency. Most Latin American English classes start in seventh grade with two hours of instruction per week. Meanwhile in Singapore, Thailand, and Malaysia, English instruction starts in first grade and in China and Korea it starts in third grade. Chinese students meet four hours a week and Singaporean students meet eight hours a week, not including private instruction outside school hours.

Teaching Is in Crisis

Perhaps no other single area presents as great a challenge for improving education in Latin America as strengthening the teaching profession. On the one hand, teachers face enormous challenges—ranging from poor training, lack of classroom resources and administrative support, and low social prestige—that make it difficult for them to do their jobs well. On the other, education management systems lack incentives to attract and retain high-quality teachers and mechanisms to remove those who continue to perform poorly after a reasonable effort has been made to help them improve. To make matters worse, governments and teachers unions generally view each other as adversaries, rather than partners, in educating children.

Most studies suggest that a large share of Latin America's teaching corps is ill equipped to provide globally competitive education to all students. Teachers seldom represent the best and brightest of their generation. Many have lower academic grades than their peers and have chosen teaching more as a last resort for getting into college than as a true vocation (PREAL-BID, 2004).[8] Poor children, who need high-quality teachers the most, generally get the teachers with the least training and experience.

To date, governments have concentrated principally on improving teacher skills through better preservice training and professional development. In most countries preservice programs are now provided at the tertiary level.[9] Several countries are creating mechanisms for teachers to learn from each other, incorporating active learning strategies and classroom follow-up into teacher education, and experimenting with ways to reach teachers and potential teachers in rural areas. However, several challenges remain. Teacher training is often disconnected from classroom needs and other elements of the education system (standards, tests, curriculum, and so on), and so far there is little evidence that training or teacher credentials have significant impact on teacher performance or student learning. The quality of training programs varies widely, and only a few countries accredit schools of education or test their graduates as a condition for employment.

The bigger challenge, however, is that systems for managing teachers do not promote professionalism. Among the major limitations are the following.

- *Teacher performance is rarely evaluated.* Most teachers in the public sector are not accountable to anyone—principals, parents, or governments. Teacher unions are opposed to reforms designed to evaluate performance, impeding effective implementation. In Chile, union leaders have refused to implement a relatively weak system of evaluation they agreed to in 2004.
- *Pay is unrelated to performance.* The issues surrounding teacher salaries are controversial and complex. However, one thing is clear—compensation systems are not producing the kind of teaching excellence the region needs. Teaching excellence is seldom rewarded, dismissing a teacher for poor performance is nearly impossible, and mediocre teachers are paid the same as outstanding educators who give 110 percent every day.

  To confront these issues, a few countries have experimented with a variety of incentive systems (including linking pay to performance), with mixed results.[10] On the one hand, evidence suggests that incentives can make a difference in attracting, retaining, and motivating high-quality teachers, and affect their behavior in the classroom. On the other, deficiencies in the design and implementation of existing teacher incentives reforms limit their effectiveness and sometimes lead to unintended outcomes. Given the small number of performance-based experiments underway in the region, it is also likely that countries have not yet found the right mix of incentives and further (well-documented) trial and error will be necessary.
- *Nonmonetary performance incentives are few.* Performance incentives that are common in other occupations—such as clear standards regarding what professionals should do and achieve; job security in return for good performance; social prestige and recognition; opportunities for professional growth, including a career advancement ladder and treatment as a competent professional; and having to satisfy clients or a supervisor—are largely absent from teaching in Latin America.

There are signs of progress, however. For example, El Salvador has revised its teacher statute, nearly doubled teachers' monthly salary, and is screening teacher candidates for academic levels. In addition to training and management challenges, significant, ongoing tension between governments and teacher unions holds back improvements to education. On the one hand, teacher unions feel underappreciated. They argue that governments, as teachers' employers, are failing to hold up their end of the education partnership. Teachers are not consulted regarding reforms, have little say in how schools are run, and often get little support in the most basic elements of their job (for example, in-service training and supervision, lesson planning, and teaching materials). On the other hand, for their part, governments argue that teacher unions are only concerned with salary and job stability, and are unwilling to accept some share of responsibility for guaranteeing education quality.

The good news is that in a few countries coalitions of actors, including teacher unions, have begun to come together to talk about national plans for improving education quality and strengthening the teaching profession. And, if experiences in Chile and Mexico are any indication, the ideas of pay for performance and teacher evaluation may be gaining ground among individual teachers and unions.

Overcoming these four major barriers to making education a more effective tool in improving competitiveness is particularly difficult given the political context in which reforms must be adopted and implemented. Leaders seeking to make tough decisions to date have had few allies. Information on school performance is often limited in scope, unreliable, out-of-date, not readily accessible, and not user friendly. As a result, most education stakeholders are unaware of deficiencies in their public schools, and so are not motivated to press for change.

Few programs monitor the effectiveness of particular interventions, leaving policy too dependent on guesswork or inertia. As a result, special interests (e.g., teacher unions and university students) opposing education reforms are strong, while demand for reform is weak. Special interests control information, defend privilege, and resist reform at the expense of those most directly affected by school quality. Parents who send their children to public schools lack information and are overwhelmingly poor, relatively uneducated, and not accustomed to playing a direct role in improving learning. Wealthier and better-educated parents send their children to private schools and so are not directly affected by—and worry less about—problems in the public system. Politics, and not just policy, hold back educational progress in the region.

Education Fundamentals for Competitiveness

Revamping education in ways that enhance competitiveness will take time. The most important changes necessary to prepare students for today's knowledge economy fall into two broad categories: (1) make learning the chief measure of educational success, and (2) make schools accountable to citizens for achieving educational objectives.

Put Learning First

In shaping education, countries need to shift away from their traditional focus on inputs—such as enrollments, spending, buildings, and teachers—and toward the most important education output: what children learn. The idea here is not to ignore inputs, but rather to recognize that outputs, in the form of learning, are what justify the inputs. Countries therefore need to reorganize educational systems to make sure the proper outputs are produced. Learning needs to be given top priority.

Putting learning first implies establishing clear learning standards. Countries need to decide what children should learn in each subject at each level. For primary schools, emphasis should be placed on mastering simple skills in reading, writing, and mathematics. These are the building blocks of competitiveness; if they are not in place, nothing else will work. At the secondary level, more complex standards that emphasize science, technology, and advanced mathematics can be phased in. Throughout, emphasis should be on understanding and applying subject matter rather than just memorizing it. And standards should include creativity, adaptability, and self-discipline.

With growing globalization, competitiveness also requires learning a second language. Training in a second language should be offered as early as possible to all children, particularly those from poor families (who are least likely to have the opportunity to acquire a second language outside of school). English is the most logical option for most of Latin America. But consideration should be given as well to Chinese or other Asian languages.

Putting learning first also implies systematically measuring how much students learn. Countries should establish robust national (or regional) testing systems that regularly measure progress toward achieving learning standards. Ideally these tests should be administered annually to all children so as to monitor progress and identify problems. The tests need to be aligned with national learning standards, and based in institutions that are insulated from partisan politics. Test results should be disseminated to parents, teachers, employers, and the general public in simple, user-friendly formats. They should be used systematically to adjust and improve education policy.

Countries should also experiment with simple diagnostic tests—at least in reading and mathematics—that teachers can apply quickly several times a year to determine which of their students need special attention. In addition, countries should regularly participate in at least one global test of student achievement. Global achievement tests, such as PISA, TIMSS, and PIRLS (Progress in International Reading Literacy Study), provide an important benchmark for assessing progress—demonstrating how national schools stack up with other (competitor) countries. Countries that do poorly in these assessments can use the results to mobilize national support for needed changes. These assessments constitute an important tool for quality control. In a global economy, however, countries are better served by participating in tests that are truly worldwide rather than in those that only include Latin American countries.

Although some officials caution that testing (and particularly global testing) is too expensive for developing countries, such arguments have little empirical base. Most estimates put testing costs at well under 1 percent of the annual cost of educating a student (Wolff, 2007, forthcoming). At those levels and given their potential for promoting quality, achievement tests appear to be remarkably cost effective. Moreover, the payoff in terms of GDP growth to improvements in learning may be high. Hanushek suggests that "if this moderately strong improvement [0.5 standard deviation] in student skills could be obtained during a 20-year reform period, a country could expect to pay for all of its educational expenditures by 2040 with the growth dividend" (2005).

Make Schools Accountable—to Parents, Employers, and Citizens

Countries should establish mechanism of accountability that link schools to parents, employers, and the broader community. The objective should be an effective, transparent system with clear standards, able providers, reasonable funding, measures of progress, rewards for success, and sanctions for failure.

Accountability—setting goals and holding students, parents, teachers, principals, and ministries responsible for results—is crucial to good education and absent from most education systems in Latin America. In the region's public schools, goals are not clearly spelled out, and progress is seldom carefully measured. Teachers receive the same salary, along with ironclad job security, regardless of their performance or their students' success. Students, parents, and employers, who constitute the schools' clients, have little information on how schools are doing and almost no mechanisms of influence.

To be sure, accountability is not a dichotomous variable. Many different forms are possible. But in all cases where accountability exists, the providers of education face strong incentives to meet standards and perform at the highest level. They are, by one means or another, held accountable by education stakeholders.

Making schools accountable is both a technical and political challenge. At least five basic elements need to be in place.

- *Standards.* Countries need to establish measurable modern education standards in at least the most basic subjects, such as mathematics and language, that clarify what students, teachers, and schools are expected to achieve.
- *Information.* Education systems need to provide reliable information on student achievement vis-à-vis standards, school performance, and the steps being taken toward improvement.
- *Consequences.* Meeting, or failing to meet, education standards must have consequences. Teachers who and schools that perform well should be rewarded. Those that consistently perform poorly should be sanctioned.
- *Authority.* All education actors—schools, local communities, and parents—should have some level of influence over educational systems. Teachers should be able to decide on teaching strategies and materials. School directors need the power to allocate their budgets, to hire and fire teachers, and to reward good performers. Communities need some influence over school management and teacher selection. Parents should have at least some choice in determining which school their children attend. In most countries, many of these elements are missing.
- *Capacity.* Good education requires ability and resources. Teachers, principals, and schools need the funding, training, autonomy, and support necessary to meet the goals that have been established. Redirecting part of the public higher education subsidy to public primary and secondary schools (which overwhelming serve the poor) would be a good step in bolstering capacity, strengthening competitiveness, and promoting equity.

By making learning the chief measure of success and by making schools accountable to citizens, countries can take a major step forward in strengthening their competitiveness. Progress will nonetheless be slow. Improving education takes time and depends on many factors working together. These two broad measures, however, constitute a powerful institutional dynamic that holds educational actors responsible for their actions as public servants. Doing that well will help tip the balance in favor of producing consistently good education.

Notes

1. This chapter draws heavily from the Partnership for Educational Revitalization in the Americas' (PREAL's) 2006 report, *Quantity without Quality: A Report Card on Education in Latin America* that is available online at www.preal.org. The authors would like to thank Kristin Saucier, Alejandro Ganimian, and Alex Triantaphyllis for their invaluable support in providing timely and dedicated research assistance.
2. Venezuela (which does not currently release figures) has had similarly high rates in the past.
3. For more on this topic see E. Hanushek, "Why Quality Matters in Education." *Finance and Development* 42, no. 2 (June 2005), http://www.imf.org/external/pubs/ft/fandd/2005/06/hanushek.htm.
4. The ranking is based on a variety of factors including alumni and faculty receiving the Nobel Prize in physics, chemistry, medicine, or economics (or Fields Medals in mathematics); number of highly cited researchers in life sciences, medicine, engineering, physical or social sciences; articles in major academic journals; and quality of education in relation to size. A similar ranking of the top 200 universities based primarily on peer review, produced in 2005 by the *Times Higher Education Supplement* in London (www.thes.co.uk), includes only two Latin American universities.
5. According to Holm-Nielsen et al., "roughly 60 percent of teachers at public and 86 percent of teachers at private universities work part time, and many of them hold more than one job" (L. Holm-Nielsen, K. Thorn, J. J. Brunner, and J. Balán, "Regional and International Challenges to Higher Education in Latin America," in *Higher Education in Latin America and the Caribbean: The International Dimension,* ed. H. De Wit, I. Jaramillo, J. Gacel-Ávila, and J. Knight [Washington, D.C.: World Bank, 2005], p. 48).
6. Paradoxically, in the same study, Mexico and Uruguay seem to do relatively well in terms of the percentage of students who are confident with high-level tasks on computers (e.g., using of software to find and get rid of viruses, using a database to produce a list of addresses, using a spreadsheet to plot a graph, creating a power point presentation, or constructing a Web-page), with rates near or above the OECD average and better than Korea for most indicators. Also note that while computer skills are important to competitiveness, it is less clear whether and how access to computers in schools affects the acquisition of those skills and learning more generally (Organisation for Economic Co-operation and Development, *Are Students Ready for a Technology-Rich World? What PISA Studies Tell Us* [Paris: Organisation for Economic Co-operation and Development, 2005]). Further study is needed to determine what technology programs will work best under what circumstances.
7. The IDB study defines internationally competitive as students scoring at levels IV, V, and VI on the PISA mathematics test.
8. However, Chile and Guatemala both appear to enroll higher-quality applicants. In Chile, this is at least in part a response to higher salaries (Navarro, 2005).

9. Until recently, several countries provided teacher training at the secondary school level.

10. For more on specific country case studies, see E. Vegas, *Incentives to Improve Teaching: Lessons from Latin America* (Washington, D.C.: World Bank, 2005).

References

Barro, Robert J., and Jong-Wha Lee. 2001. "International Data on Educational Attainment: Updates and Implication." *Oxford Economic Papers* 53, no. 3, 541–563.

Birdsall, N., A. de la Torre, and R. Menezes. Forthcoming, 2007. *Economic Policies for Latin America's Poor Majority: A Guide for the Perplexed.* Washington, D.C.: Center for Global Development and Inter-American Dialogue.

De Ferranti, D., G. Perry, I. Gill, J. L. Guasch, W. Maloney, C. Sánchez-Páramo, and N. Schady. 2003. *Closing the Gap in Education and Technology.* Washington, D.C.: World Bank.

Economic Commission for Latin America and the Caribbean (ECLAC). 2005a. *Panorama social de America Latina 2005.* Santiago: Economic Commission for Latin America and the Caribbean.

———. 2005b. *The Millennium Development Goals: A Latin American and Caribbean Perspective.* Santiago: Economic Commission for Latin America and the Caribbean.

Filmer, D., A. Hasan, and L. Pritchett. 2006. *A Millenium Learning Goal: Measuring Real Progress in Education.* Working Paper 97. Washington, D.C.: Center for Global Development.

Hanushek, E. 2005. "Why Quality Matters in Education." *Finance and Development* 42 (2).http://www.imf.org/external/pubs/ft/fandd/2005/06/hanushek.htm.

Holm-Nielsen, L., J. J. Brunner, J. Balán, K. Thorn, and G. Elacqua. 2004. "Higher Education in Latin America and the Carribbean: Challenges and Prospects." Santiago: UNESCO. http://mt.educarchile.cl/archives/2005/08/higher_educatio.html.

Holm-Nielsen, L., K. Thorn, J. J. Brunner, and J. Balán. 2005. "Regional and International Challenges to Higher Education in Latin America." In *Higher Education in Latin America and the Caribbean: The International Dimension,* ed. H. De Wit, I. Jaramillo, J. Gacel-Ávila, and J. Knight. Washington, D.C.: World Bank.

Inter-American Development Bank (IDB). 2005. *The Politics of Policy: Economic and Social Progress in Latin America, 2006 Report.* Washington, D.C.: Inter-American Development Bank and Harvard University (David D. Rockefeller Center for Latin American Studies).

———. 2006. *Education, Science and Technology in Latin America and the Caribbean: A Statistical Compendium of Indicators.* Washington, D.C.: Inter-American Development Bank.

Lopez-Claros, A., M. Porter, and K. Schwab. 2005. *Global Competitiveness Report 2005–2006: Policies Underpinning Rising Prosperity.* New York: World Economic Forum.

Murnane, R. and F. Levy. 1996. *Teaching the New Basic Skills: Principles for Educating Children to Thrive in a Changing Economy.* New York: Free Press.

Navarro, J. C. 2005. "Two Kinds of Education Politics." In *The Politics of Policies: Economic and Social Progress in Latin America, 2006 Report.* Washington, D.C.: Inter-American Development Bank and Harvard University (David D. Rockefeller Center for Latin American Studies).

Oppenheimer, A. 2005. *Cuentos Chinos: El engaño de Washington, la mentira populista y la esperanza de America Latina.* Buenos Aires: Editorial Sudamericana.

Organization for Economic Cooperation and Development (OECD). 2001–2005. *Education at a Glance.* Paris: Organisation for Economic Co-operation and Development.

———. 2004. *Learning for Tomorrow's World: First Results from PISA 2003.* Paris: Organisation for Economic Co-operation and Development.

———. 2005. *Are Students Ready for a Technology-Rich World? What PISA Studies Tell Us.* Paris: Organisation for Economic Co-operation and Development.

PREAL Advisory Board. 2005. *Quantity without Quality: A Report Card on Education in Latin America, 2006.* Washington, D.C.: PREAL.

PREAL-BID. 2004. *Maestros en América Latina.* Santiago: PREAL and Editorial San Marcos.

Shanghai Jiao Tong University. 2005. *Academic Ranking of World Universities 2005.* http://ed.sjtu.edu.cn/ranking.htm.

Vegas, E., ed. 2005. *Incentives to Improve Teaching: Lessons from Latin America.* Washington, D.C.: World Bank.

Winkler, Donald R. 1990. *Higher Education in Latin America: Issues of Efficiency and Equity.* World Bank Discussion Papers 77. Washington, D.C.: World Bank.

Winkler, D. and S. Cueto, eds. 2004. *Etnicidad, Raza, Género y Educación en América Latina.* Santiago: PREAL.

Wolff, Laurence. Forthcoming, 2007. *The Costs of Testing in Latin America.* Santiago: PREAL.

World Bank. 2006. *World Development Indicators 2006.* Washington, D.C.: World Bank.

CHAPTER 3

Competitive Capital Markets: Brazil's Capital Markets Finally Maturing

John H. Welch

The opinions in this paper are my own and do not represent those of Lehman Brothers or the sovereign strategy group. I would like to thank Thomas Glaessner for his insight in numerous conversations we have had in recent years.

Over the last 40 years, Latin American countries have tried to reform their capital and financial markets to help underwrite economic growth. Most countries at one point or another have tried to wrest their financial systems away from statutory and structural impediments and toward viable sources of long-term finance for the public and private sectors alike. The route from financial repression has proven a much longer road than originally thought, and different countries have taken different approaches to deepen their financial systems. And the results have not been uniformly successful. One of the first efforts came in Brazil in the 1960s that combined price liberalization with institution building. This was followed by more purely liberalizing efforts in the Southern Cone countries of Argentina, Chile, and Uruguay. These exercises in financial liberalizations met with serious difficulties at the end of the 1970s and in the early 1980s. Although Brazil did not avoid serious financial difficulties with the onset of the debt crisis in the early 1980s, it did not have an all-out collapse. In contrast, the financial collapses of the Southern Cone led Diaz-Alejandro (1985) to conclude that financial development along Brazilian lines might prove more fruitful from the long run.

Diaz-Alejandro's query was well taken from the point of view of financial stability but not from the point of view of efficiency. Improvements to the financial system by the Brazilian authorities after the onset of the debt crisis were limited. And in fact, accelerating inflation, the external debt moratorium in 1987, and the internal debt freeze implemented by President Fernando Collor in March 1990 all caused Brazil to move backward in its quest to improve its financial and capital markets. In the meantime, Chile, and to a lesser extent Uruguay, moved ahead with laying the groundwork for healthy financial expansion. Chile represents the lead nation in the region. After recapitalizing the banks and creating a system where salvaged banks would retire their debt with the central bank, the Chilean authorities launched a full-fledged reform effort including pension reform (starting in 1981) that moved from a pay-as-you-go system to a fully funded system. These reforms explain to a large extent the deepness of Chilean markets. They were followed by similar banking and pension reforms in Peru (1993), Argentina (1994), Colombia (1994), Uruguay (1996), and Mexico (1997), among others. All countries once again suffered serious macroeconomic instability in the 1990s but, surprisingly, only Argentina seems to have partially undone some of its reforms after the 2001 crisis and default. But others, such as Mexico, reacted to instability by accelerating the opening of the financial system and deepening of reforms. And those that had successfully deepened financial institutions, especially those that created a viable private pension fund system, such as Chile, Peru, and Colombia, weathered the financial storms of the 1990s and the early years of 2000 as well.

Meanwhile, Brazil's financial sector reform efforts really regained momentum only after the Real Plan successfully stabilized inflation starting in 1994. Because some banks, mainly state banks, had not changed their cost structures to deal with low inflation, a number of them came under severe pressure and ended up needing central bank intervention. The authorities' main objective was to stabilize the banking system and impose significant regulatory structures to ensure prudent capitalization of the system. Once past the banking crisis, the government moved quickly to improve the functioning of capital markets and markets for long-term finance.

A recent World Bank paper (de la Torre, Gozzi, and Schmukler, 2006) shows that capital market reform in Latin America has had mixed results. The authors discuss a number of explanations for these mediocre outcomes that include the types and persistence of the reform effort, timing, and expectations. Their own predilection is for reformers to go back to basics and continue improving what the authorities have already implemented. Those countries that have stuck with the reform process, namely Chile, Peru, Mexico, and Colombia, have seen their financial sectors contribute to stability and higher growth. Hence we think that despite almost inevitable difficulties that countries confront in opening and deepening their financial markets, it ultimately is worth the investment. This conclusion corresponds to the conclusion reached by Dobson and Hufbauer (2001). Seen in this light, the current Brazilian experience emerges as a particularly interesting case in point.

The fact that Brazil was relatively early in its attempts to create viable capital markets makes all the more interesting its new effort after the long stagnation of its reform efforts. In the last 15 years, Brazilian authorities have implemented a broad series of reforms from a new corporations law to better bankruptcy proceedings.

In this chapter, we look at a number of these initiatives in detail and offer an early assessment of their efficacy and what is still missing in Brazil's capital market environment. Our conclusion is that Brazil has improved the markets for long-term finance immensely but there is still much reform remaining.

Brazil's Capital Market Development

Since 1964, successive Brazilian governments have put forth considerable effort to deepen Brazil's financial and capital markets. After widespread financial market reforms in the 1960s and a first push in creating viable markets for government bonds in the 1970s, further substantive improvements in Brazil's capital markets have only come since the mid-1990s. The main reason for this stagnation was chronic and constantly accelerating inflation. What kept Brazilian markets from falling back into more severe financial repression was the hallmark of the 1960s reforms, inflation indexing. But indexing allowed Brazil to "live" with inflation and hid many of the deleterious effects of inflation on capital market development. Not until the persistent stabilization of inflation brought about by the Real Plan in 1994 and firm efforts to keep inflation low thereafter has capital market development received a new impetus.

The structure of finance in Brazil has only recently started to change. The reformers of the 1960s faced the following structure of corporate and government finance. The only long-term sources of primary funding came from international markets and the National Development Bank (BNDE), later the National Economic and Social Development Bank (BNDES). Banks primarily funded the government and financed the working capital of industry, mainly concentrated in consumer durables, through short-term loans. Private companies were closely held family-owned companies or state owned (Welch, 1993b). Things have changed dramatically since then but most of the changes have happened only since 1990. The two large efforts that led to those changes were the massive privatization program undertaken in the first Cardoso administration and the stabilization of inflation since the launch of the Real Plan in 1994.

Privatizing state-owned companies, mainly in telephony, mineral extraction, and steel, created large publicly held world-class companies that traded both domestically and then internationally (Baer, 2001; and Bacha and Welch, 1997, among many). Although the performance of the privatized companies improved over time as they implemented cost-cutting and investment programs, many of the corporate governance objectives of the reforms were common practice in these companies while they were still in state hands. Lower inflation, however, forced huge efforts to rationalize and improve the financial system that had grown fat on inflation tax revenues.

The disappearance of the inflation tax once and for all put pressure on those financial institutions that had not prepared themselves, mainly state banks, by reducing headcount, increasing investment in technology, and cutting all sorts of overheads. This put major pressure on the less-efficient banks that ultimately caused the high profile failure of the large state banks—BANESPA, BANERJ, and BEMGE—and a few private sector banks—Banco Economico, Banco Nacional, and Banco Bamerindus. It also laid bare large net worth holes at the Banco do Brasil and the Federal Thrift Caixa Economica Federal.

The huge effort to deal with the financial problems of banks, the Brazilian government, and the institutional investors in the context of lower inflation, have generated a slew of initiatives that comprise a full-fledged reform effort in Brazilian financial markets not seen since the Campos-Bulhões reforms of 1964–1965.[1] Many of the reforms were brought on by expediency stemming from the disappearance of returns to financial institutions from inflation, difficulties in the government's fiscal adjustment, and problems associated with a series of crises emanating from the global economy. Other reforms were wrought from the exigencies of more open product and financial markets. Trying to exhaustively analyze these measures in one short text is difficult. A good place to start, however, is to merely present data that reflect the improvement in Brazil's capital markets over time and juxtapose these on more advanced emerging economies to gauge how far Brazil has to go.

Brazil's Capital Markets Compared

Brazilian financial markets are dynamic but are dominated by money markets and the government bond market. We are mainly interested in the market for long-term capital, which would include domestic and foreign sales of debentures, long-term bonds, long-term loans, and stocks, preferably common stocks. Despite massive reforms in the 1960s, foreign capital markets have remained the main provider of long-term capital to both the public and private sector, until very recently. Until now, the only other provider of long-term loans was the BNDES, which uses balances of long-term forced savings funds to lend for long-term projects. Unfortunately, these reform efforts ran into governments that steadily lost control of fiscal policy, causing the governments to borrow heavily in domestic financial markets and to rely increasingly on the inflation tax to make debt payments. This lack of discipline led to not only a foreign debt moratorium in 1987 but also a freezing of 80 percent of the liabilities of the banking system in 1990.

The drop in inflation since 1994, better fiscal stance as of 1998, and improvements in bankruptcy procedures and corporate governance have combined to spur growth in Brazil's capital markets. But even with all this growth and reform, Brazilian investors still concentrate financial wealth in government bonds. Table 3.1 shows recent holdings of investment funds, the main nonbank holders of securities in Brazil. These funds hold 63.2 percent of their portfolio directly in government bonds. But a good portion of the repo operations are performed with government bonds as well. Hence, holdings are still close to 80 percent. Investment funds hold only 16.6 percent in private paper with bank paper forming the lion's share of that. Holdings of corporate bonds comprise only 4.9 percent of total holdings with equities comprising a mere 1.2 percent.

If we measure Brazil against its emerging market counterparts, Brazil fares a bit better in broad terms with Latin America but is still far behind a number of

Table 3.1 Brazil: Investment fund portfolio, November 2006

	BRL millions	% of total
Government bonds	491,214	63.2
Private bonds	129,252	16.6
Bank	91,283	11.7
Corporate	37,968	4.9
Fund shares	17,627	2.3
Repo operations	121,308	15.6
Equities	9,019	1.2
Other	9,381	1.2
Total	777,800	100.0

Source: CVM and *Monthly Report,* Banco Central do Brasil, December 2006.

Table 3.2 Stock markets and money in emerging countries

	Stock market capitalization (% GDP)	Broad money ($ GDP)
Argentina	26	29%
Mexico	31	28%
Brazil	60	29%
Peru	46	29%
Venezuela	4	23%
Chile	116	54%
Colombia	38	32%
South Africa	262	62%
Czech	44	67%
Poland	31	42%
Philippines	114	52%
Indonesia	30	44%

Source: Bloomberg and *Emerging Markets Report,* Lehman Brothers, February 2007.

emerging markets. Table 3.2 compares two indicators of capital markets and financial deepness for a smattering of emerging countries. Brazil's stock market capitalization has recovered from the lows of the 1980s to 37 percent of GDP in 1997 and now to a whopping 60 percent. Only Chile, the far and away leader in Latin America, has larger capitalization than Brazil. But compared to other emerging countries that have advanced financial markets such as South Africa and the Philippines, Brazil still lags behind.

Brazil fares worse in terms of financial deepness. With broad money only 29 percent of GDP, Brazil ranks among the shallowest financial markets in this sample of countries. Only Venezuela has a more repressed financial system than Brazil's. With the stabilization of inflation, Brazil is slowly remonetizing as depicted in table 3.3. M2 as percent of GDP is slowly growing, interrupted by the devaluation of 1999 and the huge depreciation leading into the October 2002 elections. A couple more years of stability should allow Brazil to accelerate this financial deepening and perhaps allow a long-term credit market to develop.

Table 3.3   Emerging countries: Government bond market size (% GDP)

	Internal/total debt		Internal public sector debt		Public sector debt	
	2003	2006	2003	2006	2003	2006
Argentina	26.8	52.0	37.1	32.3	138.3	62.1
Brazil	78.7	89.8	48.8	44.9	62.0	50.0
Colombia	65.7	72.0	35.4	31.0	53.9	43.0
Indonesia	100.0	91.8	64.4	40.4	64.4	44.0
Mexico	74.4	80.7	32.7	25.7	44.0	31.8
Peru	30.0	29.2	14.1	9.2	47.0	31.5
Philippines	63.8	63.1	49.6	43.7	77.7	69.2
Russia	20.8	50.3	5.8	7.6	28.1	15.2
South Africa	88.2	88.9	35.1	30.0	39.8	33.8
Turkey	84.8	83.0	66.7	50.6	78.6	61.0
Total*	70.2	80.2	39.2	31.1	55.9	38.8

Source: BIS and *Emerging Markets Report,* Lehman Brothers, February 2007.
Note: *GDP Weighted

In the meantime, this stability and some financial innovations have fostered recovery in credit with sustained growth rates not seen in decades.

In contrast to the banking system, Brazil's domestic bond markets are large relative to other emerging markets and are still dominated by government bonds. table 3.3 shows that Brazil's internal debt ratio is roughly 45 percent of GDP, with its debt to GDP ratio of 50 percent of GDP lower than only Turkey. With the new theme of many governments retiring external debt through surpluses and issuing locally, local bond markets should continue to grow over the next few years while foreign debt shrinks. The governments of Colombia, Mexico, and Russia have already started aggressive programs of buying back external debt and funding it when necessary by issuing domestic debt. This is reflected in table 3.3 by the increase in the ratio of internal to total debt.

The problem with Brazil's bond market, especially the market for government bonds, is that it has crowded out more conventional money market instruments. Although the Brazilian government has issued locally bonds with five-year maturity, these bonds were not issued with fixed rates, making their duration essentially very short. The bonds were indexed at different point in time to price indexes, the exchange rate, and to the overnight money market rate. Hence, the government essentially could only fund itself with debt of short maturity, that is, no duration. The situation was exacerbated by the readiness of Banco Central, Brazil's Central Bank to fund excess bond positions of local banks. In the bad old inflation days, banks would buy more government bonds. They could then fund with deposits and then repo out the remainder to the Banco Central. This became the main source of inflationary finance and shows how inflation imposed huge illiquidity on the banks, that is, they were constantly underfunded. The pressure from government funding needs also puts upward pressure on real interest rates, crowding out lending to the private sector.

The government's poor fiscal situation forced it to issue bonds into the market to an extent larger than the banks' capacity to absorb them and then buy them back by printing money. The fact that Brazil had a functioning bond market explains the lack of direct correlation between deficits and inflation, but it also explains banks benefiting immensely from inflation and their power to press the central bank into relaxing monetary conditions even in the face of accelerating inflation (Welch, 1993b). Government borrowing needs forced the Banco Central to become the market maker of last resort and this distortion continues to this day. Correspondingly, this situation inhibited the creation of a true secondary interbank market for debt where portfolio movements were effected by trade among banks, pension funds, and mutual funds without central bank intervention. To date, trades are effected with Banco Central and this has inhibited further development of the interbank market.[2] Typically in a sell-off, the central bank has to intervene by conducting simultaneous buy and sell auctions to different actors in the financial system. This shortcoming became abundantly clear to foreign investors during a large sell-off in May 2006.

Since inflation has fallen, the situation in the money market has completely reversed. Banks now have positive excess reserves. Their funding levels are comfortably larger than the borrowing needs of the government. This shows up in figure 3.1 as a larger net reverse repo. The Banco Central is selling bonds on repo (and now at increasing maturities) removing monetary base from the banking system. Why do banks continue to keep excess reserves so high? This is a hard question to answer. Bankers, still risk averse, do not yet trust the persistence of current inflation stability. Moreover, real interest rates in Brazil remain high and, with short-term rates above long-term rates, banks would rather lend to the Banco Central. As these credibility problems disappear with the persistence of stability, banks should decrease excess reserves by lending longer term at fixed rates to both the public and private sectors.

Although excess reserves remain high, banks have gradually absorbed more and more duration.[3] Figure 3.2 shows the median duration of bonds issued by

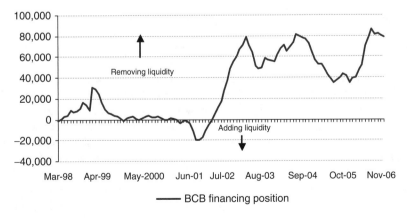

Figure 3.1 Net reverse repo (negative bond financing) position of the Banco Central do Brasil (excess reserves) with the banking system

Source: BCB and *Emerging Markets Report,* Lehman Brothers, February 2007.

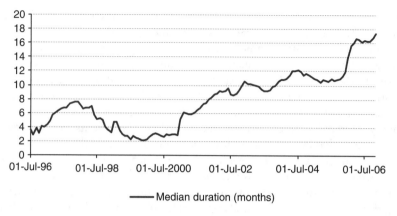

Figure 3.2 Brazil: Median duration of central government bond debt
Source: Monthly Report, Banco Central do Brasil, December 2006.

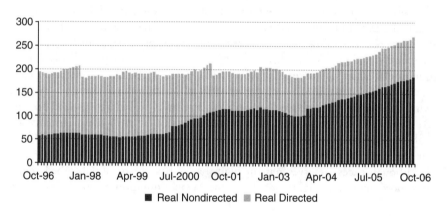

Figure 3.3 Brazil: Real nondirected and directed credit

the treasury and the Banco Central. Again, except for the interruption during the 1999 devaluation crisis and the 2002 election panic, the duration of government debt has increased steadily. Figure 3.3 shows the percentage of total government debt in fixed rate (positive duration) bonds. This has also steadily increased since the 2002 panic. The duration of government debt has increased more dramatically than the percentage of fixed rate debt because the government has increased its issuance of inflation-linked bonds although it has retired all of its dollar-linked debt. The main objective of the government is to reduce floating rate debt to a minimum and increase fixed rate debt as much as possible. Still, the only way that the government can achieve this objective is for the Banco Central to act to keep inflation low, that is, below the 6 percent level.

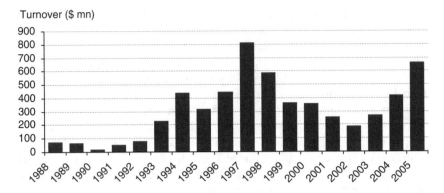

Figure 3.4   Brazil: BOVESPA average daily volume (USD)
Source: Annual Report, BOVESPA, 2006, and IIF.

The Recovery of Credit Markets

We have seen that banks and investors are more willing to take on risk in the form of increasing duration. More crucial to increasing long-term economic growth is that banks and investors increasingly lend to the private sector with longer duration. Certainly, some of this is already occurring with the help of some deregulation. Figure 3.4 shows that after some fits and starts, credit growth is starting to recover. Most notable is the growth in nondirected credit, that is, credit that banks freely lend without government restrictions. Nondirected credit grew quickly after new legislation was implemented to allow banks to lend against wages and social security benefit payments. This component of credit was the most dynamic over the last two years and will continue to grow for the next few years.

The Brazilian government's insistence on maintaining directed credit, in our view, represents one of the main distortions in Brazilian financial markets although it is encouraging that the amount of directed credit has fallen from around 71 percent of total credit in February 1996 to about 32 percent as of November 2006. State-owned banks including the BNDES, Banco do Brasil, Caixa Economica Federal, State Caixa Economics, and private banks are required to lend a certain proportion of deposits to selected industries, agriculture, and lower-income housing at the subsidized long-term interest rate (Taxa des Juros de Longo Prazo, TJLP) set by the BNDES. Perhaps these types of subsidy programs represented an effective stopgap measure for long-term financing during the import-substituting period of the 1950s; they have long since outgrown their usefulness. The existence of directed credit partially explains why interest rates in the free part of the credit market are so high. Other than the typical efficiency drawbacks resulting from government credit subsidy programs such as arbitrary criteria determination in granting loans perhaps subject to political intervention, directed credit brings with it a number of serious distortions. Given a funding interest rate, to maintain a reasonable return on capital, banks have to charge an interest rate high enough to make up for the losses on directed credit. Moreover, the existence of directed credit makes monetary policy less effective as a part of the market has a base rate well below the SELIC (Sistema Especial de Liquidação e de Custódia) rate. For example, as of December 2006, the SELIC rate was at 13.25 percent while the TJLP was 6.5 percent. The average base rate then was about 11 percent, not the 13.25 percent that most concentrate on. And to fight off an embryonic inflation, the central bank must increase the SELIC rate that much more to stabilize inflation, putting an undue burden on a highly concentrated group of industries. The Banco Central made a major effort a couple of years ago to unify the two credit markets but was defeated politically by special interest groups. A removal of these distortions would provide a further impetus to financial market deepness and lower cost of capital.

On the other hand, the Brazilian government has done a formidable job, especially the Banco Central, in cleaning up the state banking system, fostering consolidation, and deregulating and imposing effective best practice standards especially in risk management. Some view this huge effort in post-real Brazil as one of the main reasons that Brazil was able to devalue and float without a major financial and economic collapse (Gruben and Welch, 2001). But the effort has not ended there. Further regulatory innovation to allow more types of credit operations heretofore not seen in Brazil especially around real estate and securitization is currently underway. Much of this is the product of low inflation as also of the government's effort to improve the quality of collateral and improved legislation on claims by banks. Although Brazil has a long way to go in this area, we think that it will show steady progress, enough, at least, for the development of a mortgage-backed security market and long-term credit for private sector companies provided by the free market.

The Boom in Brazilian Equities Markets

Over the last decade, the Brazilian stock market has enjoyed a strong rally. The various emerging market crises over the last decade including the Mexican crisis in 1994–1995, the Asian crisis in 1997, the Russian default in 1998, the Argentine default in 2001, and Brazil's own devaluation and float crisis of 1999 and the election panic of 2002 were only able to temporarily divert the BOVESPA, Brazil's largest exchange based in São Paulo, from its upward trajectory. Figure 3.5 shows the path of average market capitalization of all listings on the BOVESPA. The index has grown more than fivefold since 1992. We have also seen significant growth in the daily volume as depicted in figure 3.4. Again, the different crises have hit volume at different points in time but volume in dollars has increased dramatically. This advancement came at a time when many thought that Brazilian exchange might close with the huge competition it confronted from New York and London. Brazil's exchange remains one of the largest and most liquid exchanges in the Western Hemisphere let alone the world.

Most importantly, capitalization in Brazil's equity markets has not only recovered but at above 60 percent of GDP, is the highest in its history. The recovery

Market cap ($ bn)

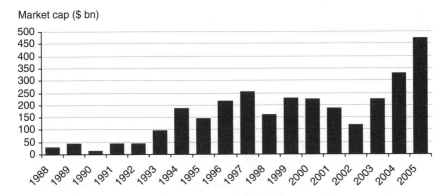

Figure 3.5   Brazil: BOVESPA capitalization (USD)
Source: Annual Report, BOVESPA, 2006, and IIF.

has much to do with the perceived stability in the economy. The fact that Brazil was able to accommodate a left wing president without major disruptions has encouraged investors to make increasing bets in Brazilian risk markets. Moreover, the enhanced credibility enjoyed by the Banco Central in inflation policy also has encouraged investors. Add to this an international environment of solid growth, high commodity prices, low real interest rates, and a savings glut, and the result is almost a perfect external environment for emerging market assets. Brazil has benefited immensely from this international environment, an environment that will probably not deteriorate any time soon.

The external environment and economic stability go a long way in explaining the recovery in volume and capitalization. And the huge privatization programs explain stock market growth in the 1990s. But Brazil's equity markets are finally starting to act like true markets for corporate control. The reformers in the 1960s thought that they could transform domestic equity markets into primary sources of investment capital. But as I have argued elsewhere (Welch, 1993a and 1993b), equity markets have never really served this purpose even in the United States with the possible exception of the dot-com period. In the event this period turned out to be temporary and equity markets returned to having a small role in underwriting corporate investment. Still, Brazil has had some success in recent years in helping small and medium-size corporations access the equities markets thorough a combination of better regulation and the creation in 2000 of the so-called *Novo Mercado* (New Market) designed after Germanys' Neuer Market. In exchange for full disclosure and issuance exclusively of common (voting) stock, small companies receive easy access to issuance. The role of the Novo Mercado is already important and explains some of the huge boom in new issuance in the BOVESPA. Figure 3.6 shows the evolution of new issuance since the mid-1990s. After fits and starts, issuance of stocks and debentures and, to a lesser extent, promissory notes, has boomed. Although the largest volume has come in the form of debentures, the increase in stock issuance is also noteworthy.

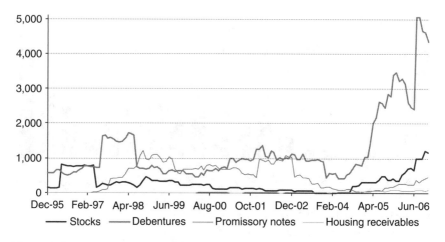

Figure 3.6 Brazil: Local market capital market issues
Source: Banco Central do Brasil and *Emerging Markets Report,* Lehman Brothers, September 2006.

Brazilian firms have mainly used the funds generated by this issuance to pay down debt, especially foreign debt. By paying down debt and raising primary capital, Brazilian firms improve their balance sheets and reduce balance sheet volatility. The fact that companies are using equities markets to restructure their balance sheets instead of using them to underwrite primary investment should not be viewed as a failure of the reforms as the reformers in the 1960s did. On the contrary, we think that this mainly reflects the proper role of the equities market as a market for control. And here is where Brazil has come a long way.

We think the newly evolving structure of corporate ownership is fast moving Brazil to a more mature and dynamic market for control. This is in contrast to more skeptical views such as Armijo and Ness (2004) who argue that this new reform push is just another repetition of cosmetic reforms that do not in the end change corporate behavior. Certainly, special interest groups and lobbying on behalf of family-owned corporations had subverted much of the reform effort in equities markets since the early 1960s. But good legislation, demographics, and a more dynamic market for managers are all galvanizing this transformation. As argued in Welch (1993a), contestable markets for corporate ownership are an extension of the market for managers. If managers of corporations act in their own interest and not that of the owners, that is, to maximize the value of the firm, underperformance of the stock makes the company a takeover target. In the event, the current management could lose their jobs. This contestability is one of the main vehicles for disciplining management and investment decisions.

In the past, either because of tradition or economic instability, Brazilian private firms were mainly closely held family-owned corporations. This effectively aligned the interests of the managers with the owners' as they were one and the same individuals. But family members are not necessarily the best people for the jobs and such a structure allocates human capital suboptimally. Hence, for an efficient market for corporate control, the economy needs a more diffused, but not completely diffused, corporate ownership structure and a dynamic market for managers. Both the market for managers and Brazil's corporate structures are moving in this direction.

Recent reform efforts have contributed to this. Brazil's Corporation Law of 1976 (Lei de Sociedade Anonima) served to protect minority shareholders, mainly through guaranteeing dividends on preferred stock. Because of inadequate protection for minority holders of common stock, which includes international mutual funds, many argued that Brazil was missing out on access to larger amounts of risk capital. Also, the Brazil National Securities Commission (Comissão de Valores Mobiliarios, CVM) was seen as weak and not independent enough to enforce disclosure and encourage common stock issuance. Hence through lobbying, corporations were able to reap the benefits of special programs created for open capital companies but were not compelled to comply with the stricter regulatory standards. After almost two decades of debate, Brazil finally revised the Corporation Law in 2001. This law protected minority shareholders in both voting and representation on the board, and their rights during public tenders. The law also strengthened the role of the CVM and limited the use of preferred shares by corporations. The other important bit of legislation was the new Bankruptcy Law in 2005. This law improved and better defined the rights of shareholders, creditors, and workers in the event of bankruptcy. In the end, the law serves to make bankruptcies proceed faster and more efficiently.

It is still too early to tell how much these laws have affected Brazil's equity markets, but early signs are encouraging especially with the significant growth in the issuance of common stock. And although the only major test to Brazil's new bankruptcy law is the current VARIG airlines bankruptcy, the relatively quick succession of decisions concerning the carrier also point to significant improvement.

Final Thoughts

After years of little reform in Brazil's capital markets since the 1960s, economic stability and a more open economy have forced the issue of reducing the cost of capital to corporations. This in turn has generated an effort to improve and reform Brazil's capital markets. Economic stability is the sine qua non behind this new reformist activity and depends upon continued adherence to prudent fiscal and monetary policies. The Brazilian government has made great strides in creating viable private sources of long-term financing but many reforms remain. Although we did not deal with the subject in this chapter, Brazil's pension funds remain small as an aggregate source of funding, with assets under management totaling only 17 percent of GDP compared to 57 percent in the United States, 73 percent in the UK, and over 100 percent of GDP in a number of European countries such as the Netherlands and Switzerland. Still, the amount of assets under management by pension funds has grown significantly in recent years. The pension system is dominated by large state-owned pensions usually associated with large state-owned corporations, including Banco do Brasil (PREVI),

Petrobras (Petros), and the Banco Central (Centros). Although urgently needing deregulation and reform, the development of a private pension fund system is also inhibited by Brazil's huge social security system, both private and public, that currently runs a deficit close to 5 percent of GDP. With Brazil's age distribution, it should enjoy current surpluses, not deficits. In other words, despite being a very young country, Brazil's social security system is de jure insolvent as also actuarially insolvent.

The social security system remains the largest barrier to better fiscal performance by the government and to the further development of a pension system that could provide cheaper long-term finance. Still, Brazil's experience of the last 12 years in opening and fostering dynamic markets for long-term risk capital is encouraging.

Notes

1. For an exhaustive treatment of these reforms see John H. Welch, *Capital Markets in the Development Process: The Case of Brazil* (Pittsburgh: University of Pittsburgh Press, 1987).
2. Some point to the problems of insider trading that were revealed in the congressional investigations into the Banco do Nordeste between one pension fund portfolio manager and that bank. But Brazil never really had a true interbank market even before this scandal.
3. Duration is a measure of maturity measured in time units (usually years but in this case, months). It is also a measure of the sensitivity of a bond to changes in interest rates.

References

Amann, Edmund. 2005. "Brazil's Economy under Lula: The Dawn of a New Era?" *World Economics* 6 (4): 149–169.

Armijo, Leslie Elliott, and Walter L. Ness, Jr. 2004. "Contested Meanings of 'Corporate Governance Reform' the Case of Democratic Brazil." Paper presented at the annual meeting of the Western Political Science Association, Portland, Oregon, March 11, 2004.

Bacha, Edmar L., and John H. Welch. 1997. "Privatização e Financiamentono Brazil, 1997–1999." In *Brazil: Desafios de um País e, Transformação,* ed. João Paul dos Reis Velooso. Forum Nacional, José Olympio, Editora.

Baer, Werner. 2001. *The Brazilian Economy: Growth and Development.* 5th ed. Westport: Praeger.

Burger, John D., and Francis E. Warnock. 2006. "Local Currency Markets." Special issue. *IMF Staff Papers* 53: 133–146.

De la Torre, Augusto, Juan Carlos Gozzi, and Sergio Schmukler. 2006. "Capital Market Development: Wither Latin America?" Mimeo. March 21. Washington D.C.: World Bank.

Dias Carneir, Dionisio. 2001. "Crescimento de Longo Prazo e a Lei das S.A." *Revista da CVM,* Dezembro, 9–12.

Diaz-Alejando, Carlos. 1985. "Good-bye Financial Repression, Hello Financial Crash." *Journal of Development Economics* 19.

Dobson, Wendy, and Gary Clyde Hufbauer. 2001. *World Capital Markets: Challenge to the G10.* Washington, D.C.: Institute for International Economics.

Eichengreen, Barry. 2006. "Brazsil Ficou para Trás na construção de um Mercado deTitulos." Interview in *Valor Economico,* August 15.

Gruben, William C., and John H. Welch. 2001. "Banking and Currency Crisis Recovery: Brazil's Turnaround of 1999." Federal Reserve Bank of Dallas Economic and Financial Review, Q4.

Hauner, David. 2006. "Fiscal Policy and Financial Development." Washington, D.C.: International Monetary Fund.

Rocca, Carlos Antonio. 2001. "Soluções para o Desenvolvimento do Mercado de Capitais." *Revista da CVM,* Dezembro, 26–32.

Welch, John H. 1993a. "The New Face of Latin America: Financial Flows, Markets, and Institutions in the 1990s." *Journal of Latin American Studies* 25, January, 1–24.

———. 1993b. *Capital Markets in the Development Process: The Case of Brazil.* Pittsburgh: University of Pittsburgh Press.

CHAPTER 4

Consumer and Small Business Credit: Building Blocks of the Middle Class

Jan Smith, Tricia Juhn, and Christopher Humphrey

Banks, Growth, and Competitiveness

The development of a formal banking system is the sine qua non of competing in an interdependent world. Resilient, complex, and deep (in the sense of reaching across all income levels, including the working poor) banking systems are synonymous with advanced economies, higher growth, and income equality. Banks are essentially intermediating institutions: their function is to convert income and savings into investment and productivity gains. All businesses need credit. In the absence of a financial services industry broadly accessible to the population at large, only the very wealthiest firms and individuals can access the credit they need—and in a closed capital market, as was Latin America's until 1990, even they are paying too much for it.

Most everyone else—small- and medium-scale entrepreneurs who make up more than 90 percent of private enterprises, middle-class consumers, and the working poor—hit their growth ceilings early, fast, and hard. This is why exclusionary banking systems, like the ones that have developed throughout Latin America, are correlated with poverty, chronic underperformance, and volatility. In Brazil, Latin America's most sophisticated financial market, 70 percent of households have no access to financial services at all. Only 15 percent have some type of formal bank account. In Mexico City, one of the more densely banked urban areas in the region, 75 percent of households have no access at all to formal financial services. Access to financial service deteriorates more the farther one moves away from the urban centers. Conservatively speaking, upward of 85 percent of Latin Americans are unbanked, compared to less than 10 percent in the United States.[1] Banking the unbanked—SMEs, the middle class, and the working poor—is the single most

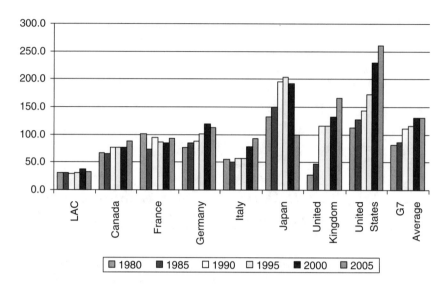

Figure 4.1 Global economies: Domestic lending to private sector (% of GDP)
Source: World Development Indicators, 2006 (Washington, D.C.: World Bank).

critical element in creating a role for Latin America in the global economy. Without it, further reforms will not take root. Figures 4.1 and 4.2 illustrate Latin America's historical underperformance in private sector lending.

Every low-income country that has successfully moved into the upper-income quintiles came to this point in its history, this point where Latin America, collectively, stands today: to choose between deepening its commitment to structural reforms and carving a role for itself on the global stage, or falling back into the bust cycle. The successful ones chose to negotiate very contentious political decisions in order to create the sort of economy its society thought it wanted. The international economic order is notoriously rigid. In the last 30 years—one generation—only four economies have gone from the lower to upper or upper-middle income quintiles: Hong Kong, South Korea, Taiwan, and Singapore. In each case, the "take-off" period, to turn a Rostowian phrase, occurred with the democratization of access to financial services.

The History of Bank Reform

Before prescribing the solutions that could take Latin America forward into an age of financial competitiveness, it is illustrative to look back to both understand and recognize the banking reforms and market maturation that has been achieved in the last 15 years. One sometimes forgets that in 1980 Latin American governments owned two-thirds of the assets of the ten largest banks in the region, including every bank in Mexico. Brazilian banks were required to direct up to 60 percent of their lending to the agricultural sector, and government credit

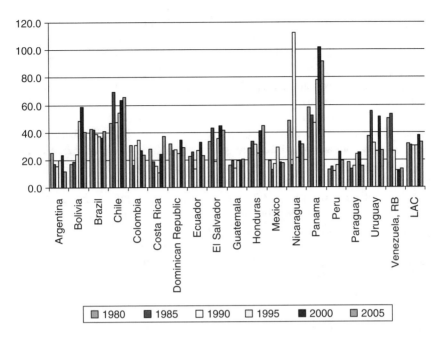

Figure 4.2 Latin America: Domestic lending to private sector (% of GDP)

Source: World Development Indicators, 2006 (Washington, D.C.: World Bank).

programs represented three-quarters of total outstanding credit to the public and private sectors. In Colombia, interest rates on directed credit were on average 12 percentage points below nondirected lending, and directed credit accounted for 60 percent of total credit by banks to industry.[2]

Latin America's foray into public-led banking was an unmitigated disaster, leaving behind a legacy of reduced credit, widened interest spreads, wasteful administration, excessive employment, a culture of nonpayment and moral hazard, political pressures on lending, and outright corruption. The fiscal costs were severe. In 2001 the Brazilian government absorbed the losses of two state-owned banks (Banco do Brasil and Caixa Economica Federal) to the tune of 6 percent of GDP. Mexico's BanRural had to be recapitalized in 1999 at a fiscal cost of U.S.$1.1 billion. The cost of subsidies ran very high also, estimated at 7 or 8 percent of GDP in Brazil in 1987.[3]

Tentative reform efforts began in the late 1970s in Argentina, Chile, and Uruguay, but it was not until the late 1980s and early 1990s, with the Washington Consensus reform movement in full swing, that essentially all of Latin America undertook full-scale reforms to their financial systems. Foreign pressure to liberalize allied with the needs of Latin conglomerates, the region's most influential organized private interests, that had exhausted domestic markets and had long been pushing to expand into untapped markets abroad. Specifically, the region's wealthiest multinationals such as Cementos de México, Femsa, Gerdau, and Grupo Carso needed the freedom to bring in lower-cost imports and technologies to compete. They wanted access to cheaper capital than could be got from domestic markets, and they wanted to export and maintain control over capital flows. Governments responded and drastically reduced their intervention in the allocating and pricing of credit, removed controls on foreign exchange and capital transactions, reduced bank reserve requirements, and allowed foreign borrowing by financial institutions.

Thus followed a brief era of widespread enthusiasm—irrational exuberance, one might say—on the part of the newly freed private bankers. Bank lending grew sharply, encouraged by relatively lax regulations and apparently calm macroeconomic environments, particularly low inflation and stable (frequently pegged) exchange rates. The owners of the newly privatized banks, who frequently paid a premium for new companies, were especially eager to lend. Alas, this happy state of affairs did not last long. Currency fluctuations, terms-of-trade shocks, sovereign debt defaults, and international financial turmoil quickly brought banks back to earth, and frequently down to their knees. The litany of banking crises is long: Argentina (1995 and 2001), Bolivia (1994), Brazil (1994), Colombia (1999), Ecuador (1996–1998), Mexico (1994–1995), Peru (1993), and Venezuela (1994), to name only some of the most prominent.

Faced with fiscal costs in the vicinity of 20 percent of GDP to get the banking sector up and running again, as well as the not-negligible political costs of such a massive and regressive redistribution of wealth, governments understandably came to view go-go laissez-faire liberalization with a jaundiced eye. Stability became the watchword in the late 1990s and in the early years of the twenty-first century. Regulators put stricter controls on lending, raised capital and loan reserve requirements, and implemented differentiated treatment for dollar deposits and loans to mitigate currency mismatch risk. Bankers, burned by nonperforming loans, needed little encouragement to reduce their risk exposure.

The real and irreversible commitment came in December of 1999 when 100 sovereigns, including all the major Latin American states, signed on to the WTO Convention on Banking, Insurance, and Financial Services (aka WTO Banking Agreement). Signatories to this convention agreed to full liberalization of their financial services, which meant that any foreign bank or insurance firm could, if they met the local requirements, be chartered to conduct business in foreign markets. (The U.S. Congress repealed Glass-Steagall in November 1999 to allow the United States to sign this convention.)

The convention was the result of almost 20 years of aggressive lobbying by the world's capital market leaders. As early as the 1980s, bulge bracket banks in New York, London, and Tokyo realized that they would exhaust domestic markets soon, and that continued expansion depended on being able to access foreign markets. The convention opened up the world's historically protected domestic banks to global competitors and set off a spate of mergers and acquisitions everywhere (see table 4.4).

In Latin America, the first wave of acquisitions was mostly large banks buying their domestic competitors. The second wave was dubbed *Reconquista,* or the

Yankee Invasion, because CitiGroup, Santander, and BBVA began gobbling up the remaining, and now considerably consolidated, banks in Latin America.

Bumps on the Road to Progress—How Reforms Initially Created Mixed Results

Bankers, being who they are, want to lend. Three important types of reform in the recent years have allowed them to do so, while at the same time not threatening macroeconomic stability or bank balance sheets. The first was an overhaul of the essential tools to issue credit and to recover assets in the case of nonpayment. Laws were modified to allow for the first time not just real estate but moveable assets as loan collateral, which previously was not possible in Latin America and which backs up roughly 40 percent of all loans in the United States. Credit and asset registries have multiplied. As well, more specialized commercial courts have begun to accelerate glacially slow bankruptcy proceedings, to afford more balance between the rights of debtors and creditors.

The second move was to open the doors to the influx of foreign banks, as described above. By 2005, foreign-owned bank assets exceeded 80 percent in Mexico and 50 percent in Argentina, Chile, and Colombia, up from 20 percent, 30 percent, 20 percent, and 15 percent, respectively, ten years ago. In Brazil, foreign bank ownership more than tripled, from 10 percent in 1995 to more than 30 percent a decade later.

The risk-return formula of lending obliged the new foreign banks to "pick the low hanging fruit" by seeking the business of large companies and wealthy Latin Americans. Within two to five years, depending upon market maturity, the upper tier of the banking market grew crowded and banks began looking toward the neglected mass market.

The change of mindset amongst bankers however did not come soon enough. The top-down strategy may have reinforced the existing prejudice that banks, particularly foreign banks, were elitist institutions out to plunder the *patrimonio nacional.* In 1997, Banco Santander commissioned 5,000 person surveys in Chile, Argentina, Mexico, and Brazil and found that banks were regarded as arrogant, slow, elitist, and fickle. With good reason—Mexico was just coming out of its 1994–1995 peso crash and 1997–1998 currency meltdown, which eventually injured every major emerging market currency in the world, did little in the way of affirming the usefulness of foreign banking practices, especially in Latin America, where 25 percent of the population lived on less than two dollars a day.

From the outset, banks had a real public relations battle on their hands. Historically, national banks had never reached out to the average (for example, not already banked) Latin consumer. In practice, the old family-owned banks had put up financial barriers (for example, very high minimum balances, elaborate working papers, arbitrary personal references to open accounts) and physical barriers (unfriendly doormen, branches on cosseted addresses) to keep accessibility exclusive.

For the new banks, this PR problem turned into a marketing problem: how to reach a mass market that had either no experience, or only negative experience, with banks, and get them to turn over their money? Many potential customers, for example, the working lower- and middle-income segments, perceived banks as elite institutions where a certain level of affluence was required a priori to becoming a customer. To grow, however, the new banks had to expand their customer base, massively and quickly. They had to reach out, not just to the under-banked, but the *never*-banked. In 1997, Citibank unveiled its internal plans to be the world's largest bank. By 2025, it aims to have 50 million customers in Latin America.

These new foreign players have brought with them all manner of new technologies and management practices to make banking more efficient and widespread: ATMs, lower-cost wire transfer services and credit scoring systems, and the like. Driven by a mass-market global strategy, the large foreign banks in Latin America have taught their own bank managers to bury their old prejudices of lending only to well-connected individuals and large companies. They know the future for retail banking in Latin America lies with bringing services to the "un-banked"—the growing middle class, the working class, and smaller companies.

Partially in response to a public outcry for more access to financing, Latin governments have cautiously undertaken "market-friendly" interventions to spur the expansion of financial services at little or no fiscal cost, and without impeding the private sector. For example, Brazil passed a law allowing the creation of correspondent bank branches, wherein a regular bank will authorize a nonbank institution (for example, a supermarket chain or a post office) to offer basic banking services such as deposits, withdrawals, invoice payments, and loan applications on its behalf. These types of branches cost an estimated 0.5 percent of opening a traditional bank branch. The results have been impressive: in 2001, 30 percent of Brazilian municipalities had no banking services at all; by 2004, all municipalities did, and a third was serviced exclusively by correspondent banks.[4] Other examples include Mexico's NAFIN- (Nacional Financiera Banco de Desarrollo-) backed reverse-factoring program for production financing and Chile's guarantee fund to back loans to small and medium enterprises—Fondo de Garantía Para Pequeños Empresarios, FOGAPE (see box).

Microfinance lending has expanded tremendously as well, partly because of the reforms noted above, and also driven by NGOs and development organizations seeking new ways to bring financial services to the poor. This has in recent years moved from a small niche of idealistic do-gooders to a profitable and rapidly growing market segment. The microfinance loan portfolio has quadrupled between 2001 and 2005 to US$5.4 billion, and the number of borrowers has risen from 1.8 million to 6 million.[5] At the same time, microfinance institutions have improved their performance, with a median return on assets of 4.1 percent in 2005—admittedly low, but more than double the 1.8 percent of four years earlier. Eyeing potential future profits for introducing the working poor and lower-middle class into the financial system, many commercial banks are getting

Chile's FOGAPE: Accelerating SME Financing with Competition

To help spur credit to small and medium enterprises in Chile, in 2000, the government reformulated the Guarantee Fund for Small Business people (Fondo de Garantía Para Pequeños Empresarios—FOGAPE), originally created in 1980. The fund, administered by the state-run commercial bank Banco Estado, now provides partial guarantees to private banks that make loans to SMEs in an innovative way to promote competition and reduce moral hazard. FOGAPE shares the risk of default on certain loans with the banks, and in return charges a fee for its services. Because FOGAPE only covers 70 to 80 percent of the loan, the banks also share the risk, and hence are motivated to pay close attention to the qualifications and track record of borrowing companies. Guarantees are put up for bidding four to six times per year, and banks bid on the number of guarantees they want and the maximum percent of risk covered. FOGAPE's commission varies between 1 and 2 percent of the guaranteed credit, depending on the claims performance of the participating bank.

The fund has been a success in Chile, and its model is being replicated in Poland, Egypt, and elsewhere. Evidence of this success is the increasing number of participating banks—up from 3 to 18 in just four years—and the fact that just 1 percent of loans have defaulted. As well, the average risk share of the guarantees fell from 79 percent to 71 percent in the first three years of the program, indicating that banks were taking on an increasing share of the risk. While certainly not the only factor, FOGAPE—a self-sustaining institution—has contributed to making credit more accessible in Chile than any other country in Latin America apart from Panama, with credit to the private sector rising to 66 percent of GDP in 2005.

into the game, including MiBanco in Peru, Banco Pichincha in Ecuador, and Banco Santander in Chile.

The result of the reforms combined with aggressive bank expansion has been a flourishing in consumer credit, particularly since the region's overall liquidity position began to improve with the rise in commodity prices in 2003. From 2003 to 2007, consumer credit across Latin America has grown at 21 percent per annum, faster than any region of the world[6] (see figure 4.3).

With a return to strong fundamentals,[7] a friendly macro environment, and a prolonged commodity boom in play, Latin America is riding the crest of another boom cycle. What sets this particular round of prosperity apart from the others is the propagation of financial services throughout the region. Never before has the region's retail banking sector been so robust and healthy, nor in a position to transform so positively the daily reality of Latin Americans. The challenge is no less than the wholesale democratization of the financial services industry in Latin America.

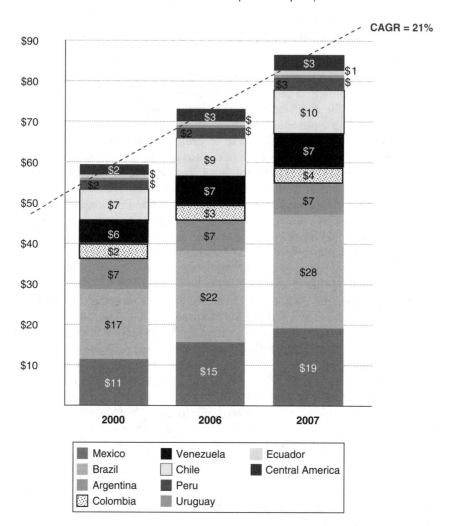

Figure 4.3   Latin America: Credit card volume growth

Why Access to Financing Enhances Competitiveness

Strong banking systems raise the equity, assets, and net worth for the middle class and the working poor, for example, the vast majority of the population who neither inherit nor marry wealth. With financing accessible, the middle class can start businesses and buy property, the two greatest vehicles of upward mobility in the developed world. High percentages of home ownership are essential for improving Latin America's dismal income distribution. Once home equity is built, workers have the economic leverage to invest in education, training, even technology, all needed to improve their productivity and marketability.

Better access to financing for small business brings needed competitive pressure to bear on large companies that continue to dominate some sectors. Quasi-monopolies still run rampant in Latin America, distorting pricing and preventing growth. One well-documented example is Telmex in Mexico that charges exorbitant rates for local telephony thanks to the lack of viable competitors, thereby eroding competitiveness in that country. Entrepreneurial opportunities help stem the flight of capital and brains from a region that has leaked both for decades, much to its own detriment. Entrepreneurialism can help rally public opinion behind tax reform, labor reform, and other important pro-business reforms as it has done in other countries that evolved from nations of factory workers to markets of business owners. Small business owners were hugely influential in the narrow victories of centrist federal governments in Mexico and Peru whose winning presidential candidates almost lost the 2006 election to populist opposition candidates.

Credit provides an essential cushion during economic recessions. In 2001 when copper prices plummeted on the heels of the telecom sector downturn, Chile's currency fell 25 percent versus the dollar, igniting a miniature financial crisis. Unlike in the past, the 2001 crisis was well survived by Chile because (1) the government had savings that it could draw upon to enact Keynesian countercyclical spending and (2) the middle class had access to credit that enabled them to assume short-term debt and continue consumption in spite of the crisis. As a result, real GDP growth in 2002 slowed to 2 percent, a dip from its strong pace in the 1990s but barely noteworthy. Compare Chile's soft landing to the infamous slowdowns in Mexico (1995, –7 percent) and Argentina (2002, –11 percent) when their currencies last tanked. Without consumer or government debt to turn to, spending in Mexico and Argentina ground to a halt, bankrupting entire industries that took years to recover. Chile, by comparison, was able to recover any lost ground in its economy within 12 months of the currency's steepest slide.

Small business credit is a powerful antidote to the region's gray economy, which goes largely untaxed. Most small businesses that operate in the cash economy do so because of red tape and a lack of capital. They find it easier to access financing in the gray market where informal financing flourishes but at onerous rates, essentially preventing them from expanding. The opportunity to go "clean" in the formal economy is welcoming to many small businesses if they can access credit and contribute to the pension system that in some markets such as Brazil and Chile is gaining traction and credibility.

From the banking community's perspective, a healthy middle class is essential to building both stability and volume. Latin America's history of extreme wealth distribution and volatility has driven much of the region's savings offshore, out of the reach of banks inside Latin America. With less than 25 percent of the region banked, the room for growth in scale is what drives Latin America's appeal to global banks. "Finance is like squash," a sovereign analyst once said. "To win the game, you have to own the center." It's true: nobody ever won a game by dawdling on the edges. For Latin America's banking system to fulfill its potential as a competitiveness driver, it needs breadth, that is, a mass market of customers.

Work Yet to Be Done

Despite the recent signs of success in some markets, there is no question that bank services still have plenty of room for growth in the region. More than 70 percent of Latin Americans lack access to such basic financial services as checking and savings accounts, compared to about 20 percent in most industrialized countries. Credit, particularly longer-term loans, is also very low. For an average of 18 Latin American countries, domestic bank credit to the private sector was a mere 33 percent of GDP in 2005, compared to 120 to 130 percent in G-7 and East Asian countries.[8] Considering the continued importance of bank lending in Latin America, with the weakness of capital and equity markets, the banking sector has a long way to go to fulfill its role as a driver of the economy.

The Remaining Policy Agenda

- *First and foremost, maintain macroeconomic stability.* Nothing will destroy a banking sector faster than high and volatile inflation, currency instability, or fiscal binges. Despite a lot of political noise, most Latin countries have performed remarkably well in this regard—for example, Evo Morales's Bolivia was more Maastricht-eligible for European Union membership on fiscal requirements than Italy in 2006.
- *Keep governments out of the banking business, both as a lender and as a borrower.* Several countries—notably Venezuela, Ecuador, and Bolivia—have or are contemplating new development bank activities for first-tier lending. It might reap short-term political rewards, but the track record is not good. Another major problem is the very high level of public debt on the portfolio of banks, which crowds out the private sector. The trend toward declining fiscal deficits and reduced public debt throughout the region will help ease this pressure (see figure 4.4).
- *Fully implement Basel II banking standards,* especially those regarding the full autonomy and enforcement capacity of bank regulators, and the assessment of risk. Further acceleration of bankruptcy proceedings and contract enforcement are also needed.
- *Have patience.* Memories of macroeconomic instability and savings-destroying crises are fresh for Latin Americans, and many have an understandably strong distrust of financial institutions. Lenders are also slow to regain trust in borrowers, who have in the past refused to pay their debts with relative impunity. These fears will not vanish overnight. But if Latin America continues on its current path, the future for banks is bright.

Risks and Opportunities Ahead

The overarching priority ahead is to bank the unbanked, aiming to reach 90 percent coverage. This is comparable to OECD (Organisation of Economic Co-operation and Development) levels as the benchmark for measuring the success of the critical next phase of deepening reforms.

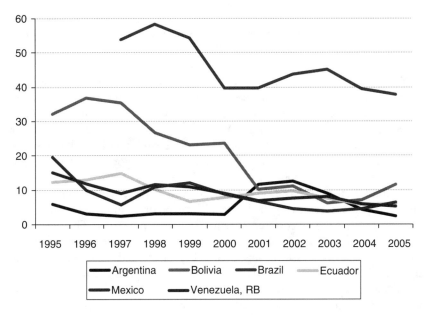

Figure 4.4 Bank spreads (interest rate % minus deposit rate %)
Source: World Development Indicators, 2006 (Washington, D.C.: World Bank).

Banking the Never-Banked

Banking the unbanked remains largely a work in progress but in some markets, progress has been significant. Those success stories provide insights as to how second-tier markets will unfold moving forward.

Coming from home markets with highly banked populations, the new global banks had to overcome both the financial and logistical barriers to rolling out their "bank the never-banked" strategy. The target customers could be segmented into three groups. SMEs, the middle class (SES levels B–C, also referred to as the 2nd and 3rd income quintile), and the working poor.

There are two major hurdles to banking the unbanked in Latin America. First, the majority of SMEs, quite rationally, operate in the black or gray market. Second, the working poor, who constitute 60 to 80 percent of Latin Americans, were always considered by banks as too poor, too illiterate, and too high risk to participate in the formal banking system.

SMEs

Although SMEs employ upward of 75 percent of the region and constitute an average of 95 percent of all enterprises, the majority of them operate outside the formal network— that is, they have no licenses, operate in cash, and pay no taxes. The process of becoming licensed has always been and remains expensive, time consuming, opaque, and humiliating. This per se is a barrier to entry. But from the banks' point of view, SMEs represent a vast swath of income-generating entrepreneurs whose money they cannot touch unless they can be persuaded to formalize their activity.[9]

Once attention was brought to bear on the vast numbers of disenfranchised entrepreneurs keeping their money out of the formal system, the new global banks used their powerful influence to push domestic regulators into easing barriers to entry: in the end, the bankers could not bank the SMEs if they could not be persuaded to have a paper trail. Although the situation for SMEs is improving, the failure to enfranchise them as a whole excludes perhaps the most vital, most entrepreneurial agents in the economically active population and is significant a net loss to the economy.

On the retail side, banks lowered minimum deposit requirements to open checking accounts, and launched aggressive marketing campaigns to change the image of banks into "customer friendly" service providers. The new banks opened branches in accessible locations or sent officials out to payroll sites on paydays to help with cash management. They financed the use, education, and infrastructure for electronic payment vehicles such as payroll cards, ATMs, non-bank branches (in retail stores, for example), and card terminals. At the same time, banks simplified the paperwork involved in opening and managing accounts, a critical initiative in developing markets where widespread semiliteracy is a barrier to the formal economy. The strategy was to hook the new customers with low- or no-cost checking and savings accounts, and then roll them over onto more sophisticated fee-generating instruments such as credit cards, mortgages, and insurance.

The results of Latin America's credit expansion are illustrative of a success story that warrants more applause and recognition.

- In Mexico, 800,000 new mortgage-financed homes were to be built in 2006, up 400 percent from 1997 and 20 percent from 2005.
- Over 1.1 million cars and small trucks were sold in Mexico in 2005, up 33 percent from 2000, and sales of household appliances in 2005 were three times greater than in 1996.
- Credit card billings in Brazil grew 70 percent in 2005 exceeding $60 billion.
- By 2008–2009 42 percent of current credit card holders will seek another card.
- GE Equity had opened, by 2006, 194 storefront GE Money outlets in Mexico offering cash loans from $100 to $1,100, credit cards, auto loans, insurance policies, and home mortgages. Mexico will rank among GE's top five consumer finance markets globally.
- In 2005, Brazilian banks earned over $10.3 billion in account management fees. The number of investment accounts grew by 18 percent in 2006.
- In Argentina, sales of household appliances grew 56 percent in 2005.
- Regionally, a record 2.2 million new mortgage-financed homes were built in 2005, and upward of 2.5 million were expected in 2006.

- At current rates of growth, banking penetration will hit 50 percent by 2010. More than 70 percent of current bank clients have been part of the financial system for less than three years and have built enough history to qualify for more sophisticated tools and services.

Infrastructure

To modernize banking in Latin America, the new owners had to dismantle both the physical and financial barriers set up by their predecessors, which meant building up entirely new infrastructure. On the physical side, banks were forced to come up with innovative ways to go, quite literally, where no bank has gone before. On average one in four Latin Americans live in rural areas; and half the small towns (under 10,000) did not have a bank branch. The strategy was to get out of the traditional, staid bank branch, anchored to immobile real estate, and get in front of the new customers. Technology was the key: ATMs, card terminals, and mobile telephony.

ATMs

ATM expansion exploded in 2004 (see table 4.1), moving beyond downtown and appearing where the new customers lived and worked—in supermarkets, drug stores, gas stations, bars, and restaurants. They were an efficient, low-cost interface with customers, especially in remote rural areas and small towns. ATMs were marketing machines: they could be used to advertise, train, and educate consumers, which bolstered brand equity and drove new product sales by as much as 35 percent.[10]

Banks have invested millions to drive uptake among the middle class and working poor. Penetration has grown an average of 7 percent per year in the last five years, with simple checking and savings customers moving into higher value-added products and services within four years.

Cards and Terminals

The proliferation of ATMs helped drive new customers away from cash transactions and toward e-payments. Cash is expensive; it gets lost and stolen, and it is difficult to track. The conversion toward e-payments was more secure, cheaper, and guaranteed VAT collection and tax reporting. Money moved faster electronically,

Table 4.1 ATMs operating in Latin America, 2005

Argentina	8,000
Brazil*	95,000
Colombia	5,500
Mexico	18,000
Dominican Republic	1,300

Source: Jan Smith, Credit Card Merchant Study, InfoAmericas, October 2005.

Note: * Includes simple ATMs that only allow consultation.

Table 4.2   Merchant outlets, 2006

Argentina	250,000
Brazil	760,000
Mexico	170,000
Venezuela	80,000
Chile	95,000

Source: Jan Smith, Credit Card Merchant Study, InfoAmericas, October 2005.

driving up credit and debit card transaction, which was good for credit card companies, issuers, and retailers, as well as consumers.

Credit cards, debit cards, and other electronic forms of cash such as payroll cards also drove bank penetration. The number of credit cards in service is projected to grow at 25 percent in 2007.

Cardholders need places to use them. By 2010, Mexico plans to triple the number of associated merchants from 12 million to 36 million, following Brazil's lucrative example. Terminals are provided free and can usually read magnetic strip and chip cards, and accept both credit and debit cards. The costs associated with maintenance, cash pickup and delivery run to $20,000 per year per ATM in the more remote areas. Banks recover the cost through the fees charged to merchants and network partners for transacting, but they are coming under market pressure to lower these fees.

Regardless, the trend toward virtual cash is booming, as consumers, merchants, and banks discover that electronic money moves faster and rolls over more often. Visa found that networks of merchants and cards contribute as much as ten percent to GDP growth (see table 4.2). Studies by Deloitte indicate that small merchants could increase sales by as much as 15 percent in the first year of adopting card terminals and decrease back office costs by as much as 6 percent. Similar studies conducted by Deloitte and Touche in Mexico and Brazil in 2005 found that sufficient presence of cards and terminals increased sales of large-ticket items such as white goods in supermarkets, while contributing to higher savings through faster turnover of inventory and lower handling costs of cash.

Mobile Banking

The next step in banking will be a collaboration between retail financial service providers and cellular phone companies. Unlike Internet access, mobile telephony has wide and growing penetration in Latin America. InfoAmericas expects banking to leapfrog technologies in the same way telephony did, that is, going from having no phone at all, skipping over the cumbersome, expensive landline, and going straight to a cell phone. The unbanked will go from having no services at all, never stepping into an immobile bank branch, and go straight to mobile phone banking, where money can be moved by using one's cell phone. This technology will also be heavily driven by the flow of dollar remittances from the United States into Latin America, as it will allow remittance earners in the United States to track the disposition of their earnings at the receiving end.

Credit Histories

The quality of Latin American credit registries varies by country, but scores high as a region, even when compared to U.S. credit bureaus, mostly due to the absence of laws prohibiting or restricting sharing of credit information within the financial sector. This stems from a need to balance credit risk in lending in a region where seizing collateral is difficult, particularly where it may not exist.

There are 34 registered credit bureaus in Latin America, the highest in the world; more than half have been in operation since 1989. The most sophisticated of these is in Brazil, where the interests of the central bank and the chamber of commerce coincided long enough to build Serasa, a centralized registry that sells and shares data. Mexico, despite the size of its market, is on the other side of the spectrum. The data in the Buro de Credito is considered of high quality (a joint effort between Dun & Bradstreet and TransUnion), but the data set is too narrow to be truly useful, restricted to the founding members of the bureau. Central America's bureaus are the youngest in Latin America and the least developed, although they are moving toward regionalization, reflecting the fluidity of capital among the five countries.

Credit bureaus make two contributions to competitiveness. First, like all the other measures outlined above, they promote capital mobility by helping money to move faster through the system. Studies conducted by the International Finance Corporation indicate that the total level of personal loans in open-sharing markets

Table 4.3 Nonperforming loans (% of outstanding loans)

	2000	2001	2002	2003	2004
Argentina	16.0	19.1	38.6	33.6	18.6
Bolivia	10.3	14.4	17.6	16.7	14.0
Brazil	8.3	5.6	4.8	4.8	3.9
Chile	1.7	1.6	1.8	1.6	1.2
Colombia	11.0	9.7	8.7	6.8	3.3
Costa Rica	3.5	2.4	3.2	1.7	2.0
Dominican Republic	2.6	2.6	4.9	8.9	7.3
Ecuador	31.0	27.8	8.4	7.9	6.4
El Salvador	...	...	15.8	12.3	12.0
Honduras	10.6	11.4	11.3	8.7	6.4
Mexico	5.8	5.1	4.6	3.2	2.5
Nicaragua	5.2	9.3	12.6	12.7	9.3
Panama	1.4	3.0	4.6	3.3	2.6
Peru	...	17.0	14.6	12.2	9.5
Paraguay	...	16.5	19.7	20.6	10.8
Uruguay	...	9.3	31.4	6.4	3.6
Venezuela, RB	6.6	7.0	9.2	7.7	2.8

Source: World Development Indicators, 2006 (Washington, D.C.: World Bank).

may increase by up to 90 percent while default rates may drop over 60 percent.[11] Similar results can be expected for SMEs, wherein the total number of approved loans is 25 percent higher in countries with open-sharing systems.[12] Other studies among Chilean SMEs find that over half of companies interviewed saw loans contribute to productivity and sales within two years.[13]

Second, credit bureaus promote transparency, compliance, and the practice of due diligence, all of which are hallmarks of advanced competitive economies. As more of the population becomes banked and credit bureaus become more expansive, it would be reasonable to predict consolidation in this industry as well with the big U.S. players looking for a foothold among local bureaus.

Conclusions

Opening the banking industry to global competition brought with it an entirely new and fundamentally more democratic attitude toward the average Latin American consumer: to treat them as a vital, proactive consumer, earner, investor—the protagonist of their own financial drama. After two centuries of being disenfranchised, it turns out that the region's competitiveness on the global market depends in large part on the participation, rather than the exclusion, of middle and lower incomes in the formal economy.

Competitiveness in a global economy may depend on a variety of factors, but first and foremost, it depends on the ability to compete *financially*. Globalization, after all the hype, is at its core a revolution in capital mobility: the ability of money to move with less and less friction through capital markets, and the resulting structural interdependence of financial systems around the world. For this reason, a modern banking system is a prerequisite of competitive economies. Moreover, in a global economy, modern banking requires mass participation to succeed: the wealth of the upper class is nothing compared to the actual and potential wealth of the working world.

The challenge is clear: how to expand the circle of financial inclusion in a region where 25 percent live at or below the poverty line; how to push ahead with difficult reforms without resorting either to authoritarian or populist rule in a region with a history of both. Although Latin America's banks have made Herculean efforts over the last ten years, the field is not yet won. In Mexico, the headquarters of some of the country's largest banks—Citi, HSBC, and BBVA—served as the staging point to protest the victory of president-elect Felipe Calderón, a neoliberal. Earlier in 2006, 15 bank branches in Sao Paulo were fire bombed by the urban gang, Primeiro Comando da Capital.

On the other hand, applications for small business loans in Argentina grew 37 percent in 2004 and contributed to halving unemployment figures to 12 percent by mid-2005. Mexico's middle-class households earning $7,500–$50,000 per year, grew 30 percent in between 2001 and 2005.

Enduring financial systems are built the same way as enduring democracies: slowly and nervously, through contention and negotiation, and ultimately, by gradually extending the circle of participation in response to contestation from below. Transitions, the ones that endure, are essentially conservative.

Table 4.4 Main acquisitions in the Latin American financial sector (percentages and millions of dollars)

Date Bank acquired	Country	%	Amount
ABN AMRO Bank, Netherlands			
1998 Banco Real	Brazil	40	2,100
1998 Banco Mercantil de Pernambuco	Brazil	100	153.6
Banco Bilbao Vizcaya Argentaria (BBVA), Spain			
2002 Grupo Financiero Banco Bilbao Vizcaya Argentaria			
Bancomer (BBVA Bancomer)	Mexico	3	216
2002 BBVA Banco Uruguay (BBVA Banco Francés Uruguay)	Uruguay	60	55
2001 Grupo Financiero Banco Bilbao Vizcaya Argentaria			
Bancomer (BBVA Bancomer)	Mexico	7	546
2001 BBVA Banco Ganadero	Colombia	14.4	70
2001 Grupo Financiero Banco Bilbao Vizcaya Argentaria			
Bancomer (BBVA Bancomer)	Mexico	9	548
2000 Grupo Financiero Banco Bilbao Vizcaya Argentaria			
Bancomer (BBVA Bancomer)	Mexico	32.2	1,850
1999 CorpBanca Argentina	Argentina	100	84
1998 BBV Excel Económico	Brazil	100	878
1998 BBVA Banco BHIF	Chile	55.52	350
1998 BBVA Banco Ganadero	Colombia	15	177
1998 Banco Providencial SAICA	Venezuela	100	103.2
1997 Banco de Crédito Argentino	Argentina	72	560
1996 BBVA Banco Francés	Argentina	30	350
1995 BBVA-Probursa	Mexico	47.9	350
1993 BBVA-Probursa	Mexico	10	53
1992 BBVA-Probursa	Mexico	10	71
Banco Santander Central Hispano (SCH), Spain			
2002 Grupo Financiero Bital	Mexico	4.7	…
2002 Banco Santiago	Chile	35.45	682
2002 Grupo Financiero Bital	Mexico	13.3	85
2001 Banco do Estado de São Paulo S.A. (BANESPA)	Brazil	63.72	1,160.7
2000 Banco Caracas	Venezuela	27.09	116
2000 Banco Caracas	Venezuela	66	200
2000 Conglomerado Financiero Meridional	Brazil	97	1,000
2000 Banco Santander Mexicano	Mexico	16	76
2000 Banco Rio de la Plata	Argentina	28.2	975
2000 Grupo Financiero Serfin	Mexico	100	1,560
2000 Banco do Estado de São Paulo S.A. (BANESPA)	Brazil	30	3,580.5
1999 Banco Santiago	Chile	21.75	600
1999 Banco Tornquist	Argentina	50	…
1999 Banco de Asunción	Paraguay	38.5	…
1999 O'Higgins Central Hispano	Chile	100	600
1999 Banco del Sur (Bancosur)	Peru	44	…
1998 Banco Noroeste S.A.	Brazil	76	564
1998 Banco Santander Brasil			
(formerly Banco Geral do Comercio)	Brazil	50	216
1998 Banco Santa Cruz	Bolivia	90	180
1998 Banco Rio de la Plata	Argentina	16	180
1998 Banco de Galicia y Buenos Aires S.A.	Argentina	9.97	100
1998 Banco Santander Chile	Chile	12	168
1997 Banco Rio de la Plata	Argentina	35	656

(Continued)

Table 4.4 (*Continued*)

Date Bank acquired	Country	%	Amount
1997 Banco Santander Chile	Chile	3.5	62
1997 Banco Santander Brasil			
(formerly Banco Geral do Comercio)	Brazil	50	150
1997 Banco Santander Colombia (formerly Bancoquia)	Colombia	60	155
1996 Banco Santander Chile	Chile	24.7	438
1996 Banco del Sur (Bancosur)	Peru	44	...
Banco Sudameris, France			
1999 Banco Wiese Sudameris Perú	Peru	64.8	180
1998 Banco America do Sul	Brazil	26.8	191
BankBoston Corp., United States			
1997 Deutsche Bank Argentina S.A.	Argentina	100	255
Scotiabank, Canada			
2001 Scotiabank (formerly Sudamericano)	Chile	0.03	...
2000 Scotiabank (formerly Sudamericano)	Chile	9.9	28
2000 Scotiabank (formerly Sudamericano)	Chile	16.4	...
2000 Scotiabank (formerly Sudamericano)	Chile	11.6	...
2000 Grupo Financiero Scotiabank Inverlat	Mexico	45	40
1999 Scotiabank (formerly Sudamericano)	Chile	33	116
1998 Banco del Caribe	Venezuela	26.6	87.9
1997 Banco Sudamericano	Peru	100	14.6
Citibank, United States			
2001 Grupo Financiero Banamex Accival (Banacci)	Mexico	100	12,500
2000 Afore Garante	Mexico	9	33
2000 Afore Garante	Mexico	51	179
1998 Banco Confia	Mexico	100	199
Crédit Suisse First Boston, United States			
1998 CSFB Garantia (formerly Banco de			
Investimentos Garantia)	Brazil	100	675
Hongkong and Shanghai Banking Corp. Holdings, United Kingdom			
2000 Chase Manhattan Bank Panamá	Panama	100	...
1997 HSBC Brasil Multiplo	Brazil	100	1,000

Source: ECLAC, Investment and Corporate Strategies Unit, *Banking Sector Report* (Chile: ECLAC, 2004).

Notes

1. Federal Reserve Bank of Atlanta, 2002; See also World Development Indicators 2006, Table 5.5: Financial Access, Stability, and Efficiency.
2. Augusto de la Torre, J. C. Gozzi, and S. Schumukler, "Innovative Experiences in Access to Finance: Market Friendly Roles for the Visible Hand?" World Bank Latin America Regional Study (Washington, D.C.: World Bank, 2006), pp. 13–15.
3. Ibid., p. 16.
4. Ibid., p. 28.
5. Sergio Navajas, and Luis Tejerina, "Microfinance in Latin America and the Caribbean: Connecting Supply and Demand," Draft working paper (Washington, D.C.: Inter-American Development Bank, 2006), p. 3.

6. InfoAmericas analysis based upon EIU data, the Nilsson Report, and Central Bank data.

7. For 2007, the consensus GDP forecast for Latin America is 4.2 percent; CPI at 5.5; and the current account at 5.5 percent of GDP. Export growth should return to 8 percent on recovery in the United States and world markets.

8. World Development Indicators database (2006), World Bank.

9. Daniel Kaufmann, Aart Kraay, Massimo Mastrussi, *Governance Matters IV: Governance Indicators for 1996–2004,* World Bank Policy Research Working Paper Series No. 3630 (Washington, D.C.: World Bank, 2006).

10. Jan Smith, "Latin America is Finally Ready for EMV Cards," *Tendencias,* no. 57 (May 2004).

11. Giovanni Majnoni, Margaret Miller, Nataliya Mylenko, and Andrew Powell, *Improving Credit Information, Bank Regulation and Supervision: On the Role and Design of Public Credit Registries* (Washington, D.C.: World Bank, 2004).

12. Inessa Love and Nataliya Mylenko, *Credit Reporting and Financing Restraints,* World Bank Policy Research Working Paper 3142 (Washington, D.C.: World Bank, October 2003), pp. 12–18.

13. Smith, "Latin America is Finally Ready for EMV Cards."

CHAPTER 5

Closing the Technology Gap

Peter T. Knight and Rosane A. Marques

Technology is a key factor determining a firm's, a city's, a region's, or a nation's competitiveness in the ever more knowledge-based global economy. Technology is knowledge embedded in labor and capital used to produce goods and services.

In this chapter we first examine some global indicators of competitiveness, future competitiveness, and technological gaps for key Latin American countries. We show that there is no evidence that the four major Latin American countries for which time series data is available (Argentina, Brazil, Mexico, and Venezuela) have made significant progress in closing the technology gap that separates them from the world's technological leaders. We then examine in more detail the polices and activities of Brazil—the largest, most technologically advanced, and economically diverse country in the region—to cast some light on what has been and can be done to close the technology gap.

To begin, we want to highlight three important aspects of technological change (Marques and Oliveira, 2006).

1. Technological change is not an isolated process. It is related to the innovative behavior and the consequent accumulation and evolution of technological capabilities in firms.
2. Technological change is a consequence of the capability of firms to manage and generate innovation as well as to acquire and diffuse technological knowledge (Freeman, 1987). The development of such capability is a process requiring that a given firm interact with other firms, research institutions, universities, and funding institutions, among other organizations.
3. Government policies have an important role in regulating and coordinating the pace (quantity) and nature (quality) of technological development. This partly explains the differences in industrial development between

countries, regions, and sectors; other factors that may influence the differences are the specific endowments and the environment (both physical and policy) within which firms operate.

In turn, differences in these three aspects of technological evolution influence the trajectory of countries attempting to catch up industrialized countries (Viotti, 2002; Freeman, 1987).

The ability to adopt, adapt, or create technology to enhance productivity (technological readiness) and the ability to create it (innovation) are two of the nine "pillars" of the World Economic Forum's new Global Competitiveness Index, or GCI (Lopez-Claro et al., 2006), shown in table 5.1. A closer look at these nine pillars indicates that they are each composed of both "hard" statistical indicators and qualitative indicators based on the WEP's annual survey of some 11,000 business leaders worldwide.

Table 5.1 Global Competitiveness Index (GCI), technological readiness, and innovation for selected countries and groups

Country	Overall GCI Rank	Score	Technological readiness Rank	Score	Innovation Rank	Score
Switzerland	1	5.81	5	5.57	3	5.72
Finland	2	5.76	12	5.44	4	5.96
Sweden	3	5.74	1	6.01	6	5.44
Denmark	4	5.70	10	5.46	10	5.04
Singapore	5	5.63	2	5.69	9	5.04
United States	6	5.61	8	5.49	2	5.72
United Kingdom	10	5.54	6	5.56	12	4.89
Germany	8	5.58	20	5.16	5	5.51
Japan	7	5.60	19	5.21	1	5.9
South Korea	24	5.13	18	5.22	15	4.71
Argentina	69	4.01	70	3.19	83	3.03
Brazil	66	4.03	57	3.5	38	3.56
Chile	27	4.85	35	4.22	39	3.56
Colombia	65	4.04	65	3.24	57	3.3
Costa Rica	53	4.25	44	3.74	36	3.65
Mexico	58	4.18	56	3.51	58	3.2
Venezuela	88	3.69	77	3.02	96	2.8
LA Select Average	*61*	*4.15*		*3.49*		*3.3*
China	54	4.24	75	3.07	46	3.44
India	43	4.44	55	3.52	26	4.14
Russian Federation	62	4.08	74	3.1	59	3.28
South Africa	45	4.36	45	3.72	29	3.92
*BRIC Average**		*4.20*		*3.30*		*3.61*
*BRICSA Average***		*4.23*		*3.38*		*3.73*
LA Select as % of US		73.98		63.54		57.69
Brazil as % of US		71.84		63.75		62.24

Source: Lopez-Claro et al., 2006, tables 4, 7, and 8.
Notes: *Brazil, Russian Federation, India, and China, unweighted average.
**Brazil, Russian Federation, India, China, and South Africa, unweighted average.

Chile stands out as the most competitive Latin American country, but even so it lags leading countries substantially in both ranking and scores (the potential maximum score is 7). The unweighted average GCI for seven leading Latin American countries is 4.15, or 74 percent of the United States' score. Measured relative to the United States, the average technological readiness and innovation scores of the selected Latin American countries stood at 64 and 58 percent, respectively.

The GCI results may be a consequence of lack of an environment that stimulates innovative capabilities in firms located in Latin American countries. In fact, Cassiolato and Lastres (1999), Katz (2000, 2001), and Bernardes (2000b) examined the technological behavior of national and foreign firms and the influences of macroeconomic policies and industrialization strategies defined by governments on this behavior. Their common argument is that the Brazilian system is fragmented and lacks long-term industrial policies. This is likely also true for other Latin American countries. Moreover, these authors assert that Brazilian firms have lacked innovative capabilities to compete successfully in the world market. There are, however, successful cases of firms that are innovative and are among the leaders in the world market, such as Petrobrás and Embraer. Thus, we need to see whether there is any evidence that on a more aggregate level Latin American has made progress in closing the technology gap.

Is Latin America Closing the Technology Gap?

Unfortunately, the GCI is available for only two years, 2005 and 2006. So to see whether Latin American countries are closing the gap, we have to use another measure that is available in a time series going back to 1993.

Measuring a technology gap over time is not simple. Perhaps the most systematic effort to do so over using a consistent methodology for a fairly large number of countries (including Argentina, Brazil, Mexico, and Venezuela in Latin America) is that undertaken by the Georgia Institute of Technology's Policy and Assessment Center under a contract with the United States National Science Foundation (Porter et al., 2006). The National Science Foundation uses these indicators in its publication, *Science and Engineering Indicators 2006.*

Table 5.2 presents calculations based on this time series data, and normalized on the value for the United States, which has shown no major trend, rising from 331.2 in 1993 to a maximum of 349.6 in 1999 and then declining monotonically to 337.9 in 2005. These numbers are the sum of four separate leading indicators of technological capability (considered as "input") leading to future competitive standing (or "output"), each having a maximum value of 100, each of which is itself a composite of statistics and answers to specific questions asked of an expert panel (see Porter et al., 2006, for a detailed explanation of the methodology used).

- National orientation: Evidence that a nation is undertaking directed action to achieve technological competitiveness. Such action can be manifested at the business, government, or cultural levels, or any combination of the three.

Table 5.2 Composite scores for four leading indicators of technological competitiveness as a percent of the US value, selected countries

Country/Year	1993	1996	1999	2003	2005
United States	100.0	100.0	100.0	100.0	100.0
United Kingdom	71.0	71.9	75.4	81.0	80.6
Germany	83.6	76.5	78.7	83.0	83.5
Japan	101.0	90.6	87.1	87.1	86.2
South Korea	72.6	69.1	69.1	75.8	74.7
Brazil	62.9	54.8	54.5	51.0	56.1
Russia	49.0	57.3	53.5	60.5	53.9
India	51.4	55.7	62.7	57.5	62.7
China	54.5	52.8	58.8	65.2	78.4
South Africa	63.4	49.4	49.4	49.5	51.0
*BRIC****	*54.5*	*55.1*	*57.4*	*58.5*	*62.8*
BRICSA*	*56.3*	*54.0*	*55.8*	*56.7*	*60.4*
Argentina	50.1	43.3	43.8	47.0	48.9
Brazil	62.9	54.8	54.5	51.0	56.1
Mexico	44.7	47.1	36.8	49.3	50.7
Venezuela	n.a.	42.2	38.8	36.0	41.6
Latin America 4 Average	*n.a.*	*46.8*	*43.5*	*45.8*	*49.3*

Source: Calculated by author from Porter et al. 2006, table 2, p. 22.
Notes: *Brazil, Russian Federation, India, and China, unweighted average.
**Brazil, Russian Federation, India, China, and South Africa, unweighted average.

- Socioeconomic infrastructure: The social and economic institutions that support and maintain the physical, human, organizational, and economic resources essential to the functioning of a modern, technology-based industrial nation.
- Technological infrastructure: Institutions and resources that contribute directly to a nation's capacity to develop, produce, and market new technology. Central to the concept are the ideas of economic investment and social support for technology absorption and utilization. These could take the forms of monetary payments, laws and regulations, and social institutions. Also included is the physical and human capital in place to develop, produce, and market new technology.
- Productive capacity: The physical and human resources devoted to manufacturing products, and the efficiency with which those resources are used.

What is evident from table 5.2 and visually from figure 5.1 is that on average, the four Latin American countries for which data is available have made marginal progress in closing the gap but not at the pace of their Asian competitors. The greatest increase in score occurred in China, with a 127 percent increase from 1993 to 2005. Latin American countries' small increase in competitiveness is neither consistent over time nor among the four countries.

Recent studies conducted by the World Bank (De Ferranti et al., 2003) and the Inter-American Development Bank (Malkin et al., 2006) have looked explicitly

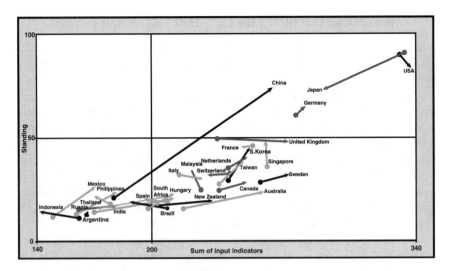

Figure 5.1 Change in competitiveness, 1993–2005

Source: Porter et al., 2006, figure 34, p. 77.

at the question of technology gap and concluded that the gap is substantial and may even be increasing.

> The overall picture that emerges is thus one of LAC countries not having given innovation and science and technology a central role in their development strategies until very recently. As a result, while their levels of indicators of technology absorption and innovation have increased, these countries have fallen behind more aggressive economies such as the Asian tigers, Israel, Ireland, and Finland. No doubt the opening of the LAC countries has given them greater access to various technologies developed abroad. However, as we argue through this report, merely having access to technology need not be enough for rapid sustainable growth. The critical question is what capabilities and institutions these countries need to use these technologies efficiently and eventually steer themselves onto a path of innovation-based development, which allows for sustainable long-term growth.
>
> The section on science and technology indicators . . . presents data in three general areas: human resources, R&D expenditures and outcomes. In all three areas there are specific improvements in some countries, but both the region as a whole and individual countries fall well below the performance levels of more advanced countries. The rate at which doctoral degrees are granted and the number of researchers in the workforce—key indicators of capacity—is several orders of magnitude below that of the OECD [Organisation of Economic Co-operation and Development] countries, and R&D expenditures as a fraction of GDP are less than half the OECD average, even for the strongest performers. While the trend in the more technologically advanced countries is to increase R&D expenditures, in the region as a whole, except for Brazil, Chile, and Mexico, the fraction of GDP invested in R&D has declined. (Malkin et al., 2006, p. 33).

Brazil: Can This BRIC Take Off—Half Full or Half Empty?

Brazil's diversified economy, creative and relatively young labor force, vast natural resources, democratic political system, and the absence of major ethnic, religious, and geopolitical conflicts are major assets. On the other hand, Brazil's education, health, public safety, social security, and judicial systems need major, politically difficult reforms. The country's physical infrastructure (roads, railways, ports, energy production and distribution) needs massive investments. And to become a knowledge economy the country also needs to increase investments in its infostructure, strengthen its digital highways to span its continental landmass, continually increase the number of citizens connected to the Internet, develop its information and communications technology industries, build a national lifelong learning system, and improve its personalized online government services to the population. We call this the e-development agenda.

To realize its potential, make the most of opportunities inherent in its assets and the global economy, and meet the challenges inherited from the past as well as new threats, Brazil must close the technology gap that separates it from the advanced countries of the OECD. In some areas, Brazil is at or near the technological frontier (see table 5.3). The country's biofuel production, agricultural and tropical forest management, deep-sea petroleum geology research and production capabilities, aircraft production, and television content (led by Globo TV), for example, are world class. In most sectors, however, there is much to do to

Table 5.3 Brazil—Selected economic sectors in relation to their distance from the global innovation frontier

Little or none	Moderate	Significant
Agriculture and tropical forest management	Vehicles: Agricultural machinery; buses; trucks; compact cars	Electronics; instruments; IT equipment
Principal agent: Embrapa (Brazilian Agricultural Research Enterprise)	*Principal strength:* Engineering of new products/processes	*Principal weakness:* Embedded chips and components
Energy: Biomass (ethanol), deep water petroleum exploitation	Auto parts, white line (stoves, refrigerators, washing machines, etc.)	Chemical products
Prinicpal agent: Petrobrás	*Principal strength:* Engineering of new products/processes	*Principal weakness:* Fine chemicals
Aeronautics: Regional jet aircraft	Software: Financial; administrative; security	Pharmaceutical products
Principal agent: Embraer	*Principal strength:* Cost/quality of software engineers	*Principal weakness:* Research on new molecules
Electric motors	Cosmetics	Capital goods related to information technology
Principal agent: WEG	*Principal strength:* Biodiversity	*Principal weakness:* Limited demand

Source: Dahlman and Frischtak, 2005, table 8, p. 188.

improve the educational, scientific, and technological infrastructure of the knowledge economy.

Brazil's position in the global economy has some similarities with the other members of the BRIC group—Russia, India, and China. All four countries have large populations and landmass, a diversified industrial base, and a critical mass of scientific and technological resources and institutions. All four are not members of either the European Union or the North American Free Trade Area (NAFTA), major economic blocs. Brazil's agricultural, biofuel, aeronautical, and electric motors potential and substantial mineral resources are major comparative advantages for trade. Strategic alliances with the other three members could help build scientific and technological resources in the areas where Brazil is moderately and significantly distant from the global innovation frontier, and in which it is possible to complement efforts. Brazil is reaching out in this direction.

Overview of Brazil's Science and Technology Policies and Innovation System

The government of President Luis Inácio Lula da Silva, which took office in January 2003 (and which will have continuity with the president's reelection in October 2006 for a second four-year term), elaborated a national policy for science, technology, and innovation (PNCT&I), as shown in figure 5.2. This plan was supported by important contributions and debates held during the Second

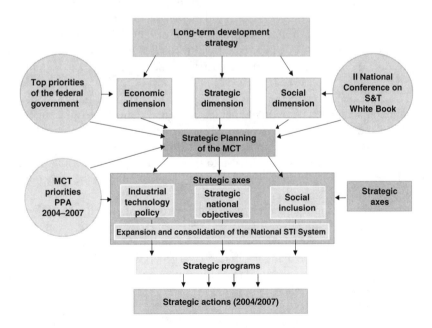

Figure 5.2 Brazil's national policy for science, technology, and innovation
Source: Adapted from Aragão de Carvalho Filho, 2006.

National Conference on Science, Technology and Innovation in 2001 and was developed within the framework of the multi-year development plan (PPA) for the years 2004–2007.

The PNCT&I involves greater activism on the part of the state than was seen during the government of Fernando Henrique Cardoso. The PNCT&I has four strategic goals:

1. Consolidate, perfect, and modernize the national system of science, technology, and innovation, expanding the national scientific and technological base
2. Create an environment favorable to innovation in the country, stimulating the business sector to invest in R&D and innovation
3. Integrate all the regions and sectors in a national effort for training for science, technology and innovation
4. Develop a broad social base of support for the national strategy for science, technology, and innovation

The Industrial, Technology, and Foreign Trade Policy (PITCE)

The PITCE is the clearest expression of Brazil's technological and scientific priorities. It considers three plans on which the Brazilian government will focus: horizontal, strategic, and future. The horizontal plan identifies innovation and technological development, external competitiveness, industrial modernization, and institutional environment together with improving production capacity as the main focus. The strategic plan considers four sectors: semiconductors, software, capital goods, and pharmaceuticals and medicine. The third plan defines the technological areas in which Brazil will focus for improving its generation, diffusion, and utilization by the industry. These areas are nanotechnology, biotechnology, and renewable energy.

The three plans were chosen because they impact all contemporary industrial production activities and are fundamental elements for the modernization of the Brazilian industrial structure. As for the four strategic sectors and three technological areas, they are viewed as having the capacity not only to improve living conditions for the population, but also to increase international competitiveness and to achieve substantial economic returns to innovation and the launching of new products and processes.

In order to strengthen the institutional environment, the Brazilian Agency for Industrial Development (ABDI) was created in December 2004 as a nongovernmental organization to "promote the execution of industrial development policies, especially those that contribute to the generation of jobs, in accordance with foreign trade and science and technology policies." Priority is given to studies and projects in the following areas.

- National Program for Space Activities (PNAE)
- National Program for Nuclear Activities (PNAN)

- Science and Technology in the Amazon Region
- Knowledge and sustainable use of biodiversity
- Ocean and water resources
- Climate change
- International cooperation

Financial Resources for Implementation of the PNCT&I

The resources used to finance actions of the PNCT&I come mainly from those available in the budget of the Ministry of Science and Technology (MCT), which includes resources for the National Council for Scientific and Technological Development (CNPq) and the National Fund for Scientific and Technological Development (FNDCT), in effect a series of sectoral funds.

The sectoral funds, beginning in 1999, are instruments for financing R&D and innovation projects. There are 16 sectoral funds, 14 for specific sectors and two transverse ones. Of the latter, one is devoted to the encouraging integration between universities and enterprises (FVA—the Green and Yellow Fund), and the other for information and communications technology infrastructure. These funds receive resources from "contributions" (in effect, taxes) on the exploitation of natural resources belonging to the federal government, parts of the Tax on Industrial Products (IPI), and certain parts of the Contribution for Intervention in the Economic Domain (CIDE) that is assessed on funds used for the acquisition of foreign technological knowledge and technology transfers. With the exception of the Fund for Telecommunications Development (FUNTEL), managed by the Ministry of Communications, the resources of the other funds are allocated to the FNDCT and administered by Financiadora de estudos e Projetos (FINEP), which acts as its executive secretariat.

The other principal source of funding at the federal level is the National Social and Economic Development Bank (BNDES, www.bndes.gov.br), which is linked to the Ministry of Development, Industry and Commerce (MDIC). BNDES has a budget of approximately U.S.$1billion for funding projects involving innovation submitted by Brazilian firms, which is made available as loans. There is also the Fundação de Desenvolvimento de Tecnópolis (FUNTEC) fund that BNDES created for projects that are more risky and related, particularly, to the strategic sectors and technological areas specified in the PITCE. At the state level there are Foundations for the Support of Research (FAPs), for example, Fundação de Amparo à Pesquisa do Estado de São Paulo (FAPESP) in São Paulo, Fundação Carlos Chagas Filho de Amparo à Pesquisa do Estado do Rio de Janeiro (FAPERJ) in Rio de Janeiro, and so on (figure 5.3). Their function is to support science, technology, and innovation activities within the states to complement actions taken at the federal level. FAPESP is particularly important.

Brazil's R&D effort stands out in Latin America in both absolute and relative terms, but actually fell from a peak of 1.35 percent of GDP in 2001 to 1.25 percent in 2004. But Brazil's R&D effort was less than half that of South Korea

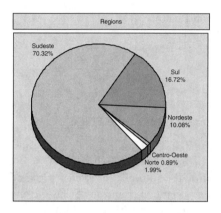
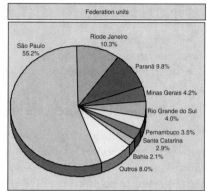

Figure 5.3   Brazil: Percentage distribution of expenditures by the state governments in science and technology by states and regions, 2002

Source: Accounts and surveys carried out by the state Secretariats of Science and Technology and related institutions.

(2.64 percent) and well below the OECD average (2.26 percent), although Brazil was investing marginally more than China and Russia in the BRIC group.

The level of finance for science and technology from the Brazilian enterprise sector (both state and private) for R&D is still relatively low, 43.9 percent of the total in 2005, though it has risen from 39.7 percent in 2000, well below the percentages of R&D carried out by "industry" in major R&D countries such as Japan (69.8 percent), Germany (69.8 percent), the United Kingdom (67.0 percent), and South Korea (76.1 percent) (National Science Foundation, Division of Science Resources Statistics, 2006, Appendix Table 4.44). Brazil's Innovation Law (Law No. 10.973/2004), was passed in 2004, and expressed an effort to create conditions to strengthen the national innovation system in three main ways:

1. Creation of a favorable environment for strategic partnerships between universities, technological institutes, and enterprises
2. Incentives for the participation of science and technology institutions in the innovation process
3. Incentives for innovation at the enterprise level

This law updates the Brazilian legal framework and seeks to facilitate the relationship between science and industry, encouraging new forms of public-private partnerships and establishing subsidies intended to encourage private expenditure in R&D (Rezende, 2006, p. 76).

Then in 2005 the "Good Law," or Law No. 11.196/2005, was passed by Congress. It provides new fiscal incentives for private R&D expenditures. Despite these advances, there remains much to do to bring consistency and coordination between public and private actions in this area according to the minister of Science and Technology (Rezende, 2006, p. 77).

Case Studies in Closing the Technology Gap in Brazil

In this section we look at how Brazil has closed or seeks to close the technology gap in aircraft and low-cost computers.

Aircraft: The Embraer/CTA/São José dos Campos Cluster Success Story

After World War II, the Brazilian Air Force decided to create an aeronautical institute to train highly qualified engineers for supporting the infant aeronautics sector. The Technological Institute of Aeronautics (ITA, www.ita.br) was founded in the late 1940s, marking the beginning of an important period for the development of this industry. The ITA was founded with the support of MIT and NASA. It had graduated approximately 200 engineers by 1970 but most of them were working in other sectors due to lack of aeronautics companies to hire them (Bernardes 2000b; Dagnino, 1999; Dagnino and Proença, 1989).

In 1969, the Ministry of Defense founded Embraer as a spin-off from the Aerospace Technical Centre (CTA, www.cta.br), in São José dos Campos, São Paulo state. The Brazilian government was its main buyer and also gave Embraer strong tax incentives and subsidies for developing production and technological capabilities for manufacturing the 19-seat aircraft EMB-110 (Dagnino and Proença, 1989; Bernardes 2000a). These incentives involved finance (through subsidies and tax exemption), marketing (through procurement and protectionism), and technological development (through the promulgation of special decrees on technology transfer and supporting research). In the first ten years of Embraer's existence, its main market was purely domestic.

Embraer's development is closely linked to the educational/scientific/industrial complex of which it is a part and the ITA around which it grew. ITA, in turn, has close ties to the Brazilian Air Force. Important milestones in the development of this industry cluster were establishment of a research center, CTA, in 1954; the first Embraer exports of the EMB 110 plane in 1975; Embraer's privatization in 1994 after a major financial crisis; and the successful development of the ERJ 145 regional jet passenger aircraft that had the cooperation of few foreign suppliers and research institutions. Almost 1,000 ERJ 145s and aircraft based on the ERJ 145 platform were delivered through early 2006 and are operating in 86 airlines throughout the world. Embraer is producing the ERJ 145 both at São José dos Campos, São Paulo, and in Harbin, China, showing its ability to develop partnerships within the BRIC framework. Embraer is developing different models to suit the needs of commercial airlines, executive travel, and the defence industry.

Embraer has improved its aircraft's performance and size since its beginning in1969—evolving from turboprop to jet propulsion and from 15 passenger seats to 108 in the latest models (see table 5.4). By 2006, Embraer was the fourth-largest aircraft manufacturer worldwide after Boeing, Airbus, and Canada's Bombardier.

Table 5.4 The evolution of aircraft models produced in Brazil

Year First plane flew	Model	Seats	Altitude (feet)	Speed (km/h)	Characteristics	(As*Vc) (1)
1972	EMB 110 Bandeirante	19	22,500	413	Light twin turboprop	7847
1979	EMB 121 Xingú	8	26,000	450	Twin turboprop pressurized	3600
1983	EMB 120 Brasília	30	30,000	555	Turbo propeller	16650
1995	ERJ 145	50	37,000	833	Twin turbofan (jet)	41650
1995	ERJ 140	44	37,000	833	Twin turbofan (jet)	36652
1998	ERJ 135	37	37,000	833	Twin turbofan (jet)	30821
2002	ERJ 170	70	37,000	870	Jet	60900
2004	ERJ 190	98	37,000	870	Jet	85260
2005	ERJ 195	108	37,000	870	Jet	93960

Source: Embraer, http://www.embraer.com.br (accessed in July 2006), and Airliners.net, http://www.airliners.net/ (accessed in January 2001).
Note: (1) As*Vc is the performance indicator that represents the number of seats (As) multiplied by the speed (Vc).

"Exports accounted for the largest share of Embraer's output that grew from U$130 million in 1996 to U$3.2 billion in 2005. Following that growth, Embraer's workforce in Brazil (excluding its Chinese plant) has increased from 3,849 in 1996 to 12,622 in 2005. Embraer was responsible for approximately 2 percent of Brazil total exports in 2005[1]" (Marques and Oliveira, 2006, p. 12).

It is important to note that the Brazilian government has supported the aeronautics sector in all stages of its development basically through (1) R&D policies, (2) joint government-private ownership, (3) protection of home markets, and (4) export development policies (Green, 1987; Bernardes, 2000b). Embraer itself has invested in R&D activities. Its R&D investments grew from U.S.$70 million in 2000 to U.S.$200 million in 2006.

Figure 5.4 shows the current arrangements for the production of Embraer aircraft. It involves not only Embraer's relationship with the ITA, but also with a network of Brazilian and international suppliers (some of the latter with Brazilian subsidiaries). An aerospace complex has developed around the ITA and Embraer similar to the Route 128 Corridor in Boston or Silicon Valley in the Bay area of California, but specialized in the manufacture and development of components for aircraft. There are also R&D laboratories of firms from other sectors, such as personal hygiene care and automotive, among others.

Few firms compose the first tier in this supply chain. With the exception of Embraer, manufacturer of the airframe structure, they are foreign firms. These first-tier firms jointly develop the aircraft models with Embraer and are also system integrators. The only Brazilian supplier in the second tier is Eleb, a producer of landing gear subsystems, which is jointly owned by Embraer (60 percent) and Liebherr Aerospace, Germany (40 percent).

There are five subsidiaries of foreign suppliers located in Brazil in the first tier and they supply airframe structures and related systems as well as propulsion

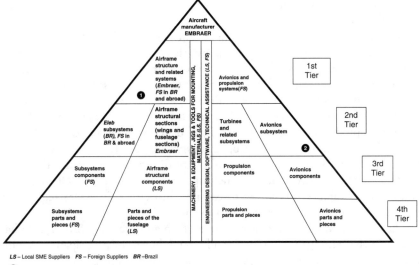

Figure 5.4 The Embraer production chain: Partnerships with Brazilian firms, foreign investors in Brazil, and foreign suppliers

Source: Marques and Oliveira, 2006, p. 7.

systems. Their activities in Brazil involve mainly customer support and assembling airframe structural sections for Embraer, as well as supporting their R&D engineers working inside Embraer's plant for developing systems for Embraer's new aircraft models. Their investments in Brazil resulted from government efforts to "nationalize" the supply chain. Embraer was responsible for attracting foreign suppliers and inducing them to set up operations in Brazil.

Other important factors for attracting foreign suppliers to set up operations in Brazil are government demand and support for some of the research, and the strategic selection of a market niche (mid-size regional passenger jets). Finance through FINEP and offset policies, which oblige foreign suppliers to produce in Brazil including technology transfer, were important, for example, for the development of the AMX Super Tucano, a training aircraft used by the Brazilian Air Force, which was the result of a partnership with Italian firms and resulted in the accumulation of technological capabilities by Embraer (for a detailed analysis of technological learning by Embraer see Frischtak, 1992 and 1994). The AMX Super Tucano was also successful in export markets.

Embraer's accumulation of technological capabilities achieving international competitiveness has been the result of a well-planned strategy. On the one hand, the national government has been an important partner in creating an innovative environment for the firm to grow up in. On the other, Embraer's executives and stakeholders have been proactive and taken risks by defining very challenging goals, such as the development of ERJ 190 and the Chinese joint venture during the September 11 crisis.

Summing up the development of the Brazilian aeronautics sector, Embraer has achieved international competitiveness. But there are questions about the development of this sectoral system of innovation in Brazil, particularly regarding the strengthening of the national firms in the supply chain. Most of these SME suppliers have maintained themselves in the supply chain by using their previously existing technological capabilities. A few of them have developed the ability to innovate in product development (for a detailed analysis see Marques and Oliveira, 2006). Only one SME, Eleb, developed advanced innovative technological capability. Most of the changes implemented by the SMEs that maintained their production capability were related to the implementation of ISO 9000 standards and quality assurance procedures to comply with either Embraer's requests or with a government export promotion program.

There are important differences between Eleb and the other SMEs. Eleb has been actively learning from Embraer and foreign buyers by participating in joint product development activities that contributed to the implementation of technological changes mostly in product, project management, and design procedures, and to the building up of advanced innovative technological capability. Eleb's other important linkages are with Brazilian and foreign universities and technological centers for research and for training employees. Another important distinction is that Eleb and a few other SMEs received technology transfer from foreign firms when participating in the offset programs organized by Brazilian military governments during the 1970s and beginning of the 1980s.[2] In the case of the other SMEs, rather than participating in joint development with customers, they rely heavily on acquiring blueprints, specifications, and technical assistance from foreign buyers and suppliers and on informal contacts with universities for testing.

The Brazilian aeronautics innovation system is similar to the national innovation system, with few successful cases of tight linkages with research institutions, national and foreign buyers, participation in government programs, and the building of innovative capability. Government policies, thus, should focus on the diffusion of the innovation culture in the sector looking at the successful cases of SMEs that accumulated innovative capability. More government support should also focus on high investments in R&D and on the development of incentives for SMEs to move from purely production capabilities to innovation capabilities.

Electronics: Low-Cost Computers for Education, Health Care, Banking, and Digital Inclusion

In Brazil, beginning in the 1990s, there have been several programs designed to bring affordable computers and the Internet to the classroom. A number of states began their own programs, and the Ministry of Education began its ProInfo program in 1997, bringing federal funding to state and municipal secretariats of education for computers in schools. By October 2006 the ProInfo program reached

25 of Brazil's 26 states plus the Federal District, with a total of approximately 70,000 computers. The minister of education announced in October 2006 that an additional 75,800 computers and 7,580 printers were to be bought by the beginning of the 2007 school year in February.

The Ministry of Communication's GESAC (Electronic Government Service to Citizens) program provided 2,409 public schools in low-income areas of all 26 states and the Federal District with broadband satellite connections as of March 2006. But despite the use of innovative bidding systems and even e-procurement, and the existence of important programs financed at the state level in most states, the cost of computers, peripherals, and maintenance combined with limited budgets left the overwhelming majority of Brazil's schools without computer laboratories or classroom computers or Internet connections of any kind.

In 2005 Nicholas Negroponte of MIT's famous Media Lab met with Brazil's President Luiz Inácio Lula da Silva and proposed that Brazil join what was then called the "One Laptop per Child" (OLPC) program, with an initial order for 1 million "$100" laptops. The Brazilian government set up a thorough evaluation system to assess the MIT offer, and eventually competing offers for low-cost laptops and alternative means of bringing computers to more Brazilian public school students (see table 5.5). As of January 2007, the OLPC had changed to "CM 1" (Children's Machine 1) and then to "XO" and the price had risen to "about $150,"[3] assuming Brazil and other countries could together come up with orders totaling 6–10 million units. Three competing systems are being evaluated by four independent Brazilian laboratories—the CERTI Foundation in Florianópolis; the MST's Paulo Renato Archer Center (CenPRA) in Campinas, São Paulo; the Laboratory for Cognitive Studies at the Federal University of Rio Grande do Sul (LEC/UFRGS); and the University of São Paulo's Integrated Systems Laboratory (LSI/USP). The initial *Mobilis* evaluations were completed by the first three laboratories in October 2006. In January 2007, classroom tests of the three systems were also being scheduled.

In September 2006, Encore, with the assistance of Telemática e Desenvolvimento Ltda., began negotiations with leading Brazilian firms to produce both the Mobilis and a $100 information appliance, the *SofComp* (without monitor or keyboard), in Brazil, and with Brazilian scientific and technical groups to work together to improve Encore's existing designs and develop the next generation of low-cost "information appliances." In October, Encore decided to enter into a technological cooperation agreement with Telavo Digital, the Center for Excellence in Advanced Electronic Technology (CEITEC), and a research unit of the Catholic University of Rio Grande do Sul, PUCRS, to further develop and adapt these information appliances to Brazilian conditions and also to work on advanced wireless and digital TV technologies. This is another concrete example of how Brazil can collaborate with a BRIC partner, in this case India, much as Embraer has done with its Chinese partner. It also fits well with the e-Brasil Program for building a more equitable and more competitive Brazil through intensive use of information and communication technologies (Knight and Aroso, 2006: Knight and Fernandes, 2006; Knight, Fernandes, and Cunha, forthcoming, 2007).

Table 5.5 Three entries in Brazil's "One Laptop per Child" competition

	Encore Software Mobilis	Negroponte/2B1 Childrens' Machine 1	Intel Classmate
CPU	400 Mhz Intel PXA-255	AMD Geode GX-500366 Mhz	Intel Celeron 900 MHz
DRAM	128–256 MB	128 MB	256 MB
Storage	128 MB–2 GB Flash	512 MB SLC flash	1 GB NAND flash
Display	7.0" TFT LCD 840x480 64 k colors, touch sensitive	7.5" Dual-mode TFT 1200x900	7.0" TFT LCT 800x480
OS	Montavista Linux	Linux (some flavor)	Win XPE / Linux
Connectivity	10/100 ethernet, GRPS, V.90 modem, Mesh Wi-Fi (one included, others options)	Mesh Wi-Fi	Ethernet or Wi-Fi
Battery	Li-ION 5–6 hours	NiMH, 22.8 Watt-hours	Unspecified 3–4 hours
Built-in peripherals	2 USB2 Host Ports, 1 USB slave ort, RS-232C, VGA Out (option), TV out (option), GPS (option) MMC Card Slot SmartCard I/F, Microphone, earphone jack, speakers	3 USB2 ports, video camera, microphone, speakers	2 USB2 ports, microphone, earphone jack, others unspecified
Price, availability	$165 for orders of 1 million units, available since October 2006	$150 target assuming 6–10 million ordered, not available as of November 2006	$250–300 estimated price, not available as of November 2006

Sources: Encore Software, www.ncoretech.com; olpc.org, www.olpc.org; Intel, www.intel.com; and direct contact with Encore Software.

The Russian government is also considering an industrial cooperation with India in this field, which involves seeking for a Russian industrial partner to cooperate with Encore, Telavo Digital, and PUCRS. It is another example of a BRIC alliance for industrial development. The OLPC program has also developed a partnership with the Taiwanese firm Quanta Computer to produce its XO laptop in Shanghai. Both competition and strategic alliances with other BRIC countries could bring benefits to Brazil to the extent that the Brazilian government will put in practice an ITC industrial development program.

Finally, Brazilian government should consider offset policies, including technology transfer, for importing low-cost computers and their components owing to the important potential spillover to the Brazilian economy. Such a policy could help reduce laptop prices in the Brazilian market as well as strengthen high-end application manufacturing in the country. While having cheap laptops is a great benefit to the economy, the benefits of the OLPC program would be greater to the extent that Brazilian firms become involved in strategic collaboration with research centers and foreign firms, in line with the PITCE objectives.

Conclusions

Latin American countries have a tough row to hoe if they seek to close the technology gap with the world's leaders. The internationally comparable statistics we reviewed show that no Latin American country has made significant progress on this front over the past decade, though Brazil and Chile may have this potential. China and South Korea stand out as countries that have made progress on this front, and we recommend that countries that aspire to close the technology gap should study their experience.

Brazil is the Latin American country with the largest domestic market; broadest industrial base, most advanced R&D institutions in many fields, and highest percentage of GDP devoted to R&D. Brazil has an explicit science, technology, and innovation policy and is at or near the technology frontier in several significant areas such as aircraft manufacture, biofuels, electronic banking and elections, electric motors, and tropical agriculture and forest management.

Brazil is in a position to make a successful effort at closing the technological gap if this becomes a national priority receiving focused attention from the nation's leadership, beginning with the president and, importantly, state governors, and supported by key civil society organizations. It is not clear at this point whether the needed leadership and mobilization of financial and organizational resources that have been announced by the government, such as increasing expenditure in S&T, will be forthcoming. Other important aspects to be considered are increasing R&D and modernizing manufacturing capacity to strengthen the Brazilian ICT firms' competitiveness. Similar measures are needed for the other strategic sectors identified in the PITCE, including aeronautics.

An important role could be played by Brazil's powerful and high-quality media establishment, led by the Globo enterprises, which includes the fourth-largest private television network in the world, and the leading Brazilian firms in the aeronautics sector owing to its important role in disseminating new technologies to other sectors. A strategic communications campaign for the dissemination of the innovation culture could build broad public understanding of and support for a major push to close the technological gap and become a first world country, which is still not widely known.

Building the needed infostructure (fiber and satellite networks and last-mile extensions using technologies such as Wi-Fi, Wi-MAX, and Powerline Communications) and harnessing ICTs, as well as strengthening technological development and international competitiveness in the aeronautics sector, can play a critical role in building Brazil's competitiveness as well as solving centuries-old socioeconomic problems. Education needs to be given the highest priority for the use of this infostructure and for the development of the aeronautics sector. The spread of digital TV, which could be very rapid in Brazil, together with cheap broadband Internet connectivity, can provide a powerful new tool for bringing quality and lifelong education and training to Brazil's future and present labor force, unleashing the creative potential of a relatively young population.

In terms of international trade, Brazil—like other members of the BRIC group—is not part of either the NAFTA or the European Union. There are potential gains to all four giant countries in selective alliances in the field of trade, science, and technology. As is true for firms, it is possible to both compete and enter strategic alliances, and the potential returns and complementarities of markets and production structures among Brazil, China, India, and Russia offer substantial opportunities for collaboration on many fronts that should be exploited.

In sum, Brazil could be the first Latin American country to close the technological gap. Whether it does so or not is a choice that Brazilians must make.

Notes

1. Embraer reports to investors at www.embraer.com.br, August 2006.
2. According to the offset programs of the military government foreign firms supplying to the government could transfer technology to Brazilian firms in accordance with the specific procurement agreement.
3. http://news.bbc.co.uk/2/hi/technology/6246989.stm (accessed January 30, 2007).

References

Agência Brasileira de Desenvolvimento Industrial (ABDI). 2006. Política Industrial, Tecnologia e de comércio Exterior: Estratégia para a competividade do Brasil.

Aragão de Carvalho Filho, Carlos Alberto. 2006. "O desafio inovador brasileiro: O papel da FINEP Agência Brasileira de Inovação." Presentation made at joint meeting of FINEP and the Brazilian Telecommunications Association directors, August 16. Aspesi, Eduardo. 2006. "IP via satellite." Connect-World, Latin America Issue, 52–53.

Bernardes, Roberto. 2000a. "O Arranjo Produtivo da Embraer na Região de São Jose dos Campos." Report. Rio de Janeiro, Federal University of Rio de Janeiro—Institute of Economics.

———. 2000b. "Oportunidades de Mercado, Produção e Acesso ao Conhecimento: Linhas de ação para o fortalecimento da performance tecnológica do setor aeronáutico". Report. Rio de Janeiro: FINEP.

Budinich, Mateo. 2006. "Digital TV—Closing in on the Digital Divide." Connect-World, Latin America Issue, 52–53.

Cassiolato, J. and H. Lastres. 1999. "Local, National and Regional Systems of Innovation in the Mercosur." Paper presented at DRUID's Summer Conference on National Innovation Systems, Industrial Dynamics and Innovation Policies.

Chahin, Ali. 2004. *e-gov.br—a próxima revolução brasileira: Eficiênccia, qualidade e democracia: o governo eletrônico no Brasil e no mundo.* São Paulo: Pearson/Prentice Hall.

Coelho, Franklin Dias. 2006. "Municipios Digitais: Caminhos do Rio." Presentation at the seminar Internet for All: A Strategy Focused on Municípios, Chamber of Deputies, Brasília, November 7.

————. "Cidades Digitais: Caminhos de um programa nacional de inclusão digital." In Knight, Fernandes, and Cunha, *e-Desenvolvimento no Brasil e no Mundo.*

Confederação Nacional da Indústria. 2006. *Crescimento. A Visão da Indústria.* Brasília: Confederação Nacional da Indústria.

Dagnino, R. 1999. "Competitividade da Indústria Aeronáutica." Nota Técnica do Complexo Metal-Mecânico. Estudo da Competitividade da Indústria Brasileira.

Dagnino, R., and D. J. Proença. 1989. *The Brazilian Aeronautics Industry.* Geneva: International Labour Office/International Labour Organization.

Dahlman, Carl, and Cláudio Frischtak. 2005. "Os desafios para o Brasil da Economia do Conhecimento: educação e inovação num mundo crescentemente competitivo." In *Reforma Política e Economia do Conhecimento: dois Projetos Nacionais,* ed. José Olympio. Rio de Janeiro: José Olympio.

De Ferranti, David, and Guillerma Perry. 2003. *Closing the Gap in Education and Technology.* Washington, D.C.: World Bank Latin American and Caribbean Studies.

Eber, Fabio Stefan. 2004. "Innovation and the Development Converntion in Brazil." Revista Brasileira de Inovação 3 (1): 35–54.

Freeman, Christopher. 1987. *Technology and Economic Performance: Lessons from Japan.* London: Pinter.

Frischtak, Claudio. 1992. "Learning, Technical Progress and Competitiveness in the Commuter Aircraft Industry: An Analysis of Embraer." Industry Series Paper. Washington, D. C.: World Bank Industry and Energy Department, OSP.

————. 1994. "Learning and Technical Progress in the Commuter Aircraft Industry: An Analysis of Embraer's Experience." *Research Policy* 23 (5): 301–312.

Gracioso, Hélio Marcos Machado. 2006. "EoIP and Industrial Policy in Brazil." *Connect-World,* Latin America Issue, 19–20.

Green, R. D. 1987. "Brazilian Government Support for the Aerospace Industry." Report. Washington, D.C.: U. S. Department of Commerce/International Trade Administration.

Katz, Jorge. 2000. *Passado e presente del comportamiento tecnológico de América Latina.* Serie Desarrollo Produtivo 75. Santiago de Chile: Red de Reestructuración y Competitividad, División de Desarrollo Productivo y Empresarial, ECLAC/UN.

————. 2001. "Structural Reforms and Technological Behaviour: The Sources and Nature of Technological Change in Latin Amercia in the 1990s." *Research Policy* 30 (1): 11–19.

Knight, Peter T., and Roberto Aroso. 2006. "E-Brasil—Accelerating Socioeconomic Development in Brazil." *Connect-World,* Latin America Issue, 15–18.

Knight, Peter Titcomb, and Ciro Christo Campos Fernandes, eds. 2006. *e-Brasil: Um programa para acelerar o Desenvolvimento socioeconômico aproveitando a convergência digital.* São Caetano do Sul, SP: Yendis.

Knight, Peter Titcomb, Ciro Christo Campos Fernandes, and Maria Alexandra Cunha. Forthcoming 2007. *e-Desenvolvimento no Brasil e no Mundo: Subsídios e programa e-Brasil.* São Caetano do Sul, SP: Yendis.

Lopez-Claro, Augusto. 2006. *Global Competitiveness Report 2006–2007: Creating an Improved Business Environment.* London: Palgrave Macmillan.

Lula Presidente—Plano de Governo 2007/2010.

Malkin, Daniel. 2006. *Education, Science and Technology in Latin America and the Caribbean: A Statistical Compendium of Indicators.* Washington, D.C.: Education, Science and Technology Subdepartment Sustainable Development Department. Inter-American Development Bank.

Marques, Rosane A. 2004. "Evolution of the Civil Aircraft Manufacturing System of Innovation: A Case Study in Brazil." In *Innovation, Learning and Technological Dynamism of Developing Countries,* ed. S. Mani and H. Romijn. Tokyo: United Nations University Press. Chapter 4, 77–106.

———. 2006. "Displays em aviões: especificidades da cadeia produtiva aeronáutica brasileira." Presentation at XIII InfoDisplay—VIII BrDisplay—VI Latin SID Seminar—VIII Display Escola, CenPRA, Campinas, SP, Brazil, November 17.

Marques, Rosane A. and L. Gulilherme Oliveira. 2006. "Sectoral System of Innovation in Brazil: Reflections about Linkages and the Accumulation of Technological Capabilities Experienced by SME Suppliers to the Aeronautic Industry." Paper presented at the Globelics India Conference, Thiruvananthapuram, India, October 4–7.

Ministério da Ciência e Tecnologia, Centro de Gestão e Estudos Estratégicos (CGEE). 2006. *3ª Conferência Nacional de Ciência, Tecnologia e Inovação, Novembro de 2005, síntese das conclusões e recomendações.* Brasília: CGEE, Ministério da Ciênica e Tecnologia.

National Science Foundation, Division of Science Resources Statistics. 2006. *Science and Engineering Indicators 2006.* Arlington, VA: National Science Foundation.

Newman, N. C., Alan L. Porter, and J. David Roessner. 2005. "Differences Over a Decade: High Tech Capabilities and Competitive Performance of 28 Nations." *Research Evaluation* 14, no. 2 (August): 121–128.

Núcleo de Assuntos Estratégicos da Presidência da República. 2004. "Projeto Brasil 3 Tempos—2007, 2015 e 2022: Apresentação." *Cadernos NAE* 1.

Pardo, Jaime Chico. 2006. "Everything over IP on the Developing World." *Connect-World,* Latin America Issue, 9–12.

Porter, Alan L., J. David Roessner, Nils C. Newman, Xiao-Yin Jin, and Alisa Kongthon. 2004. "High Tech Indicators: Who's Gaining." *Technology Exports* 6 (3): 1–16.

———. 2006. *High Tech Indicators: Technology-Based Competitiveness of 33 Nations— 2005 Final Report.* Report to the Science Indicators Unit, Science Resources Studies Division, National Science Foundation under Contract D050144. September 4, 2006. Atlanta, GA: Technology Policy and Assessment Center, Georgia Institute of Technology.

Programa de Governo da Candidatura Lula 2006: caderno setorial: comunicação e democracia.

Rezende, Sergio Machado. 2006. "Evolução da Política Nacional de Ciência, Tecnologia e Inovação e de seus instrumentos de apoio." In Ministério da Ciência e Tecnologia, Centro de Gestão e Estudos Estratégicos (CGEE), *3ª Conferência Nacional de Ciência, Tecnologia e Inovação.*

Rezende, Sergio Machado, and Conceição Vedovello. 2005. "O papel da Finep no Sistema nacional de Inovação." In *Reforma Política e Economia do Conhecimento: dois Projetos Nacionais.* Rio de Janeiro: José Olympio.

Takahashi, Tadao, ed. 2000. *Sociedade da informação no Brasil: Livro Verde.* Brasília: Ministério da Ciência e Tecnologia.

———. Forthcoming, 2007. "Rumo a um eBrasil: Pontos a Ponderar." Capítulo 3.1. In Knight, Fernandes, and Cunha, *e-Desenvolvimento no Brasil e no Mundo.*

Teixeira, Alesandro G. "O ineditismo da Política Industrial, Tecnológica e de Comércio Exterior."

Velloso, João Paulo dos Reis, ed. 2005. "O Desafio da China e da Índia: A Resposta do Brasil." Rio de Janeiro: José Olympio.

————, ed. 2005. *Reforma Política e Economia do Conhecimento: dois Projetos Nacionais.* Rio de Janeiro: José Olympio.

Viotti, Eduardo B. 2002. "National Learning Systems: A New Approach on Technological Change in Late Industrializing Economies and Evidences from the Cases of Brazil and South Korea." *Science and Technology Forecasting* 69 (September): 653–680.

Wade, Robert. 2006. "The Case for 'Open Economy Industrial Policy.'" Paper for UNCTAD. June 6.

CHAPTER 6

Fostering Innovation: Technological Innovation in Urban Clusters

Scott Tiffin and Isabel Bortagaray

Continuous innovation of new products, processes, and services creates competitiveness, profits, and employment, and encourages socioeconomic development. While this is well known to managers, regulators, and researchers in developed countries, such is not the case in most of Latin America, as reflected by investment levels, policies, and practices. Interest in innovation, the knowledge of how to manage it, and support for it are all generally low to nonexistent.

Given that constraint, this chapter, first, limits the concept of innovation to a particular subset that is fundamental for generating competitiveness in a knowledge-based economy—innovation that is related to science and technology (S&T). There is a small, but committed community that promotes this kind of innovation throughout the region (Sbragia et al., 2005). There are significant S&T resources concentrated in a few of the leading countries where these concepts have already taken root. Second, this chapter will focus on one particular type of industrial organization where innovation occurs—within urban clusters. Experience shows that an interest in competitiveness and innovation is often greater among, and more widely held by, stakeholders at local urban levels in (some parts of) Latin America, than at national and regional levels.

The term "clusters" is increasingly used by urban promoters, politicians, and policymakers as the focal point of their development plans. It is important to recognize that many of these initiatives just provide infrastructure for traditional industrial estates, or duty-free assembly enclaves, or are impractical schemes to create "world-class IT manufacturing centers" in remote provincial cities. And even in serious cases, regions and cities in Latin America are almost always short of organizational structures capable of managing and promoting the complex interactions and investments necessary to seed and fine-tune clusters. But at least

Table 6.1   National R&D expenditures for 2003

Country	Gross domestic expenditure on R&D (as % of GDP)
Argentina	.41
Bolivia	.26 [a]
Brazil	.95
Colombia	.17[b]
Costa Rica	.39[c]
Cuba	.65
Chile	.60
Ecuador	.07
El Salvador	.08[d]
Mexico	.40[a]
Nicaragua	.07[a]
Panama	.34
Paraguay	.10
Peru	.11
Uruguay	.22
Canada	1.91
United States	2.58

Source: RICYT (n/d).
Notes: [a] Data for 2002; [b] Data for 2001; [c] Data for 2000; [d] Data for 1998.

there is growing awareness. Influential stakeholders do have the capability to organize and act. While trained people, skilled organizations, and venture capital are not in abundant supply, they are concentrated in a few major centers, which represent pockets of real potential.

Patterns of Innovation in Latin America

As table 6.1 illustrates, R&D investment in Latin America—a fundamental input to innovation—is extremely low, compared to that in developed countries. Canada, a nation whose competitiveness still depends greatly on commodities, spends nonetheless six times more of its GDP on R&D than the average Latin American economy.

Publications and patents constitute alternative indicators that bring more texture to this analysis and show trends over time. The rate of change in the total number of publications tracks closely the change in the percentage of world output. Despite the total number of publications in Latin America being a small portion of world share, the constant and rapid increase in the past decade is a very promising development. Overall, Latin America's share in world publications has doubled in this period (see figure 6.1).

Unfortunately, Latin American–held US patents have grown at a much slower rate than publications (see figure 6.2). This implies that much of the research knowledge is not oriented to or linked to product development, especially products for an international market. An in-depth study of national patent data would reveal more innovation oriented toward local production, just as a study of national

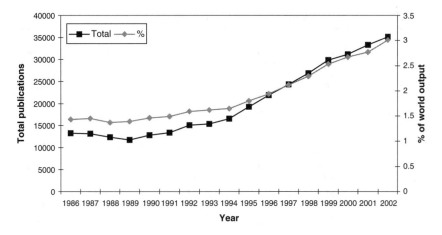

Figure 6.1 Latin American publications and world output, 1986–2002

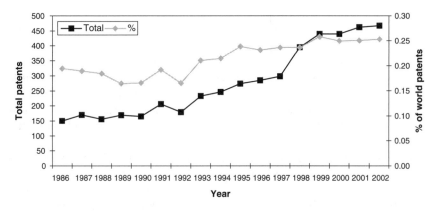

Figure 6.2 Latin American patents and world output, 1986–2002

scientific publications would show greater research output. Unfortunately, these databases are not strictly comparable across the region (let alone easily available for study). Melo (2001) has examined European patents by Latin Americans and some national databases and come to an even stronger conclusion about overall lack of innovation progress in the region, or, in terms of world average performance, a retrogression.

Why Not More?

It is important to understand that business in Latin America is quite strong. Latin Americans continually rank highly in business entrepreneurship (Minniti et al., 2005). Some business schools from the region placed in the top 50 in world rankings (Financial Times, 2005). The problem is not that Latin American

Table 6.2   Expenditure on R&D by financing sector for 2003

	Government	Firms	Higher education	Nonprofit private organizations	Foreign
Argentina	44.2	26.1	25.9	2.3	1.4
Bolivia[a]	20	16	31	19	14
Brazil	30.4	41	28.6		
Colombia[a]	13.2	46.9	38.3	1.7	
Cuba	60	35			5
Chile[b]	50.5	35.2	0.4	0.5	13.3
Ecuador[c]	39.8	32.5		4.9	22.9
El Salvador	51.9	1.2	13.2	10.4	23.4
Mexico[a]	61	30.6	7.1	0.3	1
Panama	25.5	0.6	1.8	1	71.1
Paraguay	60.9		12.1	2.1	21
Uruguay	17.1	46.7	31.4	0.1	4.7
Canada	24.8	47.5	16.5	3	8.1
USA	30	63.3	3.8	2.9	

Source: RICYT (n/d).
Note: [a] Data for 2002; [b] Data for 2001; [c] Data for 2000.

business is not innovative, but that innovation focuses on new market creation and new business models. There are relatively few new products created, little design that is embodied in them, and very little science and technology at their base. Ramos (2000) decries the prevalent "free rider" attitude in which firms expect to benefit from other companies' research and innovation without participating in the costs.

The contribution of the private sector to R&D is extremely low, when compared to the United States, Asian countries, and even many European markets where governments spend lavishly on R&D (see table 6.2). An important inhibitor to R&D investment by the private sector is the lack of enforceable intellectual property protection afforded by Latin America's judicial system. Most companies prefer to import tried and true technology solutions under licensing agreements than risk their own capital and time in developing home-grown solutions. Not only does imported technology save money, but the foreign parent company will also often help defend the exclusivity of the technology and provide legal muscle to help defend its IP when Latin American competitors try to copy it.

Both the public and private sectors in the region have long concentrated on factors of "spurious competitiveness"—low wages, low skilled labor force, lack of protection of the environment, and a reliance on natural resources. And this is part of the still broader problem of "the curse of resource wealth" that continues to be seen in the case of Canada in the R&D expenditures. Science and technology have long been divorced from production in Latin American countries. Oteiza (1992) describes it for the case of Argentina, and his analysis can be extended to almost all countries of the region. This divorce is explained by the model of economic growth fostered in the nineteenth and twentieth centuries throughout the region. The abundance of land together with the low density of

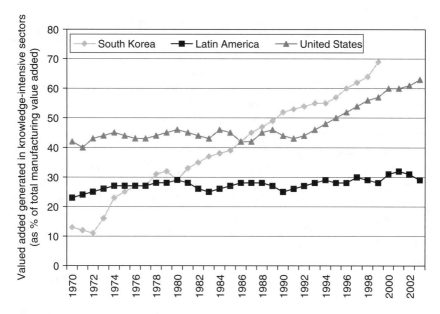

Figure 6.3 Latin American high-tech exports, 1970–2002

population nurtured an extensive mode of agriculture production in which technological change was based on direct import and adoption of technological pack-
ages, without investing in local R&D (Oteiza, 1992). Scandinavian countries
have taken a very different approach to building on the strengths of their natural
resource industries and reinforcing them with R&D and knowledge, which has
led to greatly increased value-added products (Freeman and Lundvall, 1988) and
new enterprises.

High-tech exports have represented a low share of Latin America's total exports
(Alcorta and Peres, 1995). Figure 6.3 shows the region's dramatically low performance in this respect (Cimoli et al., 2005).

There are major exceptions of course; Brazil's national oil company Petrobras
is a world leader in deep-sea operations, based significantly on its own technological innovations; and Embraer is now neck and neck with Canadair as the
third largest commercial aircraft manufacturer. Cuba has a huge biotech R&D
establishment, whose outputs are commercialized through venture capital deals
to Canada, Europe, and Brazil. Monterrey University professors are intimately
involved with business and engineering consulting activities in the large *maquiladora*
(export manufacturing) industries on Mexico's northern border. Venezuela's
national petroleum company PDVSA has been a huge source of patenting and
applied research in the petroleum industry. Costa Rican engineering schools are
closely linked to Intel and supported by the government to create software technology clusters. In Chile, a leading Norwegian salmon culture firm, EWOS, has
just set up its first product innovation laboratory.[1]

Unfortunately, these success stories do not get much attention in the public press and there are few reliable research studies of what they really entail. Worse, many of these successes never reach their potential due to generalized socioeconomic difficulties and political instability in many parts of the region. Rodriguez-Clare's (2005) frank analysis of innovation and technology adoption in Central America makes these kinds of difficulties only too clear.

Given the lack of industrial involvement with research, S&T, public S&T policy has focused on the kinds of things that it could control: management of funds for scholarships, graduate training, and research-related activities in universities and public laboratories. Until the 1980s technology policy was mainly carried out by planning institutions related to the implementation of the import substitution industrialization model such as BNDES or FINEP in Brazil, and CNEA (Comisión Nacional de Energía Atómica) or Instituto Nacional de Tecnologia Industrial (National Technological Institute) in Argentina (Bastos and Cooper, 1995).

Is this situation changing? Yes, in a few cases. For example, in Chile, there are plans in motion to double the funding of R&D, and constant attention is now being given to the finer details of improving quality in the national educational system (Waissbluth, 2006). Brazil has made enormous and sustained public investment in science, technology, innovation, and entrepreneurship infrastructure through a variety of initiatives from its National Research Council (CNPq) and industrial support agencies such as Serviço Brasileiro de Apoio às Micro e Pequenas Empresas (SEBRAE). The graph in figure 6.4 (ANPROTEC, 2005) illustrates this dramatically.[2]

At its most fundamental level, funding of the education system is a social issue. The bulk of the populace of Latin America is struggling with continued exclusion or meeting basic needs, while the upper-middle and the elite classes tend to be conservative in their views on society and economy, and like their counterparts in most developed countries, hoping for gradual social development that does not disrupt their privileged positions.

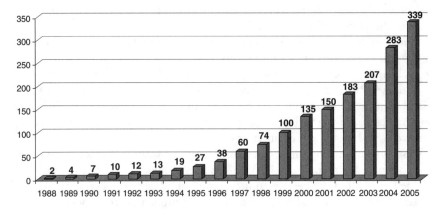

Figure 6.4 Brazil's investment in incubators

Patterns of Innovation at the Urban Level

Numerous authors (Acs, 2002; Saxenian, 1994; Jacobs, 1970; Cooke, 2002) point out how knowledge resources and knowledge-based industry concentrate at the urban level.[3] It seems that only a small number of cities really drive the frontiers of social and economic innovation, and they rise and fall over long time periods (Hall, 1999). There also seems to be a pattern of the few leading cities increasingly draining skilled people and financial and technological resources from their smaller siblings (Danell and Persson, 2003; Polese, 2003). Many of the conditions for creating innovation and entrepreneurship are simply a result of the sheer size of a city, but it appears that the natural and intellectual/social endowments of a city can be made much more effective at creating a dynamic, creative cluster by dedicated management (Castells and Hall, 1994; Miller and Cote, 1987; Florida, 2002; Rosenfeld, 2002; Feldman and Francis, 2004).

High Concentrations within Cities

The most striking feature of scientific publication is its extreme concentration in cities, and in a few cities in particular in Latin America.[4] The patents are also concentrated in a few major cities, although not to the extent of publications. There is significant correlation between location of publication and patenting, with a few notable exceptions such as Monterrey, Mexico, which is one of the major Latin American centers for patenting, but almost insignificant as a center for production of scientific knowledge (see table 6.3).

Table 6.3 Most important publication and patent cities in Latin America

City	Regional publication concentration (% of LA total)	City	Regional patent concentration (% of LA total)
São Paulo, Brazil	33.78	São Paulo, Brazil	9.52
México City, Mexico	28.56	Buenos Aires, Argentina	9.21
Buenos Aires, Argentina	25.01	Caracas, Venezuela	7.15
Santiago, Chile	16.08	Rio de Janeiro, Brazil	4.88
Rio de Janeiro, Brazil	16.02	Mexico City, Mexico	3.48
Campinas, Brazil	9.97	Monterrey, Mexico	3.20
Caracas, Venezuela	7.14	Santiago, Chile	2.69
La Plata, Argentina	6.51	Bogota, Colombia	2.06
Porto Alegre, Brazil	5.53	Leon, Mexico	1.91
São Carlos, Brazil	4.82	Porto Alegre, Brazil	1.57
Havana, Cuba	4.61	Campinas, Brazil	1.36
Córdoba, Argentina	4.48	Cuernavaca, Mexico	1.15
Belo Horizonte, Brazil	3.87	Lima, Peru	1.04
Brasilia, Brazil	2.77	Guadalajara, Mexico	0.89
Montevideo, Uruguay	2.61	San Jose, Costa Rica	0.83

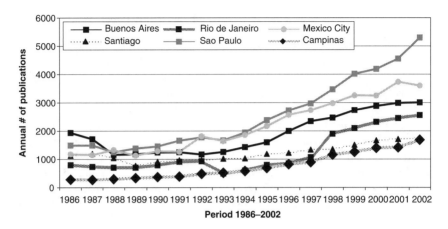

Figure 6.5 Growth in publication output for leading cities

Growth Trends

São Paulo stands out as a leading intellectual property center that is growing at a faster clip than other Latin American cities. That lead will further accelerate as Brazil attracts more investment into its ethanol industry, which is located primarily in the state of São Paulo. Over time, Buenos Aires has lost its prestige as publication leader. The belt tightening by the government in the late 1990s up to the crisis of 2001–2002 led to the dismantlement of budgets that feed the publication process. Santiago is the consistent underperformer, showing the least increase in output and gradually being left behind by the others (see figure 6.5).

When the cumulative levels of patents are tracked, Buenos Aires shows much more promise. Private sector investment continued in the late 1990s as foreign direct investment poured into the petrochemical and other infrastructure sectors. The realignment of the Argentine economy in 2002 undoubtedly led to a decline in national investment but as the Argentine economy has grown out of its crisis, many multinationals have shifted design shops to Buenos Aires to leverage the talent there, priced much cheaper than many other Spanish language markets.

Caracas began to slow its progress in 1999, as the Chavez administration won and capital flight ensued. In spite of healthy oil prices that have buoyed the economy, the investment time line for the private sector has shrunk—no one is risking long-term capital in such a high-risk political climate. The two historic drivers of patent activity in Venezuela were the state oil firm PDVSA and Procter & Gamble, which has one of Latin America's only multinational R&D laboratories based in Caracas. Recent events in Venezuela have seen the closure of the entire PDVSA laboratory and the major reduction in the number of Procter & Gamble's laboratories.

Mexico City contributes a much smaller share to Latin American patenting, and is closely tracked by Monterrey. The influence of the North American Free Trade Agreement (NAFTA) and the location of so many Canadian and U.S.

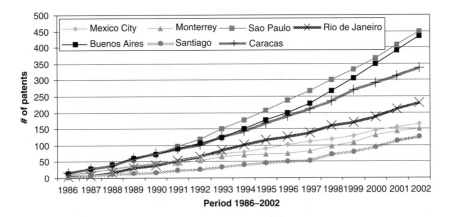

Figure 6.6 Growth in patent output

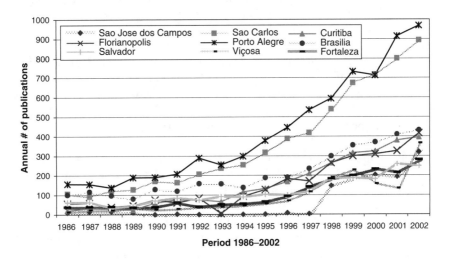

Figure 6.7 Rapid publication growth cities in Brazil

multinationals in northern Mexico seems to be the influencing factor in putting Monterrey's patenting at such a high level, while its research output is relatively low (see figure 6.6).

Rapid Growth Centers

There are numerous cases—nearly all occurring in provincial cities—of truly explosive growth in publication, typical of the Asian "miracle" countries. And we have seen São Paulo is an accelerating giant, although the acceleration is not at such a high rate (see figure 6.7). It should be noted that these kinds of rapid growth patterns also occur in some small national capitals: notably San José,

Costa Rica, and Havana, Cuba, which is a major international center for biotechnology and pharmaceutical research, and increasingly, an upstream partner in international innovation consortia.

The consensus is that innovation clusters can really be built only out of areas where there is an existing strong industrial production that is systematic and networked (Arocena and Sutz, 1998; Melo, 2001; Enright and Ffowcs-Williams, 2000; Schmitz, 2000).

Local Innovation Systems

The previous section has shown that innovation is highly concentrated in urban areas. Part of this is only a scale phenomenon, as cities have more of everything. What is more interesting is to see if Latin American cities are fostering innovation activities that are qualitatively more efficient and effective. The areas of high concentration of publishing and patenting noted in the previous section suggest the possible existence of local innovation systems, loosely known as clusters. The following section shows why clusters are important and what evidence we find for them in Latin America.

There is a very large literature on national innovation systems in Latin America, available from conference sites such as The Organization of IberoAmerican States (www.oei.es) and Globelics (www.globelics.org), in books on Brazil by Lastres et al. (2005), Cassiolato and Lastres (1999), and by Melo (2001). We agree this concept is important for Latin America, but like Bastos and Cooper (1995) and Arocena and Sutz (2001), we feel it may have been applied too freely to this region without enough measurement of what is happening here. For example, one of the unique Latin American realities seems to be "isolation" and "encapsulation" of innovation (Arocena and Sutz, 2001). Innovation takes place in what Sutz (1998) calls "innovation circuits," referring to processes in which innovation occurs to solve specific productive problems. Industrial innovation does occur, but it is not self-sustaining—let alone growing. The encounter between users and producers of knowledge and innovation is constrained to a specific request in a specific context: innovation takes place in circuits, but then disappears after the one-off task is complete.

Clusters in Latin America

Buenos Aires

One major example of an innovation cluster (see table 6.4) is the Technological Pole Constituyentes,[5] located in Buenos Aires, which comprises several large and powerful national institutions.[6] The pole is intended to generate and transfer scientific and technological knowledge among its members, within Mercosur and around the world, as well as foster linkages with the private sector. Its core areas include materials, information technologies, environment, energy, transport, microelectronics, and biotechnology. It also offers services such as human development

Table 6.4 Latin American cluster types

Cluster type	Description
Dependent or truncated	Composed of branch plants that are installed from another region or country and specialize in very limited activities, e.g., assembly (*maquiladora*) or resource extraction and processing. Technology is mature and arrives in fully packaged form of installed process equipment.
Industrial	A group of firms working together, focused on producing mature goods and services. Very limited engagement of knowledge sources except for maintaining routine quality control and hiring skilled graduates. Limited entry of new firms.
Innovative industrial	An industrial cluster with strong product upgrading, quality improvements, creation of new enterprises, and seeking of new markets. Routine engagement with local consultants, laboratories, and universities to inject new knowledge into the cluster.
Proto innovation	An innovative industrial cluster, with awareness of world markets, and the need to be at international best practice levels. It focuses on rapid acquisition of cutting-edge technology to create new products and supports a limited growth of new knowledge-intensive firms. Some key stakeholders typically missing and not clear if will continue to develop in medium term.
Mature innovation	A cluster that defines the social structure of the community it is in; creates a dynamic, expanding group of firms based on cutting-edge scientific knowl edge; sucks in talent from around the world; generates venture capital; and drives the pace and direction of scientific and technological research.

training, quality control, and support to regulatory bodies and public services, apart from functioning as a technology-based incubator. However, we find that rather than acting as an innovation cluster, it is more like a technopole emphasizing technology transfer from large government research laboratories, and strengthening of the relationships with the private sector.

Curitiba

Curitiba is the capital city of the southern Brazilian state of Parana. Long overshadowed by massive São Paulo just to the north, Parana has a tradition of an agricultural base and a small population. It was made dynamic by a charismatic mayor and a population highly receptive to change, and surged to a leadership position in Brazil in terms of urban planning, environmental awareness, and university development. Researchers, politicians, and public managers from all over the world have come to the city to see how it has developed and expanded its urban management systems, principally transportation. The lead in creating an innovation cluster centered around environmental management and software informatics, however, seems to have been taken by the state government. Thereafter, the main universities began to follow the lead of government and industry to support the quickening of the links between knowledge and enterprise. In Curitiba, the main private university, the Pontificia Catholic University, implemented a strategy to transform itself into a research-based university instead of a teaching enterprise. One of its steps is the creation of a graduate specialty in knowledge management. There is a well-established incubator, but it does not seem to be a central actor in the emerging technopole, as it is focused strongly on its immediate role of supporting technology startups. There is limited venture capital, but negotiations have begun to set up a branch of an established venture capital firm in the city.

Curitiba is recognized as the city in Brazil with probably the highest quality of life and is extremely active in promoting this status to attract environmentally friendly industries and knowledge workers. Partly as a result, Curitiba is the fastest-growing city in the country.

Porto Alegre

This city, capital of Brazil's southernmost state Rio Grande do Sul, is well known for the excellence of its urban planning and management, with a strong emphasis on democratic participation of local communities and improving the quality of life of the urban and regional environments. In 1995, the Porto Alegre Technopole project was initiated with a mission to transform the metropolitan region to a knowledge-based economy. It is led by the Universidad Federal de Rio Grande do Sul and the City Municipality. A relevant feature has been the strong and frequent dialogue among the promoters and the local stakeholders, many of whom are working together on other projects. The personal relationships are said to cut through bureaucratic obstacles. Furthermore, Porto Alegre is one of the two cities in Brazil, the other being São Paulo, where a private—and successful— venture capital firm, the Companhía Riograndense de Participações (Rio Grande Shareholder Company), or CRP, first developed. However, the CRP does not appear to be closely linked to the formally planned elements of this cluster, preferring to work independently with prospective enterprises.

The project's success stems from clear communication links among the main players and a resulting lucid sense of mission and shared goals. The lead played by the private sector in making sure that research outputs had marketable applications led to strong investment and ultimately healthy returns on investment.

Recife

Recife is a mid-sized Brazilian city on the extreme Northeast coast, the capital of the state of Pernambuco. Historically its main industry was sugarcane, but of late the region has been focusing on strengthening a modernized port and transportation facilities for raw materials and agricultural products. One of the raw materials available for technology-intensive transformation is a very diverse supply of plants that can provide alternative inputs to the local pharmaceutical industry. The state of Pernambuco has several firms producing pharmaco-chemical products, which corresponded to about 47 percent of the total production of the Northeast region of Brazil.[7] Most of this output goes to the Northeast region market.

In recent years, there has been considerable change in the production technology and products of the pharmaceutical industry, spearheaded by interaction with research teams at the Federal University of Pernambuco. A government research institute called Laboratório Farmacêutico de Pernambuco (LAFEPE) is working with the university and a private pharmaceutical firm called Hebron to develop new products based on local biological inputs. This is an incipient innovation cluster, with strong support from a variety of local stakeholders in university, industry, and government.

Costa Rica

Costa Rica has worked consistently over the past decades to develop, based on its democratic traditions, social harmony and high levels of primary and secondary education. Since the 1970s, Costa Rica has not only been synonymous with environmental tourism, but it has also managed to set the standards for this new and rapidly growing industry. Acuña, Villalobos, and Ruiz (2000) show how the environmental tourism industry has attained the complexity of a robust tourism industry cluster. We found important elements relating to the development of a strong set of management and research services oriented to tourism, principally located at INCAE—the National Training Institute, the business school in San Jose with strong links to Harvard, and the numerous NGOs working there. In addition, a number of local and regional venture capital companies, such as Empresas Ambientales de Centroamerica S.A. (Central America Environmental Companies), have been set up, as have other regional banks, focusing on the environmental business and technology areas (Tiffin, Couto, and Bas, 2000). With these related elements, we see the development of a tourism innovation cluster and of an environmental services and management innovation cluster as well. These two clusters, being focused on services instead of products, may require a different way of viewing the model elaborated before.

However, the country has managed to lay the basis for yet another innovation cluster in the last decade, based on microelectronics and software. The anchor for this cluster is the Intel plant investment in San José, which has acted as a spark and catalyst for much more cluster development not just in terms of infrastructure and companies, but also in terms of institutional and social transformation.

The growth of a few local firms in some instances has been spectacular: one software firm set up in 1993 with 4 staff expanded to 90 by 1999. With this kind of development Costa Rican software exports jumped from $10–20 million to $70–80 million between 1996 and 1999, making Costa Rica the largest exporter per capita of software in Latin America.[8] Despite these striking achievements we do not see any of these areas as yet representing a mature innovation cluster, and Rodriguez-Clare (2005) has shown that subsequent growth has not been as promising as the early phases.

Uruguay

Snoeck (1998) has carried out a detailed study of the wine industry in Uruguay. While this is a small cluster and specialized around a single agricultural product, it seems to show some characteristics that could evolve into an innovation cluster. The firms at the center of the cluster are wineries. As agricultural enterprises, they show a few of the characteristics of knowledge-based spin-offs, but in Uruguay, a significant segment of the industry has converted itself over the past decade into specialized, export-oriented companies producing small quantities of high-quality wines. Faced with financial ruin after several decades of stagnation, a group of firms in the industry decided to work together to implement radically new and different strategies, based on continuous quality and knowledge upgrading, inputs of best-practice technology, and close links with customers for developing specialty products. Overall, this industry achieved significant success in the 1990s. In relation to our model, Snoeck (1998) points out the following as key features of the industry: (i) strong integration and a highly supportive social climate, including the creation of limited time and function consortia; (ii) strong support from regulators, technology transfer agents, and business associations; (iii) transfer of skilled people, technology, and science; (iv) purchase and application of best-practice process technology and genetic stock; and (v) utilization of specialized bank credits.

On the other hand, it should be pointed out that there was virtually no support from the national school set up to train enologists, and that the main university has begun only very recently to link with the producers in terms of research and development. Most of the specialized consulting services and the technology and equipment inputs seem to come from foreign sources. In terms of our categorization scheme set up earlier, this could be identified as an innovative industry cluster.

Neither the government of Uruguay nor the city of Montevideo has had an effective policy for recognizing or promoting innovation clusters. One relevant strength of the country is its traditionally highly educated population, yet social norms and values do not favor entrepreneurship and innovation. The society as a whole is extremely conservative and has not moved significantly from its old vision of living off the sale of agricultural produce that brought such prosperity early in the century.

Havana

On the outskirts of the capital city of Cuba, Havana, the national government has made enormous investments to create biotechnology research and product development facilities. This investment was originally made as part of a commitment toward universal health care, with an emphasis on valorizing local pharmaceutical raw materials and herbal traditions (Tancer, 1995). Estimates are that in the period from 1959 to 1991, the government invested about U.S.$300 million in this pharmaceutical-medical-biotechnology system. There are about seven major research centers, employing some 1,131 research scientists and technicians.[9] It does not appear, however, that this set of laboratories is able to convert itself into an innovation cluster because of the extreme difficulties in commercializing products in a communist regime. There is no ability to create start-up firms, few specialized business services, and many restrictions on marketing and sales activities. In addition, the severe financial and regulatory restrictions on access to the

Internet make it difficult for researchers to participate in cutting-edge bioscience. However, several laboratories are acting as partners in an international innovation system with Canadian venture capitalists and basic research laboratories. The Canadians excel in basic research, the Cubans in applied research, and this work seems to be generating a fruitful partnership. The drugs are being commercialized in Canada and Cuba is being paid royalties under this scheme. The difficulty may be that the easily commercialized drugs are rapidly exploited (c. $100 million per year) while there is insufficient continuing investment maintaining the upstream supplies of new products from research.

Monterrey

This booming industrial city in the northeast of Mexico has great potential for creating innovation clusters in a number of areas. Conditions are very favorable: it is close to one of the most successful innovation clusters in the United States—Austin, Texas—and enjoys close industrial, cultural, and educational ties with the United States. Foreign high-tech investment has poured into this maquiladora center in the last few decades. One of the biggest and best technical universities in Mexico—and Latin America—the Monterrey Technological Institute, is located in the city. It is a central point in training, research, consulting, and testing, with ambitious plans to expand its reach and depth in the community, as well as its influence internationally. However, as a 30-year debate on branch plants and innovation in Canada attests, it is not at all clear that a maquiladora strategy leads to an innovation future. There is much literature to show that it can be a dead end, trapping the community in a dependent, truncated position. There seems to be no venture capital available in the urban region for new technology-based ventures. In addition, the social climate is still promoting employment in large firms, not entrepreneurship in start-ups. The research base seems to be currently oriented to testing and troubleshooting with the local industrial community. We note from the graphs in this chapters that Monterrey is not nearly as active in research as in patenting. We see great initial promise, but only time will tell if the technological and business structures will come together in a deeper partnership to form an innovation cluster.

Recommendations

A critical review of Latin America's innovation progress to date is only constructive if actionable recommendations can emerge from the analysis. Each of the key players in innovation can improve their role in raising the value and impact of innovation in the region. The motives for doing so are as much self-interest as they are a contribution to the good of their countries and the region.

University

University researchers should study clusters through measurement.[10] Up to now, most Latin American research has relied upon informal expert opinion, noncomparable case studies, and very incomplete databases. Researchers should orient their work to stakeholders, so that the opinion leaders are involved who can take action to build or strengthen the clusters the academics study.[11]

University teachers (predominantly in business, engineering, and science schools) need to teach students more about innovation and entrepreneurship, so that as professionals, these individuals will naturally be more inclined to involve their firms with these activities and know something about managing the processes. This teaching should bridge the gap between the public policy perspective on innovation and that of business management. To some extent, there could be a realignment of traditional curriculum based on disciplines toward the type of multidisciplinary activities found in innovation clusters.[12]

Government

Senior government officials at the national or state/province levels need to devolve more authority and resources to municipal governments so that they can take independent action to build clusters. Municipal governments need to acquire skills and create organizations that are responsible for building innovation clusters based on scientific and technological knowledge. This is a very new concept for most municipal administrations. Data gathering and analysis are required to understand the dynamics of the situation and orient the right course of action.

Industry

Large knowledge-based firms need to recognize that their firms can benefit from interacting with urban innovation clusters and orient their strategy appropriately. In advanced industrial economies, this is widely known and practiced, at least by knowledge-intensive firms, and there is a great deal of professional literature on the topic.[13] In Latin America, this is not the case, therefore the emphasis above on the role of business schools to incorporate such topics in their curriculum.

Managers need to work with new types of knowledge actors outside their firms in order to create new products and create more entrepreneurial structures. They need to work with them, their customers, and competitors in a much more collaborative fashion than is typical in Latin America.[14] Governments and associations can play a role in bringing together firms that do not trust each other into an environment where they share ideas and the benefits of those ideas.

Philanthropists

Wealthy individuals can set new directions for their communities and demonstrate confidence in their future by creating and endowing organizations that perform core cluster-building functions. Latin America has many billionaires, but none yet with the innovation vision and spirit of Bill Gates or Warren Buffet.[15]

Notes

1. Personal communication from Dr. Lars Huemer, business school professor at Universidad Adolfo Ibanez, from data on an ongoing research program on the Norwegian and Chilean salmon culture industries.

2. But treat these data with caution. Even in Brazilian incubators linked to engineering faculties, it seems that most of the innovation is focused on exploiting local market niches (such as software in Portuguese), not exploiting new science and technology through R&D (S. Tiffin and J. Dornelas, "Entrepreneurship and Innovation in Brazilian Incubators," in *Entrepreneurship in Latin America*, ed. S. Tiffin [Westport: Praeger Press, 2004]).

3. Where we define regional as a cluster of cities that are not greatly separated in distance or travel time (e.g., São Paulo-Campinas) or the city plus its surrounding hinterland (e.g., the conglomeration based around Mexico City, sprawling outside the boundaries of the federal district).

4. Note that the sum of the percent figures for publications exceed 100 percent as there are significant numbers of publications with multiple authors who reside in different cities, which means the same paper will be counted more than once. However, the numbers are accurate in relative terms. Patents always have one individual named as the inventor, so these numbers do sum to 100 percent.

5. Information available at http://www.ptconstituyentes.com.ar/.

6. They are the National Commission of Atomic Energy (CNEA), the National Institute of Agricultural Technology (INTA), the National Institute of Industrial Technology (INTI), the Army Scientific and Technical Institute (CITEFA), the Argentinean Service of Geological Mining (SEGEMAR), and the National University General San Martin (UNSAM).

7. Information for this industry comes from ADM&TEC, "Knowledge Based Industries, Local Development and the Role of Innovation," Instituto de Administracao e Tecnologia, 2000, a research proposal prepared for IDRC on innovation clusters.

8. Personal communication from Ricardo Aguilar, vice rector, Research and Extension, Costa Rica Technological Institute.

9. Data compiled from York Medical information circulars (a division of Yorkton Securities Inc., now Orion Securities Inc., www.orionsecurities.ca). Tiffin explored the possibility of IDRC investing in Cuban biotechnology commercialization with York Medical and the Canadian Medical Research Council in 1998.

10. The work of Landry et al. (R. Landry, M. Ouimet, and N. Amara, "Network Positions and Radical Innovation: A Social Network Analysis of the Quebec Optics and Photonics Cluster," paper presented at the DRUID Summer Conference on Industrial Dynamics, Innovation and Development, Helsingor, Denmark, June 14–16, 2004) and of E. Giuliani and M. Bell ("The Micro-Determinants of Meso-Level Learning and Innovation: Evidence from a Chilean Wine Cluster," *Research Policy* 34 [2005]: 47–68) shows how important and feasible this technique is.

11. Nowotny et al. (H. Nowotny, P. Scott, and M. Gibbons, *Re-thinking Science* [Blackwell: Polity, 2002]) go into this concept (which they call "Mode 2") in great detail.

12. It seems simple and logical, but can such a realignment realistically take place in many universities? Overall, the university system across Latin America is characterized by a sharp division between public and private schools. The public ones tend to have a research mandate, but no resources; the private schools are well off, but focus largely

on teaching. This is changing, as the leading private schools are moving more into research, but the numbers of PhD programs they have is very low (only about a dozen in management in all of Latin America). In the scramble to compete for limited research resources, A. Bernasconi ("University Entrepreneurship in a Developing Country: The Case of the P. Universidad Catolica de Chile, 1985–2000," *Higher Education* 50 [2005]: 247–274) claims that the orientation of faculty has become increasingly toward academic peers, not stakeholders. As governments have diminished funding so much to the university sector, a private "enterprise" mentality has come to pervade higher education. Bernasconi ("Does the Affiliation of Universities to External Organizations Enhance Diversity in Private Higher Education? Chile in Comparative Perspective." *Higher Education* 52 [2006]: 303–342) finds that Chilean universities, the most evolved along the privatization path, are increasingly creating homogenized products and not innovating, as they focus on immediate market demands and abandon longer-range projects involving more fundamental social change.

13. Tidd et al. (J. Tidd, J. Bessant, and K. Pavitt, *Managing Innovation* [New York: Wiley, 2001]) have written an excellent university textbook on this overall topic.

14. Miles et al. (R. Miles, G. Miles, and C. Snow, *Collaborative Entrepreneurship* [Palo Alto: Stanford University Press, 2005]) present some radical suggestions of how an "open source" style of entrepreneurship can generate strategic advantage and could become more common in the future.

15. See the *Economist* (2006) and the orientation of the Gates foundation toward improving public education as one of its thrusts.

References

Acs, Z. 2002. *Innovation and the Growth of Cities.* Cheltenham: Edward Elgar.

Acuña, M., D. Villalobos, and K. Ruiz. 2000. "El Cluster Ecoturístico De Monteverde, Costa Rica" [The Eco-Touristic Cluster of Monteverde, Costa Rica]. Santiago: CEPAL.

ADM&TEC. 2000. "Knowledge Based Industries, Local Development and the Role of Innovation." Instituto de Administracao e Tecnologia. www.admtec.org.br.

Alcorta, L., and W. Peres. 1995. *Innovation Systems and Technological Specialization in Latin America and the Caribbean.* Technical Report 9509. New York: United Nations University/Institute for New Technologies (UNU/NTECH).

Altenburg, T., and J. Meyer-Stamer. 1999. "How to Promote Clusters: Policy Experiences from Latin America." *World Development* 27, 1693–1713.

ANPROTEC. 2005. *Panorama.* www.anprotec.org.br/.

Arocena, R., and P. Senker. 2003. "Technology, Inequality and Underdevelopment: The Case of Latin America." *Science, Technology & Human Values,* 28, 15–33.

Arocena, R., and J. Sutz. 2001. Innovation Systems and Developing Countries. Universidad de la Republica de Uruguay, Montevideo.

———. 1998. *La Innovacion Y Las Politicas De Ciencia Y Tecnologia Para El Uruguay (Innovation and S&T Policies in Uruguay).* Montevideo: TRILCE.

Bastos, M. I., and C. Cooper, eds. 1995. *Politics of Technology in Latin America.* London: Routledge.

Bernasconi, A. 2005. "University Entrepreneurship in a Developing Country: The Case of the P. Universidad Catolica de Chile, 1985–2000." *Higher Education* 50, 247–274.

———. 2006. "Does the Affiliation of Universities to External Organizations Enhance Diversity in Private Higher Education? Chile in Comparative Perspective." *Higher Education* 52, 303–342.

Bortagaray, I. 1999. "Innovation Clusters in Latin America and the Caribbean." In *Innovation Clusters in Latin America and the Caribbean.* Montevideo: IDRC/LACRO.

Cassiolato, J. and H. Lastres, eds. 1999. *Globalizacao & Inovacao Localizada.* Brasilia: Ministerio da Ciencia e Tecnologia.

Castells, M., and P. Hall. 1994. *Technopoles of the World: The Making of the 21st Century Industrial Complexes.* New York: Routledge.

Cimoli, M., J-C Ferraz., and A. Primi. 2005. *Science and Technology Policies in Open Economies: The Case of Latin America and the Caribbean.* Santiago: CEPAL.

Cooke, P. 2002. *Knowledge Economies: Clusters, Learning and Cooperative Advantage.* New York: Routledge.

Cooke, P., M. G. Urange, and E. Extebarria. 1997. "Regional Innovation Systems: Institutional and Organizational Dimensions." *Research Policy,* 4, 475–493.

Danell, R. and O. Persson. 2003. "Regional R&D Activities and Interactions in the Swedish Triple Helix." Paper presented at the Conference on Knowledge-Based Economy and Regional Economic Development, St. John's Newfoundland, October 3–5.

Dei Ottati, G. 1994. "Trust Interlinking Transactions and Credit in the Industrial District." *Cambridge Journal of Economics,* 18, 529–546.

El Mercurio. 2006. "Legislación: Fondos del cobre agitan a la ciencia." Santiago: Diario El Mercurio 05/09.

Enright, Michael, and Ifor Ffowcs-Williams. 2000. "Local Partnerships, Clusters and SME Globalization." Paper presented at the OECD Conference for Ministers Responsible for SMEs and Industry Ministers, Bologna, June 14–15. http://www.oecd.org/dataoecd/20/5/2010888.pdf.

EXAME. 2000. "As Melhores Cidades Para Fazer Negócios" [The Best Cities to Do Business]. *EXAME,* 713, 77–110.

Feldman, M. and J. Francis. 2004. "Homegrown Solutions: Fostering Cluster Formation." *Economic Development Quarterly* 18, no 2 (May): 127–137.

Florida, R. 2002. *The Rise of the Creative Class.* New York: Basic Books.

Freeman, C. and B.-A. Lundvall, eds. 1988. *Small Countries Facing the Technological Revolution.* New York: Pinter.

Freire, M. and M. Polese. 2003. *Connecting Cities with Macroeconomic Concerns: The Missing Link.* Washington: IBRD.

Gibson, D., Pedro Conceição, Julie Nordskog, Jennifer Burtner y Carlos Quandt. 1999. *Incubating and Sustaining Learning & Innovation Poles in Latin America and the Caribbean.* Ottawa, Canada: Technical, International Development Research Centre.

Giuliani, E. and M. Bell. 2005. "The Micro-Determinants of Meso-Level Learning and Innovation: Evidence from a Chilean Wine Cluster." *Research Policy* 34, 47–68.

Godin, B. 2005. *Measurement and Statistics on Science and Technology.* Oxford: Routledge.

Gomes, E. J. 1995. "A Experiencia Brasileira De Pólos Tecnológicos: Uma Abordagem Político-Institucional" [Brazilian Experience of Technological Poles: A Political-Institutional Approach]. Master's dissertation, Universidade de Campinas, Institute of GeoSciences, Campinas, Brazil.

Hall, P. 1999. *Cities in Civilization.* London: Phoenix.

Harzing, A. 2005. "Australian Research Output in Economics & Business: High Volume, Low Impact?" *Australian Journal of Management,* December.

Herrera, B. and L. Orozco. 2006. "Bogota- Metropolis de Conocimiento." Paper presented at 1 Congreso Iberoamericano CTS+I, Mexico DF, June 19–23.

Jacobs, J. 1970. *The Economy of Cities.* New York: Vintage.

Landry, R., M. Ouimet, and N. Amara. 2004. "Network Positions and Radical Innovation: A Social Network Analysis of the Quebec Optics and Photonics Cluster." Paper presented at the DRUID Summer Conference on Industrial Dynamics, Innovation and Development, Helsingor, Denmark, June 14–16.

Lastres, H., J. Cassiolato, and A. Arroio. 2005. *Conhecimento, Sistemas de Inovacao e Desenvolvimento.* Rio de Janeiro: Editora UFRJ/Contraponto.

Lundvall, B.-A., ed. 1992. *National Systems of Innovation: Towards a Theory of Innovation and Interactive Learning.* London: Pinter.

Malerba, F. 2002. "Sectoral Systems of Innovation and Production." *Research Policy,* 31, 247–264.

Melo, A. 2001. *The Innovation Systems of Latin America and the Caribbean.* Washington, D.C.: Inter-American Development Bank.

Miller, R. and M. Cote. 1987. *Growing the Next Silicon Valley.* Toronto: Lexington Books.

Miles, R., G. Miles, and C. Snow. 2005. *Collaborative Entrepreneurship.* Palo Alto: Stanford University Press.

Minniti, M., W. Bygrave, and E. Autio. 2005. *Global Entrepreneurship Monitor: Executive Report.* Wellesley and London: Babson College and London Business School.

Nash, M. 1996. "Fidel Castro's Most Idiosyncratic Venture Pays Off." *Time,* May 13, 147.

Nelson, R. R., ed. 1993. *National Innovation Systems: A Comparative Analysis.* New York: Oxford University Press.

Nowotny, H., P. Scott, and M. Gibbons. 2002. *Re-thinking Science.* Blackwell: Polity.

O'Halloran, E., P. Rodriguez, and F. Vergara. 2005. *Angel Investing in Latin America.* Charlottesville, VA: Darden Business Publishing.

Oteiza, E. 1992. *La Política De Investigación Científica Y Tecnológica Argentina: Historia Y Perspectivas.* Buenos Aires: CEAL.

Polese, M. 1998. *Economia Urbana y Regional.* Cartago, Costa Rica: Libro Universitario Regional.

Polese, M. 2003. "The Future of Peripheral Regions in the Knowledge-Based Economy: Evidence from Canada." Paper presented at the Conference on Knowledge-Based Economy and Regional Economic Development, St. John's Newfoundland, October 3–5.

Porter, M. 1990. *The Competitive Advantage of Nations.* New York: Free Press.

Quintas, P. 1994. "Evaluating the UK Science Park Model: Some Methodological Issues." In *European Symposium on Research into Science Parks—European Union Sprint Programme.* Rennes.

Ramos, J. 1998. "Una Estrategia De Desarrollo a Partir De Los Complejos Productivos (Clusters) En Torno a Los Recursos Naturales" [A Development Strategy Based on Productive Complexes—Clusters—on Natural Resources]. Brussels: Technical, Comisión Económica para América Latina y el Caribe (CEPAL).

———. 2000. "Policy Directors for the New Economic Model in Latin America." *World Development,* 28.

RICYT. n/d. *S&T Indicators,* 2006.

Rodriguez-Clare, A. 2005. *Innovation and Technology Adoption in Central America.* Washington, D.C.: Inter-American Development Bank.

Rosenfeld, S. 2002. *Creating Smart Systems: A Guide to Cluster Strategies in Less Favoured Regions.* Carrboro, North Carolina: Regional Technology Strategies. www.rtsinc.org.

Sachs J. and A. Warner. 2001. "The Curse of Natural Resources." *European Economic Review* 45 (4): 827–838.

Saxenian, A. 1994. *Regional Advantage. Culture and Competition in Silicon Valley and Route 128.* Massachusetts: Harvard University Press.

Sbragia, R., I. Rodrigues, and M. Selma. 2005. *Los Seminarios de Gestion Tecnologica de ALTEC, Nota Tecnica.* Sao Paulo, Brazil: Automitacao, Inspecao, e Controle de Processos Industriais (ALTEC), July/August/September. www.fea.usp.br/altec.

Schmitz, H. 1997. *Collective Efficiency and Increasing Returns.* Technical Report 50. Brighton, UK: Institute of Development Studies, University of Sussex.

Schmitz H. 2000. "Local Upgrading in Global Chains." Paper presented at the International Conference on Local Production Systems and New Industrial Policies, Rio de Janeiro, September.

Snoeck, M. 1998. *Transición, Aprendizaje E Innovación En La Industria Vinícola Uruguaya* [Transition, Learning and Innovation in the Uruguay's Wine Industry]. Montevideo, Uruguay: Comisión Sectorial de Investigación Científica, Universidad de la República.

Sutz, J. 1998. *La Caracterización Del Sistema Nacional De Innovación En El Uruguay: Enfoques Constructivos* [The Characterizations of Uruguay's National System of Innovation: Constructive Approaches]. Montevideo, Uruguay: University of Uruguay.

Tancer, R. 1995. "The Pharmaceutical Industry in Cuba." *Clinical Therapeutics, 17.*

Tidd, J., J. Bessant, and K. Pavitt. 2001. *Managing Innovation.* New York: Wiley.

Tiffin, S., G. Couto, and T. Bas. 2000. "Venture Capital in Latin America." Paper presented at the Third Triple Helix International Conference, Rio de Janeiro, April 26–29.

Tiffin, S., and I. Bortagaray. 2000. "Innovation Clusters in Latin America." Paper presented at 4th International Conference on Technology Policy and Innovation, Curitiba, Brazil, August 28–31.

Tiffin, S. and J. Dornelas. 2004. "Entrepreneurship and Innovation in Brazilian Incubators." In *Entrepreneurship in Latin America,* edited by S. Tiffin. Westport: Praeger Press.

Tiffin, S., and Jimenez, G. 2006. "Design and Test of an Index to Measure the Capability of Cities in Latin America to Create Knowledge-Based Enterprises." *J Technology Transfer,* 31:61–76.

Tiffin, S. (Forthcoming). "Patterns of Knowledge Production and Application in Cities in Latin America." *J. Research Evaluation.*

Tiffin, S., and Simon, L. 2006. *Ciudades Creativas y Economia de Conocimiento en America Latina.* Proposal submitted to IDRC-FLACSO competition on Knowledge Society in Latin America.

Voyer, R. 1997. *Emerging High-Technology Industrial Clusters in Brazil, India, Malaysia and South Africa.* Ottawa: International Development Research Centre.

Waissbluth, M. 2006. "El Rey Esta Desnudo" [The King Is Naked]. *Que Pasa,* 20–21.

CHAPTER 7

Not All Infrastructure Is Created Equally: Learning from the Best Practices and Stunning Failures of Latin American Water Infrastructure

Lee M. Tablewski

The experience of the past 15 years can be summarized as follows. The introduction of private operators in a country that has no experience in this matter is a long and difficult process. Compared with other types of infrastructure, the water sector has been the least attractive to private investors, and the sums involved have been the smallest.

The World Panel on Financing Water Infrastructure, chaired by Michel Camdessus (2003)[1]

Competitiveness and the Infrastructure Challenge

Private sector investment flows in the 1990s amounted to a third of the investment needs of the Latin American region.[2] Contrary to the hopes of many reformers, the private sector did not become the major financier of the sector or replace the rapidly falling public investment in infrastructure, although there was rarely a call for private sector participation in projects in Latin America that went unanswered.

This trend continues until today. The consensus at the 2006 Inter-American Development Bank annual meeting was that in 2005, total investments in infrastructure (public and private, both to expand and to maintain it) amounted to U.S. $47 billion in Latin America and the Caribbean (LAC). This sum is equivalent to about 2 percent of the regional GDP, while investment rates in China and

Table 7.1   Infrastructure coverage in LAC, China, and middle-income countries

	Access to Electricity %	Roads (Km/km2)	Mainlines per 1000 people	Cellular telephones (per 1000 people)	Water access %	Sanitation reach %
LAC	87	0.008	170	246	89	74
China	99	0.189	209	215	77	44
Middle-income countries	90	0.06	178	225	83	61
Year	*2000*	*2002*	*2003*	*2003*	*2002*	*2002*

Source: Fay and Morrison, 2005, p. 1.

other Asian and East European countries are three times higher than those in Latin America, as shown in table 7.1.

There has been a significant trend toward the consolidation of infrastructure operators in the region, for a variety of local and international reasons—among them changes in global strategy, unfavorable local conditions, and low rates of return. According to Harrison Morison, the drive toward telecom consolidation, noticed in 2004, continued in 2005–2006, with América Móvil buying mobile operations in Chile, Peru, and Paraguay; Telecom Italia divesting its investments in Chile, Peru, and Venezuela; and Verizon deciding to pull out of the region altogether. In April 2006, Verizon agreed to sell Verizon Dominicana (Dominican Republic), Telecomunicaciones de Puerto Rico, and CANTV (Venezuela) to América Móvil and Telmex.[3] Unlike other sectors, there continues to be no shortage of international investors willing to buy mobile licenses.

An already significant gap has grown substantially—the change in Asian infrastructure stocks per worker relative to Latin America's grew by a huge margin over 1980–1997. Comparing simple averages for each region, the advantage of the East Asian Tiger economies grew by 48 percent for fixed phone lines, 91 percent for power-generating capacity, and 53 percent for road length (Calderón and Servén, 2003). During the period of 2001–2004, China accounted for 40 percent of the total investment in water treatment projects and half the total of the 46 plants built during that period.[4]

Research has demonstrated that the growth impact of infrastructure investment is large: for example, improving the LAC region's infrastructure to the level of Korea could result in annual per capita GDP growth gains of 1.4 to 1.8 percent. It could also reduce inequality by 10 to 20 percent, thereby helping make growth more pro-poor.[5] The investment required would, however, be substantial: at least 4 to 6 percent of GDP per year over the next 20 years. On the flip side, at the micro level, poor infrastructure quality is affecting business competitiveness—indeed, while 55 percent of private entrepreneurs complain that infrastructure is a serious problem in LAC, only 18 percent do in East Asia (Fay and Morrison, 2005).

In 1980, LAC had higher coverage of infrastructure such as roads, electricity, and telecom than the East Asian Tigers. Today, the Tigers lead by a factor of three to two. LAC also trails behind China, even though the region is richer in per capita terms. (Fay and Morrison, 2005)

The deficit observed in government and private investment across infrastructure categories in LAC during the first decade of the twenty-first century has not been an issue in Chile. The Chilean government has maintained private investment in roads, water, sewage, and energy. Autopista Central, a Spanish-owned highway operator, has made road investment look like a paying proposition, realizing an incredible 3 percent bad debts by its users. Long-term inflation-adjusted infrastructure bonds have proved to be an attractive vehicle to promote local financing, particularly with the AFPs, the Chilean pension system. Beyond traditional infrastructure concession areas, Chile is now planning private development of public hospitals, a very unusual initiative (*The Economist,* 2006).

The Infrastructure Challenge in the Water Sector

Tap water is considered unsafe to drink throughout much of Latin America; bottled water is consumed by much of the population that can afford it; and much of the region's wastewater is untreated.[6] Can necessary private sector participation in infrastructure investment in Latin America be beneficial for the public good while delivering returns to investors? This is the unanswered question that plagues the industry today. Decades of universally subsidized water utilities led to decay and financial waste. A single decade of investor-friendly reform made water unaffordable to huge segments of the population in the region's poorer countries, creating a growing public backlash against private investment in water. Policymakers now are struggling to find the middle path.

A view today that is gaining traction is that water cannot be valued properly until it is assigned a market price that reflects costs, and that private participation is necessary but not sufficient for investment in infrastructure to start to achieve Millennium Development Goals (MDGs).[7] The traditional and popular perspective, expressed most often by members of the urban popular movement, small farmers' organizations, and indigenous peoples, is that access to water is a right and a public good, that it must be free or provided at highly subsidized rates. In the view of Laura Carlsen, who directs the Americas Program of the International Relations Center, "The privatization model for water use and distribution has failed to deliver. It's time to make room for new, more democratic, alternatives."[8]

User charges and taxes have been the major funding source for building Latin American infrastructure, with relatively modest contributions by private participation in infrastructure (PPI). For some sectors with strong public good characteristic—for example, rural roads—user charges are not a feasible option. In the area of telecommunications, full cost recovery through user charges is not only feasible but is the norm in the region—telecommunications appears to have always been a profitable investment.[9] But in the water and electricity[10] sectors where cost recovery is technically feasible and economically attractive, it has been politically difficult to achieve.

By 2003, private utilities were managing 86 percent of the region's telecommunications subscriptions and 60 percent of electricity connections (Sirtaine et al., 2005). After a drop-off, private investment activity in power generation appeared to have begun to rise again during 2005–2006. A private equity fund organized to invest in the Latin American power sector closed in July 2006 with U.S. $393 million, the largest amount of capital committed since the boom times of the 1990s. According to the organizer, Scott Swensen of Conduit, "I think the success of our fund is signaling that investors believe that Latin America is a good place to invest again."[11]

This chapter will focus especially on water, historically the most difficult case for private infrastructure concessions to pay back their cost of capital. It will demonstrate that the challenge of reconciling the goals of "cost recovery"[12] vs. "social protection," lack of political commitment, increasing public skepticism about PPI, inadequate regulatory power and frameworks, and widespread corruption have resulted in the region's failure to meet both public and private investment requirements in water infrastructure in the years following the start of the new millennium. Without significant reform, it is unlikely that the majority of countries in the LAC region will meet the MDGs—falling further behind in global competitiveness.

The Promise and Perils of Public-Private Partnerships (PPPs)

Private infrastructure financial strategies in infrastructure can be categorized as shown in the matrix in figure 7.1.

In theory, PPP financing can be applied to the following sectors.[13]

- Water and sanitation: Treatment plants; distribution system concession
- Solid waste: Construction of disposal site; collection, transport and storage system
- Social services and administration: Hospitals, universities, and administrative centers
- Urban transport: Centralized system and tariff administration (buses)
- Public transit systems: Dedicated rail systems, trolley systems
- Roads: Urban highways, and so on
- Urban cadastre and property tax administration

Alas, transport projects have had a history of poor regulation, corruption, and poor business planning regarding demand projection. New investors are now buying existing concessions, presumably at large discounts on the costs encountered by the previous concessionaire. But as tainted as transport concessions have been, water has the deserved reputation for being the most challenging sector for private participation, in spite of considerable reform activity (see table 7.2). In the words of Inter-American Development Bank President Luis Alberto Moreno,

Private investment is not a panacea for Latin America's sanitation problems. More than 90 percent of the region's population still depends on public utilities, and in

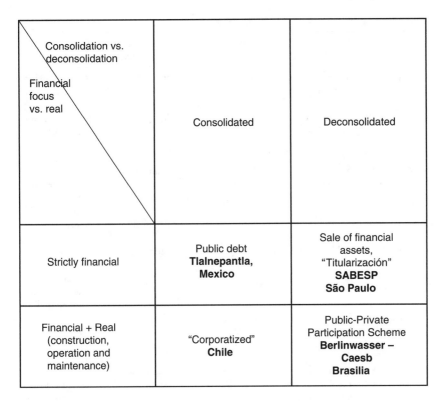

Figure 7.1 Financing options: PPP

Source: Fabrice Henry, "Los Esquemas de Participación Público-Privada: Una Alternativa Atractiva para el Financiamiento de los Municipios Intermedios en México" (paper presented at the Institute of the Americas' Conference on Long-term Municipal Finance, Mexico City, Mexico, February 1, 2005). Henry was the executive director of structured finance at Astris Finance, a subsidiary of Dexia Credit Local. Examples in bold have been selected by the author.

the near term investors are not likely to provide the tens of billions of dollars that are needed to close the sanitation gap. But as they look for ways to extend drinking water and sewer services to the millions of citizens who still lack them, governments should leverage the experience and creativity of private providers on their home turf.[14]

The Rise of the Cost Recovery Pricing Model

During the final decade of the twentieth century, the majority of LAC countries instituted reform legislation committing to cost recovery for water services. Governments were responding to the fiscal burden of water service and the requirements set by private and multilateral bank lenders to entice private sector participation. However, ten years later, "it is apparent that the transition to cost recovery pricing has been much more challenging than originally supposed."[15]

Table 7.2 Reforms in the water and sanitation sectors

Country	Start year	New legal standard	Creation of a new regulator	Decentralization	Private sector participation
Argentina	1990	Various laws at the provincial level	Various at the provincial level	Provincial and municipal	Various provinces; 2 largest cancelled
Bolivia	1994	SIRESE law Sector law	SISAB	Municipal	La Paz, El Alto cancelled. Smaller municipalities
Brazil	1990s 2004– 2005	Sector law PPP law	Varios a nivel estadual	Municipal	Various municipalities, São Paulo listed on NYSE
Chile	1989	Sector law	SISS	Regional	Concessions in all regions
Colombia	1994	Public services law	CRA	Municipal	Various municipalities including Cartagena and Barranquilla
Costa Rica	1996	Legal framework	ARESEP	No	No
Nicaragua	1998	Sector law	INAA	No	No
Panama	1998	Sector law	ERSP	No	No
Paraguay	2000	Sector law	ERSSAN	No	No
Peru	1995	Sector law	SUNASS	Municipal	Yes
Uruguay	2002	Legal framework Citizen initiative to make private ownership illegal	URSEA	No	Punta del Este; private ownership now illegal

Source: ADERASA, "Las Tarifas de Agua Potable y Alcantarillado en América Latina, Grupo de Tarifas y Subsidios (Borrador Final)," Asociación de Entes Reguladores de Agua y Saneamiento de las Américas, 2005, p. 6.

In contrast to national commitments to cost recovery, many utilities have actually lost ground in attaining this objective through tariff increases. Currency adjustments have erased almost the entire real value of tariff increases (see figure 7.2) for the LAC's major water utilities, yielding an average rate of tariff increase of less than 1 percent.[16]

Analysis of household income distribution by Foster and Yepes shows that, except in a handful of the poorest countries, "only a small segment of the population in Latin America (around 20 percent) faces genuine affordability problems in paying cost recovery tariffs, far fewer than in other developing regions—that is that they must pay more than 5 percent of monthly income"[17] (see table 7.3). Why is there such resistance to higher rates?

It is interesting to see how these tariff rates and cost recovery levels compare across regions (see figure 7.3). Less than half of the LAC region's water firms

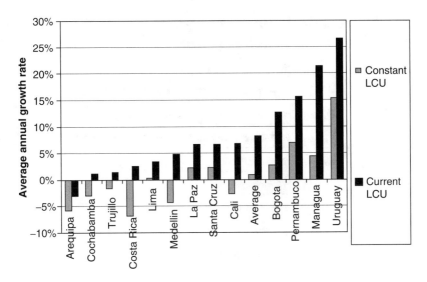

Figure 7.2 Average annual rate of water tariff increase, in constant and current local currency (1997–2003)

Source: Foster and Yepes, 2006, p. 3.

Table 7.3 Thresholds for evaluating cost recovery of water tariffs (GWI)

	Developing countries	*Industrialized countries*
<US$0.20/m	Tariff insufficient to cover basic operating and maintenance costs	Tariff insufficient to cover basic operating and maintenance costs
US$0.20–0.40/m3	Tariff sufficient to cover operating and some maintenance costs	Tariff insufficient to cover basic operating and maintenance costs
US$0.40–1.00/m3	Tariff sufficient to cover operating, needs maintenance, and most investment	Tariff sufficient to cover operating and maintenance costs
>US$1.00/m3	Tariff sufficient to cover operating, needs maintenance, and most investment in the face of extreme supply shortages	Tariff sufficient to cover full cost of modern water systems in most high-income cities

Sources: ADERASA, 2005; Foster and Yepes, 2006.

apparently recover partial investments both in operation and maintenance (O&M) and partial investments in capital, but they are doing better than other developing regions, falling short only of the OECD (Organisation for Economic Co-operation and Development) group. Within the LAC region, relatively high connection charges also contribute to problems of affordability and political resistance, as seen in the case of El Alto, Bolivia, where riots led to the cancellation of the concession.

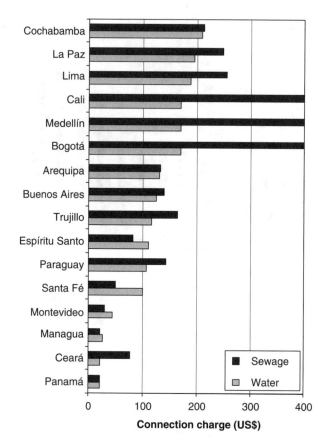

Figure 7.3 Charges for connection to services (U.S. $)
Source: Foster and Yepes, 2006.

It is interesting to compare the cost-recovery experience of Latin American water and wastewater with the experience of electric power. According to Foster and Yepes (2006), the average residential electricity tariff in 19 Latin American countries rose from U.S. $0.07 to U.S. $0.10 per kilowatt-hour between 1990 and 1996, falling back down to U.S. $0.09 per kilowatt-hour by 2002. Correspondingly, the percentage of countries recovering some degree of capital costs for power projects rose from 32 percent to 68 percent between 1990 and 1996, falling back down to 63 percent by 2002. However, the percentage of countries offering residential electricity service at tariffs lower than O&M cost fell from 16 percent to 0 percent over the entire period. Overall, residential power tariffs in Latin America are the highest of any area in the developing world, in real terms. The fact that electricity privatization was tackled beforehand or simultaneously with water privatization in several markets points to the lesson that no one utility sector can be viewed in isolation when trying to forecast viability—the consumer must balance all of his costs.

Given the challenges seen in achieving higher real tariff levels, it may not be surprising that private utilities have been seeking to change the terms of the contracts. About 42 percent of infrastructure contracts in Latin America have been renegotiated within three years of the date of award, in two-thirds of the cases at the request of the operators. The renegotiation incidence was, in fact, much higher in the transport and water sectors. Guasch (2004) and Sirtaine et al. (2005) have concluded that this is indicative of a pattern of low bidding to win the concession, with the hope and expectation of subsequent negotiation of better terms. This expectation tended to be correct with the negotiations resulting in improved terms benefiting the concessionaire.

Estimated Investment Requirements

To meet the MDGs for LAC by 2015, 50 million more people would need to have access to safe drinking water and 87 million additional people would need to receive connection to basic sanitation.

> An estimated 75 million inhabitants, representing 7 percent of the urban and 39 percent of the rural population, do not have access to clean water. Sixty percent of urban and rural dwellings with water hookups do not have continuous water service. Some 116 million people do not have access to sanitation services. This represents 13 percent of the urban and 52 percent of the rural population. The rate of access to drinking water in the region rose by 26 percent during the last decade of the twentieth century, but in order to meet the Millennium Development Goals, access to the service must increase by 33 percent between now and 2015. The rate of access to sanitation services in the same period was 27 percent, and it must increase by 35 percent by 2015.[18]

Given the growing animosity to water and sanitation privatization, the region is not going to reach its goals by relying on private investment. Government, at all levels, will have to invest much more aggressively, particularly in rural and small-town regions where cost-recovery investment models are simply incapable of attracting private investment.

There are many learned estimates for the required investment in the water and wastewater sector to achieve the 2015 goals, as shown in table 7.4.

Table 7.4 Estimates of additional annual global investment to meet MDG in water and sewage

French Water Academy	US$10 billion per year
Camdessus Report	US$10 billion (basic service)
	US$49 billion (full water and sewerage)
Water Supply and Sanitation Collaborative Council	US$10 billion (basic)
World Bank (2003)	US$15 billion
Global Water Partnership	US$16 billion
WSSD Johannesburg	US$14–30 billion
Water Aid	US$25 billion

Whether the region will meet its MDGs is a subject of great disagreement. According to the Americas Regional Document presented at the 4th World Water Forum, "If the effort made by the Latin American and Caribbean countries in the 1990s is maintained, it seems like the region, as a whole, will meet its commitments to the MDGs." This may be true for Brazil, Mexico, and Chile but it appears that public spending and private spending on water and wastewater in the balance of countries in LAC have fallen below the rates necessary to achieve the MDGs.

Return on Investment in Infrastructure

Contrary to popular perceptions, infrastructure concessions in Latin America have returned very modest yields and many have had returns below the cost of their capital.

> The analysis has shown that concessions are profitable (although risky) businesses overall, capable of generating adequate returns in the long term. Concessions in the water sector appear relatively less attractive than others, while concessions in the telecommunications sector appear to be the most profitable in relative terms. On average, concessions seem to become profitable after about 10 years of operation. However, about 40 percent of our sample concessions do not seem to have the potential to generate attractive returns, with this number climbing to 50 percent in the energy and transport sectors. Concessions are thus risky businesses.[19]

According to Sirtaine (Sirtaine et al., 2005), if historical growth rates in Latin America hold, only telecom concessions are inherently profitable, generating adequate returns to cover both operations and maintenance and the cost of capital. In all other sectors, shareholders can hope to gain long-term remuneration commensurate with their risk only if the sector "consistently and significantly outperforms historical market growth." This finding would not change according to Sirtaine even if the concessionaires paid up to 20 percent less for their concession.

Sirtaine concludes that concession returns are highly volatile from year to year in Latin America—high-risk ventures—explaining the observed requirement for such high rates of return by operators and their financiers.[20] On average, telecommunications and energy concessions have been more successful than transport and water concessions.

Water and Sewage: Best Practice Benchmark Set by Chile

It is important to remember that the story of water in Latin America is not entirely a tale of waste, fraud, abuse, and mismanagement. There are many governments, municipalities, villages, companies, and user associations working to provide good service and good coverage to their customers and citizens (see figure 7.4).

According to most government experts, balancing the public good of providing social protection from poverty-exacerbating tariffs and the need to

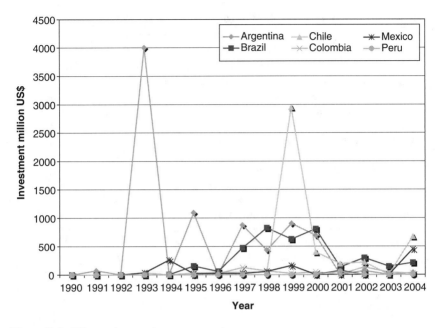

Figure 7.4 Water and sewage investment trend

bring investment into the water infrastructure requires creation of a social tariff scheme with subsidies. A review of the successful Chilean strategy is instructive.

The Chilean subsidy scheme has been devised so that households do not have to spend more than 5 percent of their income on water. The amount of the subsidy varies between 15 and 85 percent and is limited to the first 15 cubic meters of monthly water consumption. Eligibility is determined using a multidimensional poverty scale based on information collected and verified every three years through a household interview. The national government funds the system, which is run by the municipalities. When the user pays their portion of the bill the municipality transfers the subsidy directly to the utility. Around 20 percent of the population, or 600,000 people, participate in the system, which costs around U.S. $40 million per year.[21]

There have been few public demonstrations about rates and service in Chile. Water companies and other utilities have been sheltered by the Chilean government from the strong anti-privatization sentiment. They have managed in general to meet performance and profitability expectations—demonstrating again the success of political support for economic policy and aggressive but balanced regulation in Chile.

Elsewhere in the LAC region, subsidy programs such as the "increasing block tariff" (IBT) are often badly designed and subsidize ineffectively.[22] IBT and its cousin, the volume-differentiated tariff—the most common forms of cross-subsidization, and of subsidies to utility customers in general—invariably have had a regressive impact not just in LAC but worldwide.[23]

> [S]ubsidies have adverse consequences that can actually work against improving the quality of service to existing consumers and extending access to unconnected households. Subsidies engender distortions in the use of water and electricity, thereby leading to an inefficient use of resources and thus indirectly raising the costs of service provision. Subsidies can also induce inefficiency in utility operations, as utility managers face soft budget constraints. The costs of subsidies in terms of inefficiency may rival or exceed any benefit derived from the provision of the subsidy. Moreover, utility subsidies have tended to produce financially weak utilities with stagnant service areas and with declining service quality, because fiscal transfers are not always dependable and cross-subsidies are frequently insufficient to cover the subsidies provided to consumers. This endemic financial weakness means that the poorest unconnected households face the prospect of relying on alternative and often more expensive water and fuel sources for many years to come. Given the high cost of utility subsidies and their potential for creating this collateral damage to utilities and households, there is much interest in evaluating and improving utility subsidies.[24]

Indeed, Komives et al. (2005, p. 166) have shown that the poor tend to benefit half as much from these consumption-based subsidy schemes as they would from random subsidies spread across the entire society. In part this is due to the lack of strong, consistent correlation between consumption and household income—many poor households consume large quantities of water while many nonpoor families consume very little.

There is strong policy interest in improving and reducing subsidies as far as practical. But, as these subsidies have tended to favor almost the entire consumer base of the utility, frequently extending to cover higher-income people, it has proven relatively easy to build coalitions against lowering subsidies or changing subsidy structures.

The historical record of investment in water and sewage in Chile is the best in Latin America, with an impressive amount of equity investment flowing into the sector. The quality of regulation, transparency, social tariffs, the ability and desire to regulate quality of service, and the effectiveness of consumer action against poor performance have proved to be a successful combination in support of private participation and investment.[25]

Why Global Investment Dried Up

> The most important finding from the research is that households, even though they had free and reliable stand post water service, were willing to spend well in excess of 5 percent of total household expenditures to finance an individual metered water connection and the subsequent monthly commodity charges. For many of the respondents, the amount bid for this service was slightly more than what they were already paying for electricity and was considered more important than any other household expenditure except food and clothing.[26]

Latin Americans do place a high value on reliable and plentiful potable water but like any household around the world, there are limits to how much one is willing to pay for any utility. Foster and Yepes's research has found that

> [a] careful analysis of income distribution in the region suggests that only about 20 percent of Latin American households would have to pay more than 5 percent of their income for water or electricity services if tariffs were set at cost recovery levels. However, in the region's lower income countries [Bolivia, Honduras, Nicaragua, Paraguay], reaching cost recovery tariffs would represent a significant affordability problem [spending more than 5% household income] for around half of the population. Even in cases where tariffs might have to double to reach cost recovery levels, the overall impact on poverty levels in Latin America would be negligible.[27]

World Health Organization's Guy Hutton and Laurence Haller assert that the main beneficiaries do not always understand the full benefits of water initiatives until well after the investment. They also point out that most costs are incurred in the first year of the intervention, while benefits accrue over time. "These factors together lead to a type of market failure," say Hutton and Haller, "[implying] that many private consumers cannot be expected to finance the initial investment costs up-front."[28]

It seems that many private operators have preferred to try to raise tariffs quickly without regulator restraint, guidance, or adequate subsidies. In early 2000, foreign-owned water companies in Cochabamba, Bolivia, increased tariffs by up to 200 percent, to fund infrastructure improvements. These increases were spread to all consumers equally, meaning that the poor were forced to spend up to half their income just on water bills. This unsustainable policy was only terminated after public outrage led to widespread street protests in March 2000 (Public Citizen, 2001).[29]

Failure to be granted requested tariff increases and public outrage over rates and service have led to high-profile contract disputes and terminations in Argentina, Brazil, Bolivia, Mexico, and Chile. Not surprisingly, "early breaks of concession contracts may have a highly negative impact on expected returns," with hundreds of millions of dollars of losses registered (Sirtaine et al., 2005). These *fracasos nacionales* (national failures) have tainted the public view of private-public cooperation and private supply of water in particular.

Another factor causing public dissatisfaction with PPI regimes and rates has been the perception that both government and companies are thoroughly corrupt. "Corruption is at the core of the governance crisis in the water sector. Whereas the scope of corruption varies substantially across the sector and between different countries and governance systems, estimates by the World Bank suggest that 20 percent to 40 percent of water sector finances are being lost to dishonest and corrupt practices."[30]

Corruption in the water sector in Latin America is typically quite tightly organized, internally stable with a logic of reciprocity, and supported by dysfunctional

Table 7.5 PPI projects canceled or distressed, 1990–1920

Argentina	39	(43% of total investment)
Mexico	17	(9% of total investment)
Brazil	9	(4% of total investment)
Peru	5	(4% of total investment)
Colombia	3	(2% of total investment)
Chile	1	(2% of total investment)

Sources: Guasch, 2004; Guasch, Laffont, and Straub, 2003; and Guasch, Kartacheva, and Quesada, 2000.

public administration and a weak civil society. The Argentine water reform was characterized by substantial corruption of the entire process, from terms, to bids, to awards, to the innumerable contract and tariff renegotiations.[31] Table 7.5 provides a listing of troubled projects. Regardless of the approach or proposed reforms of the system, the numbers indicate that it will be extremely difficult to bring the private sector back into the water sector in the majority of countries in the LAC region.

How to Survive the Anti-PPI Tsunami

In a tidal shift that wasn't entirely clear until the recent public protest march in Mexico City, popular opinion has moved against private-sector management and reclaimed water as a basic human right to be managed outside the market, by the people. In a remarkable demonstration of how water issues have filtered into public consciousness, thousands of people marched through Mexico City during the 2006 4th World Water Forum, with signs reading "Public Water Forever," "Life, not Profits," and "You Can't Buy What Has Never Been for Sale: Land and Water are Sacred." It marked the first time that water had mobilized so many people.[32]

Around the world, water is seen as a basic right, along with air, given its basic human survival function. Wherever governments have attempted full cost-recovery of water infrastructure, controversy has ensued; Latin America is no exception. On the other hand, it is manifestly true that "you can't build when you have no money."

For PPPs to succeed, it is imperative that regulation must align cost of capital and rate of return (Sirtaine et al., 2005, p. 43). Profit is not only dependent on the quality of management and market conditions but also a result of regulatory regimes and regulators decisions on tariffs. The record of quality of regulatory regimes and decision making is not good, according to Sirtaine et al.'s research, explaining about 20 percent of the observed unprofitable cases of infrastructure projects in Latin America.

Regulators have historically focused on maintaining tariffs as low as possible, without regard for the financial health of the investor. The consistent pattern of failure to increase tariffs to adequate levels under rising public anger across the Americas points to a failure of political leadership on the part of regulators, operators, and senior government officials.

What Can Be Done?

Grassroots participation throughout the infrastructure development project will be essential to private water project success. A review of 33 country cases by the OECD encourages maintaining the affordability of infrastructure services for the poor by introducing competitive markets, under proper legal frameworks, and improving subsidies effectiveness, if subsidies are used. "[C]ommercialization of infrastructure services, which often entails tariff reforms, need to go hand-in-hand with the introduction of other policies that keep people connected, that improve access to and expand depth of services, and that make services affordable to the poor."[33]

Several other important reforms have been identified. These include the following:

- Improved regulatory frameworks and institutions
    1. Legal solidity, embedded in law
    2. Adequate financial capacity and strength
    3. Decision-making autonomy[34]
- Development of effective social tariff/subsidy schemes with a needs formula
- Transparency initiatives led by multilateral financial institutions
- Creation of incentives to expand local investment
- Development of local financial markets, particularly bond markets
- Municipal government transparency, fiscal responsibility, and management capacity
- Enhancement of municipal revenue management and creditworthiness
- Implementation of painful reforms before private participation is proposed

Finally, there is a need to inform the public about the positive outcomes of the PPIs of the 1990s. Argentina embarked on one of the largest privatization campaigns in the world, including the privatization of local water companies, covering approximately 30 percent of the country's municipalities. It is only now that we are finding that child mortality fell 8 percent in the areas that privatized their water services and that the effect was largest (26 percent) in the poorest areas.[35] Not a bad return on an investment.

Notes

1. Global Water Partnership. *Financing Water for All: Report of the World Panel on Financing Water Infrastructure.* Also known as the Camdessus Report (2003). http://www.gwpforum.org/gwp/library/FinPanRep_MainRep.pdf. Camdessus, M., and J. Winpenny. 2003. *Financing Water for All.* Report of the World Panel on Financing Water Infrastructure. Stockholm, Sweden: World Water Council and Global Water Partnership.
2. M. Fay, "The Infrastructure Needs of Latin America," mimeo (Washington, D.C.: World Bank, 2000) quoted in AntonioEstache, J. Luis Guasch, and Lourdes Trujillo, "Price Caps, Efficiency Payoffs and Infrastructure Contract Renegotiation in Latin America," paper prepared for the conference on the UK Model of Regulation: A Retrospective of

the 20 Years since the Littlechild Report" organized by the London Business School's "Regulation Initiative-CRI," at City University, London, April 9, 2003. Fay states that the annual investments needed for 2000–2005 would amount to about U.S. $ 57 billion, equivalent to 2.6 percent of Latin America's GDP.

3. Harrison Morison. "Americas—Telecom Overview by Region" (unpublished draft, Institute of the Americas, La Jolla, 2006).

4. A. Izaguirre, and C. Hunt, "Private Water Projects," *Public Policy for the Private Sector,* no. 297 (July 2005): 4. http://rru.workdbank.org/PublicPolicyJournal.

5. C. Calderón and L. Servén, "The Effects of Infrastructure Development on Growth and Income Distribution," Policy Research Working Paper No. 3400 (Washington D.C.: World Bank, 2004).

6. "In most countries, only a marginal percentage (less than 10 percent) of the wastewater is treated, resulting in continued environmental degradation and health impacts in downstream populations. . . . [For example,] in Peru, the economic impacts associated with environmental degradation accounts for approximately 4 percent of the country's GDP." 4th World Water Forum, *Regional Document for the Americas* (Mexico City: World Water Council and CONAGUA, 2006), p. 7, http://www.worldwaterforum4.org.mx/uploads/TBL_DOCS_106_12.pdf.

7. M. Fay and M. Morrison. *Infrastructure in Latin America and the Caribbean: Recent Developments and Key Challenges,* vol. 1, Main Report (Washington, D.C.: World Bank, 2005).

8. Laura Carlsen, "World Water Forum Not the Place to Solve Global Water Crisis," March 28, 2006, http://americas.irc-online.org/am/3168.

9. Fay and Morrison, *Infrastructure in Latin America and the Caribbean,* p. v.

10. In view of the fact that the correlation between consumption and income is much stronger in the case of electricity than water, it has been easier to build subsidy structures to achieve social protection objectives.

There have been significantly fewer instances of protests over power rate increases. International investors are increasingly interested in Greenfield projects in Mexico, Chile, Peru, and Central America, among other countries.

But also see the massive protests in 2002 in Arequipa, Peru, over President Toledo's plan to privatize the local power utility—with blockades, urban barricades, and battles with police that resulted in 1 death and 152 wounded. After a declaration of martial law failed to quell the protests in the region, the government agreed to postpone its privatization plans indefinitely.

11. See for example Alex Burgess, "Conduit Closes $393M Latin American PE Fund," *Venture Equity Latin America* 5, no. 12 (July 31, 2006): 1. This is the largest private equity energy fund for Latin America raised since the 1990s boom.

12. "Cost recovery" means use of tariff levels to generate income sufficient to cover operation and maintenance (O&M) costs and full capital costs.

13. F. Henry, "Los Esquemas de Participación Público-Privada: Una Alternativa Atractiva para el Financiamiento de los Municipios Intermedios en México," paper presented at the Institute of the Americas' Conference on Long-term Municipal Finance, Mexico City, Mexico, February 1, 2005.

14. Luis Alberto Moreno, "Water Works," *The Wall Street Journal,* March 10, 2006.

15. V. Foster, and T. Yepes, "Is Cost Recovery a Feasible Objective for Water and Electricity? The Latin American Experience," World Bank Policy Research Working Paper 3943 (Washington, D.C.: World Bank, June 2006), p. 1.

16. Ibid., p. 3.
17. Ibid., p. 2.
18. Inter-American Development Bank, *The Millennium Development Goals in Latin America and the Caribbean: Progress, Priorities and IDB Support for Their Implementation* (Washington, D.C.: Inter-American Development Bank, 2005), http://www.iadb. org/idbdocs.cfm?docnum=591088.
19. Sophie S., M. E. Pinglo, J. L. Guasch, and V. Foster. "How Profitable Are Infrastructure Concessions in Latin America?" *Trends and Policy Options,* no. 2 (January 2005), 42. http://www.ppiaf.org/Trends&policyseries/ConcessionsLACpaperNo2.pdf.
20. Ibid., 43.
21. Foster and Yepes, "Is Cost Recovery a Feasible Objective for Water and Electricity?" p. 25.
22. Fay and Morrison, *Infrastructure in Latin America and the Caribbean,* p. 29. IBTs are tariffs that increase based on increased consumption of water.
23. K. Komives, V. Foster, J. Halpern, Q. Wodon, and R. Abdullah, *Water, Electricity and the Poor: Who Benefits from Utility Subsidies?* (Washington, D.C.: World Bank, 2005).
24. Ibid., p. 5.
25. The major social criticism of the Chilean subsidy scheme is that it misses substantial numbers of poor people, perhaps as many as 78 percent. Komives et al., *Water, Electricity and the Poor,* p. 241.
26. A. McPhail, "The 'Five Percent Rule' for Improved Water Service: Can Households Afford More?" *World Development* 21, no. 6 (June 1993): 969.
27. Foster and Yepes, "Is Cost Recovery a Feasible Objective for Water and Electricity?" p. 1.
28. G. Hutton, and L. Haller. "Evaluation of the Costs and Benefits of Water and Sanitation Improvements at the Global Level" (Geneva: World Health Organization, 2004), http://www.who.int/water_sanitation_health/wsh0404/en/.
29. Public Citizen (2001), "Water Privatisation Case Study: Cochabamba, Bolivia," http://www.citizen.org/documents/Bolivia_(PDF).
30. P. Stålgren, "Corruption in the Water Sector: Causes, Consequences and Potential Reform," Swedish Water House Policy Brief No. 4 (Stockholm: Stockholm International Water Institute [SIWI], 2006).
31. Based on author's personal interviews with participants in the processes in the provinces of Santa Fe and Buenos Aires and in the federal capital.
32. Carlsen, "World Water Forum."
33. Organization for Economic Co-operation and Development, Development Assistance Committee Network on Poverty Reduction, "Role of Infrastructure in Economic Growth and Poverty Reduction—Lessons Learned from PRSPs of 33 Countries," DCD/DAC/POVNET (2004)16 (Berlin, Germany: Organization for Economic Co-operation and Development, Development Assistance Committee Network on Poverty Reduction, October 21, 2004), p. 6, http://www.oecd.org/dataoecd/57/60/ 33919674.pdf.
34. Sirtaine et el., "How Profitable Are Infrastructure Concessions in Latin America?" p. 43.
35. S. Galiani, P. Gertler, and E. Schargrodsky, "Water for Life: The Impact of the Privatization of Water Services on Child Mortality," *Journal of Political Economy* 113, no. 1 (2005): 83.

References

4th World Water Forum. 2006. *Regional Document for the Americas.* Mexico City: World Water Council and CONAGUA.

ADERASA. 2005. "Las Tarifas de Agua Potable y Alcantarillado en América Latina." Grupo de Tarifas y Subsidios. PPIAF and World Bank, Washington, D.C. http://www.aderasa.org/en/documentos3.htm?x=654.

Burgess, Alex. 2006. "Conduit Closes $393M Latin American PE Fund." *Venture Equity Latin America* 5, no. 12 (July 31).

Calderón, C., and L. Servén. 2004. "The Effects of Infrastructure Development on Growth and Income Distribution." Policy Research Working Paper No. 3400. Washington, D.C.: World Bank.

Camdessus, M., and J. Winpenny. 2003. *Financing Water for All.* Report of the World Panel on Financing Water Infrastructure. Stockholm, Sweden: World Water Council and Global Water Partnership.

Carlsen, L. 2006. "World Water Forum Not the Place to Solve Global Water Crisis." *IRC Americas Program Column.* March 28. http://americas.irc-online.org/am/3168.

The Economist. 2006. "Infrastructure in Latin America: Slow! Government Obstacles Ahead." June 15. http://www.economist.com/displayStory.cfm?story_id=7065735.

Estache, A, J. L. Guasch, and L. Trujillo. 2003. "Price Caps, Efficiency Payoffs and Infrastructure Contract Renegotiation in Latin America." Policy Research Working Paper No. 3129. Washington, D.C.: World Bank.

Fay, M. 2001. "Financing the Future. Infrastructure Needs in Latin America, 2000–2005." Policy Research Working Paper No. 2545. Washington, D.C.: World Bank.

Fay, M., and M. Morrison. 2005. *Infrastructure in Latin America and the Caribbean: Recent Developments and Key Challenges.* Vol. 1. Main Report. Washington, D.C.: World Bank.

Foster, V., and T. Yepes. 2006. "Is Cost Recovery a Feasible Objective for Water and Electricity? The Latin American Experience." Policy Research Working Paper 3943. Washington, D.C.: World Bank.

Galiani, S., P. Gertler, and E. Schargrodsky. 2005. "Water for Life: The Impact of the Privatization of Water Services on Child Mortality." *Journal of Political Economy* 113, no.1: 83–120.

Guasch, J. L. 2004. *Granting and Renegotiating Infrastructure Concessions: Doing It Right.* Washington, D.C.: World Bank Institute Development Studies.

Guasch, J. L., A. Kartacheva, and L. Quesada. 2000. "Concessions Contracts Renegotiations in Latin America and Caribbean Region: An Economic Analysis and Empirical Evidence." Washington, D.C.: World Bank.

Guasch, J. L., J. J. Laffont, and S. Straub. 2003. "Renegotiations of Concession Contracts in Latin America." Policy Research Working Paper No. 3011. Washington, D.C.: World Bank.

Henry, F. 2005. "Los Esquemas de Participación Público-Privada: Una Alternativa Atractiva para el Financiamiento de los Municipios Intermedios en México." Paper presented at the Institute of the Americas' Conference on Long-term Municipal Finance, Mexico City, Mexico, February 1.

Hutton, G., and L. Haller. 2004. "Evaluation of the Costs and Benefits of Water and Sanitation Improvement at the Global Level." Geneva: World Health Organization. (WHO/SDE/WSH/04.04). http://www.who.int/water_sanitation_health/wsh0404/en/.

Inter-American Development Bank. 2005. *The Millennium Development Goals in Latin America and the Caribbean: Progress, Priorities and IDB Support for Their Implementation.*

Washington, D.C.: Inter-American Development Bank. http://www.iadb.org/idbdocs. cfm?docnum=591088.

Izaguirre, A. K., and C. Hunt. 2005. "Private Water Projects." *Public Policy for the Private Sector* 297 (July). http://rru.workdbank.org/PublicPolicyJournal.

Komives, K., V. Foster, J. Halpern, Q. Wodon, and R. Abdullah. 2005. *Water, Electricity and the Poor: Who Benefits from Utility Subsidies?* Washington, D.C.: World Bank.

Latinobarómetro Surveys, 1998 and 2004.

McPhail, A. 1993. "The 'Five Percent Rule' for Improved Water Service: Can Households Afford More?" *World Development* 21, no. 6: 963–973.

Moreno, Louis Alberto. 2006. "Water Works." *The Wall Street Journal,* March 10.

Organization for Economic Co-operation and Development, Development Assistance Committee Network on Poverty Reduction. 2004. "Role of Infrastructure in Economic Growth and Poverty Reduction—Lessons Learned from PRSPs of 33 Countries." DCD/DAC/POVNET(2004)16. Berlin, Germany: Organization for Economic Co-operation and Development, Development Assistance Committee Network on Poverty Reduction. http://www.oecd.org/dataoecd/57/60/33919674.pdf.

Panizza, U., and M. Yañez. 2006. "Why are Latin Americans So Unhappy about Reforms?" Research Department Working Paper Series No. 567. Washington, D.C.: Inter-American Development Bank.

Public Citizen. 2001. "Water Privatization Case Study: Cochabamba, Bolivia." http://www.citizen.org/documents/Bolivia_(PDF).

Sirtaine, S., M. E. Pinglo, J. L. Guasch, and V. Foster. 2005. "How Profitable Are Private Infrastructure Concessions in Latin America? Empirical Evidence and Regulatory Implications." *The Quarterly Review of Economics and Finance* 45, nos. 2–3: 380–402.

Stålgren, P. 2006. "Corruption in the Water Sector: Causes, Consequences and Potential Reform." Swedish Water House Policy Brief No. 4. Stockholm: Stockholm International Water Institute (SIWI).

World Bank. 2005. Private Participation in Infrastructure (PPI) Project Database. http://ppi.worldbank.org/.

CHAPTER 8

Logistics: The Software That Drives an Economy

John Price

The 2005 World Bank study of Latin American infrastructure[1] revealed some of the region's shortcomings in road, rail, and port assets and the negative impact these have on trade and wealth generation. A common political rallying cry across the region during the election season of 2006 was a promise to increase infrastructure investment. But creating an efficient transportation system requires more than new roads and ports; it also calls for the active participation of modern logistics companies. If infrastructure is the hardware of a productive nation, then logistics services is the software that drives it.

Over the last quarter century, Latin America's investment in transportation infrastructure has failed to even keep up with population growth, while greater investment levels in Asia have been paramount to that region's wealth creation (see table 8.1). Latin America has also been unable to create its own large-scale competitive transportation service firms and has had limited success at attracting the investment and technology transfer of international logistics service companies.

Why Logistics Matters to Latin America

Logistics is a powerful economic enabler, one of the fundamental building blocks of external and internal trade. Countries such as the United States and Germany, which ranked first and second in terms of supply chain efficiency according to a recent study by SRI,[2] derive major economic benefits from their logistical strengths. Enjoying lower logistics costs per widget output enables factories to competitively deliver products and procure inputs over a larger geography than equivalent factories in less-efficient countries. This allows industry to consolidate into larger players, achieving economies of scale and efficiencies that lower costs

Table 8.1 Paved highways (meters of paved highway per capita)

	Latin America	South-east Asia
1980	1.1	0.58
1990	1.18	0.87
1995	0.93	0.95
2000	0.86	1.29*

Source: Ricardo J. Sánchez and Gordon Wilmsmeier, agosto del 2005, "Provisión de infraestructura de transporte en América Latina: experiencia reciente" (CEPAL-United Nations).
Note: *1999 data.

Table 8.2 Logistics costs as a percent of imported goods (CIF)

Regions	1980	1990	2000	2001
Industrialized Economies	5.5	4.4	5.2	5.1
Latin America	8.9	8.2	8.7	8.6
Mexico*	7.0	5.0	4.7	4.5
Rest of Latin America*	10.1	10.8	12.7	14.0
Emerging Markets	10.4	8.6	8.9	8.7
World Average	6.4	5.2	6.2	6.1

Source: UNCTAD *Review of Maritime Transport 2003.*
Note: *John Price, *Latin America International Logistics Trends, Risks & Opportunities Whitepaper* (Miami, Florida: InfoAmericas, April 2005).

to consumers and raise profits and wages. In most industries, size matters, and the ability to compete in global markets or withstand global competition in one's home market requires a healthy environment for large company development. Latin America has only a few dozen homegrown, globally sized firms. Now as the region tries to compete with Asian manufacturers, it is learning how difficult it is to match the production costs of Chinese and South East Asian large-scale manufacturers that are ten times the size of their Latin American counterparts. Logistical inefficiencies tax the private sector that is trying to grow by increasing the cost of goods sold, costs that either limit the ability of a company to reinvest profits or cut into the savings and investment of the consumer depending upon who bears the added cost. Other than Mexico, which efficiently imports products from the United States, transportation costs in most Latin American countries represent 10 to 20 percent of the cost of imported goods (see table 8.2). Worse still, while the rest of the world has reduced logistics costs since 1980, in most of Latin America, they have risen.

Financing Supply Chain Inefficiencies

One of the often-overlooked costs of logistical inefficiency is the financial burden of a slow-moving supply chain. Companies in Latin America require on average 30 days to ship goods out of the country, including the export documentation, port and terminal handling, customs and inspection, and pre-arrival documentation.[3] Comparatively, a German exporter requires only six days.

Supplying competing supermarkets in Eastern Canada, to illustrate by example, the German exporter can rotate the same working capital 61 times per year (365 days/6 days to export) versus the Latin American company that can only rotate its working capital 12 times (365 days/30 days to export). The Latin American company must tie up five times more capital than the German company, and this is when the cost of capital in Latin America is probably double the comparative cost in Hamburg. The additional financial costs for the Latin American firm are as much as 10 times that of the German company. How can the Latin American firm compete?

Studies have shown that a doubling of a country's transportation costs leads to a reduction in that country's trade by 80 percent.[4] Other econometric studies have shown that "on average, each additional day that a product is delayed prior to being shipped reduces trade by at least one percent."

A recent study by SRI (see figure 8.1), sponsored by FedEx, draws a direct correlation between access and economic development. "Access" is a broadly defined term in the study that combines the free movement of goods in and out of markets as well as ready access to information, communications, finance, and services that act as enablers of trade. What is evident is that countries cannot achieve either domestic efficiency or fulfill their trade potential without an economy that enjoys physical access.

Latin America has not been shy about negotiating trade agreements around the world. Mexico and Chile each enjoy free trade with nations that together are responsible for over 60 percent of the world's imports. Yet, so much of the region's comparative trade advantage is found in products that rely on swift and/or cost-efficient logistics to reach a market and maintain a consistent

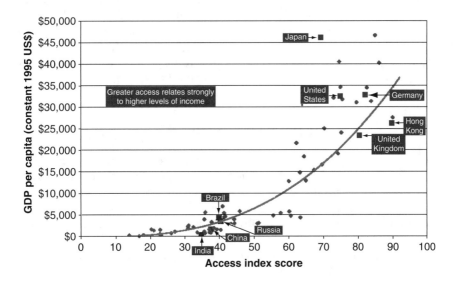

Figure 8.1 Access Index and GDP per capita

supply. Heavy commodities that have been the lifeblood of Latin America's recent export boom are highly sensitive to transportation costs and delivery times given the high cost of storage, especially in Asia where industrial real-estate pricing is stratospheric. With close to 50 percent of the world's arable land, South America has a great potential to be the leading horticultural exporter yet its logistics systems do not allow growers to reach prized markets in Japan, Europe, or the United States in a timely fashion. Central America's assembly industries, increasingly under threat by Chinese factories, must compete on speed to market when exporting northward but they lack the air cargo links and efficient road links to earn their place in the U.S. supply chain.

Why Did Investment Dry Up in Latin American Infrastructure?

The last time that the region enjoyed significant investment in its transportation infrastructure was in the 1970s when Latin America and its large-scale governments were awash with cash thanks to record sales of natural resources. The debt crisis of the 1980s, beginning with Mexico, led to a drastic contraction in government spending as foreign debt tripled and payment obligations drove several countries into devaluation-triggered crisis. The neoliberal formula for fiscal turnaround in the 1990s as espoused by the IMF and the World Bank, left little money for infrastructure and recommended that private investors fill the place of public investment in building the next generation of roads, ports, and rail links.

However, private investment in transportation infrastructure never fulfilled its potential in the 1990s. To begin with, investors were wary of Latin America's high country risk levels and placed large risk premiums on financing projects in those markets, which only priced such projects beyond a viable range. When foreign investors did venture into port privatizations or bid on new road tolls, they were too often discouraged by the nepotistic bidding processes that favored local players over international consortia. Not surprisingly, Chile, which has invested reasonably well in its infrastructure, is also the least-corrupt country in the region, according to Transparency International.[5]

Financing Infrastructure—A Tale of Two Countries

The massive price tags of infrastructure and the long-term financing needs they bear often lead Latin American governments to seek credit from prominent leading development institutions, namely the World Bank, the Inter-American Development Bank (IDB), and International Finance Corporation (IFC). Some countries have also succeeded in attracting the private investors to help fund transportation projects.

Here are two contrasting examples of how infrastructure projects were recently developed in Latin America.

Brazil

In 1995 the World Bank began the appraisal of a U.S.$300 million loan to Brazil for a federal highway decentralization project. The project was approved in 1997, and the results were appraised in June 2006.[6]

The report declared that the overall performance by the bank and the borrower were satisfactory but it went on to highlight several factors that delayed and weakened the results of the project. The first factor mentioned was the weak fiscal position of the Brazilian government and its inability to push through fiscal reforms. This resulted in insufficient funds with which to fulfill its public investment obligations. The Brazilian government did not have money to maintain its existing highways, let alone embark on a decentralization project. The second factor mentioned was political opposition to the project as a response to perceived loss of influence by federal politicians with the reorganization of the federal transport ministry. There was also strong political opposition to increasing private involvement in infrastructure at a time when the region was most sharply rejecting neoliberal reform.

In a constrained fiscal environment, government focused on short-term budgetary obligations, such as paying the civil servants their salaries, social security, pension, and social programs obligations. With neither the Cardoso nor the Lula first-term governments able to reform Brazil's costly pension and social security programs, they continued to drain the government of needed resources. Then there was the productivity of the Federal Road Administration. This was a department in flux, as the old Departamento Nacional de Estradas de Rodagem (DNER) was restructured into the new, more-efficient Departamento Nacional de Infra-Estructura de Transportes (DNIT). The resulting departmental reengineering took time and struggled in the process.

Cost increases also impacted the project. "The main reasons for these cost increases include: (a) higher degradation of road condition (resulting from large delays in contracting of works) which increased rehabilitation costs; (b) irregularity of payments to contractors which led to various neutralization of works, and thus requirements to pay interests on late payments, pay higher price adjustments, and revise work schedules; and (c) an increase in the price of bituminous material of close to 100 percent over the project implementation period."[7] Furthermore, financing costs ballooned when the currency depreciated in 1999. Total financing costs were 36 percent higher than originally forecast in the planning stages.

One of the general conclusions of the report was that the project was affected by "fiscal difficulties and weak political coordination," and that "despite lots of efforts both on the federal Government and Bank sides, no immediate solution could be found to resolve these issues."[8]

Colombia and Infrastructure Development

Colombia plans to invest almost U.S.$11 billion in transportation and logistics infrastructure between 2004 and 2010 (see table 8.3), most of which is destined

Table 8.3 Colombian transport infrastructure investment plan, 2004–2010

All figures in USD millions

	Total investment	2004	2005	2006	2007	2008	2009	2010
Roads	6,910	1,187	1,229	1,089	840	816	827	831
Superhighways	3,067	563	606	466	347	323	334	338
Highways	2,777	443	443	443	362	362	362	362
Secondary highways	1,066	180	180	180	131	131	131	131
Incomes in contributions and compensations	354	48	56	60	54	45	45	45
Maritime	75	14	15	15	8	8	8	8
River transport	149	32	32	32	32	10	10	10
Aerial transport	730	121	117	115	99	96	86	86
Urban passenger transport	2,615	261	261	261	261	261	261	261
Totals	10,832	2,849	2,939	2,661	2,134	2,052	2,064	2,072

Source: Colombian Transport Infrastructure Investment Plan 2004–2010, Ministry of Transport, Colombia, 2004.

Table 8.4 Private sector investment in Colombian transport infrastructure

All figures in USD millions

Sector	1994	1995	1996	1997	1998	1999	2000	2001
Highways	22	76	103	103	126	81	21	48
Other	9	23	39	82	64	57	6	9
Railroads						36	0	0
Ports	9	23	27	29	33	21	4	5
Airports			12	53	31	0	2	3
River								
Urban								
Total	40	122	181	268	253	195	32	65

Source: Colombia Proexport, Foreign Direct Investment Statistics, 2004.

for highway construction. The majority of the financing is to come from the government's budget, which in turn is financed by a variety of government taxes and charges, including road tolls, airport taxes, exit taxes at the airport, and other public sources.

The Colombian government, however, has earmarked certain projects for private investment, both as a means of spreading costs and also to invite new ideas and best practices from the private sector. But private sector investment has proved fickle when macroeconomic conditions or the political climate grow polemic, as they did in 2000 and 2001 (see table 8.4).

Results up to 2006 of Colombia's infrastructure expansion have been largely positive. Projects in road, air, and ports transportation were finished ahead of time and within budget and succeeded in dramatically improving transport efficiency. Most visible have been the positive results of both ports and urban transportation.

The downside of the project is the failure of the market to deliver higher traffic volumes on private concessions, which triggered guarantee penalties to the tune of U.S.$700 million against the government. The volume guarantees were a risky but necessary incentive utilized by the Colombian government to entice a skeptical private sector. The mixed results demonstrate the need to reach out to the logistics industry and involve them in all stages of the project, from feasibility to implementation, to ensure that the infrastructure fits the needs of the market.

Politically, Colombia was successful where Brazil failed because it had widespread support for the infrastructure plans across federal ministries and also at the state level. With its political ducks in a row, the government was able to pass through five decrees within a period of two months in 2003 (see table 8.5), which helped to restructure the transportation ministry and overcome existing regulatory bottlenecks.

Colombia started off with a stronger fiscal position than Brazil, and was able to cover a large part of the infrastructural development with the use of public

Table 8.5 Colombia's transport investment enabling regulatory decrees

All decrees passed in 2003

Organization	Regulation	Date	Objective	Judicial nature
Fondo Nacional para Caminos Vecinales (FNCV)	Decree 1790	June 26	Abolition of FNVC	With the expiry of the settlement, the legal existence of the FNVC as a Public Establishment of National Order comes to an end
Instituto Nacional de Concesiones (INCO)	Decree 1800	June 26	Creation of INCO	Public Establishment of National Order attached to the transport ministry with own legal status, independent funds, and administrative and financial autonomy
Empresa Colombiana de Vías Férreas Ferrovías	Decree 1791	June 26	Abolition of FERROVIAS	Liquidation of the State Industry and Comercial Enterprise
Ministerio de Transporte	Decree 2053	June 23	Restructuring of the ministry	Ministry
Instituto Nacional de Vías (INVIAS)	Decree 2056	June 24	Restructuring of the ministry	Public Establishment of National Order attached to the transport ministry with own legal status, independent funds, and administrative and financial autonomy

Source: Colombia's Transport Investment Enabling Regulatory Decrees, Ministry of Transport, Colombia, 2004.

funds, raised from taxes, international loans, and project bonds. Colombia was also successful in attracting private investment, and was able to push through institutional reforms that allowed for more efficient regulation and management of the investment projects. Colombia's approach to transportation infrastructure improvement may be the most viable model today for Latin America, a combination of significant public investment in basic projects along with the construction of business conditions to lure private investors in more specialized fields where their technology transfer is best utilized.

Bringing Modern Logistics to Latin America

A vital component of globalization is the role played by modern logistics service companies that bring together supplier and buyer around the world. Building a healthy climate to entice the arrival of these companies should be viewed in a similar light to the exercise of attracting R&D investment. Logistics service providers and the experts they employ bring the know-how and often the know-who to local companies seeking foreign markets and supply channels.

Logistics companies are traditionally very conservative when it comes to expanding into new markets. They almost always follow their biggest customers into a new market. Latin America, a region historically wrought with political and economic risks, has attracted limited investment from 3PL players, almost all of whom have taken an asset-light approach to market entry and to date have invested only in the region's largest and safest markets.

Demand for Latin American logistics (see figure 8.2) , both international and domestic, has been driven, above all, by foreign direct investment (FDI). Multinationals bring with their investment a global network of suppliers and customers and a scale of operations that demands significant logistics spending.

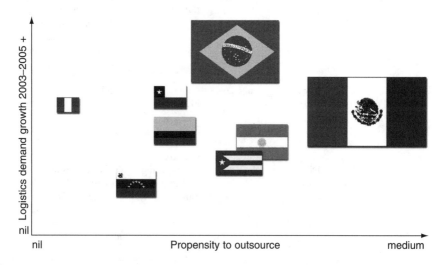

Figure 8.2 Logistics demand forecast

With enough FDI in any one market, the competitive landscape is changed (Mexico, Argentina, Brazil, Chile) and large domestic companies begin to adopt the use of outsourced logistics in a response to regain lost market share.

International logistics is also driven by the trade of manufactured products and dangerous cargo, both of which require more costly logistics planning and handling. Nations that trade beyond the norms of their market size (Panama, Puerto Rico, Chile) consume significant levels of international logistics and, as a result, have attracted global logistics providers. In a region known for its commodity exports and finished good imports, the inbound logistics market is at least 50 percent larger than its outbound equivalent, adding a logistical challenge to a region that exports on ships its commodities and imports by plane and truck its value-added goods.

Logistics demand across the region's 20 markets is highly concentrated in two tiers of markets (see figure 8.3). Tier I, comprisingMexico, Puerto Rico, and Brazil, represents 79 percent of regional demand.[9] Brazil's market is described as in the early to middle stages of growth. After two lost years due to political risk and capital flight, investment is streaming back into Brazil and in 2004, Brazil's logistics market led the region with 20+ percent growth, built on four engines: 3.5 percent GDP growth, 30 percent growth in FDI, 15+ percent trade growth, and a 25 percent appreciation of the real.[10]

Mexico's logistics market, like its economy, is split into two distinct segments: the export economy that relies on cross-border logistics for 95 percent of its traffic and the domestic economy. The logistics market servicing Mexico's exporters is sophisticated and relatively mature with consolidation of suppliers ongoing.

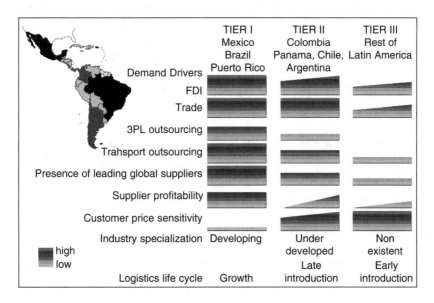

Figure 8.3 The three tiers of Latin American market

Three hundred multinationals are responsible for 90 percent of Mexico's exports.[11] Mexico's domestic economy is driven by consumption, which has enjoyed a renaissance since 2000, when the peso regained significant purchasing power and consumer credit began its run of record growth. The sectors that most buy logistics in Mexico are now dominated by multinational players, so demand for logistics has grown quickly in recent years and should continue to do so.

Puerto Rico is a relatively mature market, classified in the latter stages of growth. While logistics demand is declining in some manufacturing fields where it no longer competes, growth is found in IT and pharmaceutical industries where investment is growing. As a U.S. protectorate, Puerto Rico is a stable market but as a dollarized economy, its ability to compete in global markets is limited to its capacity to move up the value chain into more sophisticated industrial development. Nonetheless, as a distribution hub for the Caribbean basin, the island supports a disproportionately large market for its small size, thanks to its investments in logistics.

Tier II markets are smaller logistics markets, comprising Panama and Chile (trading nations) as well as Colombia, a diversified industrial economy. Global logistics players, to date, focused on Mexico and Brazil, and only dabbled in the tier II markets, to a greater degree in its safe-haven dollarized market (Panama) and to a lesser degree in Chile and Colombia, where currency and security risks respectively have kept some players away. Most logistics players have structured their operations in tier II markets in a very asset-light fashion, either through a partnership with an independent agent or through a skeleton greenfield operation that subcontracts all mid- and lower- value service segments. Such associations limit technology transfer because the foreign company does not want to lose possession of its proprietary software or methods.

Tier III markets are still undeveloped, with an extremely low awareness of value-added logistics. Within these still-barren markets are pockets of activity where focused FDI has created growth and demand for logistical support. However, the multinationals that invested by and large bring with them relationships with logistics players. Often a one- or two-client market, it is too risky for most logistics players to consider market entry into tier III markets ahead of a contractual sale with one of these clients.

What Continues to Hold Back Logistics in Latin America?

Significant barriers exist to normal market maturation in Latin America. These will be overcome soon in a few markets but could take a generation or more to conquer in most countries.

Customs Reform

When asked what holds back their investments in Latin America, the largest logistics providers will start their laundry list with the desperate need for customs reform. Governments across Latin America, with few exceptions, have made great strides in removing the administrative and customs barriers facing their nation's exporters but have left importers continually frustrated by the bureaucracy and expense of bringing a foreign product into the country. For integrators such as FedEx, UPS, or DHL, any mismatch between inbound and outbound volumes and speeds leads to flying empty planes, that is, operating losses that make routes unviable. In Taipei, an inbound airplane full of cargo is cleared through customs within 18 minutes of landing. In Buenos Aires, it can take more than one week.

Trust

Latin America, like many emerging markets, is plagued by mistrust of its core institutions, most especially its corrupt legal system. In this environment, Latin American entrepreneurs are naturally hesitant to trust vital functions such as inventory control, product distribution, and billing to unknown outside suppliers. This cultural factor is a huge impediment to outsourcing. It alone explains why even large domestic firms outsource at half the rate of multinationals and why mid-size firms are yet to outsource en masse.

Trucking Regulations and Lack of Standards

In several Latin American markets, regulations are made that, intentionally or not, inhibit the consolidation and modernization of the region's trucking. In Brazil, trucks that pass state borders face a state tax, based upon the value of merchandize. This effectively converts a potentially large and competitive Brazilian trucking industry into a highly fragmented supply of small and mid-size trucking firms operating largely within state borders. Without scale, trucking firms cannot achieve the profit levels needed to modernize.

In Peru, the government has imposed minimum rates to be paid to truckers based upon a complex formula of volume and type of product shipped, routes, and so on. The rules help protect small independent trucks, which are the last to invest in modernization of their fleet.

In Mexico, foreigners are prohibited from owning any stake in domestic truck cargo services. Without foreign capital, Mexican trucking remains woefully behind the standards demanded by its clients, including logistics firms that subcontract Mexican truckers.

A general lack of truck safety, environmental compliance, and driver safety regulations allows small trucking firms and independents across Latin America to keep their dilapidated fleets on the road. With no depreciation to amortize in their pricing, small players keep market prices down, and trucking profits near zero. This prevents Latin American trucking from modernizing.

Conclusions

Transportation and logistics in today's world are the hardware and software of a trade-linked global economy. Countries with more efficient supply chains can better integrate into the global economic system, and have a significant competitive advantage in what is now a global race for jobs, wealth, and development. Latin America, with its wealth in commodities and raw materials, makes most of its foreign exchange through exports. Lack of investment in its transportation and logistics systems (infrastructure, companies and management) creates bottlenecks, denying the region vital export wealth. Weak institutional, political, and fiscal systems are some of the reasons for the historical underinvestment in the transportation and logistics system.

But the need for investment just to recapture the lost ground of two decades of decay, let alone catch up with Asia, is so vast that public and private investment must be combined and coordinated. Governments must work hand in hand with funding agencies and private enterprise to plan and build one integrated transportation and logistics system that creates efficiencies and economies of scale not just across countries, but across regions and ultimately continents with financially viable projects. This is already occurring slowly between the United States and Mexico as a result of North American Free Trade Agreement (NAFTA).

The real architects of tomorrow's modern transportation and logistics systems are the logistics services providers (3PLs, 4PLs, integrators, and freight forwarders) whose livelihood is built upon bringing their customers' products to market efficiently. This community of professionals understands where today's bottlenecks lie and therefore where investment and reform must be prioritized. Their knowledge makes them invaluable advisers to infrastructural planners. As service providers who do not invest in infrastructure themselves, logistics companies bring much-needed objectivity to an industry (infrastructure) that is traditionally fraught with waste and corruption. When governments integrate logistics advisers into their logistics planning committees, they inspire a greater degree of confidence in private investors that project bidding will be transparent and fair. More serious bidders at the table translate into better quality and lower cost infrastructure projects—precisely what Latin America needs to catch up with its global competitors.

Notes

1. World Bank, *Infrastructure in Latin America and the Caribbean: Recent Developments and Key Challenges* (Washington, D.C.: World Bank, 2005).
2. SRI International, *How Greater Access Is Changing the World*, August (Washington, D.C.: World Bank, 2006).
3. 2006, *Doing Business in 2006: Creating Jobs,* The International Bank for Reconstruction and Development/World Bank.
4. Limao, N. and A. J. Venables (2001), "Infrastructure, Geographical Disadvantage, and Transport Costs," *World Bank Economic Review* 15.
5. Transparency International Global Corruption Index, 2006.
6. Aymeric-Albin Meyer, "Implementation Report on a Loan in the Amount of $300 Million to the Federative Republic of Brazil for a Highway Decentralization Projects" (Washington, D.C.: World Bank, June 2006).
7. InfoAmericas, *Latin America International Logistics Trends, Risks & Opportunities Whitepaper* (Coral Gables, Florida: InfoAmericas market research company, 2004).
8. Ibid.
9. Ibid.
10. Ibid.
11. Ibid.

CHAPTER 9

Legal Reform: Some Emerging Paradoxes of Latin America's Legal and Judicial Reform Movement

Linn Hammergren

A
mong the several factors cited by observers as affecting Latin America's global competitiveness, the legal and judicial system is increasingly being given a prominent place. Concerned critics argue that outdated laws, flawed judiciaries, and their combined impacts on juridical and citizen security, as well as on political and policy stability, raise the costs of economic transactions, constrain credit availability, and discourage long-term investment. Building on the work of neoinstitutional economics as developed by Douglass North (1990) and others, researchers have attempted to quantify the relationship between a "well-functioning" legal and judicial system and economic growth (Kaufman et al., 1999 and 2002) and to calculate the impact of improvements in the former on national growth rates (Sherwood et al., 1994; Castelar Pinheiro, 2003). Meanwhile, a variety of cross-national surveys (summarized in CEJA, 2003 and 2005) reveal entrepreneurs' belief that the region's legal systems pose several impediments to their own actions.

Despite an early and still largely independent effort to modernize key economically relevant legislations (for example, bankruptcy and secured credit laws, civil and commercial procedures codes), there is an emerging consensus that most effort should go into reforming the institutions (courts, private bar, etc.) responsible for the laws' application. This consensus draws on the disappointing results of isolated legal change, better understandings of institutional operations, and a realization that their negative impacts extend far beyond the handling of "commercial" cases. It also coincides with Latin American tendencies to focus on judicial reform and its presumed broader benefits for national societies. As we will see, the region's reforms privilege noneconomic objectives, sometimes to the extent of conflicting with economic aims, but overall their goals are compatible with the needs of a more competitive economy and their achievements and failures are significant in that light.

The Regional Reform Movement

Beginning in the early 1980s, the Latin American countries began a process of legal and judicial reform that continues to this day (Hammergren, 2003; Pásara, 2004). The national programs are characterized by extensive cross-fertilization and as a consequence, by considerable similarity as regards their contents, methodologies, and objectives. The cross-national continuities have been encouraged by a series of additional factors: the impetus provided by the simultaneous process of redemocratization in a majority of the region's countries; the financial and technical support offered by the donor community; the influence of a renewed, worldwide interest in judicial reforms; and the greater ease of communication in the current globalizing society. Sequential imitation of reform processes also characterized Latin America's earlier history, but the past two decades are unusual for the speed at which it occurred and the substantial changes transpiring within a relatively short period.

The similarities are also explained by the consistency in the reasons for undertaking the reforms. Whether called reform or modernization, the national efforts inevitably aimed at (1) overcoming certain traditional weaknesses in the courts and other justice sector institutions especially as regards their failure to provide high-quality services to a greater portion of the population and to do so in a timely fashion; (2) reversing the inattention to the sector experienced throughout the period of de facto governments and, according to some authorities, for a good part of the past century (Correa, 1999); (3) strengthening the sector's role as an equal branch of government and thus fortifying the balance of powers; and (4) increasing its contributions to such national developmental objectives as citizen security, poverty reduction, and economic growth. Over time, the list of objectives has, if anything, expanded, as have the expectations as to the broader benefits to be derived from their achievement. There may be few development programs that have promised so much on the basis of a relatively modest financial investment,[1] and thus, it is not surprising, that in only 20 years' time, some disillusionment has set in.

The changes that have been achieved have provided their own mixed blessings. "Strengthened" institutions are not necessarily improved institutions, and in some sense the reforms' real accomplishments have introduced new problems and new dilemmas. This chapter reviews the changes achieved through the standard reform package and then focuses on the emerging questions or paradoxes these same accomplishments have revealed.

The Accomplishments

There can be absolutely no doubt as to the reforms' impact on Latin America's justice sectors. There may be few public institutions that have experienced as radical a change in their outward appearance, internal operations, and interface with users. As demonstrated by available statistics (see for example World Bank, 2005c) and a series of recent evaluations (Pérez Perdomo, 2006; Riego, 2002), several generalizations can be applied across the board. First, within barely 20 years, the region's justice sectors have experienced revolutionary alterations to their size and structure. The number of judges, courts, and of auxiliary organizations and personnel has doubled or tripled in many countries. Whereas Latin America's current average of 8.1 judges per 100,000 inhabitants is lower than that of Eastern (20.6) and Western (15.2) Europe, several countries (Argentina, Costa Rica, and Uruguay) reach or come close to the Western European average, and nearly all surpass the United Kingdom's 4.2 or Denmark's 6.8.[2] Where they did not exist before, public defense and prosecutors' offices were created, and where they did exist, their size and geographic distribution were increased. The sector as a whole has a far greater geographic penetration than it did 20 or 30 years ago, making services directly accessible to populations formerly far removed from their reach.

Second, the sector's financial weight has increased commensurately. Budgets and salaries have grown, in some cases exceeding international benchmarks.[3] The former "Cinderella" branch of government is now capable of investing in modern equipment and attracting more qualified employees. Supreme Court judges are paid as well and sometimes more than other high-level officials. Salaries for lower-level professionals and support staff are generally superior to what they were before.

Third, workloads have increased substantially. Despite considerable variation among and within the region's countries, nearly all have experienced an increase in demand for services exceeding the growth in supply. Some countries demonstrate near world records as regards caseload per judge, reaching averages of over 1,300 annual filings and dispositions in Brazil and Costa Rica, and over 800 in Argentina (World Bank, 2003a and b; 2005c). While a majority of countries still have average annual filings below 500 per judge, even they have experienced a substantial increase in demand. If their average caseloads remain low, this is partly because a greater number of judges has taken up the slack.

Fourth, the manner of operations of the courts and the rest of the sector has also changed. This is most evident in the near-universal adoption of accusatory criminal procedures, featuring oral trials in which the defense and prosecution present their arguments before a judge or panel of judges, sometimes accompanied by a jury; investigation by a prosecutor (instead of an instructional judge); abbreviated procedures and alternative sentencing (including conciliation between the victim and offender for lesser crimes); efforts to reduce the use of pretrial detention; and the insertion of a long list of due process guarantees to ensure the defendant is treated fairly (Binder and Obando, 2004; Correa, 1999; Riego, 2002). Other changes include increased transparency (not only oral trials, but also the publication of judgments and of statistics on institutional output); procedural simplification; more emphasis on pretrial conciliation and mediation; and increased use of automation and online filing and consultations. On the organizational side, there have been alterations in procedures for selecting, evaluating, and disciplining employees with more emphasis on merit criteria, transparency, and the invitation of public input; new forms of judicial governance (especially via judicial councils); and improvements to internal administration (both of service units and of entire organizations).

Fifth, in response to common complaints about the inaccessibility of justice services, countries have introduced mechanisms aimed at facilitating use by traditionally marginalized groups. These include provision of free legal aid, either by the state or by nongovernmental organizations and universities; introduction of court interpreters for parties not conversant with the dominant language; small claims and other special courts; itinerant services for groups living in remote areas or in large urban slums; court-annexed or free-standing alternative dispute resolution; and educational and information programs to facilitate citizens' understanding of their rights and the means of accessing them (Alvarez and Highton, 2000; Instituto de Defensa Legal, 1999; Sadek, 2004). Some countries have waived legal fees for those without the means to pay them.

Finally, throughout the region, courts have begun to play a greater role in curbing unconstitutional or abusive government actions and policies (Taylor, 2004; Wilson et al., 2004). Two structural factors, usually a consequence of constitutional changes, are critical here: the expansion of the judicial review powers of ordinary courts and/or the creation of constitutional tribunals (or chambers). Their impact has expanded as a consequence of redemocratization; the additional institutional-strengthening measures discussed above; greater activism on the part of private attorneys and civil society organizations; and a decreased tendency to overt political interference with court operations.

In short, the past 20 years have produced revolutionary changes in the sector, starting with, but hardly limited to the courts. Nonetheless, popular evaluations of sector performance have not been as positive. The region's judiciaries, and by extension other sector entities, continue to occupy among the lowest rankings on public opinion polls rating the performance of and citizen confidence in various public institutions (CEJA, 2003 and 2005). The few exceptions (Chile, Costa Rica, and Uruguay) started with higher scores, and even they have experienced some decline. While clearly related to increasing levels of public skepticism about all governmental bodies, the sector's failure to make improvements relative to other organizations (the executive, the legislature, or agencies within their sphere of action) is perplexing given the concerted efforts and substantial financial investments placed in justice reform. Thus, the question inspiring the title of this chapter and occupying the rest of its contents—why does it appear that the sector has to "run faster" to maintain the same ground or to avoid backsliding still further?

The issues are explored in three parts. These include quantitative and qualitative paradoxes and a series of issues constituting a set of emerging problems, not anticipated for the most part by the reforms' proponents. They can be considered paradoxes, but unlike the others, a consequence not of what was not achieved, but rather of the unpredictable effects of the successful implementation of certain changes.

The Quantitative Paradoxes

The most obvious paradoxes can be expressed in a quantitative form: the sense that no matter how much is invested and how many more entities are created, the sector is no more able to keep up with the increased demands for its services. Here we look at three aspects of the quantitative riddle—the supply-demand gap; the issue of financing; and the problem of access.

The Paradox of the Supply-Demand Gap

The supply-demand gap takes two forms, depending on the countries considered. In a minority of countries (for example, Argentina, Brazil, Costa Rica) the demand for services has increased exponentially as have judicial caseloads (Mora Mora, 2001; World Bank 2003b; 2005c). Despite judicial productivity, backlogs and delays have grown more rapidly. In the rest of the region, while demand has grown, the average caseload per judge remains moderate to low. Nonetheless, backlogs and delays have also risen in a still more paradoxical fashion. A part of the explanation is similar for both categories and encompasses trends with comparable impacts universally. Recently drafted or amended constitutions include more guaranteed rights and means of accessing them; increasing globalization, greater urbanization, and new forms of economic and social interactions provoke more conflicts and thus more business for the courts; these same developments and the democratic transition itself have been accompanied by rising crime rates, which again, must be handled by the sector. However, the differences within the two groups of countries may be still more significant.

In the high-caseload countries, average annual filings received and disposed by judges reach what one Brazilian jurist called "surrealistic" proportions. Brazil's 11 Supremo Tribunal Federal (Constitutional Court), or STF, justices now decide over 100,000 cases annually. Although a regional, if not world, record, the numbers are only an extreme example of a broader phenomenon; Latin American constitutional, supreme, and superior courts handle thousands of cases annually.[4] The surrealistic numbers also affect the rest of the judiciary. Each of Brazil's first instance judges currently receives and decides over 1,400 cases annually (World Bank, 2005c), but again the number may be matched by Costa Rican judges and by those of a few other countries. How this is possible was explained in part by the former president of Brazil's STF—the 10,000 opinions he wrote annually were in reality "only 25 conflicts" (Jobim, 2003). In short, much of the workload comprises a large number of repetitive conflicts, many involving at least one of the same parties—often government agencies, banks, or public utilities that have refused services to users—and others representing standard dilatory practices initiated by a party attempting to delay an inevitable negative decision.

Latin America's legal codes allow such maneuvers, what can be called the use of the justice system to avoid or postpone a just decision, and thus encourage the congestion of courts with cases with a foregone, but delayed conclusion (World Bank, 2002, 2003a and b, 2005c). Aside from congestion and the costs of adding judges and staff to handle this burgeoning workload, a focus on these routine matters may delay attention to the more complex cases on which judges should be spending greater amount of time. The repetitive and less important cases, because they are easier to deal with, may thus create delays in the inherently more significant—pleasing beneficiaries of disputes over adjustments to pensions (a classic repetitive case) or excessive fees for banking services, but leaving parties to more complex contract disputes bereft of a timely resolution. The remaining explanation, the use of multiple appeals and other dilatory practices to postpone or escape justice, represents a more traditional problem of all Latin American systems.

In short, in the minority of Latin American countries where unusually large judicial caseloads are the rule, the underlying problem is abusive use of the courts by ordinary parties and repeat defendants, whether governmental or private agencies (Brazil, Poder Judiciário, 2004). This is facilitated by a legal framework that, first, does not provide for a more direct attack on the problem (for example, a better system of administrative law, better consumer protection agencies, or a means of penalizing public and private agencies routinely engaging in such abuses) and, second, permits multiple appeals of final and interlocutory decisions and other dilatory practices.

Such practices are not limited to the high-workload countries, but in the rest of the region the more basic problem is that judges and other sector professionals are not very productive by any reasonable standards. Consequently, exceptional dilatory actions are unnecessary because those who might resort to them can count on routine, judicially caused delays.

In some of the poorest performing countries, supply (the number of judges and courts) has grown even faster than demand so that judges may be still less productive today than they were ten years earlier (World Bank, 2005a). Because these same countries also commonly demonstrate an extremely unequal distribution of the work, it is not unusual to find, as in Honduras and Paraguay, that over half the bench (usually members located in more removed areas) receive fewer than 200 filings a year, while their urban colleagues face "surrealistic" numbers not unlike those found in Brazil or Costa Rica. However, the larger problem is the lack of change in work methods and expectations so that judges in both circumstances have a kind of "set point," a number of cases, based on historical experience that they regard as the maximum. They do not try to find ways to handle more cases, and in fact, when the workload drops may decide even fewer (another set point being the reasonable percentage of incoming cases to be disposed) (Magaloni and Negrete, n.d.). While one can blame the judges for this mindset, the major responsibility lies with the body charged with overseeing them and setting standards, be it a judicial council or a high court. In the high performers, it is not unusual for the governing body to track output and discipline or assist the lower producers. This fairly novel approach is rarely found elsewhere. In fact, interviews around the region usually demonstrate that the governing body has little idea as to the qualitative or quantitative nature of the judicial workload.[5]

In summary, the region's persisting demand-supply gap has various explanations, but the constant factors are a failure to recognize, first, that it is not unusual; second, that by international standards caseloads in most Latin American courts are not excessive; and third, that the gap has remedies other than adding judges and courts. These additional remedies all require a proactive approach to setting organizational policy, to devising and adopting new work methods, including, but not limited to, the use of automation, to finding ways to control abusive litigants, and to monitoring individual performance. Few reforms have addressed these issues, meaning that the expectations of helping courts match the quantitative demands for their services are rarely met. Whether judiciaries are actually running faster to stay in the same place, or merely adding judges to maintain the traditional rhythm, the results have only increased public dissatisfaction. Much the same can be said of other sector organizations—police, prosecution, defense, and even private attorneys. The reforms emphasize "modern" codes and technology, but the more critical change is attitudinal, and in most cases it remains untouched.

The Paradox of the Insufficient Sector Budget

In both relative and absolute terms, judicial budgets have grown throughout the region. The once-orphan branch of government in some cases accounts for a near-record share of the national budget, and in most cases, receives an acceptable percentage (Díaz and Linares, 2005). Conceivably, Latin American needs are different from those of the United States or Europe, but that is also true of most other sectors; countries with extraordinary judicial needs usually face extraordinary challenges in education and health as well. Hence, the question is why, with few exceptions, the region's courts and other sector organizations still claim poverty even after substantially increasing their claims on the public coffers.

There is a second aspect to the paradox—the lack of a strong relationship between the percentage spent on the courts and their performance. The strong performers include one (Chile) with among the lowest shares of the national budget and two (Costa Rica and Uruguay) with relatively high amounts. Others with generous proportions (El Salvador with nearly 4.5 percent of GDP; Nicaragua with 3.23; and Honduras with 2.24) are not notable for their good performance.[6] Brazil, which also has a high percentage (although one hotly disputed by the judges), and Argentina, with 4.5 can be considered moderately efficient, albeit with other problems. Part of this aspect of the paradox is explained by the tendency to use most of the budget on personnel, with the high spenders having relatively more judges (Chile, Costa Rica, El Salvador, Honduras, Uruguay), higher salaries (Brazil, Nicaragua, for higher-level judges), or both (Argentina). Several court systems also seem to have an excessive number of support and administrative staff, whether well paid or not.[7] The issue is that neither high salaries nor large numbers of judges or staff guarantee good performance. Latin American courts, perhaps courts everywhere, are notorious for somewhat haphazard financial administration, and there is a reluctance to "waste money" on nonlawyers or to delegate them sufficient responsibility.

It should also be recognized that despite the regional tradition of court management of its own resources, there are frequently extra-sector obstacles to doing better. First, in many Latin American countries, a more progressive approach to budgeting has not developed. In those cases, it is difficult to imagine the courts doing any better than the rest of the public sector. Second, courts often face significant constraints in improving the quality and distribution of their financial and other resources. Salaries of professional and support staff may be set by the executive and legislature; the congress may have to approve changes in the number and location of judges and courts; it may be legally, even constitutionally, impossible to shift judges from one type of court to another; judicial staff may be relatively immovable under current civil service laws; and there may be further requirements as to where judges will be placed. Colombia, for example, constitutionally requires a judge in every population center, regardless of the likely workload. Third, judicial budgetary proposals may be subject to alteration by the executive or manipulation by the congress, which in any case is responsible for approving the final amounts. Unfortunately, as the sector begins to take budgeting more seriously it often finds its efforts to do so limited by a traditional legal, political, and structural straitjacket, offering little room for innovation.

As regards the budgetary paradox, the fundamental explanation again rests on attitudes and practices. Latin American courts now have the funds to do much more and are unlikely to increase their share of the budgetary pie. That they continue to protest poverty is a result of poor resource management combined with certain external obstacles. Very few have accepted, as one Supreme Court president has said (Mora Mora, 2001), that today's challenge is to find ways to do more with what they have, not to hope that their protests will continue to enlarge their funding.

Paradoxes of Access

One common reform goal is to increase "access to justice," especially for marginalized populations. What exactly this means has never been clear. Based on the measures adopted, it appears most often equated with getting more individuals from these groups to courts or to comparable alternative services as a means of ensuring they can have their problems resolved and their legal disputes settled in the same manner as other, better-off citizens. A second, less-common set of measures seems to equate access with using the courts and related institutions to give these same groups "access" to nonjudicial services and goods guaranteed in the post-1980s constitutions. Here the emphasis is less on the number of new users than on the results achieved through legal actions entered in their name. More recently, access has also been linked to a goal of "legal empowerment," another vaguely defined term that seems to imply that access of either of the first two types will encourage citizens, and especially the poor, to become more active in pursuing their interests, within or outside the courts.

There has been important progress in broadening the use of courts and related services to a wider variety of citizens and in using the courts to obtain concrete benefits for them. Unfortunately, poor record keeping makes it difficult to quantify the beneficiaries or benefits, and most of the evidence tends to be either anecdotal or limited to single programs or events. The multitude of state and privately sponsored legal services do provide a body count of beneficiaries, but reach only a small portion of the universe. If getting people to court is the goal, allowing pro se representation as in Brazil's small claims courts (Sadek, 2004) might be more practical.

Determining the relative importance of the benefits achieved, especially vis-à-vis real needs, is virtually impossible. It is hard to say who the beneficiaries are, whether they are the most needy, and whether the victories won respond to what they would request were they to set their own priorities. For critics of the approach, this scatter-gun strategy may not be the most efficient means of improving the situation of the poor, either in terms of its immediate results or as compared with other nonjudicial means of reaching them. A dollar spent on legal aid is a dollar not spent on education or housing; and at some point, the state may be investing more in getting theoretical access to rights than in actually providing them.

The paradox of access is in the end a question of strategy, objectives, and downstream impacts. Access proponents, of whatever stripe, have tended to take a more-is-better approach to their theme, consequently leaving little means for evaluating the efficacy of their efforts beyond the quantity of cases and parties affected. The apparent conclusion that the best system is one where every citizen gets his or her day in court is patently absurd in the abstract and as compared with the situation in countries deemed to have well-functioning systems. It also, at least over the short to medium run, conflicts with other reform goals—juridical security, conflict reduction, and possibly efficiency.[8] Ultimately, access is a means not an end, and the paradox might be better understood, or perhaps disappear, were the access proponents to specify the end actually being pursued. Their failure to do so condemns them to an impossible battle against logistical and financial obstacles. They will never reach their goal until they decide what their goal actually is.

The Qualitative Paradoxes

The goals of the region's reforms are not limited to quantitative change—in fact some of the most important emphasize improvements in the quality of services rendered. Reform programs are filled with measures to address these problems, ranging from higher salaries and training, to new selection systems and greater transparency in all operations. Many new codes and laws have also aimed at improving quality—by reducing opportunities for manipulating outcomes and adding due process guarantees. Even automation has played its part—by reducing certain traditional types of discretion (for example, in assigning cases to judges) and leaving a more permanent record of case handling. However the results have been disappointing, and in certain cases, the remedies have aggravated existing vices. Here we look at three areas: corruption, formalism, and enforcement of judgments.

Corruption

Corruption (whether of judges and their staff, or of police, prosecutors, defenders, private attorneys, and others) is a frequent complaint about nearly all the region's justice sectors (Abaid and Thieberger, 2005; Kaufman et al., 1999 and 2002). Only a few systems (Chile, Costa Rica, Uruguay) escaped the criticisms, but they, like virtually every judiciary in the world, were never entirely immune. Factors believed to encourage corruption include excessive political intervention in judicial selection and career management, continued interference in internal operations, low salaries and lack of secure tenure, and inadequate systems for monitoring performance and receiving and following up on complaints. To the extent many supreme courts were already "tainted" (as they had been selected under the politicized systems), there was some reluctance to transfer or leave selection and career management of the other judges with them. Thus, many countries shifted a part or all of these responsibilities to newly formed judicial councils, modeled on local understandings of European practices (Hammergren, 2002). Wherever these functions were lodged, there was also an effort to change selection procedures, introducing merit-based criteria, greater transparency, and at times, the participation of civil society groups and ordinary citizens. Similar changes also extended to systems for investigating complaints and disciplining judges, although still another body was sometimes set up to handle these themes. Both Argentina and Paraguay thus have separate disciplinary boards while Colombia's Judicial Council has one chamber handling court administration and judicial selection and another responsible for discipline. Where such matters were shifted to an external council, it was not uncommon for the Supreme Court to retain a hand in judicial evaluation and investigation of complaints, an arrangement that has, not surprisingly, given rise to some conflicts (Díaz and Linares, 2005, 79–80).

Beyond selection and career management, additional mechanisms were introduced to fight corruption. These included raising salaries of judges (and occasionally of staff), drafting ethics codes and offering training in their contents, instituting and occasionally publishing assets declarations, modifying criminal codes to specify more exactly the types of behavior prohibited, and automating case assignment to discourage judge shopping. Publication of judgments and other information on case handling and monetary awards were believed to provide disincentives for judges tempted to do the wrong thing.

The impact on reducing corruption has unfortunately not been as great as the large number innovations might suggest. Of course, real measures of corruption, as opposed to opinion polls, are virtually impossible to come by. It is conceivable, as some courts now argue, that the increased attention to the topic has encouraged citizens to complain about it more. Nonetheless, there are enough documented cases to indicate that the battle has a long way to go, especially in countries where corruption has long been endemic. Thus, the paradoxical aspect—with so much effort put into fighting the problem, why do complaints and real cases persist?

One answer is that the remedy of choice—the new selection and career management systems—was too easily contaminated by the preexisting vices (Hammergren, 2002; World Bank, 2005a). Some new judicial councils are rumored to be worse than the systems that preceded them. Ironically, the first council introduced in the region—that of Venezuela (in 1969)—was long notorious for its corrupt, politicized practices, described as the reign of "judicial tribes," or groups of judges and lawyers who controlled their own corruption networks (Pérez Perdomo, 2006). Although eliminated by President Hugo Chavez for other reasons (reputedly a desire to exercise more control over the courts), it was a poor model for the others to follow. The councils of Bolivia and Paraguay are plagued by similar problems. While Argentina's council has been less problematic, it is not regarded as a great success (Abaid and Thieberger, 2005). President Nestor Kirchner recently succeeded in modifying its composition on the grounds of general inefficiency and a failure to control corruption. Modified systems left in the hands of the supreme courts have not been markedly more successful, and there are some councils (Colombia, El Salvador, Peru) that whatever their other problems, have not been accused of fomenting corruption. However, the general lesson stands: where the motives for corrupting judges are strong, simply changing the identity of those controlling their nominations and careers is unlikely to be a sufficient solution.

Separate disciplinary bodies, whether internal or external to the court system, have suffered similar contretemps. Paraguay's external disciplinary board is regarded more negatively than is its council, believed, inter alia, to threaten judges who do not rule in favor of clients of the board's members (World Bank, 2005a). Argentina's is less frequently criticized, but citizens perceive it as ineffectual in combating corruption. Internal bodies are often seen as too soft, more inclined to impose minor sanctions, encourage suspects into early retirement, or sideline them to positions where they can do less harm. Some are also accused of insufficient transparency, not allowing an accused judge to offer a defense, or in some cases to know what the charge is. Where the problem is not corruption of the discipliners, it is often a judicial reluctance to air dirty laundry and a tendency to sympathize excessively with the culprit.

The move to merit appointments and more transparent selection systems has had some positive effect on raising the quality of the bench, as have higher salaries. However, neither constitutes a strong weapon against corruption and many "merit" systems still rely on subjective criteria and have not eliminated the use of recommendations from well-placed lawyers or judges.[9] In the countries where the largest raises have gone to the supreme court, the financial incentives do not operate for ordinary judges and staff. A few of the additional mechanisms (randomized case assignments, automated case files and tracking, publication of statistics and judgments) have had positive effects, but they tend to work only against certain forms of corruption. Moreover, many legal changes have actually added opportunities. It is a common complaint, for example, that the new criminal procedures codes, by adding steps and actors, increased the places where a bribe might be applied. Due process guarantees, while important for combating other abuses, have been successfully used by lawyers to "get their clients off on technicalities" or simply draw out a proceeding until the legal time limits run out. Time limits, intended to decrease delays, have worked against successful investigation and prosecution of complex crimes. These unforeseen effects are not inevitable, but guarding against them requires understanding where they might backfire.

One place where too little has been done is in providing checks on attorney abuses. Throughout the region, private bar associations have never been strong on disciplining members. Even the most powerful, like the Order of Attorneys of Brazil (OAB), have a poor record of catching and sanctioning their errant members. Elsewhere, the associations function more like private clubs or lobbies; often membership is not compulsory or can be acquired by simply paying a fee. As lawyers are the source of many of the problems, and as the new methods for keeping track of judicial performance often make the judges more fearful of offending the litigators, this is a serious oversight.

It is hard to say whether judicial corruption has increased, decreased, or remained the same throughout the region's countries. What is certain is that the complaints have augmented, and that judiciaries have, for whatever reason, not taken this seriously enough. The common fear, that by admitting the existence of corruption they will decrease public confidence, seems entirely misplaced. It should instead be realized that by recognizing the problem and dealing with it decisively, courts can only move forward.

Formalism versus Effective Conflict Resolution

An essential part of improved judicial services is ensuring that cases are dealt with in an effective as well as timely fashion. It has long been said that too many judges operate in a highly bureaucratic fashion, processing papers rather than disputes. This is another source of declining faith in the sector—the belief that the least effective way to resolve a problem is to ask a judge to do it. Formalism stands those seeking to avoid justice in good stead. A shrewd attorney can find hundreds of ways to protect his client by raising incidental issues, asking for endless reviews, and otherwise obfuscating the questions at the core of the case. The introduction of oral hearings for criminal proceedings had sought to attack these vices, but the new procedures too often enhanced the ability of parties bent on postponing justice by adding stages and actors, and imposing arbitrary deadlines that, if exceeded, stop the action entirely.[10]

Even without changes to the codes, the theoretically simple debt collection proceedings that constitute a large portion of the civil caseload have evolved into lengthy ordeals in which lawyers commonly speak of "selling time" to the debtor. They cannot win the case, but they can extend it for years. In countries that have added, on the theory that specialization is better, a second group of judges responsible for the enforcement of these and ordinary actions, the judgment is followed by what is effectively another trial, in which the same dilatory practices can be indulged. A study done in Mexico's Federal District in 2002 found that while the median time to judgment in a debt case was 223 days, the subsequent enforcement process took at least twice as long (World Bank, 2002, 2003a).

It is no wonder that in the face of these examples and their own experience, citizens so often conclude that the courts are of little help in resolving a legitimate complaint. That the efforts to make them more effective have produced such disappointing results again is the product of a series of factors. First, excessive formalism is often related to corruption. Judges and other actors, paid or pressured to delay results or otherwise defeat just ends, often do so by entertaining frivolous or abusive requests from the interested party. However, that explains only a part of the problem. A second set of reasons derives from the efforts to combat corruption. Judges are increasingly afraid of being charged with favoritism and thus are reluctant to say "no" to any request because this could lead to a complaint and a disciplinary action. Similar reasoning explains the tendency of government attorneys to register multiple appeals against any decision of the agency they represent. They may well recognize the ultimate futility of such actions, but find it easier to make the appeal than to explain why they didn't and face possible charges of dereliction of duty. However, third and most important, is the impact of judges' own education and background and of the environment in which they operate.

The idea that the court user's interest, at least that of the honest user, is to get a fair and rapid decision is often simply not understood. Judges' internalization of that concept is complicated by the intervention of the parties' lawyers, whose incentives may be quite different; by the impact of their own legal training that puts a premium on citing doctrine and finding unexpected details and angles; and occasionally by their own evaluation systems that may reward complexity over simplicity.

At the same time, there are judges who seem to err in the other direction, interpreting their roles as social workers or revolutionaries.[11] While these functions are important, one can ask whether they are consistent with the judicial responsibility for applying the law and so enhancing juridical security. Nonetheless, for the majority of the region's judges, rather than what could be called an excessive focus on extralegal results, the problem would appear to be an exaggerated emphasis on process and a failure to see legally based conflict resolution as their principal role. Bureaucratization and formalism have not disappeared, in part because there has been so little attention given to the problems. Even the efficiency measures have done little here, as their main emphasis is to accelerate the proceedings, not to heighten the relevancy of their outcomes. Additionally, acceleration often provides still more opportunities for introducing extraneous issues—lawyers can now file their pleadings online and increase their length by computerized cutting and pasting. Judges and their staff can respond in the same fashion and so the process goes on and on. Formalism has not decreased because it was never attacked adequately—the paradox's explanation is that the objective was not incorporated into the reforms.

Enforcement

As court observers in Latin America and elsewhere have recently realized, a good judgment is worth little if it cannot be enforced. Latin Americans refer to this phenomenon in a series of adages—*gané pero no cobré*, or in Portuguese, *ganhei mas não levei* (I won but I didn't collect). The experience is well known, but it only recently became a focus of reforms (Henderson et al., 2004). The one exception is the introduction of separate *jueces de ejecución* (enforcement judges), a remedy increasingly recognized as worse than the problem. These judges, whose workload commonly exceeds that of a trial judge by a factor of two or three, have become a bottleneck in their own right, leading to a still more recent tendency to eliminate their positions. Whatever the benefits of the Latin American preference for specialization, this is one specialized role that rarely seems to work.

Enforcement of judgments is a universal problem and is often complicated by extrajudicial factors. Aside from the fact that there is little to do against an insolvent debtor (and that insolvency often originates in poor practices among creditors or economic downturns), the additional obstacles include (1) legal constraints as to the types of assets that can be attached or seized; (2) limited access to information on bank accounts, tax records, and individuals' other holdings; (3) corrupt or poorly managed property registries; (4) prohibitions on direct seizures of assets; and (5) requirements on how assets will be liquidated (usually by a complicated, and sometimes corrupt, judicially managed auction). To the extent these problems were not recognized, the paradox was that efforts to speed up prejudgment processing of cases often resulted in the winner walking away with nothing. Transferring the responsibility for enforcement to another judge tended to discourage attention to the problem, as did the fact that so many of the impediments originated outside either judge's control. Although not as well documented, similar problems appear to affect alternative dispute resolution. Proponents claim that parties' agreement to a solution increases compliance levels, but there is little evidence to support their claims.

As the paradoxes presented by inadequate enforcement are only now being recognized, there has been little progress in eliminating them. The fact that so many causes are extrajudicial in origin complicates matters; any solution will require working with agencies other than the courts. It would help if courts kept better track of enforcement. The ability to do so may be the one advantage offered by the use of enforcement judges, but it was one also realized in the breach.

The Impact Paradoxes

A primary explanation for the popularity of legal and judicial reforms is their promise of so many extra-sector impacts at such a relatively low cost. For all the talk of strengthening justice institutions, the real payoff for many external supporters was the impact this process would have on various social, economic and political goals. A series of macroeconomic analyses (Kaufmann et al., 1999 and 2002; Castelar Pinheiro, org., 2000 and 2003; Djankov et al., 2002; Sherwood et al., 1994; La Porta et al., 1998; World Bank, 2005b) fortified the arguments by finding statistically relevant correlations between levels of judicial development and such extra-sector values as economic growth, political stability, levels of poverty, or other development variables. In fact, as critics of this work sometimes comment, that all other goals could be achieved by reforming courts and the rest of the sector. Educational, economic, and health programs would be superfluous. Even the proponents do not go to that extreme, but the extrapolation does raise certain doubts about predictions drawn from the macroeconomic analyses. Still, it is fair to ask if, on a more modest scale, the reforms could and did have an effect in promoting extra-sector change, and if so, where and how.

The Classic Justifications and the Downstream Effects of Justice Reform

Perhaps the most famous predicted impact is that on economic development— as summarized in the frequent statement that a well-functioning rule of law system is a prerequisite for market-based economic growth (Dakolias, 1995). Positive examples, such as Chile, could be taken as an endorsement of the predictions, although in Chile, as in the case of the slow growers, there are many other factors at play. Similar conclusions might be drawn on the societal side— the region's failure to make substantial progress in reducing levels of inequality and poverty is another example either of what did not happen because the justice reforms did not go far enough, or evidence that the progress in areas such as access has not had the predicted impacts on improving the welfare of the poor.

As regards the relationships posited between justice reforms and socioeconomic development, critics have raised many caveats. On the economic side, one major issue is causality—are better-functioning systems the cause or consequence of higher levels of economic development? While authors such as Kaufman et al. (1999 and 2002) claim to have established causality, the skeptics remain unconvinced (Hewko, 2002). Even if the economists are correct, there is a second issue as to the nature of the linkages. Reformers tended to assume that whatever causality exists is channeled through the performance of civil and commercial courts, those dealing most directly with business-related conflicts. However, it has been suggested that the critical linkages lie elsewhere—the justice system's impact on crime and violence or the remedies and disincentives it offers for administrative abuses. Crime and violence do pose direct and indirect costs on business, and at an extreme, discourage investment. Cities and regions experiencing escalating criminal violence often suffer a reduction in or outflow of investment to other, less troubled areas. True, much of the investment in justice reforms has gone into the criminal justice systems, but if this has had an impact on levels of crime in violence, it has not stopped their escalation.

Administrative law is a largely untapped area. Increased constitutional protections and the greater activity of courts in upholding them have offered some redress to individual entrepreneurs facing administrative abuses, but the disincentive impact is notoriously limited. The individual gets relief, but the agency or bureaucrat responsible for the abuse is usually not sanctioned and so can continue the objectionable practice with others (World Bank, 2003b). Moreover, increased judicial activism has occasionally impacted economic actors negatively by raising costs of government services (and thus the tax burden), by reversing new or long-standing policies benefiting investors, and by enforcing workers' and consumers' rights, increasing costs of business operations. As this last comment suggests, the purported external impacts and objectives of judicial reforms are not always consistent with each other. What is good for business is not necessarily good for workers, the poor, or the environment, and vice versa. In the longest run, all good things may eventually coincide, but over the short to medium term there are conflicts among many of the goals pursued.

Aside from the very important and still-controversial issue of the direction of causality, the additional paradoxes or conflicts posed by the reforms' purported extra-sector impacts are ultimately no different from those inherent in all development strategies. Justice reform continues to be all things to all people despite the failure to satisfy any of them and the likelihood that full satisfaction for one group will conflict with the desires of the others. The first part of this situation may finally be changing, as suggested in the following section on the balance of power issues.

The Balance of Power Issues

Behind many of the "institutional strengthening" reform components are still another objective—increasing the sector's, and especially the courts' status as an independent branch of government, capable of checking the actions of other governmental powers (Mainwaring, 2003). It would be fair to say that this objective has been advanced in most countries and that courts and other agencies (especially defense and prosecution) have increased their actions in combating many traditional abuses (Barker, 2000; Sousa Santos et al., 2001; Wilson et al., 2004; Uprimny, 2001). The phenomenon has not always been welcomed, partly because of suspicions that court rulings are still influenced by political and other irregular inputs, and partly because the results are disturbing to some stakeholders. For example, when the Argentine courts began to grant *amparos* (orders for protection against the actions of authorities) against the government's emergency economic measures in 2001 and 2002, the executive and the international financial institutions were fearful that this would complicate the country's economic crisis. The supreme court was in fact suspected of economic blackmail, using the threat of more reversals to hold off the pending impeachment of its members (Abaid and Thiesberger, 2005).

The phenomenon of courts' greater involvement in reviewing and checking government policies has been observed worldwide. It is often linked to a tendency for losers in political battles to take their case to the courts. As parties take to the courts conflicts they have lost in more political arenas, they may effectively prevent government policies from moving forward. A related concern is that especially in countries with rights-rich constitutions, a tradition of very inequitably distributed "acquired rights,"[12] and active public interest bars, the courts may become a means for making as well as blocking policies by insisting on the implementation of constitutions "never meant to be enforced" (Wilson et al., 2004).

The problem here is the drain on the public treasury, as well as the likelihood that the benefits will not be distributed equitably, instead rewarding the squeaky wheel.

Observers are divided on the longer-term benefits of these trends. They generally agree that the immediate impact of these trends has been to reduce juridical security, increase court congestion, feed public controversy, and provoke renewed efforts at political interference. In Argentina, Bolivia, Ecuador, Paraguay, Peru, and Venezuela, executives have promoted the ousting of justices or entire supreme courts. While often popular, these quick fixes rarely constitute an improvement and they set a dangerous precedent. The larger problem, which the region will soon have to address, transcends the judiciary, extending to the roles, responsibilities, and interactions of all branches of government. Courts' performance of their checks and balance function depends not only on the judges, but also on the quality of the inputs from the other institutional actors as well as some implicit or explicit understandings of the limits on each. While often blamed on the courts, the imperfect coordination of institutional roles and the consequent institutional clashes cannot be resolved by them alone, and will require, as the judicial reformers never envisioned, the concerted efforts of all.

Toward a Conclusion—Institutional Accountability as the Other Face of Increased Independence

The justice sector can resolve few of these paradoxes on its own. Its members can take a more active role in recognizing the problems and promoting the necessary remedies. That they have so often failed to do so is in part a result of the way in which the reforms were introduced and implemented—usually by small groups of extrajudicial and sometimes entirely extra-system (for example, donors) actors who did the diagnosis, developed the remedies, and implanted them, all too frequently with the sector organizations as passive participants. Even when the courts and others received the proposals favorably (as in most cases they sooner or later did), the process did not encourage a proactive approach to monitoring and assessing their own performance, let alone to adopting reform (or self-improvement) as a permanent rather than a one-time undertaking. Increased independence has made courts more aggressive in demanding resources, but these too often are invested in improving the judicial situation, not that of the user, or in innovations that imperfectly address the fundamental problems. Brazil and Costa Rica have, for example, invested heavily in automating case processing, but without attacking the procedural complexities that account for most delay. Several countries have introduced public information and education campaigns that will do little for parties who cannot get to court because of their inability to hire a lawyer.

Courts often see these basic problems as outside their control, requiring, for example, a new law, or different performance from other sector actors (the prosecutors, the private bar, the police). In this they are correct, but it should not prevent them from campaigning as actively for these changes as they do for higher budgets and salaries or for the retention of their own acquired rights. Aside from a basic responsibility to identify external constraints, there is an issue of self-interest. It may indeed be corrupt prosecutors or police that account for "criminals escaping justice," but the public usually blames the judges. To be fair, this narrow focus on "my own rights and duties" is not exclusive to the courts, and indeed seems shared by most sector actors—a lack of shared accountability for system outputs.

Accountability has also been a missing element in a narrower sense and in areas where each institution could do more on its own. While a few countries have made progress in tracking the quantity and quality of outputs, the sector still has a long way to go here, as well as in the responsible and transparent use of its resources, internal discipline, and explanations of its internal policies and decisions. It is understandable that organizations only recently removed from high levels of external intervention might resist having to render accounts to anyone, but they will never improve their public images or their performance without adopting these practices. Ideally, judicial reform should be led by the courts on the basis on demands generated by the full complement of stakeholders. Over the past 20 years, reforms have either been worked on the courts by a small group of external proponents, or, in more recent times, the goals and methods have been set by the judges themselves. Judges are not always good at second-guessing user priorities and they do have their own vested interests. If the paradoxes are to be resolved, the sector organizations will have to recognize first and foremost that the remedies lie not in each playing its narrowly defined role, but rather in a mutual effort to produce the collective results required by the citizenry.

Because of the lower priority Latin American judicial reformers have assigned to economic goals and the emerging resistance to efforts to give them more emphasis,[13] those interested in improving the sector's contribution to the region's competitiveness may have to work through the broader programs. This is logical inasmuch as the structural and attitudinal obstacles to better performance have undercut the impact of go-it-alone endeavors. The cultural sea change required to induce judges to speed up their decisions, privilege substance over form, control abusive litigants, and apply (often already existing) legislation intended to facilitate these ends cannot be easily restricted to one type of proceeding. Moreover, in areas such as criminal and administrative law, poor performance, whatever its causes, tends to have indivisible effects. The most dramatic claims about the economic benefits of a "well-functioning" legal and judicial system, while helping donors justify their work, are increasingly contested by researchers,[14] but no one is arguing that improvements are unnecessary. In highly competitive work, a slight edge can make a difference in attracting and retaining investment and in defining its returns. However, the changes producing that slight edge can make justice work better for all citizens, and by stressing that point, economically oriented reformers may have more success and stir up less opposition than with arguments focusing only on their particular goals.

Notes

1. It bears mentioning that the projected investments, whether forthcoming from the national budgets or from donor loans and grants, come nowhere near the amounts required for reforms in other sectors (for example, health, education, agriculture) and that the donor contributions in particular were far smaller than those provided for programs in these other areas.
2. Statistics from various sources, collected by Borja Díaz Rivillas and on file in World Bank.
3. Op cit. See also Douat (2001) for comparative statistics on Western Europe and a discussion of some of the problems in calculating budgets.
4. Some statistics are found in Centro de Estudios de Justicia de las Américas (CEJA), *Reporte sobre el Estado de la Justicia en las Américas, 2002–2003* (Santiago, Chile: Centro de Estudios de Justicia de las Américas, 2003) and CEJA, *Reporte sobre el Estado de la Justicia en las Américas, 2004–2005* (Santiago, Chile: Centro de Estudios de Justicia de las Américas, 2005). Others, on file in the World Bank, have been collected from various sources by Borja Díaz Rivillas.
5. One example taken from Peru is not unique to that country. A World Bank–sponsored study (Mantilla Gonzales, Jean Carlo Serván Gorki, Luciano López, and Hernando Burgos, *El sistema judicial en el Perú: Un enfoque analítico a partir de sus usos y de sus usuarios.* Draft report prepared for the World Bank, 2002. [On file with the author.]) found that the Lima district court was unaware that the bulk of its justice of the peace workload was initiated, not by women seeking child support or employees disputing dismissals, but by banks and pension funds trying to collect fees owed them.
6. These and other budget figures come from various official sources, as collected for the World Bank by Borja Díaz Rivillas. Figures are on file in the bank.
7. For Paraguay, see Rojas et al. (2006) who found a 45:55 ratio between administrative and jurisdictional staff. The latter includes support staff assigned to individual courts and judges.
8. More access would appear to mean higher system costs and more delays. As Prillaman (2000) notes of Brazil, where everyone has access, no one does. This is not a call for limiting access, but rather for rationalizing it to advance prioritized results.
9. As just one example, in a personal interview in Lima in May 2006, a Peruvian prosecutor told the author that while she had passed the written test to become a judge, she decided not to go forward with the process because, albeit informally, the recommendation of a prominent politician or judge was also required.
10. In interviews in Paraguay in June 2006, the author was told that the *jueces de garantía*, responsible for supervising the investigative stage, had begun to conduct their own mini-trials, turning a simple request to conduct a search of a private office into a lengthy debate with witnesses, appeals, and all.
11. See for example Castelar's (Armando Castelar Pinheiro, "Judiciário, Reforma e Economia: A Visão dos Magistrados," Discussion draft number 966 [Rio de Janeiro: IPEA, 2003] [On file with the author] findings in a survey of Brazilian judges where many of the younger interviewees claimed they would put the interests of a poor claimant over the dictates of the law in a contract dispute.
12. These are privileges, often with no legal basis, won by groups in former political conflicts, or simply as a consequence of traditional practice.
13. In recent years, there has been a notable reaction to legal and judicial reforms (and especially those associated with donors) perceived as favoring economic interests.

While the group raising these objections is small and often poorly informed on donors' activities, its claims of a pro-globalizing plot do get a hearing among a wider public. The effect has been most evident in Brazil, but it is also visible in Mexico, Colombia, and Argentina.

14. Most often targeted are estimates (like those offered by Robert M. Sherwood, Geoffrey Shepherd, and Celso Marcos de Souza, "Judicial Systems and Economic Performance," Special issue, *The Quarterly Review of Economics and Finance* 34 [1994]: 101–116 and Castelar Pinheiro, 2000) of the increases in national growth rates derivable from an "improved" justice system.

References

Abaid, Pablo, and Mariano Thieberger. 2005. *Justicia Era Kirchner: La construcción de un poder a medida.* Buenos Aires: Marea.

Álvarez, Gladys S., and Elena I. Highton. 2000. "Resolución alternativa de conflictos estado actual en el panorama latinoamericano." *California Western International Law Journal* 30 (2): 409–428.

Barker, Robert S. 2000. "Judicial Review in Costa Rica: Evolution and Recent Developments," *Southwestern Journal of Law and Trade in the Americas* 7(2): 267–290.

Binder, Alberto, and Jorge Obando. 2004. *De las "Repúblicas Aéreas" al Estado de Derecho.* Buenos Aires: Ad-Hoc.

Brazil, Poder Judiciário, Tribunal de Justiça do Rio de Janeiro. 2004. *Perfil das Maiores Demandas Judiciais do TJERJ.* Rio de Janeiro, August.

Castelar Pinheiro, Armando. 2003. "Judiciário, Reforma e Economia: A Visão dos Magistrados." Discussion draft number 966. Rio de Janeiro: IPEA. (On file with the author.)

———. 2000. *Judiciário e Economia no Brasil.* Sao Paulo: Editora Sumaré.

———. 2003. *Reforma do Judiciário: Problemas, Desafios, Perspectivas.* São Paulo: IDESP.

Centro de Estudios de Justicia de las Américas (CEJA). 2003. *Reporte sobre el Estado de la Justicia en las Américas, 2002–2003.* Santiago, Chile: Centro de Estudios de Justicia de las Américas.

———. 2005. *Reporte sobre el Estado de la Justicia en las Américas, 2004–2005.* Santiago, Chile: Centro de Estudios de Justicia de las Américas.

Correa Sutil, Jorge. 1999. "Judicial Reform in Latin America: Good News for the Underprivileged?" In *The (Un)Rule of Law and the Underprivileged in Latin America,* eds. Juan E. Méndez, Guillermo O'Donnell, and Paulo Sérgio Pinheiro, . Chicago: University of Notre Dame Press. 255–277

Dakolias, Maria. 1995. "A Strategy for Judicial Reform: The Experience in Latin America." *Virginia Journal of International Law* 36 (1): 167–231.

Díaz Rivillas, Borja Lejarraga, and Sebastián Linares Lejarraga. 2005. "Fortalecimiento de la Independencia judicial en Centroamérica: un balance tras veinte años de reformas," *América Latina Hoy,* 39: 47–96.

Djankov, Simeon, Rafael La Porta, Forencio Lopez-de-Silanes, and Andrei Schleifer. 2002. "Courts: The Lex Mundi Project." Draft report prepared for the World Bank, March. (On file with the author.)

Douat, Étienne. (2001). *Les budgets de la justice en Europe.* Paris: La Documentation Française.

Fuentes, Alfredo, and Carlos Amaya. 2001. "Demanda y oferta judicial: Dificultades de ajuste." Paper prepared for World Bank Conference, New Approaches to Meeting the Demand for Justice, México City, May 11.

Garavano, German C., Héctor M. Chayer, Milena Ricci, and Carlos Alejandro Cambellotti. 2000. *Los usuarios del sistema de justicia en Argentina.* Final Report for the World Bank, Foro de Estudios sobre Administración de Justicia (Fores), Buenos Aires, Argentina.

Gonzales Mantilla, Jean Carlo Serván Gorki, Luciano López, and Hernando Burgos. 2002. *El sistema judicial en el Perú: Un enfoque analítico a partir de sus usos y de sus usuarios.* Draft report prepared for the World Bank. (On file with the author.)

Hammergren, Linn. 2002. *Do Judicial Councils Further Judicial Reform? Lessons from Latin America.* Working Papers, Rule of Law Series, No. 26. Washington, D.C.: Carnegie Endowment for International Peace.

_____. 2003. "International Assistance to Latin American Justice Programs: Toward an Agenda for Reforming the Reformers." In *Beyond Common Knowledge: Empirical Approaches to the Rule of Law,* eds. Erik Jensen and Thomas Heller. Stanford: Stanford University Press. 290–335.

Henderson, Keith, Angana Shah, Sandra Elena, and Violaine Autheman. 2004. *Regional Best Practices: Enforcement of Judgments; Lessons from Latin America.* IFES Rule of Law Paper Series, April. Washington, D.C.: IFES

Hewko, John. 2002. *Foreign Direct Investment: Does Rule of Law Matter?* Working Papers, Rule of Law Series, No. 26. Washington, D.C.: Carnegie Endowment for International Peace.

Instituto de Defensa Legal. 1999. *La Justicia de Paz en debate.* Lima, Peru: Instituto de Defensa Legal.

Jobim, Nelson. 2003. "O processo do reforma sob a ótica do Judiciário." In *Reforma do Judiciário: Problemas, Desafios, Perspectivas,* ed., Armando Castelar Pinheiro, 13–40. São Paulo: IDESP.

Kaufmann, D., A. Kraay, and P. Zoido-Lobatón. 1999. *Governance Matters.* World Bank Policy Research Working Paper 2196. Washington, D.C.: World Bank.

_____. 2002. *Governance Matters II.* World Bank Policy Research Working Paper 2772. Washington, D.C.: World Bank.

La Porta, Rafael, and Florencio Lopez-de-Silanes. 1998. "Capital Markets and Legal Instititions." In *Beyond the Washington Consensus: Institutions Matter,* eds. Shahid Javed Burki and Guillermo Perry. Washington, D.C.: World Bank Latin American and Caribbean Region. 67–86.

Magaloni, Ana Laura, and Layda Negrete. n.d. "El Poder Judicial Federal y su política de decidir sin resolver." Unpublished draft, Mexico, Centro de Investigación y Docencia Económicas. (On file with the author.)

Mainwaring, Scott. 2003. "Introduction: Democratic Accountability in Latin America." In *Democratic Accountability in Latin America,* eds. Scott Mainwaring and Christopher Welna. Oxford: Oxford University Press. 3–33.

Mora Mora, Luis Paulino. 2001. "El Acceso a la Justicia en Costa Rica." Unpublished draft prepared for World Bank Regional Conference on New Trends in Justice Reform, México City, April. (On file with the author.)

North, Douglass. 1990. *Institutions, Institutional Change and Economic Performance.* Cambridge: Cambridge University Press.

Pásara, Luis. 2004. "Lecciones ¿aprendidas o por aprender?" In *En busca de una justicia distinta: Experiencias de reforma en América Latina,* Luis Pásara (org). Lima, Peru: Consorcio Justicia Viva. 515–570.

Pérez Perdomo, Rogelio. 2006. "Una evaluación de la reforma judicial en Venezuela." Paper prepared for CSIS Conference on Judicial Reform in Latin America: An Assessment, Washington, D.C., June 7.

Prillaman, William C. 2000. *The Judiciary and Democratic Decay in Latin America.* Westport, CT: Praeger.

Riego, Cristián. 2002. *Informe Comparativo.* Proyecto de Seguimiento de los Procesos de Reforma Judicial en América Latina. Santiago de Chile: Centro de Estudios de Justicia de la Américas.

Rojas, Flora Orlando Bareiro Aguilera, and Lourdes Cassanello. 2006. *Informe Final: Corte Suprema de Justicia.* Asunción: Centro Superior de Estudios Matemáticas y Financieros.

Sadek, Maria Tereza. 2004. "El poder judicial brasileiro." In *En busca de una justicia distinta: Experiencias de reforma en América Latina,* ed. Luís Pasara. Lima, Peru: Consorcio Justicia Viva. 89–140.

Sherwood, Robert M., Geoffrey Shepherd, and Celso Marcos de Souza. 1994. "Judicial Systems and Economic Performance." Special issue, *The Quarterly Review of Economics and Finance* 34: 101–116.

Sousa Santos, Boaventura de, and Maurico García Villegas, eds. 2001. *El caleidoscopio de las justicias en Colombia: Análisis socio-jurídico.* Bogota: Siglo de Hombre Editores and Universidad de los Andes.

Taylor, Matthew. 2004. *Activating Judges: Courts, Institutional Structure, and the Judicialization of Policy Reform in Brazil, 1988–2002.* Unpublished PhD dissertation, Department of Government, Georgetown University.

Uprimny, Rodrigo. 2001. "Legitimidad y conveniencia del control constitucional a la Economia." *Revista de Derecho Público* (Universidad de los Andes, Bogota) 12: 245–183.

Wilson, Bruce M., Juan Carlos Rodríguez Cordero, and Roger Handberg. 2004. "The Best Laid Schemes . . . Gang Aft A-gley: Judicial Reform in Latin America— Evidence from Costa Rica." *Journal of Latin American Studies* 36 (3): 507–532.

World Bank. 2002. *The Juicio Ejecutivo Mercantil in the Federal District Courts of Mexico: A Study of the Uses and Users of Justice and Their Implications for Judicial Reform.* Report No. 22635-ME. Washington, D.C.: World Bank.

———. 2003a. *An Analysis of Court Users and Uses in Two Latin American Countries.* Report No. 26966. Washington D.C.: World Bank.

———. 2003b. *Brazil: Judicial Performance and Private Sector Impacts.* Report No. 26261-BR. Washington, D.C.: World Bank.

———. 2005a. *Breaking with Tradition: Overcoming Institutional Impediments to Improve Public Sector Performance.* Report No. 31763-PY. Washington, D.C.: World Bank.

———. 2005b. *Doing Business in 2005: Removing Obstacles to Growth.* Washington, D.C.: World Bank, International Finance Corporation, and Oxford University Press.

———. 2005c. *Making Justice Count: Measuring and Improving Judicial Performance in Brazil.* Report No. 32789-BR. Washington, D.C.: World Bank.

CHAPTER 10

Property, the Rule of Law, and Development in the Americas

Peter F. Schaefer and P. Clayton Schaefer

The principal impediment to Latin America's competitiveness is the lack of credible commercial law, especially concerning property. Good property law is the foundation of free, impersonal, contract-based economies in the West. Without property law, entrepreneurship, commerce, and growth are stifled. Were the Latin American states able to create a modern legal environment, their transformation would open enormous new commercial markets with significant purchasing power that would demand First World goods and services.

To date, the region has been politically and technically unable to reform itself. Property rights, defined and protected by law, are missing from the commercial environment in nearly all of Latin America. Addressing this deficiency is critical for Latin America's competitiveness in the regional and global marketplace.

Up to now, private businesses have dealt with the lack of a national rule-set by creating their own special rules through negotiation with government officials. Although businesses understand the costs and disadvantages of such an ad hoc system, they have been unable or unwilling to push for comprehensive reform and impartial enforcement. However, negotiated rule-sets are always vulnerable to arbitrary changes, and they create political unrest by alienating citizens who do not enjoy the same rights as the national elite or multinational firms. Official development assistance (ODA) has not been able to foster this transformation despite decades of work and trillions of dollars. This failure suggests not that the task itself is impossible but that the means employed so far are flawed. If this transformation is to take place, private businesses themselves will be instrumental in bringing it about.

Global Commercial Law

Despite the existence of national legal systems that arose from a variety of very different traditions, there is an extensive and powerful global rule-set that applies to economic actors across the modern world. A businessman in New York City can purchase a house in the south of France without ever leaving his office because the legal systems have been harmonized for the purposes of commerce.

The contract to purchase the house is more than a piece of paper, and it represents more than a simple transfer of assets. The ability to enter into a contract with another person depends on such things as standards for disclosure, implied or explicit tax and lien liabilities, and the rights held by the contracting parties in both countries. The agreement to purchase also contains details of the payment schedule, currency, and the means of transferring the funds; and above all, it is sanctioned by law.

Globalization of Pre-Modern Countries

Transactions based on the global rule-set may also be conducted in parts of many developing countries because global rules have been extended to isolated pockets by elites who manage these rules for their own commercial benefit. These elites have been able to insulate their international transactions from their own imperfect national legal systems by, in effect, purchasing special rights not granted to the population.

To take part in the global economy in premodern countries, individuals and firms must exempt themselves from their own national system of law. Although systems of law exist mainly on paper, whatever force they have is bypassed by the elites and avoided by the poor. As a result, the nominal legal system applies to few, if any, citizens. The countries surveyed by the Institute for Liberty and Democracy (ILD) in its 2006 report make this point clear (figure 10.1).

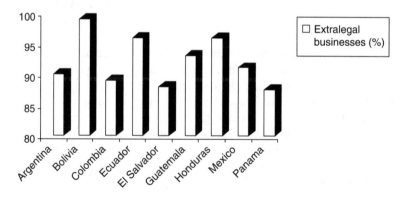

Figure 10.1 Extralegal business representation

Source: Institute for Liberty and Democracy, *Preliminary Evaluation of the Extralegal Economies of 12 Countries in Latin America and the Caribbean* (Lima, Peru: Institute for Liberty and Democracy, 2006).

The growing body of research on informality shows that elites throughout the world participate in the global economy by finding ways to accommodate their businesses to the various informal rule-sets that have evolved in place of a functioning national rule-set. In order to bring goods from producers in a poor country to consumers in a rich country, there are large numbers of firms, brokers, and government officials who earn profits by mediating between the myriad of local rule-sets and the relatively uniform global rule-set. However, these mediators drive up the transaction costs to the point that exports are often uncompetitive and imports are not affordable to the poor.

In countries with imperfect or repressive legal systems, as in most of Latin America, an individual or a business and their assets are invisible to the law and so do not exist in a legal sense. Because they and their property have no rights under the law, they cannot be subject to binding legal contracts. This decreases the value of assets and limits the efficiency of markets.

For extralegal businessmen and home owners, their contact with the law is almost nonexistent, although their contact with the "authorities" is nearly constant. Because the legal and regulatory environment is arbitrary and the state stands squarely in the way of legitimate economic activity, people establish their own informal rule-sets to acquire the predictability and security they need.

In modern countries, the structure of rights and obligations relating to people and assets is such that nearly everything is visible to the law and nearly all transactions adhere to rules and conventions accepted by all economic actors. Without this uniformity, transparency, and predictability, modern production and exchange would be impossible. A simple cash-and-carry market is the most that can be maintained without the confidence inspired by an impartial legal system.

A country may have a private market economy without it being a "capitalist" economy. Because predictability and security are essential to any market economy, rule-sets are formulated by every economic group no matter how small. To be "capitalist," however, the rule-sets governing exchange must define and protect assets and actions, both now and in the future for transactions that have not been completed. Commercial rule-sets define types of assets, what may be privately owned, and delineate what may be done with them. This is the essence of rules governing property both formal and informal. Formal systems necessarily harmonize all national rule-sets and so expand the market to the entire nation (and internationally) by rationalizing competing rules and enforcement mechanisms.

The essence of a modern, law-based economy is this ability to create a system of production and exchange based on agreements about future actions. For a national economy to compete globally, it must be integrated into the global rule-set by first creating an effective national rule-set that supports virtual transactions.

In May 2000, *Time* magazine published an article on the transformation of the world through the Internet. The picture they used to illustrate this was of a native Peruvian standing at an open-air Internet kiosk. This person wore a *serape* and a bowler hat, and looked every inch a poor Peruvian peasant. In reality, however, he represented a group of farmers who grew the ancient varieties of potatoes that were the staple of the pre-Colombian Andean society. By marketing on the Internet, he had found a group of gourmet restaurants in New York willing to buy the produce directly for ten times its local price.

Focusing on this as a success of the Internet is a mistake, however. The Internet is a useful tool, but the success story is really about the rule of law that enabled this transaction to take place. As detailed in Hernando de Soto's first book, *The Other Path*, rural property rights in Peru in support of small farmers had been an essential part of the strategy against the Shining Path and coca production. Having a national rule-set that could be integrated into the global economy was what allowed the technology to be put to productive use.

"Global competitiveness" means that individuals and firms are able to participate directly in the international marketplace, something denied to those people unlucky enough to be located in states whose laws do not meet the minimum requirements of the global rule-set. Although a small company's production may end up on the global market, the entry of these products must be brokered by elites.

The ability to compete in the international market is not just important to small businesses trying to sell goods on the global market but to multinational corporations trying to procure primary and intermediate goods in poor countries. The inability to sell to or buy directly from the world market excludes somewhere between 2.5 and 4 billion people from competitive exchange.

This competitive deficiency is one of ideas, not of money or things. What Latin America lacks is the rule of law that defines the rights and privileges of economic entities (people, businesses and property, both real and intellectual) and establishes the rule-sets that allow them to enter into binding contracts with one another. Many have argued that poverty is the reason that the markets of the developing world remain isolated from the global economy, but this formulation attributes causation to what is just another outcome of bad law.

The central problem of governments operating without the rule of law is that if a state is powerful enough to protect and enforce the arbitrary economic rules it creates (for contracts, taxes, trade, ownership, etc.), then it is necessarily powerful enough to endanger everyone's interests through confiscation or policy reversal. Without a credible guarantee that this will not take place, no one's property is safe. If making and applying rules is unconstrained by a more fundamental law that dictates which actions are impermissible to the state, then only corruption can arbitrate competing interests.

By and large, both the governments and the legal systems in Latin America are an incomplete and ineffective composite of liberal and authoritarian institutions managed by economic elites who continue to maintain relatively closed political economies. Fujimori in Peru used Hernando de Soto to liberalize parts of the Peruvian political economy, but used former spymaster Vladimiro Montesinos to maintain control. Hugo Chavez's rise is not a reaction to a failure of true liberalism, but rather to the failure of the "democratic mercantilism" of previous governments. Until the traditional economic elites in Latin America accept the need for—and most especially, see their own interests served by—true reform, Latin America must live with pendulum swings from radical left to radical right.

Above all other factors, the *main* requirement for the countries in the region to become modern is to create the necessary institutional reforms required for the transition to states that operate under the true rule of law. This issue is explored empirically in a paper entitled *The Primacy of Institutions over Geography and Integration in Economic Development* (Rodrik et al., 2002). The authors estimate the importance of institutions, geography, and trade on income levels. Their conclusion, using the most current analytic techniques, is that "the quality of institutions trumps everything else," although location and trade "have a strong indirect effect by influencing the quality of institutions."

The Latin American Context

After years of troubled reforms inspired by the Washington Consensus that advanced policies important to the developed world—specifically privatization, more open trade and investment, lower corporate taxes, and fiscal discipline—the rejection of neoliberalism is gaining momentum on the continent (see Table 10.1). The question often asked in developed countries is, why have we failed? How can Castro and Chávez and Morales be explained? How do we explain the return of an utterly failed former president of Peru, Alan Garcia, as anything but a failure of democratic capitalism itself? Unfortunately for the business community, the Latin American reality is anything but simple.

Table 10.1   Regional repressiveness in Latin America

Regional repressiveness rank	*Country*	*Fraser Institute index of economic freedom (10=Best)*
1	Venezuela	4.3
2	Colombia	5.5
3	Argentina	5.8
4	Ecuador	5.9
5	Brazil	5.9
6	Nicaragua	6.3
7	Paraguay	6.4
8	Bolivia	6.5
9	Mexico	6.5
10	Honduras	6.5
11	Guatemala	6.5
12	Uruguay	6.8
13	Peru	6.9
14	El Salvador	7.2
15	Panama	7.3
16	Costa Rica	7.4
17	Chile	7.4
	Latin America Average	6.4
	Zimbabwe	3.3
	India	6.4
	Hong Kong	8.7

Source: Gwartney and Lawson, 2004.

Nobel laureate Joseph Stiglitz, in a speech entitled *More Instruments and Broader Goals—Moving toward the Post-Washington Consensus* (1998), said: "The policies advanced by the [West] . . . are sometimes misguided. Making markets work requires more than just low inflation: it requires sound regulation, competition policy and policies to facilitate the transfer of technology and to encourage transparency."

Moreover, elections in many developing countries do little more than swap one corrupt autocrat for another, thus limiting reform. George Pendle, in *A History of Latin America,* says: "The social structure in the majority of the Latin American republics is still profoundly undemocratic. The widespread illiteracy and poverty . . . the concentration of land and political power in the hands of small minorities, these are factors inimical to the setting up of true democratic government—especially when they are combined with a tradition of authoritarianism and a highly personalist interpretation of politics." Pendle wrote this in 1963, and his analysis still holds.

The irony is that the left in Latin America is ideologically unprepared to fix the problems of law and institutions despite the fact that its primary constituents, the informal poor, would be the main beneficiaries of institutional reform. The solution of the radical left is to wield the arbitrary power of the state to punish elites and redistribute resources. This ignores the fact that the arbitrary exercise of state power itself perpetuates the underdevelopment of the nation.

In Mexico alone, the formalized assets of the poor, protected by law and connected with global credit markets, would provide them with hundreds of billions of dollars in new liquidity that, in turn, would have profound benefits for the government and domestic businesses. The apparent inability to enact these reforms is not a failure of democracy or of capitalism; it is a failure of ideas and understanding. To learn from this failure, we must examine three main elements: (1) the commercial law systems in Latin America (property rights/contracts), (2) the role of corruption, and (3) the importance of intellectual property rights.

The Rule of Law (ROL) and Competitiveness

Without a *common* rule-set—a legal *lingua franca* understood and accepted by all market participants—contracts are essentially meaningless. When different rule-sets overlap, their mandates and enforcement mechanisms may be incompatible with one another, thus driving up transaction costs and opening the door to corruption.

Good property law and its supporting economic institutions reduce transaction costs by lowering insecurity and diffusing information throughout markets. With competing or inconsistent rule-sets, commerce—whether across town or across national frontiers—is restricted and difficult.

International trade and investment pushes the process of harmonizing different national legal systems, but it does so first in those areas that are most important to multinational corporations. However, isolated pockets of good law in lawless societies are unsustainable. Either the rules will be expanded to cover the economic lives of the entire population or they will be destroyed by the redistributive demands of the extralegal poor whose work can never raise them out of poverty.

Anything less than a well-regulated, formal, national rule-set is inefficient and stifles economic activity. As such, the interests of all economic agents are served by sensible reform.

The Results of Imperfect Law

- Corruption will be pervasive because it is the accepted (often the only) way to resolve conflicts that arise from conflicting rule-sets.
- The majority of economic activity will be informal, resulting in fragmented national economies that exhibit little growth due to these inefficiencies.

In a recent report for the Inter-American Development Bank, the ILD demonstrates that the poor of just 12 Latin American countries hold 1.2 trillion dollars in extralegal assets, nearly all of which is held in real property and none of which is recognized by law. The central problem for these extralegal properties, which are the savings of most citizens, is that the state ascribes legal ownership to the state itself or to people other than the actual owners.

The informal savings of the poor are illiquid, literally trapped in immovable objects. Yet, the people who created this enormous pool of illiquid capital continue to save, despite their limited investment opportunities. With any surplus capital, they improve their homes and expand their businesses, but then these new savings become frozen so they have no access to their equity and no ability to leverage their growing assets in pursuit of better returns.

Informal ownership means that the full value of savings can never be made liquid through sale or used as collateral for loans. The inefficiency and limited scope of real estate markets mean that the sale price of property is often little more than the replacement value of labor and building materials. In a law-based system that protects property effectively, the sale price of these assets would also incorporate present and future land values and so would increase dramatically.

As a result of imperfect property law, the savings of the poor are in constant jeopardy since they cannot be diversified, protected by the police, or converted to something that can be protected by a bank. The irony here is that the informal poor require government action creating new rule-sets to liberate them from their poverty.

The poor are well aware of the huge costs of their informality, but the institutions that shape their economic lives leave them no choices. The few well-implemented property reforms of the last century suggest that the poor are eager to be a part of a legal system that protects their assets. Perhaps the most powerful example of this can be found in Peru. In his book *The Other Path* (revision 2002), de Soto describes in detail how his program allowed President Fujimori to literally destroy the Shining Path insurgency through the provision of property rights for their small coca farms. In less than a year, the Shining Path went from an 84,000-man army in control of large areas of Peru to almost nothing. The formalization of property in the coca regions was entirely voluntary but, nevertheless, nearly universal. Even more surprising, the destruction of the Shining Path was not the main objective but rather was a natural reaction of the poor farmers who chose the state's formal defense of their property over the Shining Path's informal guarantee.

Creating a Formal Legal and Regulatory Regime

Historically, the United States led the way for the establishment of the norms of civil law that underlie all modern states. However, in Latin America, governments have relied on U.S. models for change, both voluntarily and involuntarily, but with little success. In fact, policy prescriptions of American origin are increasingly impossible to sell to the publics of Latin America (Green, 2003).

Fortunately, the United Nation's (UN's) *Universal Declaration of Human Rights* (1948) states that "everyone has the right to own property alone as well as in association with others [and] no one shall arbitrarily be deprived of his property." All the countries of Latin America are signatories, and so with the UN as the philosophical basis for policy reform, the program may be sold as an extension of existing Latin American values, not the imposition of Western values.

The process of extending the protection the poor demand begins by discovering their own informal rule-sets. The features of these existing informal rule-sets must be adapted in the drafting, marketing (after all, subscribing to formal rules is voluntary, based on personal cost benefit that has to be explained), and implementation of a formal rule-set that variously harmonizes, co-opts, and replaces their informal norms.

It is the combination of stability and efficiency that, when offered to the informal poor, will draw them out of the shadow economy. Those managing this transformation must understand that while most people will "opt-in" to a formal system that is well conceived, they will opt back out if it degenerates into a corrupt, rent-seeking process that will probably become too costly. This raises two issues that need a more full discussion for the business community: corruption and intellectual property rights.

Corruption

In modern countries, we consider corruption to be a personal, moral failure. The impulse to corruption in the United States is nearly always due to greed. However, in developing countries, corruption is a far more complex phenomenon. Corruption is both a logical and even necessary result of complex mercantile systems that function without the rule of law.

On June 16, 2006, the US Millennium Challenge Corp. (MCC) removed Gambia from its list of countries approved for assistance. In contrast with the United States' traditional diplomatic stance toward the corrupt leaders of the developing world, it was a courageous decision, but it was also a risky one since most developing countries are governed by autocrats, even when they are elected. Some are thugs, some are benign, some are even well-meaning reformers, but their administrations all have little choice but to engage in corruption. They have no alternative because it is impossible to "play by the rules" if there is no established rule-set.

Rule of law, adjudicated by even-handed justice, simply does not exist *anywhere* in the developing world, and this is the real culprit that stifles development and condemns the poor to life in zero-sum societies. *All* developing countries are failed states to one degree or another, and most of their citizens are miserably poor. In fact, even calling them "developing" is misleading because it suggests an upward spiral. These people are the great-grandchildren of individuals who were poor a half-century ago when the significant expansion of foreign aid began.

In the eyes of the people, the state becomes inseparable from the system of tribute and bribery that keeps it in business. Since this system is not just accepted but actively reinforced by a dispersed network of beneficiaries, corruption becomes the organizing principle of society. This is the situation in most of Latin America.

Once corruption is institutionalized, demands by aid donors that governments "control corruption" are not just impossible to meet, but could even be dangerous and destabilizing for recipient governments. You cannot simply eliminate a basic ordering principle of a society and economy without replacing it. At present, the options are corruption or chaos, and no one can seriously believe that either government officials or the people would choose the latter. Only the ROL can supplant corruption as an ordering principle, but the commitment to make the transition is not present at the moment in Latin America.

Intellectual Property Rights (IPR)

There is an enormous global establishment that believes—indeed is often organized around the belief—that IPR are not important to poor countries. Opposition to IPR is a mainstay of the antiglobalization movement as evidenced by such NGOs as NoLogo and many more. They seem to believe that in the developing world, medicine, software, books, records, clothing, CDs, DVDs, new designs and technology, and an array of other modern and modernizing items should be provided for free or nearly free, ignoring the huge research, design, and development costs.

This situation is compounded by many governments that, at best, turn a blind eye to counterfeiting and, at worst, officially sanction such policies by allowing businesses that do not respect IPR to operate under their protection. The production of generic AIDS drugs in places such as Brazil, South Africa, and China, and the widespread piracy of Microsoft products by Latin America's governments themselves are prime examples of the institutional disregard for IPR.

Government complicity, in one form or another, highlights the important point that the lack of both IPR and real property rights are evidence of failed property law systems, a failure that profoundly inhibits investment, innovation, commerce, and, thus, the growth of Latin America. A country may have low taxes, tariffs, and duties; a good location; and low labor costs, but if potential investors cannot protect their capital, their technology, and their products, they will not invest. As Alvaro Vargas Llosa notes in his recent article "Will Mexico 'Jump to the Top?'" (2006), many companies have migrated from Mexico to China because of the high hidden costs of doing business there, and yet even China has a poor record of protecting property rights, especially IPR.

Some years ago, the government of China simply expropriated a McDonald's franchise in Shanghai. Even the poorest Chinese observer would intuitively understand that the owner had been wronged, notwithstanding the law or, in this case, the legal justification. This is because they own homes, probably shops, or workplaces, so they sympathize with McDonald's because they can relate to the prospect of their property being confiscated. No matter what the justification under Chinese law, they would resist the forfeit of their real property and believe that they were victims of injustice. In fact, there have been ongoing riots over land confiscations in rural China for the last several years to such a degree that they are threatening national stability.

The Chinese person who stands up against his government in such a situation has no qualm buying a pirated copy of Windows in order to run his computer. To the average Chinese person, there is no relationship between their own real property rights and IPR of foreign firms.

For a poor, uneducated person who lives with no property rights, just trying to survive day to day, the notion of owning an idea is hard to grasp. As a result, resisting the illegal use of intellectual property is a difficult notion to sell.

On the streets of every large U.S. city there are people hawking "designer" clothes, glasses, and watches. Some of these are top quality; in fact, they are often made "off the books" on the same production line as the branded goods. To the person selling a "Gucci" pocketbook on the corner, the value of that item is in the plant, equipment, labor, raw materials, and his profit, not in such abstractions as copyright, design, and development and marketing costs. Yet, it is just these intangibles that represent the "value added" for a firm such as Gucci. This is what a knockoff salesman is stealing.

Life-saving medicines create even more difficult issues than illegally downloaded music or knockoff products because the debate is cast in highly charged terms of life and death. Poor patients rarely, if ever, have access to medical insurance and so lack good medical care. Still, modern drugs can provide miraculous cures. When large numbers of people can benefit from a new therapy, national drug policy quickly becomes politically charged and subject to considerable demagoguery. When drugs seem to be too expensive for most people, governments blame the manufacturers rather than evaluating the total cost of drugs and working on different approaches that can lessen political and commercial confrontations.

At the 2006 G-8 Summit, leaders of the Group of Eight industrialized nations called for lower customs duties on drug imports to bring medicine and medical technology within easier reach for people in the world's poorest countries. Another option is the licensing of generic medicines, in effect a contract negotiated between the states of the developing world and the drug companies of the West.

Such creative solutions based on compromise between producers and consumers across the globe are necessary because, realistically, no educational program in a poor country will enhance respect for IPR enough to be noticed by large owners of intellectual property. In fact, because the consumers are poor, there is little that can be done to change the structure of market demand for pirated goods. Even enforcement is difficult in a country where the police are likely no better off than their fellow citizens.

Unfortunately, in a political economy where the use of corruption to protect business interests is pervasive, neither the manufacturers nor the magistrates are able to make a distinction between one kind of extralegal business or another. In Mexico, approximately 60 percent of assets are informal. In Haiti, it is close to 100 percent. Why should a Haitian care about Microsoft's IPR? The man patching flat tires in his backyard is just as "illegal" as the man selling DVDs on the corner. They both pay the bribe and keep earning a living.

The first step in combating the problem of piracy is to promote widespread property rights. Only someone whose own rights are protected can develop respect for the rights of others, whether real property or IPR. The possession and exercise of a right is, by definition, reciprocal; if your fellow men do not believe that you have a particular right, you do not have it. If no one believes you own your home, then your claim is not valid, no matter what legal codes say. With that said, establishing a widely accepted national property law system is a *necessary* first step in untying the knot of extralegality that allows counterfeiters to operate openly. The full protection of real property requires an understanding of assets not as objects in space but as virtual representations, pieces of information attached to objects. The representations are transportable, divisible, transferable, and controlled exclusively by the owners.

This leap from the physical to the virtual is not inconsequential. The notion is fundamental to the capitalist market system, and from it flows the understanding that intellectual property is fundamentally the same as real property. When they come to the market, both real and intellectual property are little more than data in a true capitalist system. Correcting this fundamental misunderstanding of the mercantile world and unraveling centuries of Latin American cronyism will not be quick or easy.

However, the weak point in the entire global system of counterfeiting is with the counterfeiters themselves. Someone illegally copying software, medicine, or handbags is a software producer, a pharmaceutical company, or a clothing manufacturer. Their daily activities change very little just because they are pirates. The only thing that will end the theft of intellectual property is bringing them into the legal economy, not putting them in jail. People schooled in supply and demand will, as they do with international drug markets, answer that so long as there is a demand for drugs (or software or medicine) there will be illegal producers.

However, as counterfeiters evolve into legal producers under a legitimate property rights system, they become innovators with their own intellectual property to protect. These newly legal producers will become the agents of change in pressing for the protection of their own IPR, but to do so they will necessarily support a system that protects all IPR. Counterfeiting will be a threat to them just as it is to Microsoft or Merck, and opposing it will be part of their cost of entering the global market.

National Transformation

So the question now is, how do we fix such complex and politically charged problems? The first step, of course, is to sell the idea of reform to the various domestic constituencies, which is say the average citizen, the government, and the business community. This is discussed in detail in the following section. For multinationals, the question is how do firms and individuals in the rich countries help governments put property law in place? The techniques were discussed at length above, but it is important to keep in mind that formalization begins by accepting those informal rules already shared in common and continues through the selection of the best from any competing rules that remain. For sophisticated, new functions—such as protecting IPR or defending international contracts—the process may incorporate foreign institutional designs, adapted to local conditions as necessary, to fill the gaps. Once a nation has forged a common, national rule-set that is adjudicated openly and altered politically, there are a number of benefits that will accrue to a country that follows the rule of law in commerce.

Selling Reform

Property rights and good civil law are not sufficient to stimulate a process of modernization, but they are certainly necessary. No country has become modern without such a legal and regulatory environment, and there is no reasonable scenario that can project the creation of a modern state without modern law. To improve competitiveness in Latin America, countries in the region must address their informality.

While the process of formalization begins with writing good law, publishing the legal codes in a public registry is only the first step. It is impossible to force an entire society to obey the law if they decide it is not in their interests to do so. What the "consent of the governed" really means is that individual citizens and groups decide that it is in their best interest to live under a common rule-set and so *choose* to obey the law. People and groups have different interests, and so the common rule-set must accommodate the majority interests to succeed. Protecting wealth and economic opportunity is a common objective of all groups and any successful rule-set begins with this.

Because there is little growth, informal societies often have zero-sum economies. If groups compete by dividing a fixed pool of resources, conflict will be intense and often violent. For instance, the government needs revenue while the individual wants to conserve the maximum amount of his capital by paying the least amount of taxes.

Once both taxation and capital accumulation are understood to be indispensable parts of a functioning economy and that governments provide useful services with the money they take in, debate about the optimal levels of taxation and accumulation can be meaningful. To make the case that the "the modern state should exist," we must consider the interests of the three most important groups of stakeholders: (1) the poor and informal, (2) the formal businesses and elites, and (3) the government. The following discussion concerns the respective benefits to each group.

Benefits to the Poor

In the Field and Torero study (2002) of Peruvian "new towns," the reason given for a near doubling of family income was that they no longer needed to maintain continuous occupancy to protect their homes because the state now protected their assets. Since the bulk of informal assets are held by the poor, the surge of economic growth resulting from their formalization will create a more equitable distribution of income.

It isn't just income and wealth that will change for the poor. Their quality of life will improve substantially due to increased visibility and access to utilities. Now, water, power, and telephone service are simply not available in extralegal settlements. This is not because informals have no money to pay (in fact they usually pay more than middle-class residents who are on the grid) but because utility companies cannot verify addresses or enforce contracts with these clients.

Hookups are sold to the poor by moonlighting power company electricians because utilities cannot penetrate this market. One report indicated that in Mexico City, 40 percent of all power produced by the local power utility was stolen (Sullivan, 2004). With formalization, utility companies are able to identify the home owner, thus making hookups sufficiently safe and profitable to businesses.

In addition to greatly increasing family income, the Field study also found that in newly formalized communities in Peru, there was an almost 30 percent increase in school attendance, mainly consisting of girls who no longer had to stay home and help their housebound mothers or guard the family's property. Informal assets are illiquid savings. By becoming liquid, the assets can be both invested and saved safely by the poor.

Government Benefits

Because formalization is a necessary condition for balanced growth, because prosperity is good for politicians, and because a bigger and more transparent economy means increased tax revenues, governments have an enormous incentive to carry out formalization programs. By definition, any country that acquires an enormous pool of new, liquid investment capital will grow. This will create the basis for both individuals and governments to prosper because there will be increased tax revenues based on appreciating assets and rising incomes. De Soto's research shows that the extralegal economy in Mexico has nearly US$400 billion in assets and nearly US$600 billion in annual economic activity. A modest, reasonable property tax and turnover tax of 1 percent per year, calculated against an expanded tax base of US$1 trillion annually, would yield US$10 billion per year in new public revenues. According to the 2005 *World Development Report,* this amount is the same as *all* foreign direct investment into Mexico, and it could easily cover Mexico's US$3 billion per year budget deficit.

In addition to property and business taxes, personal income taxes will rise. As noted, the Field study of Peruvian communities after formalization found that family income nearly doubled (Field and Torero, 2002). With a dramatically larger tax base and better cash flow, Latin America's governments could end their reliance on confiscatory and trade-distorting taxes and deficit spending, while still improving and expanding their services.

In a formalized legal environment, governments are better able to license utility companies to deliver services to poor communities rather than borrowing money from development banks. As a result, they will be able to reduce their reliance on foreign aid and loans from the West. This lowered government debt will impact the currency as well. An even greater impact on the currency will be the process of creating money. The creation of currency to monetize the debt of newly formal property owners would strengthen the currency, not weaken it through deficit spending, since this new money would be backed by hard assets used for investment rather than to feed consumption.

There is also a national security interest in formalization. Informal shanty towns are faceless, and this anonymity allows criminals and revolutionaries to live in relative security. This will be diminished by identifying owners and addresses of residences.

Business Community

In history, no country has ever become modern through government action alone. Governments create the environment for economic activity, but *only* the private sector can run a modern economy. Pursuing a process of formalization is only meaningful if the private sector—from micro to large businesses—participates.

All sizes of business in Latin America operate by purchasing privileges in the absence of clearly defined rights. Small businesses pay bribes just for the right to exist, and, as a class, these poor extralegal businessmen are undercapitalized. It is not uncommon for microentrepreneurs to pay 10 percent *per day* for loans. Normal, securitized credit will be a tiny fraction of their former capital costs and as a result, it must be expected that there will be substantial demand for new loans that in turn will generate new business activity.

Lending costs for both small and large businesses will be reduced, since loans to local financial institutions from foreign lenders will be less risky. As extralegal savings become liquid, they will add to the pool of capital national savings that can then be used for lending to businesses and government.

If the market value of previously informal assets increases substantially and can be made liquid through sale or credit, consumer demand will increase to the benefit of any business that can produce the things the poor want. And they will have the cash to pay for it. The World Bank notes that the value of rural land in Brazil, Indonesia, the Philippines, and Thailand increases by anywhere from 43 percent to 81 percent after being titled. For urban land, titling increases the value by 14 percent in Manila and up to 58 percent in Davao, Philippines.

As the poor enter the national market, their demands for goods and services, capital equipment, and credit will be met mainly by the local business class. As a result, both domestic businesses and their foreign suppliers will benefit from emerging markets.

Trade will expand because export-oriented manufacturers will be more competitive since their cost of money and input prices will be reduced. Since the time of Adam Smith, the essence of productivity has been seen as specialization, so the growth of large businesses through trade will present more opportunities to small businesses by allowing them to engage in processing raw materials or subcontracting for components. Presently, these sorts of contractual arrangements are nearly impossible for extralegal businesses that operate without contract enforcement mechanisms.

One of the greatest privileges conferred by law is the right to incorporate and, so, limit liability. In *The Company* (Mickelthwait and Woolridge, 2003), the authors state that "the most important organization in the world is the company: the basis of the prosperity of the West and the best hope for the future of the world." Starting in the United States in the early nineteenth century, incorporation became a right, not a privilege. The innovation spread throughout the country and Europe within a decade and, by the end of the century, to Britain's colonies in Asia. Almost a century later, the right of incorporation became an important part of the economic miracles of the former Crown colonies of Singapore, Malaysia, and Hong Kong.

But in an extralegal economy, there is simply no mechanism by which entities can incorporate. Therefore, the enormous benefits of incorporation are denied to all but a small handful of firms, and even they purchase this right that is maintained through the goodwill of the politicians.

An economy with a good property rights system will also increase respect for IPR not only of large, established foreign firms but also for firms of all sizes throughout Latin America that will have greater security and motivation to develop their own intellectual property. The recent economic history of such formerly flagrant IPR violators such as Taiwan and Korea (and increasingly India) shows that the ability to protect your own property through law creates strong, law-based momentum to protect all intellectual property, domestic as well as foreign.

Conclusion

Formalization by providing property right systems is the only way to create the elusive "rising economic tide" in Latin America. Every group—citizens, governments, and businesses—will benefit profoundly from formalizing the extralegal economy. Being legal means that transactions are protected by law so the mechanisms of a modern economy—contracts, loans, financial instruments, incorporation—are available to anyone who chooses to have them.

Moreover, connecting the most basic interests of the voters to the political system will create a greater sense of responsibility of citizenship and, thus, a greater interest in good government, which can only be realized by electing officials willing to act for the majority interests. By connecting changes in the rules to an open political process, democracy will become relevant to the lives of the poor majority of the population, giving people a stake in the political system and making them co-owners of their societies instead of wards of the state.

References

DeLong, Seth. 2005. "Venezuela's Agrarian Land Reform: More Like Lincoln Than Lenin" *Venezuela Analysis.* http://www.venezuelanalysis.com/articles.php?artno=1384.

De Soto, Hernando. 1989. *The Other Path: The Invisible Revolution in the Third World.* New York: Basic Books.

———. 2000. *The Mystery of Capital: Why Capitalism Triumphs in the West and Fails Everywhere Else.* New York: Basic Books.

Easterly, William. 2006. *The White Man's Burden: Why the West's Efforts to Aid the Rest Have Done So Much Ill and So Little Good.* New York: Penguin.

Field, E., and M. Torero. 2002. *Do Property Titles Increase Credit Access among the Urban Poor? Evidence from Peru.* Research Program in Development Studies Working Paper. Princeton: Princeton University Press.

Green, Duncan. 2003. *Silent Revolution: The Rise and Crisis of Market Economies in Latin America.* New York: Monthly Review Press.

Gwartney, James, and Robert Lawson. 2004. *Economic Freedom of the World: 2004 Annual Report.* Vancouver: Fraser Institute.

Locke, John. 1690. *Two Treatises on Government.* Book 2, *Of Civil Government,* London: John Bumpus.

Mickelthwait, John, and Adrian Woolridge. 2003. *The Company.* New York: Modern Library.

Miles, Marc, Edwin Feulner, Mary Anastasia O'Grady. 2005. *2005 Index of Economic Freedom.* Washington: Heritage Foundation.

Millenium Challenge Corporation. 2006. *Fiscal Year 2006 Country Data.* Washington, D.C.: Millennium Challenge Corporation.

Neuwirth, Robert. 2005. *Shadow Cities: A Billion Squatters, A New Urban World.* New York: Routledge.

Pendle, George. 1963. *A History of Latin America.* Baltimore: Penguin.

República Bolivariana de Venezuela. 2001. *Lineas Generales del Plan de Desarrollo Económico y Social de la Nación 2001–2007.* Caracas: República Bolivariana de Venezuela.

Rodrik, Dani, Arvind Subramanian, Francesco Trebbi. 2002. "Institutions Rule: The Primacy of Institutions over Geography and Integration in Economic Development." NBER Working Paper Series, Working Paper 9305. http://www.nber.org/papers/w9305.

Stiglitz, Joseph. 1998. "More Instruments and Broader Goals—Moving toward the Post-Washington Consensus." Wider Annual Lecture, Helsinki, January.

Sullivan, Kevin. 2002. "Power Pirates Leave Mexico City in the Dark." *Washington Post,* January 20.

United Nations. 1948. *Universal Declaration of Human Rights.* New York: United Nations.

Valdes, Juan Gabriel. 1995. *Pinochet's Economists: The Chicago School of Economics in Chile.* New York: Cambridge University Press.

Vargas Llosa, Alvaro. 2006. "Will Mexico 'Jump to the Top?'" *Wall Street Journal.* July 6.

World Bank. 1998. *Assessing Aid: What Works, What Doesn't and Why.* Oxford: Oxford University Press.

———. 2005a. *Doing Business in 2005: Removing Obstacles to Growth.* Oxford: Oxford University Press.

———. 2005b. *World Development Report: A Better Investment Climate for Everyone.* Oxford: Oxford University Press.

Zakaria, Fareed. 2003. *The Future of Freedom: Illiberal Democracy at Home and Abroad.* New York: Norton.

CHAPTER 11

Tax Reform: Tax Policy, Reform, and Competitiveness in Latin America

*Mauricio Carrizosa**

Taxes are often regarded as a major determinant to competitiveness. Taxes rank second, after policy uncertainty, in the list of major or severe obstacles identified in the World Bank's Investment Climate Assessments (ICAs) that survey business firms across the world.[1] Taxes also enter into the World Economic Forum's competitiveness index published annually in the Global Competitiveness Report (GCR) and into the Indices of Economic Freedom constructed by the Heritage Foundation and the Fraser Institute.[2] Other major or severe obstacles listed in ICAs are, in descending order, macroeconomic instability, corruption, finance, employment barriers, licenses and customs, courts, labor, crime, and infrastructure.

Expenditure, Taxes, Competitiveness, and Growth

When assessing the impact of taxes on competitiveness, it is inevitable to consider how taxes are linked to public expenditures. Under Milton Friedman's well-known observation:

> You cannot reduce the deficit by raising taxes. Increasing taxes only results in more spending, leaving the deficit at the highest level conceivably accepted by the public. Political Rule Number One is government spends what government receives plus as much more as it can get away with.[3]

There are two other competing hypotheses,[4] but none disputes that both variables are closely related. Increased expenditure, say in response to demand for public services or to political pressure (e.g., for higher public wages), is primarily met with present and future tax increases, including increases in the inflation tax, the 100 percent implicit taxation of "non-tax" revenues (e.g., profits of public enterprises), and borrowing. In the other direction, tax increases raise expenditure through revenue sharing and earmarking arrangements, and by providing governments with the space to spend even more.

Be that as it may, public expenditures also help determine competitiveness. Accordingly, the GCR index mentioned above also captures multiple indicators of public sector outputs or outcomes from its expenditures. Property rights, diversion of public funds, wastefulness of government spending, reliability of police services, infant mortality, primary education enrollment, and government debt are a few examples. Similarly, some of the major obstacles listed in ICAs (e.g., courts) are closely linked to public expenditures.

If we define competitiveness as the set of country attributes that help generate economic growth, it makes sense to assess the competitiveness impact of taxes and public expenditures by focusing directly on their growth impact. The most readily available indicator of the public sector burden is general government consumption, which is closely correlated with taxation.[5] As in most regions, Latin America's average government consumption, expressed as a percentage of gross domestic product (GDP), has increased over the years. As shown in figure 11.1, government consumption increased by 4 percentage points of GDP during the 30-year period ending in 2004, more than in any other region. Despite its faster growth, government consumption in Latin America is still lower than in the OECD (Organisation for Economic Co-operation and Development) countries, but it is now higher than in Asia. Government consumption expenditure growth varied considerably from country to country.

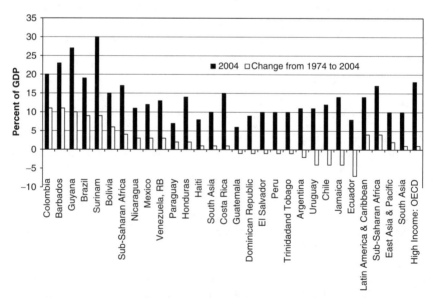

Figure 11.1 General government consumption

Source: National Accounts, World Development Indicators, CD-ROM, World Bank, 2005.

What is the growth impact of increased public consumption expenditures? In Latin America, cross-country econometrics has estimated that doubling the ratio of government consumption to GDP reduces per capita growth by around one percentage point,[6] not an insignificant amount.

The impact of government consumption also depends on its quality, of course. In econometric cross-country growth equations, governance often appears with a significant positive impact on the rate of growth, perhaps capturing the beneficial effect of the quality of public services. For 2005, the governance indicator shows, as expected, that the average rank of Latin American countries was above the Africa average and below the OECD average. Within Latin America, Chile ranked best[7] while five countries ranked at low levels similar to those of several African countries.

What about the growth impact of public investment? In 2004, the ratio of public investment to GDP in Latin America amounted to, for example, 3.1 percent in Chile, 3.5 percent in Mexico, 5.3 percent in Ecuador, 9.8 percent in Nicaragua, and 11.4 percent in Guyana. While public investment responds to development and competitiveness needs, particularly infrastructure needs, it is sometimes associated with poor project choice (e.g., white elephants), poor management, and excessive public indebtedness. For Latin America, some research suggests that both public and private investment contribute to growth, but that government consumption expenditures have a negative effect on growth, as discussed in the previous paragraph.[8] The potentially positive contributions of public investment reflect its role in creating infrastructure, a variable that many growth regressions show as having a positive effect on growth. However, causality analysis suggests that the effect may run the other way; that is, from growth to public investment.[9] Be that as it may, the impact of investment on growth depends on its quality, which is often undermined by poor project choice or implementation.

The total tax burden typically has an adverse effect on growth, as discussed above, but the tax structure may also affect growth. It is well acknowledged that a higher share of trade taxes in total taxes discourages growth. Recent research on specific countries suggests that the share of taxes on income may also affect growth adversely. And it is often argued that funding subnational expenditures with intergovernmental transfers raises subnational expenditures more than locally raised taxes would (the flypaper effect), and thus may both increase the total size of the public sector and discourage growth.

What do these expenditure and tax considerations imply for growth-friendly fiscal policy? First, constraints on public expenditure growth and reduced expenditure rigidities will help break the cycle that has led a number of countries to excessive public sector sizes. Second, countries with huge public sectors will benefit not only from reducing expenditure but also from improving the sector's effectiveness. Third, reallocating expenditure from public consumption to public investment, improving public investment management, and opening up opportunities for replacing public investment with private investment will more often than not raise growth.

These expenditure policies have a bearing on what the appropriate tax policies should be. Depending on the direction of causality, constraints on expenditure (taxes) growth will reduce pressure to increase taxes (expenditures). Changing the size of government will change the needed tax burden accordingly. Reallocating expenditures to investment may allow a reduction in the tax burden (if it leads to a substitution of private for public investment) and may also change the appropriate tax structure toward more borrowing (i.e., future taxes). Restructuring taxation away from trade taxes and toward consumption taxes will also help growth. Finally, encouraging funding of local expenditures with local taxation will also contain the public sector burden.

With this background on the effect of taxes and expenditures on competitiveness and growth, we now turn to a review of tax policies in Latin America.

Tax Policy Trends

There are, perhaps, three key, broad tax policy trends in Latin America. First, between 1960 and 2004, government consumption expanded at an average rate in several Latin American countries, and at a considerably higher rate in some. The tax revenue/GDP ratio increased correspondingly. Second, tax structures have changed, with trade taxes declining and income, value-added, inflation, and deferred (borrowing) taxes increasing. Third, although subnational taxation has increased somewhat, it remains weak and dwarfed by increased intergovernmental transfers toward subnational governments. On the other hand, Latin America's competitiveness, as measured by the path of relative per capita GDP,[10] has declined with respect to much of the rest of the world. Measured at purchasing power parity, the ratio of Latin America's per capita GDP to the world's per capita GDP declined by about 20 percent between the mid and the late twentieth century. Compared to the "Asian Tigers," it declined by 60 percent.

Taxation needs are, of course, larger than public consumption needs because taxation must also cover investment, interest, and transfer payments (primarily pensions), with the latter two often resulting from prior unfunded commitments (e.g., unfunded pension arrangements or debt-financed investments without cost recovery). Taxation will have a stronger adverse effect on growth to the extent that interest and pension payments crowd out investment and service delivery. For example, in Argentina, public consumption (expenditure on wages and goods and services) was 11 percent of GDP in 2004; other expenditures, including investment, pensions, interest, and investment raised total expenditures to 25.2 percent of GDP. Argentina raised revenues of about 29 percent of GDP primarily in taxes and social security contributions in 2004 to help defray these costs. Thus, while Argentina is a fairly small state from the perspective of service provision, it is large from the perspective of total expenditures and thus of taxation. Public expenditures expanded to 31 percent of GDP in 2001 from 22 percent in 1990, and then declined to 22 percent in 2002. The excess of total public expenditure over government consumption expenditures is also significant in several other Latin American countries, including Brazil, Colombia, Honduras, Nicaragua, Paraguay, and Uruguay.

There are several theories that have aimed to explain expenditure expansion. The Leviathan Hypothesis, whereby "government is a monolithic entity trying to maximize size and revenue"[11] is implicit in the Friedman quotation cited earlier. Other hypotheses view public sector size, and hence taxation, as responding to other phenomena. Among these are (a) as nations industrialize, the share of the public sector in the national economy grows continually to meet increased demand for administrative and protective actions, social and welfare actions, and large investments; (b) the variance of private employment (with public expenditure an insurance mechanism); (c) "high" public sector wages, set by governments to increase political support from government workers; (d) income inequality, triggering more redistribution through the public sector; (e) trade openness, where a government's size increases to fund compensatory subsidies to losers of trade reform; and (f) the "natural resource curse," where governments spend the revenues of commodity price booms and thereby increase the size of the state.

Did changes in the tax structure also contribute to Latin America's disappointing competitiveness? There are two aspects to this question. First, changes in tax structure reflect improvements in tax collection technology. The widespread introduction of value added taxes (VAT) partly reflects governments taking advantage of this tax over the income tax to collect taxes more effectively. Second, changes in tax structure altered the overall distortionary makeup of the tax system. Most likely, the decline in the importance of trade taxes improved economic efficiency. This decline has been systematic in all countries, although trade taxes remain an important source of revenue in many of the smaller countries. The removal of exemptions, stronger enforcement, and lower tax rates on income may also have increased tax neutrality and reduced distortions; but higher VAT rates have increased distortions in this tax, which also remains strongly non-neutral. Moreover, in a number of cases, new taxes reduced efficiency. This particularly includes the tax on financial transactions, a very productive albeit distortionary tax applied in Argentina, Brazil, Colombia, Peru, and Venezuela.[12]

The other broad development is increased decentralization of expenditures financed by transfers. Decentralization of expenditures has been a very strong trend in a few countries during the last two decades, encouraged by enhanced local political power and the desire to improve effects "on the ground." Its effect on expenditures has been important in countries such as Colombia and Brazil, and is likely to have a similar impact in the many countries that are pursuing it. It is frequently noted, nonetheless, that in many cases decentralization of expenditures has gone too far for the absorption capacity and governance of local governments.

Selected Tax Reform Experiences

What follows is a brief review of tax policies in selected countries since the 1970s to illustrate the common trends and diversity of those polices in Latin America. It shows the considerable impact of radical political change, the frequent expansionary response of expenditures to attempts at closing deficits with tax increases, the trend toward VAT taxation, and the more recent trend toward reduced income tax rates. The review covers tax policy in Guyana and Nicaragua, where the role of political change has been considerable; Ecuador and Mexico, where oil revenues have played a strong role; and Chile, where tax policy has been the most consistent with competitiveness and growth.

Nicaragua

Nicaragua illustrates well the role of political change and of expenditure growth in shaping tax policies. Political change to the left in the late 1970s led to a decade of extreme distress in public finances, where declining GDP and rapidly expanding expenditures combined to fully derail macroeconomic stability. In the early 1990s, new political change to the center marked the beginning of efforts to reestablish fiscal balance through tax reforms. The country's tax reforms since then have systematically responded to financing gaps created by growing expenditures. This increased the overall tax burden and may have contributed to lower growth, but the measures contained in the early 1990s reforms improved the quality of the tax system for the growing size of the overall tax burden. The reform measures reduced discrimination against imports, improved horizontal neutrality of the core taxes, reduced the inflation tax, and made some progress in reducing income tax rates and improving compliance.

Nicaragua faced two major shocks during the 1970s: the 1972 earthquake and, later, a full-scale civil war that led to a regime change when the socialist Sandinista revolutionary forces deposed the old Somoza dictatorship in 1979. The earthquake and the war produced major economic, human, and physical losses and disruption. Macroeconomic stability began to weaken after the earthquake and output began to fall in 1978. In 1979 alone, per capita GDP declined by almost 30 percent. By the end of the Sandinista regime in 1990, per capita GDP had declined by about 58 percent compared to its peak in 1977 (see figure 11.2).

The Sandinista government nationalized a considerable share of private properties. To finance higher expenditures, the government printed more money, causing higher inflation (the inflation tax), and also borrowed money. By 1983, and with a smaller economy, the government's current revenues were more than twice the revenues of 1979 as a percent of GDP. Correspondingly, public expenditures more than doubled as a share of GDP between 1979 and 1983. At the same time, inflation increased from 5 percent in 1978 to more than 14,000 percent in 1988, and external debt increased from 70 percent of GDP in 1979 to 800 percent of GDP by 1990.

Nicaragua's economic and fiscal conditions were thus ripe for a tax reform in 1990. Nicaragua's tax system at the time included an income tax, VAT (introduced in 1975), taxes on trade, and selective consumption taxes. A new regime, now toward the right, came to power in April. The new government introduced a tax reform during the second half of 1990 that indexed taxes, repealed most exemptions, unified corporate income tax (CIT) rates, reduced personal income tax (PIT) rates on nonwage income, improved the income tax–withholding system, increased the VAT rate from 10 percent to 15 percent, and reduced most of the

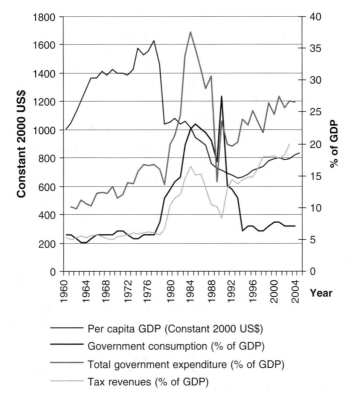

Figure 11.2 Nicaragua—Selected macro variables

Sources: Per capita GDP and Government Consumption: National Accounts, World Development Indicators, CD-ROM, World Bank, 2005; total government expenditure and tax revenues: 1960–1989: author estimates based on data from Central Bank of Nicaragua, Estadísticas Macroeconómicas de 40 Años, December 13, 2006, http://www.bcn.gob.ni/estadisticas/macroeconomia/default.shtm; total government expenditure: 1990–2004: International Monetary Fund, Article IV, Consultation Reports and Statistical Appendices, December 13, 2006, http://www.imf.org/external/country/nic/index.htm; and tax revenues: 1990–2004, Central Bank of Nicaragua, December 13, 2006, <http://www.bcn.gob.ni>.

other taxes, including the repeal of most selective consumption taxes. Furthermore, the average customs tariff was reduced from 47.9 percent to 14.7 percent, and exporters were exempted from tariffs and sales tax on their purchases of machinery and intermediate goods. The tax reforms were part of a broader package aimed at stabilization by further reducing government expenditure through adjustments of government wages and public sector prices and tariffs, restoring currency convertibility, obtaining external financing, devaluing, and privatizing.

The tax reform, the stabilization of economic activity following its free fall through the 1990s, and the reduction of inflation helped increase tax collections from their low of 8 percent of GDP in 1990 to 16 percent of GDP in 1996. Nevertheless, the increase in revenues did not match the gap that now had to be filled to attain fiscal sustainability, for expenditures went on the rise again.

This generated pressure for more tax revenues and led to the 1997 tax reform following the change in administration. This reform sought to increase the tax base by repealing a large number of discretionary tax and customs exemptions, by introducing a 1.5 percent tax on corporate assets and a fixed tax per unit of land (creditable against income tax liabilities). The reform also increased income incentives by introducing a PIT exemption and by lowering the CIT and top PIT rates from 30 percent to 25 percent by 1999. Finally, the reform simplified the customs tariff schedule to two rates of 5 percent and 10 percent (albeit with many goods exempted to allow for higher tariffs), repealed nontariff restrictions, and introduced an export tax credit of 1.5 percent on the FOB value.

Tax revenues continued to increase in the same trend as before the reform, despite further changes in 1999 and 2000 that increased tariff and other tax exemptions and reduced excise tax rates. But public expenditures also increased, in good measure responding to the damage wrought by Hurricane Mitch in October 1998 and the failure of several commercial banks in 2000–2001. As a result, the new government that took office in January 2001 instituted a fresh set of tax reforms that included removing import tariff exonerations, repealing tax exemptions for the financial system, establishing a gradual repeal of preferential VAT rates and limiting VAT exemptions, increasing withholding rates on many activities, and broadening the base for taxes on beverages. Reforms continued in February 2003 with an increase in tax rates for automobiles and cigarettes, and a new tax on commercial banks based on the level of deposits. They concluded in April 2003 with another round of reforms that the government expected would yield 1.7 percent of GDP in additional taxes.[13]

In the future, transfers and pension payments will be two important sources of additional pressure on expenditures. The Fiscal Transfers Law approved in 2003 committed the government to transfer 4 percent of total revenues to the country's 151 municipalities in 2004. The amount of the transfer is scheduled to rise to 10 percent by 2010. As in other experiences in Latin America, the transfer of revenues was not accompanied by a corresponding transfer of expenditure responsibilities, with the latter being constrained by insufficient municipal capacity. Under the recent pension reform, which will replace the existing defined-benefit, pay-as-you-go system by a defined-contribution system, the government's pension deficit will rise well into the future before declining again in the absence of new parametric changes. Consequently, due to the rise in transfers to the municipalities and medium-term increase in pension system obligations, further fiscal adjustments are necessary.

Guyana

Interest in Guyana's tax reform process stems from the country's sharp policy shifts after independence from the British in 1966 and from the sheer size of the difficult-to-tax informal economy. Guyana's tax policy directions have been shaped by developments during three very different periods: one of extreme government control of the economy (1966–1989), followed by another of successful free market reforms (1989–1997), and then the more recent period characterized by several shocks (political and social unrest and adverse weather and terms of trade from 1997 to the present). With regard to informality, tax enforcement and compliance have been constrained by the large size of the underground economy, estimated at anywhere between 50 percent and nearly 100 percent of the official economy (see figure 11.3).

Guyana's first fiscal crisis as an independent republic began to brew in the 1970s, when the government of Linden Forbes Burnham (1964–1985) proclaimed Guyana as the first "Cooperative Republic." This meant a republic where the government would own at least 51 percent of enterprises. By the early 1980s, the government had nationalized most of the economy. This control included

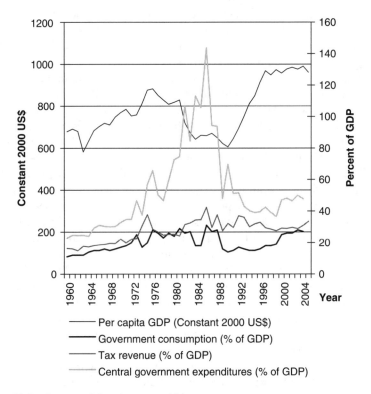

Figure 11.3 Guyana—Selected macro variables

Sources: Per capita GDP and government consumption: National Accounts, World Development Indicators, CD-ROM, World Bank, 2005; total government expenditure: 1960–1981, *Central Bank Bulletin;* 1982–1988, from Ebrima Faal, "Fiscal Adjustment and Reform of the Public Sector," in IMF, *Guyana, Experience with Macroeconomic Stabilization, Structural Adjustment, and Poverty Reduction,* Washington, D.C.: IMF, 2003, p. 8, table 3.5; 1991–2004, ECLA, CEPALSTAT, http://www.cepal.org/estadisticas/. Tax revenue: 1960–1981, Bank of Guyana, *Economic Bulletin,* various numbers; 1982–1989, from Ebrima Faal, "Currency Demand, the Underground Economy, and Tax Evasion: The Case of Guyana," *IMF Working Paper* WP/03/07, 2003, p. 21, figure 3; 1990–2004, ECLA, CEPALSTAT, http://www.cepal.org/estadisticas/. Percent of GDP expenditure data exceeds 100% in some years because official GDP is underestimated.

the major bauxite and sugar companies that comprised the core of economic activity as well as the majority of retailing and distribution systems.

Government expenditure depended directly on its profits from the bauxite, sugar, and other industries that comprised the formal economy, now owned by the government. These profits benefited from robust world commodity prices through much of the 1970s and permitted considerable growth in government expenditures. Government consumption increased from about 12 percent of official GDP in the early 1960s to about 28 percent by 1976.[14] However, as commodity prices weakened during the late 1970s and 1980s, and productivity and investment in the government-owned companies declined, government revenue declined. Exports also declined and foreign exchange became scarce; in response, the government created parallel foreign exchange and product markets by introducing exchange and price controls. Furthermore, to cover import needs, the government borrowed money. By 1985, when President Forbes died, Guyana's foreign debt was four times the level of its GDP. By 1987, it had increased further to 6.7 times the GDP. By 1990, per capita GDP had declined by 31 percent compared to its previous peak in 1977.

During the 1980s, total government expenditures of about 92 percent of GDP were financed by taxes (about 32 percent of GDP), inflation (averaging 34 percent p.a.) and external debt (accumulating at an average annual rate of about 27 percent of GDP). The severe fiscal and debt crisis at the end of the decade triggered an economic reform program that included a reversal of government ownership of enterprises and prices, and foreign exchange liberalization, trade liberalization, and the reestablishment of fiscal order through expenditure cuts and tax reform. Spending was cut to the effect that government consumption declined by 15 percentage points of GDP between 1986 and 1994. The tax reform focused on broadening tax bases (raising collection of the consumption tax and reducing import tariff exemptions), advancing payment of the CIT from the previous to the current year, and lowering excessively high marginal income tax rates (up to 55 percent). Other tax reforms during the 1990s included the conversion of consumption taxes from specific to ad valorem taxes, the elimination of consumption tax exemptions favoring state-owned enterprises, the reduction in the number of consumption tax rates, the simplification of the tariff structure, the merging of the Inland Revenue Department with customs, and the use of market exchange rates for customs tax purposes.[15]

The reversal of state intervention and the reestablishment of fiscal order, the latter brought about by expenditure cuts and increased tax collection, succeeded in raising economic growth. Per capita GDP increased by 60 percent between 1990 and 1997. Some of the growth reflected a recovery from the deep slump that the economy suffered as a result of the misguided policies of the 1970s and much of the 1980s. However, public expenditures began to increase again after 1996, largely in response to wage pressures and capital spending, and tax collection weakened. Furthermore, economic growth stopped as political stability deteriorated in the aftermath of the 1997 election and was further affected by adverse weather conditions and a deterioration of the terms of trade.

Stagnant output, increased expenditure, weak taxes, and the debt overhang triggered a new tax reform beginning in 2003. This reform substantially modernized Guyana's tax provisions. Initial reforms included the extension of the consumption tax to all services provided by hotels and restaurants as well as to services provided by professionals, the introduction of a presumptive tax on the self-employed, and the introduction of limits on discretionary exemptions on the consumption and customs taxes. In 2005, a 16 percent VAT was levied, replacing the consumption tax and a number of other minor taxes. With this, Guyana simplified the tax system and followed in the footsteps of many other Latin American countries that already have VATs in place.

Guyana's present stance is one of continued growth of public expenditures. These increased, following their decline through 1999, from 37 percent of GDP that year to 48 percent in 2004. They are expected to continue increasing as strong public investment plans are carried out, especially to support the modernization of the sugar sector. This is likely to call for additional taxation primarily focused on broadening the statutory base and improving compliance, as tax rates are still too high for competitive purposes.

Ecuador

In addition to the standard taxes, Ecuador has received considerable oil revenues since the early 1970s and provides an example of how an abundant natural resource may undermine fiscal policies. This is so because revenues from natural resources are unstable and do not last forever, and because governments have a strong incentive to spend those revenues instead of saving them for future expenditure. Hence, the instability of revenues translates into unstable expenditures. Furthermore, as these revenues reflect the consumption of a nonrenewable asset, Ecuador's reliance on this source of income, which has been used primarily to finance subsidized internal prices of oil products, has reduced the public sector's net worth. The loss is estimated at about 30 percent since oil revenues started in the early 1970s.[16] As oil revenues cover expenditure, tax effort has been correspondingly low (see figure 11.4).

Although reforms have improved Ecuador's tax system, it still faces a number of critical challenges to make it more competitive in today's international setting. The challenges include the large number of taxes in force, the non-neutral application of those taxes, the rigidities in the allocation of taxes to expenditures, and the administration of taxes. These need to be addressed to improve resource allocation and sustain competitiveness and growth.

During the 1970s and 1980s, Ecuador's main taxes included a PIT with a very complex rate system; a CIT with a 20 percent tax rate on retained profits and an 18 percent rate on distributed profits, the latter also taxed at the individual level; VAT, introduced in 1970 as the "Mercantile Transactions Tax" (MTT) with a 4.1 percent tax rate;[17] and excise taxes on tobacco and alcoholic beverages. In total, the PIT and CIT yielded about 1.8 percent of GDP in 1986. VAT yielded 2.7 percent and the excise taxes yielded 0.8 percent of GDP. The other 100 or so minor taxes yielded 0.5 percent of GDP.[18]

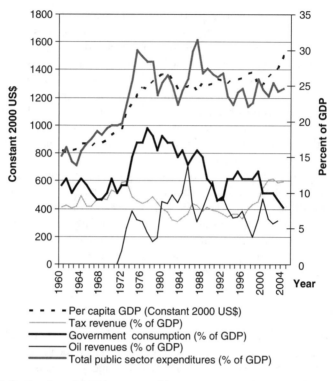

Figure 11.4 Ecuador—Selected macro variables

Sources: Per capita GDP and government consumption: National Accounts; World Development Indicators, CD-ROM, World Bank, 2005; tax revenue 1960–1982: Banco Central del Ecuador, 70 Años de Información Estadistica, 1997; tax revenue 1983–2004: Banco Central del Ecuador, Operaciones del Sector Público No Financiero, December 13, 2006, http://www.bce.fin.ec/contenido.php?CNT=ARB0000943; total public sector expenditures and oil revenues 1960–1982: Banco Central del Ecuador, 70 Años de Información Estadistica, 1997; and 1983–2004: Banco Central del Ecuador, Operaciones del Sector Público No Financiero, December 13, 2006, http://www.bce.fin.ec/contenido.php?CNT=ARB0000943.

Public sector expenditures increased sharply during the first half of the 1970s, driven by rising oil revenues. General government consumption expenditures rose from 12 percent of GDP in 1970 to 19 percent of GDP in 1977. By 1982, the economic crisis triggered by misguided fiscal policies, falling oil prices, and rising international interest rates left Ecuador's public finances in distress, with inflation and external debt increasing fast. In response, the government established taxes on the consumption of beer and cigarettes, on vehicle registrations, and on increases of property value linked to public works, and raised the existing tax on luxury goods. Furthermore, it reduced tax incentives by 50 percent for all sectors except agriculture. Tax collection increased only temporarily, and the reforms did not reestablish fiscal sustainability, for total public expenditures were rising fast, financed by debt and the inflation tax. Public external debt increased from 29 percent of GDP in 1982 to 99 percent of GDP in 1987. Inflation also increased from an average of 14 percent (1973–1982) to an average of 33 percent (1983–1987). This set the ground for the 1988–1989 tax reform.

In 1986, the MTT rate was raised to 10 percent. The 1988–1989 reform extended the 10 percent MTT (now renamed VAT) to some services; introduced withholding and advance payments, reduced the number of tax rates in the progressive schedule to four rates ranging from 10 percent to 25 percent, and unified the PIT rates. The tax revenue/GDP ratio did not increase after this reform. It remained level at 7 percent from 1983 until 1999. However, fiscal adjustment began in 1988 by exercising control on expenditure growth. The ratio of total expenditure declined from 31 percent of GDP in 1987 to 24 percent of GDP in 1993, the level at which it remains today.

The government made few tax changes during the 1990s. Tariffs were lowered in 1991, several nontariff restrictions (e.g., licenses, quotas) were removed, and excise taxes were raised. By Ecuador's prior record, most of the 1990s was relatively calm from the economic perspective, with the external debt/GDP ratio falling and inflation under some degree of control. However, a deep recession in 1999, triggered by the El Niño devastation, led to considerable macroeconomic distress. The inflation rate soared from 36 percent in 1998 to almost 100 percent in 2000, and external debt rose from 71 percent to about 100 percent of GDP. This distress triggered an increase in the VAT rate to 12 percent in 1999, an additional tax reform in 2001 comprising the introduction of a 1 percent tax on financial transactions, a decrease in the maximum PIT rate to 15 percent, and a revamping of the revenue collection agency. These reforms have had an important impact thus far, for revenues increased from 8 percent of GDP in 1998 to 12 percent of GDP in 2001, the level where they remain at present. After 1999, inflation declined to 2 percent in 2005, to a large extent due to dollarization in 2001, and growth accelerated, much of it due to oil.

Ecuador's comparatively low level of tax effort is, of course, largely due to the government's oil revenues. These revenues accounted for about a quarter of total nonfinancial public sector revenues during 2000–2004.

Compared to the 1960's tax system, Ecuador's new tax system is better in at least three respects: the archaic income tax of the 1960s has been replaced with a more modern one; tax administration has improved; and taxation of trade has reduced. Among the areas where tax reform will need to focus to improve competitiveness, the repeal of most exemptions, of most minor taxes (84 taxes at the last count),[19] and of extensive earmarking stand out. A critical challenge is to contain expenditures, which have already increased from 24 percent of GDP in 1999 to about 26 percent of GDP today.

Mexico

Mexico's tax reform efforts over the years have created particularly difficult tensions among the government, the private enterprise sector, and the population at large. With the opening of the economy since the mid-1980s, competitiveness considerations are increasingly having a bearing on the quality of tax reform efforts.

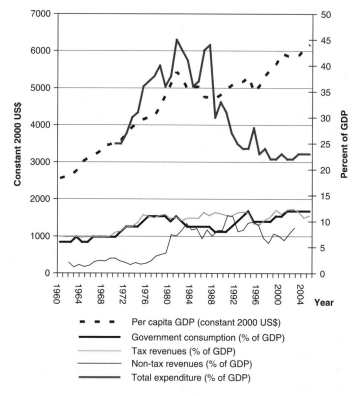

Figure 11.5 México—Selected macro variables

Sources: Per capita GDP and government consumption: National Accounts, World Development Indicators, CD-ROM, World Bank, 2005; tax revenues: OECD Revenue Statistics, http://www.oecd.org, and Country Economic Memorandum, *Challenges and Prospects for Tax Reform,* World Bank, 1992; total expenditure: 1970–1998, I. Katz, "Hacia una Politica Fiscal de Esatbilidad: La Reforma del Marco Institucional," *Gaceta de Economia* 5(9); 1998–2005, ECLA, CEPALSTAT, http://www.cepal.org/estadisticas/; nontax revenues: 1960–2000: author estimate with revenue data from Oxford Latin American History Database, http://oxlad.qeh.ox.ac.uk/, and tax data cited above.

These competitiveness considerations are affected by the need to work on the expenditure side to improve public service provisions (see figure 11.5).

Mexico's tax collection has been low relative to those in most other Latin American countries. In 1960, tax collection amounted to 6.3 percent of GDP and Mexico ranked 70th in a sample of 72 countries with available information. Taxation included primarily an income tax, with only wage earners de facto paying progressive rates (at a maximum of 35 percent), and innumerable exemptions and different tax bases for different sectors; a turnover tax (the "tax on mercantile transactions"); a set of excise taxes; and state taxes (so-called *alcabalas,* often deemed illegal[20]) on all manner of goods, reflecting a long-standing method of subnational finance.

Much progress has been made since, but along a very rocky path. Economic conditions became favorable to tax reform, or at least to tax increases. Government expenditures began to increase toward the end of 1972, partly supported by rising oil revenues, and the overall public sector expanded, with the number of public enterprises expanding from 84 in 1970 to 845 in 1976.

With solid economic growth after 1977 and sharply rising nontax revenues (i.e., oil), the government was able to focus on structural changes to the tax regime. These included, in 1978, an income tax reform that made the PIT more progressive (with the maximum marginal rate raised from 50 percent to 59 percent) and increased its base (by adding rents, capital gains, and dividends). It was also at the end of the 1970s that the fractionalized personal income tax system began to be unified. Furthermore, in 1980, a VAT replaced the old turnover tax and several excise taxes (in total, 25 federal taxes and 300 local excises were repealed). The main VAT rate was set at 10 percent, with a preferential 6 percent rate on goods along the northern border in order to facilitate competition with the United States and zero rates on basic agricultural products and foodstuffs. However, with growing evasion/avoidance, this did not change the level of tax collections. Instead, rising expenditures led to more inflation (inflation increased further to an average of 42 percent between 1978 and 1983) and debt. Confidence in growth of oil revenues allowed the government to continue borrowing at a rate that reached its peak in 1983 (10 percent of GDP).

The 1982 economic and banking crisis inevitably triggered by falling oil prices and rising international interest rates completed the setting for further tax reform measures, this time aimed at increasing collection. VAT was raised to 15 percent in 1983, with medicines added to the 6 percent preferential rate and a 20 percent rate added for some luxury goods. A surtax of 10 percent on income was established. In 1986, a more comprehensive corporate tax reform reduced collection lags by introducing monthly payments, introduced full indexation (in particular to ensure inflation-proof depreciation of assets), and reduced the tax rate to 35 percent. It was in the mid-1980s that policymakers concluded that higher tax rates were not compatible with growth or tax compliance.

However, the tax revenue/GDP ratio stayed put. With inflation at 131 percent in 1987 and external debt at 82 percent of GDP, the government was running out of options and had then to adjust the hard way: reducing public expenditures and, in addition, deepening the trade liberalization recently initiated through tariff reductions. Total public expenditure, which averaged 40 percent of GDP during 1978–1983, ultimately declined to 22–23 percent by 1998 and has remained there since then. The income tax was also reformed in 1987 by establishing a gradual reduction of the top marginal rate from 60.5 percent in 1986 to 35 percent in 1990, and reducing the corporate rate from 39 percent in 1988 to 35 percent in 1990.

With stability more or less recovered by 1989, the government increasingly focused on tax changes that improved growth, combining lower tax rates with better tax compliance. However, in 1995 the VAT rate (reduced to 10 percent in 1991) was raised back to 15 percent to generate revenue needs created by the recession that began at the end of 1994. Further revenue increases were sought in 1998 with the increase in several excise tax rates. In 1999, the corporate tax rate was increased back to 35 percent and dividends began to be withheld.

In 2002, the special corporate tax rate for reinvested profits (30 percent) was repealed so that these now paid the standard 35 percent rate. The preferential CIT tax treatment of agriculture and transportation sectors was also repealed. In the PIT regime, full consolidation of all sources of income was finally achieved. An attempt to broaden the VAT base was not successful. In 2005, the corporate rate was reduced to 30 percent, to be reduced by one point more each year in 2006 (29 percent) and 2007 (28 percent). The individual income tax rate was lowered and simplified to two marginal rates (25 percent and 28 percent). The VAT rate remains at 15 percent.

Mexico's tax regime today continues to face reform challenges. The most important need is to end the fiscal dependence on oil revenues. PEMEX, the public oil company, has had to borrow heavily to finance investments, and oil sector investments are low because so much of PEMEX's revenue flows to government. Other challenges include reducing tax expenditures, which amount today to more than 6 percent of GDP, and reducing tax evasion. Most observers writing on tax issues argue that the tax burden needs to be increased to provide more and better public services. The current political environment also appears to be moving in that direction. Nevertheless, although there have been pressures to raise taxes before, the tax burden has remained constant for many years.

Chile

Chile's tax reform record during the last three decades shows a consistency, stability, and direction that are difficult to find in the rest of the region. It illustrates the application of consistent taxation and macroeconomic principles. It exemplifies the country's trademark stability of economic policy during the last 30 years. Despite its stability, it exhibits movement toward constant improvement. Nevertheless, Chile still faces a number of tax reform challenges including, most importantly, the relatively high tax rates and the burden of tax regulations.

Prior to 1974, Chile's tax structure consisted primarily of income tax (established in 1924–1925); sales (transactions), copper, social security, and property taxes; and customs tariff. The years 1975 and 1984 are milestones in Chilean tax reform toward a system that relies primarily on indirect taxation.

In 1974, the new government's first fiscal policies were to reduce expenditures and increase taxes within the existing tax structure, in order to address the deep fiscal imbalances—a fiscal deficit of about 30 percent of GDP in 1973—that had emerged from increased expenditure and falling tax revenues during the previous three years. To reduce expenditures, the government cut public salaries and employment and returned formerly intervened and money-losing enterprises to their owners. To raise taxes, the government introduced a wealth tax, raised the assessed values of real estate, and increased direct and indirect tax rates. It was indeed a tough but an effective adjustment that reduced the deficit to only 2 percent of GDP in 1975.[21]

The 1974 actions went far in resolving the macroeconomic imbalances but did not address the structural pitfalls of the system, primarily myriad special regimes, cascading indirect taxation, and non-neutrality with respect to the price level. Addressing the second of these problems led to the kernel of the new system: a flat VAT on goods (extended to services in 1977) that replaced the cascading transactions tax. In addition, the reform eliminated the special tax regimes, indexed the tax system, and reduced the CIT tax rate. As a result, the share of VAT in the tax system increased considerably, reflecting the government view that tax systems should be designed to collect revenues efficiently and that the role of improving income distribution should fall instead on public expenditure.

The policies initiated in 1974 resulted in a sharp increase in tax collection and a more gradual decline in expenditure, except for the drastic cut during the 1975 recession. The 1984 tax reform in Chile came in the aftermath of the severe recession that started in 1982, whereby per capita GDP contracted by about 16 percent between 1981 and 1983.

The 1984 reform pursued a strategy that would also encourage saving and growth. The reform partially exempted savings from income taxation and integrated individual and corporate taxation to avoid double taxation of income from capital. As a result of this reform, the government advanced toward a system primarily based on indirect taxation of consumption. This approach paid off. Saving and investment increased and Chile was launched on an accelerated growth path (figure 11.6). Falling public expenditures, from 33 percent of GDP in 1985 to 22 percent of GDP in 1990, and the aggressive trade liberalization that Chile pursued also contributed to this acceleration.

The late 1980s and 1990s witnessed additional reforms, including increased social expenditures to help address poverty. The government then designed a program to raise $580 million annually during 1991–1993. It speaks very well for Chile's fiscal consolidation that the raising of taxes came before implementing the additional expenditure, not after, as in the majority of the cases in the region. It is also laudable that the raising of taxes came with recourse to mainstream taxation and not through resorting to new distorting taxes, as has occurred in many other adjustment efforts in the region. To meet the target, the government raised the corporate income tax rate from 10 percent to 15 percent, shifted from taxation of retained earnings to taxation of all profits whether distributed or not (but maintaining the integration of the PIT and the CIT), changed individual income tax brackets to increase the number of persons in the highest rate, and raised the VAT rate from 16 percent to 18 percent. The tax revenue/GDP ratio increased by about two percentage points following these reforms. Import tariffs were reduced further, first gradually from 15 percent to 11 percent in the early 1990s, and then gradually to 6 percent after 1998.[22] Revenue losses from the tariff reduction were offset with increased excise tax rates. Furthermore, in 2003, the VAT rate was further raised to 19 percent and, in 2004, the corporate rate was raised to 17 percent.

Taxes remain an important concern for the private sector in Chile, and the World Economic Forum has cited the level of tax rates and tax regulations as the major obstacle to the growth of the private sector in Chile. To these we must add that the strong reliance of the system on indirect taxes remains a subject of much

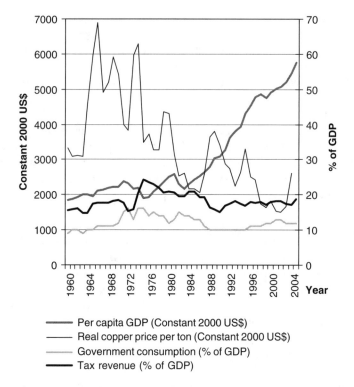

Figure 11.6 Chile—Selected macro variables

Sources: Per capita GDP and government consumption: National Accounts, World Development Indicators, CD-ROM, World Bank, 2005; real copper price: UNCTAD, Commodity Price Statistics, http://www.unctad.org/Templates/Page.asp?intItemID=1584&lang=1; tax revenue: General Government Accounts and IMF.

debate. More broadly, the size of Chile's public sector is often in question, with some claiming it is too small and others pointing out that it is too large. However, it is difficult to dismiss the very likely positive growth and poverty reduction impact that Chile's moderation in public expenditure and consumption-based tax system has had thus far. In both of these dimensions, growth and poverty reduction, Chile has done better than Latin American countries with larger public sectors and thus remains in an enviable position in the Latin American context.

Concluding Comments

In discussing taxes and competitiveness in Latin America, this chapter focused on the close link between taxes and public expenditures, the impact of fiscal burden on growth, and the tax policy experience of a selected group of countries. A central point that was highlighted is the clear relationship between the quality of tax policies and economic performance. Average annual per capita growth during the 45-year (1960–2005) horizon covered in the reviews puts Chile at the top (2.5 percent), followed by Mexico (2.0 percent), Ecuador (1.4 percent),

Guyana (0.8 percent), and Nicaragua (–0.6 percent). Of course, other policies and factors were also at work, but tax policy ought to have played a role in these differences in outcomes. To some extent, the differences in the quality of tax policies were driven by differences in the degree of political stability, with sharp shifts in the political stance having a considerable impact on tax policies.

The experience of the five countries highlights the limits of tax increases in resolving fiscal distress. An increased tax burden has too often led to more expenditure, not to a resolution of fiscal imbalances. Indeed, higher taxes, inasmuch as they raise the fiscal burden, may well have reduced growth and the rate of poverty reduction. A better policy approach is to control expenditures, improve the effectiveness of expenditure, and let competitive tax provisions encourage the private sector to invest, employ, and generate growth.

Finally, the review shows an improvement in the makeup of taxes. This improvement is the shift from a strong reliance on trade taxes, very segmented income tax systems, and cascading taxes to systems that rely more extensively on VATs and better income taxes with lower tax rates. Much improvement still remains to be made. Exemptions abound, rates remain far from neutral, and several poor taxes are still alive. Furthermore, the extensive informal sectors in many Latin American countries continue to block the reach of taxes to those sectors, thereby impeding a more neutral and lower tax rate incidence.

Do we get more competitiveness from Latin America's taxes today than in the past? It is hard to tell. Fiscal burdens are generally larger but taxes are probably better. The balance will vary from country to country.

Notes

* The comments and suggestions provided by Ernesto May, David Rosenblatt, David Gould, Antonella Bassani, Vicente Fretes-Cibils, and James Parks are gratefully acknowledged. The findings, interpretations, and conclusions expressed in this chapter are entirely those of the author. They do not necessarily represent the views of the World Bank, its executive directors, or the countries they represent.

1. See Raj M. Desai and Sanjay Pradhan, "Governing the Investment Climate" (March, 2005). Available from http://www1.worldbank.org/devoutreach/mar05/article.asp?id=282.

   In a recent survey of Latin America, taxes do not rank as high as an obstacle. Taxes and tax regulations reported by the 2006 World Economic Forum Report for Latin America ranked respectively in the seventh and eighth place on the average. However, these relatively low ranks may be misleading. The obstacle that ranked second in Latin America is policy instability and the history of tax reforms in Latin America, as illustrated in this chapter, suggests that changes in tax policy must be one of the major components of this instability. See Klaus Schwab and Augusto López-Claros, 2006, "The Latin America Competitiveness Review 2006: Paving the Way for Regional Prosperity" World Economic Forum, http://www.weforum.org/pdf/Latin_America/Review.pdf (accessed December 13, 2006).

2. See World Economic Forum, 2006, "Global Competitiveness Report 2006–2007," http://www.weforum.org/pdf/Global_Competitiveness_Reports/Reports/gcr_2006/composition.pdf (accessed December 13, 2006).

3. Milton Friedman, Interview with *Washington Times,* June 2, 1982. Cited by William Anderson, Myles Wallace, and John T. Warner, "Government Spending and Taxation: What Causes What," *Southern Economic Journal* 52, no. 3 (January 1986): 630–639.

4. The three possible hypotheses are (i) the "tax-and-spend hypothesis formulated by Milton Friedman, that with increased taxation capacity, a government raises the tax burden and consequently government spending (see M. Friedman, "The Limitations of Tax Limitations," *Policy Review,* Summer, 1978, 7–14); (ii) the spend-and-tax hypothesis formulated by Peacock and Wiseman, that crises are more likely than taxes to change public attitudes on government size (see A. T. Peacock and J. Wiseman, *The Growth of Public Expenditure in the United Kingdom* [Princeton, NJ: Princeton University Press for the National Bureau of Economic Research, 1961]); and the "fiscal synchronization hypothesis" advanced by Richard Musgrave, that governments change taxes and expenditures concurrently (see R. A. Musgrave, *Principles of Budget Determination in Public Finance, Selected Readings,* eds. A. H. Cameron and W. Henderson [New York: Random House, 1961, 15–27]). Econometric tests show different directions of causality for different countries; e.g., see James E. Payne, "A Survey of the International Empirical Evidence on the Tax-Spend Debate," *Public Finance Review* 31, no. 3 (2003): 302–324.

5. Government consumption expenditures, as calculated in national accounts, include compensation of employees and net purchases of goods and services. They are then an estimate of the cost of government services (e.g., public education and health).

6. See Norman Loayza, Pablo Fajnzylber, and César Calderón, *Economic Growth in Latin America and the Caribbean: Stylized Facts, Explanations, and Forecasts* (Washington, D.C.: World Bank Publications, 2005). This study uses data from 1960 to 1999. A similar result is obtained for a wider sample of countries (75) and using data from 1960 to 2003. See World Bank, *The Foundations of Growth and Competitiveness, Dominican Republic,* (Washington, D.C.: World Bank, 2006), Table A2.6, 44.

7. See World Bank, 2006, "A Decade of Measuring the Quality of Governance," http://siteresources.worldbank.org (accessed December 13, 2006).

8. See Miguel D. Ramirez and Nadir Nazmi, "Public Investment and Economic Growth in Latin America: An Empirical Test", *Review of Development Economics* 7, no. 1, (2003): 115–126.

9. See Niloy Bose and M. Emranul Haque, "Causality between Public Investment in Transport and Communication and Economic Growth," Research Paper 2005/10, The University of Nottingham, 2005.

10. Per capita GDP not only indicates general welfare; it also reflects the extent of a country's prior accumulation of physical and human capital. As such, it is closely linked to competitiveness.

11. G. Brennan, and J. M. Buchanan, *The Power to Tax: Analytical Foundations of a Fiscal Constitution* (Cambridge: Cambridge University Press, 1980).

12. This tax became known as the BAD (Bank Account Debit Transactions) Tax in Australia, where it was introduced in 1983 (and repealed in 2005). Its pernicious effects have been well documented. See Pedro H. Albuquerque, "BAD Taxation: Disintermediation and Illiquidity in a Bank Account Debits Tax Model," *International Tax and Public Finance* 13 (September 2006): 601–624. For a review of the BAD tax experience in Latin America, see Jorge Baca-Campodónico, Luiz de Mello, and Andrei Kirilenko, "The Rates and Revenue of Bank Transaction Taxes," Organisation for Economic Co-operation and Development, Economics Department

Working Papers, No. 494 (Paris: Organisation for Economic Co-operation and Development, June 30, 2006).

13. See International Monetary Fund (IMF), Nicaragua—First and Second Reviews under the Three-Year Arrangement under the Poverty Reduction and Growth Facility and Request for Waiver and Modification of Performance Criteria, IMF Country Report 03/349." (Washington, D.C.: IMF, November 2003), http://www.imf.org/external/pubs/ft/scr/2003/cr03349.pdf (accessed December 13, 2006).

14. Severe underestimation of GDP is a major problem for interpreting indicators that rely on this variable for intertemporal and cross-country comparisons. See Ebrima Faal, "Currency Demand, the Underground Economy and Tax Evasion: The Case of Guyana," IMF Working Paper WP/03/07, 2003. This paper argues that the underground economy may have been as large as the measured economy, particularly during the 1980s, and that it has surely varied in its relative size through time.

15. See Ebrima Faal, "Fiscal Adjustment and Reform of the Public Sector," in *Guyana, Experience with Macroeconomic Stabilization, Structural Adjustment, and Poverty Reduction* (Washington, D.C.: IMF, 2003), 21–25.

16. See IMF, "Article IV Consultation, Staff Report," April 2003, Box 1, p. 8.

17. Ecuador was the second country in Latin America after Brazil to introduce VAT.

18. For more details and other useful information see Mauricio Villafuerte, "Reforma Tributaria En Ecuador: Su Impacto sobre los Ingresos Tributarios y el Comportamiento de los Contribuyentes". Central Bank of Ecuador, *circa* 1994.

19. See WorldBank, *An Economic and Social Agenda for the New Millennium* (Washington, D.C.: World Bank, 2001), Table 3, 48.

20. Luis Aboites Aguilar provides a fascinating account of the alcabalas. See L. A. Aguilar, "Alcabalas Posporfirianas. Modernización Tributaria y Soberanía Estatal", *El Colegio de México,* HMex, LI:(2), 2001. For other noteworthy reviews of tax developments, providing much of the information used in this chapter, see C. Elizondo, "In Search of Revenue: Tax Reforms in Mexico under the Administrations of Echeverrìa and Salinas," *Journal of Latin American Studies* 26, no. 1 (February 1994): 159–190, and Carlos M. Urzua, "An Appraisal of Recent Tax Reforms in Mexico," in *Fiscal Reform and Structural Change in Developing Countries,* vol. 1, eds. G. Perry, J. Whalley, and G. McMahon (London: Macmillan, 2000), 75–96.

21. Much of the information in these paragraphs comes from a very useful review of fiscal developments in Chile: Felipe Larraín B. and M. Rodrigo Vergara, "Un Cuarto de Siglo de Reformas Fiscales," in *La Transformación Económica de Chile,* eds. F. Larraín and R. Vergara (Santiago: Centro de Estudios Públicos, 2000). Useful information was also obtained from the thorough analysis of the 1990 reform available in Delya M. Boyland, "Taxation and Transition: The Politics of the 1990 Chilean Tax Reform," *Latin American Research Review* 31, no. 1 (1996): 7–31.

22. Today, the average tariff in Chile is actually 2.5 percent due to the free trade agreements that Chile has signed with numerous other countries.

References

Aguilar, L. A. 2001. "Alcabalas Posporfirianas. Modernización Tributaria y Soberanía Estatal." El Colegio de México, HMex, LI: (2).

Albuquerque, Pedro H. 2006. "BAD Taxation: Disintermediation and Illiquidity in a Bank Account Debits Tax Model." *International Tax and Public Finance* 13 (September): 601–624.

Anderson, William, Myles Wallace, and John T. Warner. 1986. "Government Spending and Taxation: What Causes What." *Southern Economic Journal* 52 (3): 630–639.

Baca-Campodónico, Jorge, Luiz de Mello, and Andrei Kirilenko. 2006. "The Rates and Revenue of Bank Transaction Taxes." Economics Department Working Papers, No. 494, June 30. Paris: Organisation for Economic Co-operation and Development.

Barro, Robert, and Xavier Sala-i-Martin. 1995. *Economic Growth*. New York: McGraw-Hill. 153–156.

Blunck, Franzisca. "What is Competitiveness?" *Competitiveness*. The Cluster Practitioners Network. June 26, 2006. The Competitiveness Institute. http://www. competitiveness.org/article/articleview/774/1/32/.

Bose, Niloy, and M. Emranul Haque. 2005. "Causality between Public Investment in Transport and Communication and Economic Growth." Research Paper 2005/10. The University of Nottingham.

Bose, Niloy, M. Emranul Haque, and Denise Osborn. 2003. "Public Expenditure and Economic Growth: A Disaggregated Analysis for Developing Countries." The School of Economic Studies. http://www.ses.man.ac.uk/cgbcr/DPCGBCR/dpcgbcr30.pdf (accessed December 13, 2006).

Boyland, Delya M. 1996. "Taxation and Transition: The Politics of the 1990 Chilean Tax Reform." *Latin American Research Review* 31 (1): 7–31.

Brennan G., and J. M. Buchanan. 1980. *The Power to Tax: Analytical Foundations of a Fiscal Constitution*. Cambridge: Cambridge University Press.

Clements, Benedict, Rina Bhattacharya, and Toan Quoc Nguyen. 2003. "External Debt, Public Investment, and Growth in Low-Income Countries." IMF Working Papers WP/03/249.

Desai, Raj M., and Sanjay Pradhan. 2005. "Governing the Investment Climate." *Worldbank. Development Outreach*. March. http://www1.worldbank.org/ devoutreach/ mar05/article.asp?id=282.

Elizondo, C. 1994. "In Search of Revenue: Tax Reforms in Mexico under the Administrations of Echeverrìa and Salinas." *Journal of Latin American Studies* 26 (1): 159–190.

Faal, Ebrima. 2003a. "Currency Demand, the Underground Economy, and Tax Evasion: The Case of Guyana." IMF Working Paper WP/03/07.

———. 2003b. "Fiscal Adjustment and Reform of the Public Sector." In *Guyana, Experience with Macroeconomic Stabilization, Structural Adjustment, and Poverty reduction*. Washington, D.C.: International Monetary Fund.

Friedman, Milton. 1978. "The Limitations of Tax Limitations." *Policy Review,* Summer.

———. 1982. Interview. *Washington Times.* June 2.

International Monetary Fund. 2003a. "Ecuador—Article IV Consultation, Staff Report Country Report 03/90." April. International Monetary Fund. http://www.imf.org/ external/pubs/ft/scr/2003/cr0390.pdf (accessed December 13, 2006).

———. 2003. "Nicaragua—First and Second Reviews under the Three-Year Arrangement under the Poverty Reduction and Growth Facility and Request for Waiver and Modification of Performance Criteria, IMF Country Report 03/349." November. International Monetary Fund. http://www.imf.org/external/pubs/ft/ scr/2003/cr03349.pdf (accessed December 13, 2006).

Katz, I. 2000. "Hacia una Política Fiscal de Estabilidad: La Reforma del Marco Institucional." Instituto Tecnológico Autónomo de Mexico. *Gaceta de Economía* 5(9).

Larraín B., Felipe, and Rodrigo Vergara M. 2000."Un Cuarto de Siglo de Reformas Fiscales." *La Transformación Económica de Chile,* eds. Felipe Larraín B. and R. Vergara. Santiago: Centro de Estudios Públicos.

Loayza, Norman, Pablo Fajnzylber, and César Calderón. 2005. *Economic Growth in Latin America and the Caribbean: Stylized Facts, Explanations, and Forecasts*. Washington, D.C.: World Bank Publications.

Musgrave, R. A. 1961. "Principles of Budget Determination." In *Principles of Budget Determination in Public Finance, Selected Readings*, ed. A. H. Cameron and W. Henderson. New York: Random House. 15–27.

Payne, James E. 2003. "A Survey of the International Empirical Evidence on the Tax-Spend Debate." *Public Finance Review* 31 (3).

Peacock, A. T., and J. Wiseman. 1961. *The Growth of Public Expenditure in the United Kingdom*. Princeton, NJ: Princeton University Press for the National Bureau of Economic Research.

Ramirez , Miguel D., and Nadir Nazmi. 2003. "Public Investment and Economic Growth in Latin America: An Empirical Test." *Review of Development Economics* 7 (1): 115–126.

Sala-i-Martin, Xavier, and Elsa V. Artadi. 2004. "The Global Competitiveness Index." In *The Global Competitiveness Report 2004–2005*. Hampshire: Palgrave Macmillan. 51–80.

Schenone, Osvaldo. 2001. "Tax Policy and Administration." In *Ecuador—An Economic and Social Agenda for the New Millennium,* eds. Vicente Fretes Cibils, Marcelo M. Giugale, and Jose Roberto Lopez Calix. Washington, D.C.: World Bank. 43–63.

Schwab, Klaus, and Augusto López-Claros. 2006. "The Latin America Competitiveness Review 2006: Paving the Way for Regional Prosperity." World Economic Forum. http://www.weforum.org/pdf/Latin_America/Review.pdf (accessed December 13, 2006).

Thornton, J. 1998. "The Growth of Public Expenditure in Latin America: A Test of Wagner's Law." *Cuadernos de Economía* 35 (105): 255–263.

Urzua, Carlos M. 2000. "An Appraisal of Recent Tax Reforms in Mexico." In *Fiscal Reform and Structural Change in Developing Countries*. Vol. 1. Eds. G. Perry, J. Whalley, and G. McMahon. London: Macmillan. 75–96.

Villafuerte, Mauricio. 1995. "Reforma Tributaria En Ecuador: Su Impacto sobre los Ingresos Tributarios y el Comportamiento de los Contribuyentes." Notas Tecnicas, February 11. Banco Central de Ecuador. http://www.bce.fin.ec/frame.php?CNT=ARB000037 (accessed December 13, 2006).

World Bank. 2001. *An Economic and Social Agenda for the New Millennium*. Washington, D.C.: World Bank.

———. 2002. *Mexico: Country Economic Memorandum*. Washington, D.C.: World Bank.

———. 2006a. "A Decade of Measuring the Quality of Governance." The World Bank. http://siteresources.worldbank.org (accessed December 13, 2006).

———. 2006b. *The Foundations of Growth and Competitiveness, Dominican Republic*. Washington, D.C.: World Bank.

World Economic Forum. 2006. "Global Competitiveness Report 2006–2007."

World Economic Forum. http://www.weforum.org/pdf/Global_Competitiveness_Reports/Reports/gcr_2006/composition.pdf (accessed December 13, 2006).

CHAPTER 12

Labor Reform: Undercompetitive Economies and Unprotected Workforce

Christopher Sabatini[1]

It is difficult to imagine a more dysfunctional labor situation than what currently exists in Latin America. Costs for hiring new employees and firing unnecessary ones make Latin America one of the most inflexible labor markets in the world, throttling the private sector's capacity to increase productiveness and discouraging new investment. On the labor side, the laws have done little good as well. Constraints on formally hiring new employees have dampened employment growth, increasing the ranks of the jobless and those employed outside the law. These informal workers, who represent close to half of the region's workforce, exist on the margins of the economy and society, often with few legal and social protections.

In this environment, it is no exaggeration to say that almost everyone loses: employers, employees, and the region's competitiveness in general. To argue for reform in this dysfunctional deadlock of labor regulations does not imply a rejection of labor rights or the removal of all benefits. Unarguably, the current arrangement has failed workers, particularly those now in the informal sector. In contrast to the relatively narrow areas of trade, tax, and fiscal reform, labor reform, for historical and institutional reasons, is a far more political nut to crack. The effect of labor law on regional competitiveness and the growing numbers of informal sector workers has opened an innovative path for resolving this collective action problem.

This chapter provides a brief overview of employment trends after the economic reforms of the 1990s and then looks deeper at the current state of labor laws in the region, focusing specifically on examples in Argentina, Peru, and Chile. Following this, the chapter examines the reasons for the lack of reform and its cost in terms of competitiveness. The chapter then looks at the relationship between labor laws and the growth of the informal economy since the 1990s.

It concludes with some tentative recommendations for breaking the current deadlock to improve competitiveness and labor conditions in the hemisphere.

Reforms and Employment

According to regionwide surveys, unemployment and job security remain the number one concern of Latin American citizens today, and with good reason. Unemployment rates in Latin America have increased since the 1990s at the same time that job quality has declined dramatically.

Despite the hopes of technocrats, multilaterals, and some politicians, the economic and fiscal reforms that marked the 1990s (what became known and now disparaged as the Washington Consensus) failed to generate employment at the anticipated rates. The privatization of state enterprises and the restructuring of private firms resulted in huge layoffs of employees in the formal sector. In a study of seven privatized firms in Argentina alone, the Inter-American Development Bank (IDB) concluded that approximately 113,000 people lost their jobs as one-time public holdings passed into private hands.[2] In addition, modernization of the public sector throughout the region produced thousands of layoffs, as governments struggled to reduce fiscal expenditures by reducing their bloated public sectors. The same IDB study of Argentina determined that "approximately 406,000 federal government jobs were cut in the Argentina between 1990 and 1992."[3]

The assumptions of those backing these reforms were that the workers who bore the brunt of the adjustment would quickly be reabsorbed in other areas of the economy. The expectation was that by addressing fundamental inefficiencies in the macroeconomic environment, reforms would create a more competitive economy that could induce economic growth and ultimately increase labor demand. Further, it was believed that the integration of Latin American economies into the global market would favor the region's advantages of cheap labor and lead to greater demand for unskilled labor.

While the uneven levels of economic growth that followed did help to create new jobs, the growth was insufficient to sop up the increase in the labor force resulting from the public and private sector layoffs and the entrance of new workers into the labor market. The unanticipated "jobless growth" produced regional urban unemployment rates from 1990 to 2004 that grew by 37 percent from 7.3 percent to 10 percent, with rates in countries such as Argentina, Brazil, and Ecuador more than doubling in that period. In stark contradiction to conventional wisdom, those most affected by the downturn in employment were unskilled and semiskilled workers and youth. Throughout the region, trade actually increased wage disparities between skilled workers (who benefited from the growth of export and service sector jobs) and unskilled and semiskilled workers (many of whom lost jobs in the restructuring). Sadly, many unskilled workers who bore the brunt of adjustments were doubly affected: not only did they lose jobs, but they also lost many of the welfare benefits that the state and labor unions had typically provided for them.

But more important was the *quality* of the jobs generated during the period. Throughout the region, the 1990s continued the trends of the 1980s: a contraction of employment in manufacturing and the public sectors, the expansion of employment in services, and the dramatic growth of employment in the informal sector. According to a 2005 International Labour Organization (ILO) report, during the 1990s, the number of jobs in the informal sector increased by 3.9 percent per year, compared with 2.1 percent growth in the formal sector.[4]

The persistence of unemployment and informal sector employment was largely a consequence of unfinished reforms to labor markets. In the post–Washington Consensus environment, in which the public sector no longer provided the primary source of employment and the state no longer coddled industries, firms that had to compete internationally had to increase productivity. Doing so meant reducing labor costs, but without changes to the hidebound labor codes that characterize Latin America, where labor markets lack the flexibility to effectively reabsorb laid-off workers in the now-competitive private sector. The failure to seriously reduce costs for employing and shedding workers kept non-wage labor costs artificially high, and constrained the growing sectors of the economy from hiring new workers. When employers looked to hire new employees, they often did so informally, contributing to the growing gap between skilled and unskilled workers.

In every country in Latin America, there is a welter of laws that govern employer/employee relations. Labor laws, as they affect what has been called "labor flexibility," comprise three areas: (1) laws or established practice governing the dismissal of an employee; (2) government-mandated payroll contributions by employers for unemployment and health insurance and pensions; and (3) regulations governing collective contracts between workers and employers. Many of these laws were passed in the 1930s and 1940s, and while there have been some reforms during the 1990s, most of them remain largely unchanged.

Despite a series of reforms in the 1990s and more recently in Chile and Peru, Latin American labor legislation is among the most restrictive, rigid, and cumbersome in the world. This is true primarily in the regulations affecting the hiring and firing of employees—what are called job-security provisions. The provisions typically involve three components: advance notification of dismissal of up to three months in which employers must either give the full notice or pay the employee the equivalent wage in full; compensation for unjustified dismissal (and in many cases economic difficulties of the firm do not apply) based on multiples of the most recent wages and years in service; and additional payments to long-term employees called a seniority premium in which a worker will receive an additional payment whether he or she is fired or (as in Ecuador, Colombia, Panama, Peru, and Venezuela) quits. For employers calculating the costs of hiring or firing, these can be staggering.

In the case of Argentina, current labor law establishes a two-month notification period before dismissal. To comply, the employer can either give the full two-month notice or pay two months' full wages upon immediate dismissal. Upon dismissal, a worker is entitled to one-twelfth his or her salary from the previous

Table 12.1 Payroll taxes in Argentina

Category	Employee contribution		Employer contribution %	Total paid by employer and employee %
	Private fund A.F.J.P. %	Public fund Pay as you go %		
LAW 24241—Savings for retirement	7	11	10.17	21.17
LAW 19032—I.N.S.S.J.yP (retirement regime)	3	3	1.5	4.50
LAW 23660—Social security	3	3	6	9.00
LAW 22105—Labor union (mandatory)	2	2		2.00
Insurance in charge of labor union (optional)	3	3		3.00
LAW 24714—Family contributions			4.44	4.44
LAW 24013—Fund for unemployment			0.89	0.89
LAW 24557—Work risks				0.00
Life insurance				
Retirement insurance (mandatory)			3.5	3.50
TOTAL	18	22	26.5	48.5

Source: Summary of payroll deductions according to Argentine federal labor law compiled by Norberto Auld and Juan Matias Zaldua.

year, which includes the twice-yearly bonus equivalent to a thirteenth month of salary each year, plus vacations, all multiplied by the total number of years worked. Moreover, to avoid massive layoffs during the financial crisis in 2001, dismissal payments were temporarily doubled. In addition, there is the cost of payroll taxes, which contain a heavy employer contribution. These are detailed in table 12.1.

Other countries have variations of the same theme. In Peru, labor legislation guarantees a package to dismissed employees totaling one and a half times his or her monthly salary (in contrast to one month's annualized salary in Argentina) times the number of years worked, capped at 12 years.

In Chile, there has been an evolving process of reform that has reduced the costs associated with hiring and firing. As a result, job security payments in Chile are lower compared to other countries in the region, though still high globally. Chilean labor laws provide for one month's salary, plus vacation multiplied by the number of years worked, up to 10 years.

In the 1990s, a number of countries tinkered with these laws. Most of these changes centered on allowing firms to contract temporary workers formally. Peru introduced a parallel and more flexible system that allowed for temporary hiring and probationary periods by small and medium-sized enterprises and several key industries. In addition, severance payments were reduced by half, retirement contributions and health insurance were made optional, and mandatory vacation periods were reduced. In Chile, the legislature approved reforms permitting the use of temporary and less-binding labor contracts, and established a government subsidy for the first four months of a contract with a private company. Later reforms also changed the requirements for the registration and authority of new unions. Argentina approved a three-month probationary period for new employees. As a result, the percentage of workers employed under temporary contracts shot up across the region.[5]

But these reforms were a palliative—a halfway measure by governments to address the problem of business demand for greater labor flexibility without having to face the political opposition implied in a broader reform of labor legislation. In this, the reforms failed on two fronts. First, by only permitting for temporary employment, they left untouched the larger issue of the cost associated with hiring permanent employees, the root problem of the labor market. Second, by creating a back door for hiring, the laws reduced the rights of workers, limiting their access to the benefits of full employment and undercutting their ability to organize.

As a result, the overall labor markets in Latin America remained largely unchanged during the wave of economic and structural reforms in the 1990s. Figure 12.1 compares labor reforms to other sectors that were affected by the wave of reforms of the 1990s: trade, the financial sector, tax, and privatization. While many of the reforms of the 1990s succeeded in liberalizing financial markets and trade and reduced the role of the state in production, labor markets remained stuck in the past, serving as a drag on the capacity of the economy to improve productivity efficiently and thereby compete internationally. In the end, according to Heckman and Pages, by the late 1990s the "average cost of dismissing

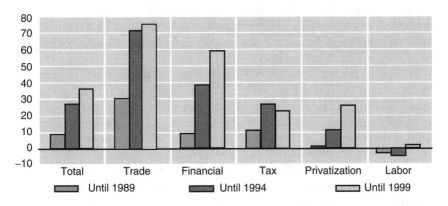

Figure 12.1   The extent of reform in Latin America (margin of reform used)

Source: Lora and Panizza, 2002.

Notes: The index measures the following: trade liberalization: average tariffs imposed on imports and exports; financial reforms: reserve requirements, interest rates, and Basilia rules; labor markets: difficulties for hiring (short probation periods, limits for temporary employment); restrictions on labor (high costs related to overtime and holidays); social contributions (pensions, health insurance, vacation, and dismissal costs); tax reforms: introduction of value-added taxes, sales taxes, efficiency in collecting taxes, and income taxes; and privatization: number of privatizations as a percent of GDP. Eduardo Lora, Eduardo and Ugo Panizza, "Un escrutinio a las reformas estructurales en América Latina," Inter-American Development Bank, *Documento de Trabajo # 471* (Washington, D.C.: Inter-American Development Bank, 2002).

Table 12.2 World Bank employment rigidity

Country	Difficulty of hiring (0–100)	Difficulty of firing (0–100)
Argentina	44	40
Chile	33	20
Peru	44	40
China	11	40
Hungary	11	20
Malaysia	0	10

Source: Compiled by authors from the World Bank and the International Finance Corporation, *Doing Business in 2006: Creating Jobs* (Washington, D.C., 2006), pp. 110–161.

a worker in Latin America [was] still higher than the average of industrial countries," as well as the developing countries of Eastern Europe and Asia.[6]

These unreformed, outdated labor provisions add up to one of the most onerous systems for employers around the world. According to an index of employment rigidity compiled by the World Bank that quantifies the difficulty in hiring and firing new employees, Latin America ranks as one of the most inflexible labor markets with a gross score of 42.2 (on a scale of 100) compared to East Asia and Pacific (27.2), South Asia (38.5), and the high-income OECD (Organisation for Economic Co-operation and Development) countries (35.7).

The breakdown is even starker country by country, particularly when stacked up against the emerging markets that Latin Americans must compete with. Table 12.2 shows the World Bank index broken down into its two separate indices: difficulty of hiring and difficulty of firing. In Argentina, Chile, and Peru, obstacles to hiring are significantly higher than those in China, Hungary, and Malaysia. In the difficulty of firing, only Chile ranks lower or the same as China and Hungary while the other Latin American countries present far greater obstacles to shedding employees than their competitors.

The stalled state of labor reform, despite being on the agenda of multilateral banks, such as the World Bank and the IDB, is largely a story of political opposition and the traditional volatility of Latin American markets that favor social guarantees and protections. Many of the unions in Latin America grew from the political movements that gave birth to these labor laws. Thus, as Ronaldo Munck has written in the case of Argentina, "labor reform is essentially a political process and not just a response to competitiveness."[7] As a result, without comment or regard to the individual merits or weakness of the individual proposals, efforts in countries such as Argentina and Mexico to reform labor legislation have consistently met with considerable opposition from organized labor through strikes, protests, and political lobbying that have scaled back or even killed labor reform.

Apart from the political factors, however, the historical macroeconomic volatility that has marked Latin American economies has tended to favor greater reliance on legal guarantees for social and economic security. Legal disincentives to firing and strong contributions for social programs provided an important cushion against the wild fluctuations of Latin American economies. Job security provisions, in particular, served as a brake on the affect on employment of sharp, unexpected busts, while social protections and insurance guaranteed that the benefits of the boom were shared more broadly.

In this vein, as the pool of the underemployed and unemployed swelled after the economic reforms of the 1990s, political momentum for reforms that would diminish benefits and guarantees of the remaining (organized) workers came to a grinding halt. A reform of labor code, ironically, would ultimately have benefited those who had lost their jobs; unfortunately, in the classic collective action problem, those who could have benefited were not organized or as politically powerful as those who had retained their employment and its organizational and political perquisites. The result, unfortunately, was the kicking down the road of a key reform, with the economic, social, and political costs it would bring.

Employment Rigidity and Informality [8]

Businesses must, of course, take into careful account the long-term legal and financial costs and commitments associated with hiring new regular employees. The high incidence of job-security provisions serves as a disincentive to reducing unproductive laborers or shifting them to other areas. At the same time, the risk of being saddled with expensive, hard-to-fire workers discourages firms from engaging in new hiring. The result, more often than not, has been for expanding businesses to seek extralegal means for contracting employees. Recently, a series of studies has attempted to measure the cost of job-security provisions to labor demand, patterns of unemployment, and the growth of the informal sector.

While many of these studies are still single-country in nature, they found that the effect of reducing the costs of firing or dismissing employees is threefold.[9] First, while reducing the costs to firing employees increases the turnover rate in the formal sector, it is also associated with a decline in the overall unemployment rate. Basically, firms can formally shed workers more efficiently—and do—but the reduction in firing costs also permits firms to hire formally; thus the absorption rate in the formal sector increases, though often with a lag.

Second, studies have also found that high barriers to the dismissal of workers are associated with high rates of self-employment and informality. While the correlation is not perfect, research shows a correlation between labor regulations and job security provisions and informality.[10] The reasons are obvious. The high risk of hiring employees formally increases the incentives for workers to avoid those costs by hiring outside the law in the informal sector.

Third, studies have shown that high job-security provisions segment the labor market and have highly discriminatory effects on youth, women, and unskilled workers. By creating an expensive disincentive for firing existing employees, particularly ones that have been in the job for a while (because of the years-at-work multiplier) job security provisions lock in older workers and discriminate against the employment of new entrants into the workforce, primarily youth and women. According to one study, the effect of job-security provisions is twice as great on youth as it is on other sectors.[11]

Of course, not all of the factors affecting firms' decision to hire informally are shaped by costs of hiring and firing implied in labor law. In addition, to avoid the financial and administrative costs associated with formal, full-time employees, there is also a more intangible benefit to firms for hiring informally. Hiring formally brings the risk that regular employees will be more likely to organize or join unions that can later press for higher pay and benefits. Informal workers are not only cheaper; they are also a more quiescent labor force. Yet the very precariousness of informally contracted labor may arguably dampen productivity in the long run, making it less obviously a good bargain for employers or society as a whole.

Nevertheless, informal employment is a two-way street, with both firms and workers calculating costs and making choices. Research also suggests that the border between formal and informal employment is fairly porous and more voluntary than previously thought.[12] Workers sometimes opt for the informal sector to avoid having to direct some of their salary to benefit plans. The decision is often based on both the low level of formal wages and a lack of confidence that benefits, such as pensions and unemployment insurance, will ever materialize in countries where employers can refuse to pay while governments drag their feet in making them. Rather than pay part of their salary into a system with few guarantees that they can collect their contribution and the expected match between the contribution and collection, many—logically—just prefer to be paid directly in cash.

Whether because of workers' lack of alternatives or by their choice, the ranks of the informal sector have swelled over the last two decades. According to a 2005 ILO report, during the 1990s the rate of job growth in Latin America's informal sector was almost twice that in the formal economy.[13] While estimates vary depending on how "informal" employment is defined, most current studies calculate that close to half of Latin America's nonagricultural workforce is now informal.[14] In countries such as Ecuador, Honduras, and Peru that number is probably closer to 60 percent, while in Chile—whose rate of informality is the region's lowest—just under 40 percent of nonagricultural workers are not formally employed.

While informal employment may have helped to cushion the blow of economic reforms in the absence of a more efficient labor market, it is hardly a desirable employment outcome. There is a fair amount of variation in how people enter the informal sector and the degree of choice in doing so. Yet, there can be little doubt that informal-sector employment is, on the whole, a suboptimal situation for a worker. Those who toil on the fringes of the formal economy all too often have limited access even to minimal job security or basic benefits and safety protections.

Frequently, women and youth suffer most. According to a number of studies, women and younger workers make up the majority of those employed informally.[15] That women and youth should be overrepresented in the informal sector is to be expected given the proven discriminatory effect that existing labor law has on aspiring entrants to the labor market. This effect looms particularly large in a region where more than a third of the populace is under 16.[16] This "youth bubble" will mean that Latin American labor markets will have to absorb a flood of new workers when already, according to the ILO, unemployment among youth (18.8 percent) is more than double the overall unemployment rate of 9 percent.[17]

Unionization

The effect of the reduction of employment in public and manufacturing sectors that followed the economic reforms of the 1990s, the increased use of temporary work contracts, and the dramatic increase in the informal sector have meant plummeting rates of unionization throughout Latin America. As a result, unions find their traditional structures and orientations under pressure as never before.

The large public sectors and protected industries on which union organizers and leaders once focused gave way during the decade of the Washington Consensus to privatization programs and a reduced role for state intervention. In the past, the heavy role of the state in the economy meant that union advocacy efforts and relationships were oriented primarily toward the government and elected officials. Economic reforms that passed public enterprises into private hands cut the roles of public employees and reduced state intervention, decentralized the locus for negotiation for the unions, and demanded a new strategy for organization and bargaining.

At a time when unionization has declined across the world, it has dropped especially sharply in Latin America. While comparable data are difficult to find, levels of unionization have decreased by almost 50 percent in Argentina, Colombia, Peru, and Venezuela since 1980. In Colombia and Peru, the portion of the workforce that is unionized hovers at just 5 to 8 percent.[18]

In only two countries has union membership grown: Brazil and Chile. In the case of Brazil, the government of President Luis Inacio Lula da Silva (Lula) has launched a campaign to grant informal sector workers semiofficial recognition as laborers by giving them workers' cards, thus providing access to state-provided health and pension benefits. While the loose incorporation of informally employed workers into the ranks of the unions has sparked tensions within the formal union movement, the plan has increased membership (albeit in an ill-defined category) in formal labor unions. The policy points to a future path for reform for the region.

In Chile, the increase in union membership has been the result of a labor law reform that has left few limits on the ability of small workers' groups to gain recognition as unions and bargain collectively. Membership in these groups went up after the reform, but at a cost. The lower barrier for the formation of new unions has led to the proliferation of new, shop-floor unions, fragmenting worker representation.

The movement of so much of the working class beyond the reach of traditional union-organizing efforts has had implications for both economic and political representation. Established unions have become increasingly marginal, as did the influence of many of the old-line labor-based parties that these unions have long supported. Argentina's General Confederation of Workers (CGT) and the Peronist Party, Mexico's Confederation of Mexican Workers (CTM) and Institutional Revolutionary Party (PRI), Venezuela's Confederation of Venezuelan Workers (CTV) and the Democracy Action (AD) Party are classic examples of mass unions and the political parties that depended on them. With the organized segment of the working class in eclipse, such parties have either declined or, in the case of the Peronist Party, sought new constituents amid the growing ranks of informal workers.

For unions, the task of organizing the informal sector presents a dilemma. Heterogeneous and dispersed, this sector has few easily identifiable or unified interests and little sense of common identity. The informal sector is a world of small producers, casual laborers, street vendors, illegally contracted workers, and domestic employees. In this world, it is hard to apply the usual union model of banding large numbers of workers together to negotiate with employers by leveraging the collective power of the workers' labor. The workers' organizations that exist in the informal sector typically take the form of sector-specific groups or neighborhood associations. While such small groups may have coherent interests, they do not scale up to meaningful nationwide movements able to facilitate large-scale inclusion.[19] Nevertheless, the traditional orientation of unions toward the state in Latin America, rather than a more employer-focused approach, does make them better organized and equipped to take on the political task of advocating on behalf of informal sector.

What Is to Be Done?

Despite these organizational obstacles, there may be a path for reform. A solution could lie in changes to law and policy that will grant workers, including those in the informal sector, better protection for core labor rights and access to social services in exchange for reductions in the burdens that employers must shoulder when making hiring and firing decisions. The latter holds the prospect of longer-term change that will improve the competitiveness of Latin American countries by creating a more flexible labor market. The former, improving the conditions for informal laborers, would provide governments with the political capital to rewrite outdated labor law.

Since there are a number of interests that have a serious stake on both sides of the equation, in seeking an improvement in labor conditions today, there is a possibility of change. The basic equation is this: reach out to a new constituency that will benefit from labor law reform to support a fundamental reform of labor flexibility codes that will improve the region's competitiveness and its capacity to generate new jobs. The problem is that many of the potential beneficiaries are unorganized and exist outside the establishment.

In order to navigate such a course, governments will first need consistently to defend the basic rights of labor. Successfully granting citizenship and protecting organized and unorganized workers requires as a first step that governments protect labor rights already on the books: freedom of association and bargaining, freedom from forced labor and invidious discrimination, and the eradication of child labor. Throughout the region, these rights have received imperfect protection at best. Labor courts remain notoriously slow, corrupt, and politicized, and there is tremendous room for improvement that could help address labor leaders' basic demands.

Second, governments should develop effective means of ensuring basic benefits (including pension programs and health-care access) for workers, including informals, through a creative mix of private and public initiatives. As mentioned earlier, some employees opt for informality because they expect that the benefits promised by formal employment will never materialize. The Lula government in Brazil has launched an innovative program to grant limited benefits to employees in the informal sector. The effort has spawned some concern among labor leaders that the policy may lead to an attenuation of worker representation and collective power. Nevertheless, it represents one of the first serious efforts to incorporate the nonorganized informals in the labor movement around the demand for public benefits.

While the goal for the incorporation of informals in Brazil has been to bring them under the umbrella of state protections—rather than formal political representation—in many ways unions, in Brazil and in Latin America in general, are particularly well suited for this form of representation and negotiation. The primary orientation of unions in Latin America has been advocating for increased benefits and wages for state employees before governments. Now, with fewer state employees, many have struggled to reorient their strategies to relations with private employers. The informal sector dilemma plays in many ways to unions' traditional strength.

Third, the keystone of reform has to be the updating of outmoded labor codes, especially insofar as these make the cost of dismissing workers unreasonably and destructively high. Unreformed, these laws serve as a deadly drag on new hiring, investment, economic expansion, and prosperity. Important change could be achieved by lowering or eliminating the sums that firms are required to pay in order to shed unnecessary workers and in several cases (where such provisions do not exist) allowing for economically motivated dismissals. Ultimately, the long-term path to creating more formal jobs for Latin American workers lies in this area. Without more freedom to make economically rational personnel decisions, firms will continue to be shackled by high labor costs and more workers will continue to be forced into the marginal world of informal labor. Labor law reform is by no means a panacea, but labor markets need the flexibility to be able to respond to the inevitable expansion and contraction of the market.

Fourth, new job training programs must accompany any scaling back of job-security provisions. Studies show that when companies no longer face high costs for shedding workers, layoffs go up. The same studies indicate that time between dismissal and reemployment is shorter when these costs are lowered (easier firing also means easier hiring). Training programs can provide a speedier route to new jobs and a buffer against the painful, even if relatively short-term, dislocations that labor market fluctuations can cause.

What will unions get out of all this? For one, a broad reform of labor law promises to augment the ranks of formal economy workers, and with them the recruiting and organizing prospects of old-line unions. They and their leaders could find themselves newly relevant—precisely at a time when the pressures and demands associated with globalization make stronger voices for workers' rights so urgently needed. But getting to such a point will require unions to sharpen their vision and rethink their traditional strategies and political positioning.

The larger question, however, is what these reforms can mean for competitiveness. Ultimately, by allowing international firms greater flexibility in contracting labor and expanding employment, while being able to tie labor costs to productivity, Latin America will become a more attractive place for new and increased investment. As described earlier, in comparison to its competitors for investment in Asia and Eastern Europe, Latin America remains one of the most inflexible regions in terms of labor markets. Reforming those laws, while it may bring immediate returns for investment, is one more component of improving the region's ability to compete globally for investment and higher-end jobs. In the end, Latin America's ability to absorb the growing influx of youth into its already struggling labor markets will depend on its capacity to attract this new investment.

Notes

1. I would like to thank in particular Juan Matias Zaldua who conducted the initial and follow-up research for this chapter and Maria Lotito who provided comments on an earlier draft. Portions of this chapter appeared earlier in the *Journal of Democracy,* October 1, 2006, and have been reprinted with the permission of Johns Hopkins University Press.
2. Inter-American Development Bank, *Economic and Social Progress Report: Good Jobs Wanted: Labor Markets in Latin America 2004,* (Washington, D.C.: Inter-American Development Bank, 2004).
3. Ibid.
4. World Bank Development Indicators database, Latin America and the Caribbean, Unemployment, total (percent of total labor force), 1989–2003, http://devdata.worldbank.org/data-query/.
5. Víctor Tokman, "Integrating the Informal Sector in the Modernization Process," *SAIS Review* 21 (Winter–Spring 2001): 45–60.
6. James Heckman and Carmen Pages, "The Cost of Job Security Regulation: Evidence from Latin American Labor Markets," NBER Working Paper No. W7773, June 2000.
7. Ronaldo Munck, "Introduction," *Latin American Perspectives* 31, no. 4 (July 2004).
8. What do we mean by informal employment? There is a huge amount of debate about what is meant by "informal"—a fact that has clouded efforts to effectively quantify informality. What is meant here by informal employment is firms that either operate informally and therefore hire workers outside the law, or firms that operate formally or even legally (i.e., paying taxes) but hire informally (i.e., outside the labor code).
9. A series of individual countries have found a negative relationship between high barriers to firing and employment demand. See for example, on Colombia, Adriana Kugler, "The Incidence of Job Security Regulations on Labor Market Flexibility and

Compliance in Colombia," *Research Network Working Paper, R-393* (Washington, D.C.: Inter-American Development Bank, 2000); on Barbados, Andrew Downes, Niandu Mamingi, and Rose-Marie Belle Antoine, "Labor Market Regulation and Employment in the Caribbean," *Research Network Working Paper R-388* (Washington, D.C.: Inter-American Development Bank, 2000); on Peru. Jaime Saavedra and Máximo Torero, "Labor Market Reforms and Their Impact over Formal Labor Demand and Job Market Turnover: The Case of Peru," *Research Network Working Paper R-394* (Washington, D.C.: Inter-American Development Bank, 2000); and on Argentina, Guillermo Mondino and Silvia Montoya, "Effects of Labor Market Regulations on Employment Decisions by Firms: Empirical Evidence for Argentina," *Research Network Working Paper R-391,* (Washington, D.C.: Inter-American Development Bank, 2000). The most rigorous cross-country analysis of the effect of firing costs and employment concludes that a reduction in the costs associated with shedding workers reduces worker tenure but is associated with a decline in the duration of unemployment. Heckman and Pages, "The Cost of Job Security Regulation."

10. See for example, Norman Loayza, Ana María Oviedo, and Luis Servén, "The Impact of Regulation on Growth and Informality: Cross-Country Evidence," *World Bank Working Paper,* April 2005.

11. Heckman and Pages, "The Cost of Job Security Regulation," 29.

12. See for example, William Maloney, "Does Informality Imply Segmentation in Urban Labor Markets? Evidence from Sectoral Transitions in Mexico," *World Bank Economic Review* 13, May 1999: 275–302; and Jaime Saavedra, "Labor Markets during the 1990s," in *After the Washington Consensus: Restarting Growth and Reform in Latin America,* ed. Pedro-Pablo Kuczynski and John Williamson (Washington, D.C.: Institute for International Economics, 2003), 213–264.

13. The growth rate in the informal sector was 3.9 percent while in the formal sector it was 2.1 percent. See International Labour Organization, *Global Employment Trends Brief* (Geneva: International Labour Organization, February 2005), 6.

14. Most research on the informal sector in Latin America places the total size of the sector regionwide at around or just over 50 percent of the urban workforce. The International Labour Organization's 2002 Labor Overview calculated the rate at 46.3 percent. Nicolai Kristensen and Wendy Cunningham ("Do Minimum Wages in Latin America and the Caribbean Matter? Evidence from 19 Countries," *World Bank Policy Research Working Paper,* 3870, March 2006) estimate the range throughout the region as 30 to 70 percent, and Tokman ("Integrating the Informal Sector in the Modernization Process"), citing ILO numbers, says that the sector provides about 57 percent of total urban employment in Latin America.

15. International Labour Organization, *Global Employment Trends Brief,* 6.

16. Economic Commission for Latin America, *Boletín demográfico: América Latina y Caribe—Estmaciones y proyecciones de población, 1950* (Santiago, Chile: United Nations, 2002), 38, Table 11a, "América Latina: Estimaciones y Proyecciones de la Población Total."

17. International Labour Organization, *Global Employment Trends Brief,* 7.

18. Jaime Saavedra, "Labor Markets during the 1990s," 246.

19. Ruth Berins Collier and Samuel Handlin, "Shifting Interest Regimes of the Working Classes in Latin America," *Institute of Industrial Relations Working Paper Series* (Berkeley: University of California, 2005), 7.

Chapter 13

Regulatory Reform: Increasing Competitiveness through Regulatory and Investment Climate Improvements in Latin America; the Case of Mexico

José Luis Guasch and Benjamin Herzberg*

The past two decades have witnessed two trends in regulation. First, there has been an unparalleled rise in new regulations related to health, safety, and the environment. Second, there has also been substantial economic deregulation of certain industries in some countries, including airlines, trucking, railroads, financial markets, energy, and telecommunications. More recently, and to complement the objectives of their far-reaching privatization programs, a third trend is in place in developing countries. They have begun to examine regulations, the investment climate, and administrative procedures that keep prices inefficiently high, deter entry, increase transaction costs, and so on; this is the focus of the present chapter.

The increased interest in regulatory reform can be explained in part by a growing understanding of the impacts of regulation. The costs that regulations can impose on the economy are now much better understood. Indeed, scholars now appreciate that regulation is subject to political influences and is rarely implemented with the sole purpose of improving economic efficiency; in many cases, regulation has had adverse effects on the economy. That argument forms the basis for the trend toward regulatory reform as globalization increases the pressure to reduce production costs and as officials react to the increased mobility of capital and labor by adjusting their policies to reflect the likely impact of regulations on transaction costs and on attracting foreign direct investment.

Benefits of Deregulation

The literature on the benefits and costs of regulation demonstrates that this issue can be explored systematically using standard economic analysis. It also shows that regulation can have a significant, adverse impact on economic growth. Specifically, regulation aimed at controlling prices and entry into markets that would otherwise be workably competitive is likely to reduce growth and adversely affect the average standard of living. In addition, process regulation can impose a significant cost on the economy. The benefits of deregulation in both developed and developing countries are quite significant and have been well documented (Guasch and Hahn, 1999; Hahn, 1998; Hahn and Hird, 1991; Christainsen and Haveman, 1981; MacAvoy, 1992; World Bank, 2004; Dollar, Hallward-Driemeier, and Mengistae, 2003a, b; Castelar et al., 2001; OECD, 1997; SECOFI, 1997). In countries that have deregulated, the efficiency gains have been quite significant. A few examples illustrate the point.

A study of Argentina (Fundación de Investigaciones Económicas Latinoamericanas, 1991) assesses the welfare cost of regulations and other government interventions in the 1980s. The total costs of regulation and state intervention amount to more than $4 billion a year (1990 dollars), and this is only for the selected interventions. The Mexican Institute for Competitiveness (IMCO) produced its own benchmarking report in 2005, which concludes that the cost of the regulatory burden currently represents 15 percent of Mexico's GDP, while the benefits from regulatory improvement could yield a 5 percent increase in GDP. In Brazil, regulations have forced industry to ship by road rather than rail, although the costs are almost three times higher than railroad charges; only 12 percent of relatively short trips and a negligible 3 percent share of longer trips are made by rail. Similar effects are seen in Argentina. Additional anecdotal evidence of regulation and of its impact in developing countries is quite ample.

The costs of various kinds of process regulation caused by inefficient bureaucracies and high levels of corruption can add substantially to consumer burdens in developing countries. For example, customs administrations tend to be plagued by inefficiency and corruption, imposing a high cost on traded goods. According to the Nigeria Manufacturers Association (1996), permission to clear goods in that country requires 27 stages and takes five to eight weeks. Inefficient regulation of port operations and customs procedures has contributed to implicit tariffs of 5 to 15 percent on exports in Latin America (Guasch and Spiller, 2004). Surveys indicate that managers spend between 10 and 30 percent of their time managing process regulation, incurring costs on produced goods or services in the range of 5 to 15 percent (World Bank, 2006). Mexico has been reviewing regulations for major federal agencies. The purpose of the review is to eliminate unnecessary regulations, simplify regulations that are unnecessarily burdensome, and make the process more transparent.

Developing countries have begun to realize the benefits of reforming economic regulation, but much remains to be done in the area of economic and administrative regulation. Yet, it is beginning to appear on the policy agenda, if not from domestic pressure, then from interest groups in industrial countries. The overall lesson is not that regulation is generally undesirable but that it often has undesirable economic consequences. Moreover, these effects result partly from political forces that lead to inequitable redistribution of wealth (Stigler, 1971). We believe such forces can be mitigated by more sharply evaluating the consequences and tradeoffs involved before a regulatory policy is set in stone.

Investment climate reform, designed to unleash the private sector as an engine of economic growth, is a key component of poverty reduction and economic reform strategies. This entails providing a sound legal and regulatory framework that encourages investment and business development, and strengthening the capacity of government to respond efficiently to enterprise needs.

A good investment climate fosters productive private investment—the engine of growth and poverty reduction. It creates opportunities and jobs for people. It expands the variety of goods and services available and reduces their cost, to the benefit of consumers. It supports a sustainable source of tax revenues to fund other important social goals. Many features of a good investment climate improve the lives of people directly, whether they work or engage in entrepreneurial activities or not. Improving the investment climate—the opportunities and incentives for firms to invest productively, create jobs, and expand—is the key to sustainable progress in attacking poverty and improving living standards. Latin American economies cannot escape the imperative to improve their investment climate, especially in the face of the rising competitive threat that increased globalization (and China in particular) represents.

Where does Latin America Stand on Investment Climate, Red-Tape Regulation, and Administrative Procedures?

In Latin America, structural reforms are necessary, but so is the simple elimination of red tape caused by cumbersome and outdated laws and administrative procedures. Figure 13.1 illustrates but one of the problems of red tapism in licensing issues—and the burden of administrative procedures in Latin America.

A large, pending agenda of reforms remains daunting. The time and costs to register firms, to secure construction licenses, to move imported or exported goods through ports and customs, to resolve contractual disputes, to deal with red tape and administrative procedures, are all still too large. The labor market regulations are still too rigid, taxes are high and unbalanced, collateral requirements too high, recovered value of disputed contracts too low, and so on. The most current data on Latin America's business climate may be found in the World Bank's *Doing Business* series (World Bank, 2006).

Most Latin American countries are aware of their predicament with regard to administrative burdens and a number of them have begun to seriously engage in a program of reform in order to reduce the costs and burdens. Among the most active reformers are Colombia and Mexico. In fact, Mexico was one the top ten reformers in the world for the year 2006. The government of the municipality of Mexico D.F., with the largest share of economic activity, is taking the lead

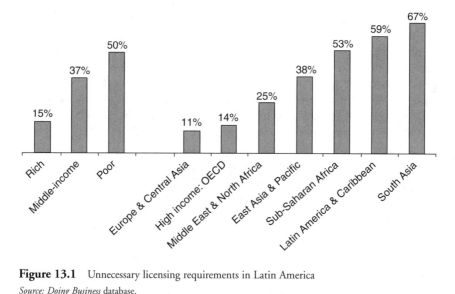

Figure 13.1 Unnecessary licensing requirements in Latin America
Source: Doing Business database.

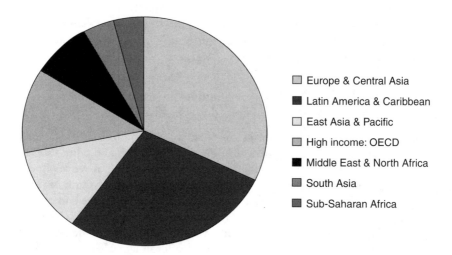

Figure 13.2 Latin America—Moving forward with reforms
Source: Doing Business database.

with an aggressive program to reduce the time and costs to register firms, obtain construction permits, register property, enforce contracts, and resolve contract disputes. Latin America is moving ahead with reforms (figure 13.2), including those that improve investor protection (figure 13.3).

Promoting competitiveness through regulatory improvement has attracted growing attention in the past decade. Nevertheless, there is still significant confusion and misunderstanding about what specific returns can be expected

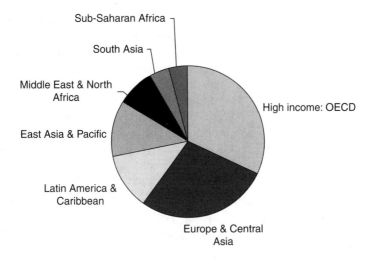

Figure 13.3 Latin America—Improving investor protection
Source: Doing Business database.

of regulatory mechanisms and how they can best promote competitiveness. Such mechanisms, policies, and institutional means come in as many different shapes and forms as there are different political and economic situations. Rather than trying to catalog all the regulatory improvement initiatives in Latin America and to capture them in a grand framework—always a temptation for the economist, but hardly beneficial in the case of this nascent process—the rest of this chapter will look at the example of Mexico and explore how the federal authorities have set in place a regulatory governance process operated by the Federal Regulatory Improvement Commission, which is now looked at by other Latin American economies as a precedent in best practice for enhancing competitiveness through regulatory improvement. We are presenting our argument in three parts. We will first look at how federal regulations still hinder competitiveness by contemplating time and cost indicators of doing business in Mexico compared to other Latin American countries and key competitors. Then, we will briefly review the history of how Mexico started to handle its regulatory challenges by reviewing the different regulatory initiatives that were engineered over the past three decades. In this section we will also describe the current functioning of regulatory improvement mechanisms and their mostly positive impact on the investment climate. Finally, we will analyze the important implications of regulatory improvement for governments and aid partners in Latin America.

Regulatory Challenges

Although recent reforms have been far reaching, Mexican entrepreneurs still face microeconomic constraints. Over the last two decades, Mexico has undergone a reform process that has redefined the economic role of the state. Market liberalization, especially through the establishment of North American Free Trade

Agreement (NAFTA), privatization of state-owned enterprises, and regulatory reforms affecting 90 percent of the legal framework, have moved the country closer to free and competitive markets. However, much remains to be done to address the structural weakness that constrains productivity and growth. Poverty remains high; approximately 52 percent of the population lives in poverty, a level similar to the early 1990s, and 20 percent live in extreme poverty. The informal sector represents 33 percent of GDP. At a time when Mexico is facing increased competition from China and Central American countries, the Mexican entrepreneur's competitiveness is hindered by a series of microeconomic constraints, including the increased cost of doing business created by the regulatory burden.

Mexico needs to reduce its regulatory burden to improve productivity. Several studies demonstrate how the regulatory burden in Mexico is still hindering business growth. The Organisation for Economic Co-operation and Development (OECD), in its most recent review of the effect of product market regulations on investment and growth found that when regulation is restrictive, productivity growth is generally below the OECD average. As the OECD points out, this does not imply that governments should dismantle regulations. Regulation is necessary for well-functioning market economies, but regulation may also impede competition with detrimental consequences on resource allocation, innovation, and productivity. The challenge for Mexico is to design regulations that help to safeguard the public good without compromising economic performance. It is an area where learning from best performers is crucial. The OECD estimates that if those sectors that lag in terms of productivity were to modernize their regulatory framework and align it on best practices, then productivity could increase by as much as 10 percent.

Benchmarking the cost of doing business in Mexico is telling as to where improvements can be achieved through targeted regulatory improvement reforms. The *Doing Business* report of the World Bank Group has benchmarked indicators of the cost of doing business in Mexico against more that 150 countries around the world. The report covers entry regulations, licensing regulation, employment regulations, registering property, court efficiency, corporate governance, creditor rights and credit information, bankruptcy, and tax issues.

Compared to other countries in Latin America, Mexico clearly faces disadvantages in (a) time and cost to open a business; (b) time and cost to obtain a license; (c) cost of hiring; and (d) cost of tax compliance. The indicators contribute to a better understanding of progress in regulatory reform and demonstrate the efforts that remain to be made to improve the regulatory environment so as to allow the Mexican private sector to become more competitive. Despite these shortcomings, Mexico's overall performance in *Doing Business* indicators is better than the average, reaching the top 40 percent. However, competitors such as Chile, Malaysia, and Thailand are in the top 20 percent (figure 13.4).

The time and costs required to open a business in Mexico are high compared to China and Latin America. According to the *Doing Business 2007* benchmarking report of the World Bank, it is cheaper to open a business in China (9 percent of income per capita) than in Mexico (14 percent). The picture darkens considerably

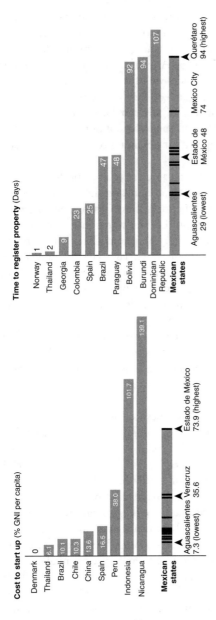

Cost to start up (% GNI per capita)

Denmark	0
Thailand	6.1
Brazil	10.1
Chile	10.3
China	13.6
Spain	16.5
Peru	38.0
Indonesia	101.7
Nicaragua	139.1

Mexican states

Aguascalientes 7.3 (lowest) Veracruz 35.6 Estado de México 73.9 (highest)

Time to register property (Days)

Norway	1
Thailand	2
Georgia	9
Colombia	23
Spain	25
Brazil	47
Paraguay	48
Bolivia	92
Burundi	94
Dominican Republic	107

Mexican states

Aguascalientes 29 (lowest) Estado de México 48 Mexico City 74 Querétaro 94 (highest)

Doing business in Mexico: where is it easiest?

1 Aguascalientes (Easiest)
2 Guanajuato
3 Chihuahua
4 Jalisco
5 Nuevo León
6 Veracruz
7 Yucatán
8 San Luis Potosí
9 Coahuila
10 Mexico City
11 Estado de México
12 Puebla
13 Querétaro (Most difficult)

Figure 13.4 Start-up cost and time to register property—Mexico and other selected countries

Source: Doing Business database.

when comparing some states of Mexico to its Latin American neighbors. While the *Doing Business* database uses the Federal District of Mexico as a reference point for cross-country benchmarking, some states of Mexico, according to a subnational *Doing Business* study, fall short of enabling their business community to compete with Latin American neighbors. In Chile, which competes with Mexico in trade with the EU, it takes just about a quarter (27 days) the time it takes in Querétaro (94 days) to create a business. States such as Estado de Mexico (48 days) also fall well short of countries such as Argentina (32 days) or Colombia (44 days). On the upside, Auguascalientes fairs well for the ease of doing business with 29 days to open a business compared to 92 days in Bolivia. As mentioned, the government of the municipality of Mexico D.F. is engaged in an aggressive reform program to improve the time and costs of obtaining operating licenses for new firms, for registering property, for obtaining construction licenses, and for resolving contractual disputes.

The regulatory cost associated with operating a business is one of the main factors that drive companies into the informal sector, reducing the competitiveness of entire sectors of the economy. The construction sector is particularly affected. It used to take 222 days to obtain a license to build a warehouse in Mexico in 2005, placing it in the bottom quarter of Latin American countries. In comparison, obtaining a license took 150 days in Colombia, 187 days in Bolivia, and 191 days in Chile. Costs to obtain a license in Mexico (159 percent of income per capita) in 2005 are not bad compared with many countries in Latin America, but there is still significant room for improvement. For instance, it only costs 48 percent of income per capita in Argentina and 125 percent in Chile. These times and costs are indicators of the weight that the regulatory burden can play on investment and/or compliance decisions that investors have to face while trying to grow their market share. In 2006, it seems that Mexico reacted, as the *Doing Business 2007* numbers indicate that the number of days required to obtained a construction license went down to 74 days.

Other indicators also point to regulatory weaknesses. Mexico is in the bottom third of the worldwide distribution of the ease of enforcing contracts. Regarding property registration, there are as many procedures in Mexico (5) as in Australia (5) and Ireland (5), but it takes at least twice as long (74, 38, and 5, respectively). The registration property is the main source of bottlenecks; this procedure may take between one and three months. Costs to register property are high in Mexico, encouraging informal transactions that leave the property registry out of date and reducing the availability of collateral for firms trying to access financing. Another example is the cost of hiring workers. *Doing Business* estimates that hiring an employee costs just under a quarter of that employee's annual salary in Mexico (23.8 percent), well above all but three Latin American countries. Comparable numbers (percentage of salary) are 3.3 percent in Chile, 9.75 percent in Peru, and 13.7 percent in Bolivia. Finally, tax regulations are complicated enough to take the average Mexican entrepreneur 552 hours per year to pay taxes. Meanwhile, entrepreneurs in Colombia and Chile only spend 456 and 432 hours paying taxes, respectively.

The IMCO produced its own benchmarking report in 2005. It concludes that the cost of the regulatory burden currently represents 15 percent of Mexico's GDP, while the benefits from regulatory improvement could yield a 5 percent increase in GDP. The IMCO and *Doing Business* reports make clear that the costs related to the complex regulatory framework, nontransparent business procedures and weak judicial structures remain factors inhibiting investment in Mexico. They create indirect costs that impede Mexican manufacturers in their competition with other countries, and translate into job loss and growth reduction.

Lack of harmonization in the regulatory environment negatively impacts businesses. Since regulatory responsibilities are shared among the federal, state, and municipal levels, coordination is necessary to eliminate the overlaps, duplication, and inconsistency with federal regulations. A 2003 study commissioned by the Business Coordination Council (CCE) showed marked differences in the quality of the regulatory framework among states. On the positive side, improvements in some subnational entities have attracted reforms in others, as has been the case with the Sistema de Apertura Rápida de Empresas (SARE, Rapid Business Start-Up System). Benchmarking different states and municipalities can spur this positive competition to improve regulations. The result of two state-by-state studies was released in December 2005 by IMCO and the World Bank's Foreign Investment Advisory Service (FIAS)/*Doing Business,* from which the numbers cited above were drawn.

These studies and reports have stirred up healthy debates in Mexico, and there are indications of regulatory improvement, as Mexico is singled out as the sixth best reformer of the 2005–2006 period in the *Doing Business 2007* report. This stellar improvement demonstrates the validity and efficiency of the regulatory governance mechanisms (table 13.1).

The Mexican Government Initiatives in Bettering Regulation

The Federal Regulatory Improvement Commission (COFEMER) is an agency that was created in 2000 to improve regulation. In 2000, amendments to the Ley Federal de Procedimiento Administrativo (LFPA, Federal Administrative Procedures Law) institutionalized the COFEMER. COFEMER is a technically and functionally autonomous agency of the Ministry of Economy created to coordinate and to supervise the Regulatory Improvement Program of the government. It aims to ensure the transparency of the regulatory process and promote regulations that produce benefits greater than the costs. Mexico is one of the few developing countries that created a mechanism to challenge the quality of new regulation through the establishment of mandatory Regulatory Impact Assessment (RIA) for all new regulations that impose costs on citizens. COFEMER plays the key role of systematically reviewing RIAs and regulatory improvement proposals (figure 13.5).

The systematic review of administrative proposals is now well grounded in law, and COFEMER is fairly effective in improving "new regulations." Nevertheless, although COFEMER can push for the structural reform agenda, it cannot carry

Table 13.1 The top 10 reformers, 2005–2006

	Country	Starting a business	Dealing with licenses	Hiring and firing	Registering property	Getting credit	Protecting investors	Trading across borders	Paying taxes	Enforcing contracts	Closing a business
1	Georgia	✓	✓			✓		✓		✓	
2	China	✓		✓		✓					
3	France		✓			✓	✓	✓		✓	
4	Romania		✓	✓		✓		✓			✓
5	Tanzania	✓			✓		✓	✓			✓
6	Mexico	✓					✓				
7	India	✓				✓	✓		✓		
8	Armenia	✓	✓		✓	✓			✓		
9	Nigeria				✓			✓		✓	
10	Ghana				✓			✓	✓		

Source: Doing Business database.

Note: Countries are ranked on the number of reforms. When countries have the same number of reforms, they are ranked on the impact of the reforms on the *Doing Business* indicators. The larger the improvement in ranking on each set of indicators, the higher the ranking.

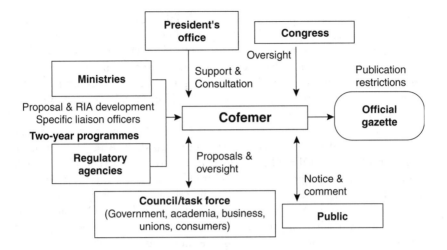

Figure 13.5 Institutional design for regulatory review

Source: Carlos Garcia-Fernandez, "Regulatory Reform in Mexico," paper presented at the Special Session of the OECD Working Party on Regulatory Reform, Paris, September 28, 2005.

it out on its own. Accountability and transparency of the regulatory review process is supported by the right to apply severe sanctions for noncompliance. Sanctions are applied by the Secretariat of Civil Service (SFP). A key enforcement power of COFEMER is that regulations cannot be published in the national gazette without its explicit opinion.

Certain specified federal agencies must send each of their draft proposals, together with an RIA, to COFEMER, which makes them public on its website, www.cofemer.gob.mx. COFEMER has the authority to issue a public opinion concerning each draft proposal and RIA. It also has the authority to request changes in the RIA, and, in specific cases such as high impact regulations, it can seek expert opinions on the draft proposal. For other agencies, COFEMER has "optional or not optional" authority to review and analyze all proposals with general exemptions in fiscal policy, criminal justice, and national defense. COFEMER can hence develop reform proposals in collaboration with these agencies. In the Fox administration, COFEMER has made use of its optional authority to propose new measures in at least three areas: (1) with Interior, it cosponsored the Transparency Act (2003); (2) with Treasury, Foreign Affairs, and Labor, it cosponsored administrative reforms to reduce federal procedures for start-ups; and (3) with states and municipalities, it sponsored the federal/subfederal fast track start-up program SARE.

Regulatory planning activities are being undertaken via the Regulatory Betterment Program (RBP), a mechanism to organize future regulations that give the Mexican public the opportunity to participate in regulatory planning. RBPs were created by amendments to the LFPARBP. At least every two years, Mexican ministries and regulators must prepare an RBP to inform the public of their plans for regulation proposal and the possible creation of new formalities. These RBPs are beginning to build a discipline of periodical review and planning of the regulatory framework and its amendments. The RBPs also help to achieve the central purpose of the federal regulatory improvement policy: to create and to modify regulations and formalities according to processes based on planning, transparency, analysis potential effects, and public consultation, in order to obtain the highest social benefit.

The first draft of the RBPs is submitted to COFEMER and posted for public comments on COFEMER's website for at least 20 days. After the period of public consultation, COFEMER sends each ministry and decentralized agency its comments on the programs, as well as other public comments received. Each regulatory agency then makes any corresponding changes to its program or explains the reasons for rejection, publishing the final version in the Official Gazette within a month. Each agency must submit to COFEMER a periodic report on compliance with the program, and possible modifications to the programs are assessed.

The version of the RBP presented in the summer of 2005 included a novelty: the RBP was prepared with a private/public dialogue that took place before the first draft of the RBP was prepared. This approach made it possible to unify efforts in a new "systemic approach" to regulation, creating a coordination mechanism between the public, academic, and private sectors. The idea was to set regulatory priorities in conjunction with the private sector. The systemic approach also aimed to incorporate a holistic analysis of regulatory systems in particular economic sectors. Together, the Mexican public and private sectors defined 36 specific actions related to regulatory improvement that could influence competitiveness in a positive way. Those actions have impact in specific areas such as transport and telecommunications, labor and social security, health, energy, foreign trade, finance, technical standards, migration, and states and municipalities.

Progress has also been achieved at the subnational level. COFEMER does not have direct jurisdiction over states and municipalities. However, one of COFEMER's functions is to provide technical assistance in regulatory improvement to states and municipalities. Also, the Programa de Mejora Regulatoria 2001–2006 (Program for Regulatory Improvement 2001–2006) establishes the promotion of a culture of regulatory improvement in the three levels of government as one of COFEMER's strategic objectives. COFEMER has thus signed coordination agreements with all states and the Federal District in which states agree to implement regulatory programs similar to the ones at the federal level. COFEMER has also signed 50 memorandums of understanding with municipalities. COFEMER's support to states and municipalities has varied from providing technical assistance in establishing registries of formalities to conducting reviews of regulatory authorities to designing enforcement schemes. As an illustration, in 2006, 67 municipalities' regulatory improvement systems were being inventoried by the COFEMER.

COFEMER works with municipalities to simplify business-opening procedures. The SARE was created by COFEMER and issued at the federal government level in 2002. It allowed businesses to complete two federal procedures—obtaining a fiscal identification number and registering their name—in one business day. Building on this mechanism, as of 2006, some 85 municipalities (representing 35.7 percent of Mexican GDP) have also implemented the SARE, reducing the time to start up a business from over thirty days to one to two days. COFEMER is to have had implemented the SARE in a total of 100 municipalities by 2007. The SARE is also considered an important tool in developing compatible systems at the state and local levels. However, the SARE has been only partially implemented in some locations. Moreover, even with the SARE, the entrepreneur still has to register separately with labor and social security authorities as well as with the statistical office.

COFEMER allows labor and business representatives to advise the government on regulation. The Federal Regulatory Improvement Program, designed and co-coordinated by COFEMER, is supported by the Consejo para la Mejora Regulatoria Federal (Federal Regulatory Improvement Council), whose membership was also modified by the LFPA. The president of the council is the Minister of Economy. Other members are the minister of finance, the minister of labor, the minister of the public function, the general director of COFEMER, the governor of the Bank of Mexico, five business sector representatives, and at least one representative from the labor, agricultural, and academic sectors. The president's legal counsel, the president of the Federal Competition Commission, and the president of the Federal Consumer Protection Agency (PROFECO) were added as new members after 2000. This council mirrors the experience of other OECD countries, involving labor and business representatives in official advisory bodies to the government for regulatory matters.

In a meeting of the council in April 2004, President Fox announced a one-year moratorium on regulations as part of an effort to further reduce burdens on businesses. Under this moratorium, any new federal regulations must be shown to have benefits that significantly surpass the costs, or be driven by an emergency situation. This moratorium has caused a significant reduction in issue and renewal of regulations. The moratorium process has been effective in reducing the number of regulations being issued, illustrated by the fact that 38 percent fewer regulations are now "produced" by the federal authorities, compared with the number before the moratorium. It also has had a positive impact upstream within agencies and institutions, which are now submitting 34 percent less proposals for new regulations, compared with the volume of proposals they used to forward for review before the moratorium. In 2005, the moratorium was extended for another year at the demand of the private sector.

COFEMER has increased transparency in the implementation of regulations. Through open communication with the public and the private sector in particular, transparency has been reinforced. COFEMER has emphasized its importance not only with RIAs and commentary on draft regulations, but also with public participation in comment procedures and with clearer legal requirements for notifications. Within the government, COFEMER disseminates knowledge about RIAs among institutions through training courses and its electronic portal, which has proved to be a major success. COFEMER has also developed a Registro Federal de Trámites y Servicios (RFTS, Federal Registry of Procedures and Services) that contains all formalities and services of the federal administration with general exemptions in fiscal formalities.

Transparency mechanisms have also been strengthened through the creation of the Instituto Federal de Acceso a la Información Pública (IFAI, Federal Institute of Access to Public Information). IFAI enforces the Ley Federal de Transparencia y Acceso a la Información Gubernamental (Federal Law of Transparency and Access to Public Information), enacted in 2002. It also guarantees the effectiveness of both the right to access public information and the right to privacy through data protection, and promotes transparency and public sector accountability.

Lessons for COFEMER: Type of Institutions

While the improvements have been quite significant and in the direction of best practices for other countries, there is room for improvement both for Mexico and for other countries considering the type of reform.

- **COFEMER needs continuing support.** COFEMER can lead the above-mentioned tasks, but it can exercise its full powers only if it enjoys broad support and acts decisively. One challenge is sustaining the support of the private sector and official institutions. Earlier, rallied by the domestic crisis and strong political support, the private sector took on an active role in pressuring agencies to improve regulation. Today, many factors contribute to the more passive role of several public and private actors, including the loss of founding members of the council through turnover. Additionally, political circumstances and a fragmented Congress have shifted the private sector's lobbying efforts from the executive branch and its agencies toward Congress. This trend can only be counterbalanced by a reinforcement of COFEMER's role vis-à-vis the institutions issuing regulations. In that sense, ensuring continuous training of public administration officials on the RIA framework is key to maintaining momentum while improving the upstream quality of proposed regulations. The cornerstone of this effort lies in demonstrating the benefits of the RIA process in terms of cost reduction to the entrepreneurs. In that regard, the establishment of an ex post evaluation framework for RIAs would help benchmark regulatory compliance of key administrations and create strong political incentives for those administrations to streamline and simplify their regulatory environment.
- **Public consultation needs to be strengthened.** Consultation in making, modifying, or repealing legislation and regulation in Mexico is still weak. There is still no legal obligation to undertake active public consultation for certain federal regulatory proposals. Nevertheless, COFEMER has included a section in the RIA questionnaire on public consultation. Institutional bodies are requested to specify if they established some type of public consultation and who was consulted about the proposals. The RIA also requests a list

of all the submissions that were taken into account for the draft regulation that is being presented. But the input of the private sector, when it comes to regulation affecting the cost of doing business, should be reinforced.

- **Better harmonization of regulation between the different levels of jurisdiction is necessary.** Today, any regulatory improvement process, including red-tape reduction at the sub-federal level, depends on states' and municipalities' will and capacity to coordinate with each other. COFEMER, through the SARE system, can play a key role in helping set up similar frameworks and systems between jurisdictions. It is crucial to deepen the voluntary relationship between COFEMER and the states and municipalities. As a first step, it is equally important to diagnose binding constraints at the state and municipal level in order to identify the different sources of competitiveness loss of specific industries or value chains. A benchmarking exercise between the states and municipalities could help identify best practices and drive the regulatory cost reduction agenda in that regard.

- **Expanding the implementation of the SARE will reduce the time and cost of business-opening regulations.** The target is for COFEMER to help implement the SARE in more than 100 municipalities, representing more than 40 percent of Mexican GDP by 2007. The output is to be measured in the start-up time for small and medium-size businesses (from an average of 52 days to 3 days only) and a reduction in the associated cost. The outcome is to be measured in the number of new companies created, the value of investment in these entrepreneurial projects, and the number of jobs created. Beyond the numerical targets, COFEMER shall also create a system to measure the SARE's effectiveness and monitor its implementation in order to keep improving the processes and facilitate the introduction of the system to new municipalities.

- **The RIA process in federal institutions needs to be reinforced.** This component aims at generalizing the current RIA process among all agencies and institutions when applicable. This includes raising the number of RIAs being conducted (355 in 2005), as well as the quality of the RIAs being submitted for review. In that regard, training of public servants in impact assessment practices remains crucial. In order to ensure compliance and accountability in the RIA process, enactment of the bylaws of the Ley Federal de Procedimiento Administrativo (Federal Administrative Procedures Law) is also important.

- **COFEMER needs to create a monitoring and evaluation framework for RIAs.** To date, COFEMER does not compare the cost it estimates for regulatory proposals to actual cost, which could be measured ex post. Similarly, COFEMER does not track how the regulatory alternatives it suggested during the RIA process were actually applied and implemented. Finally, COFEMER does not formally benchmark the quality of RIAs originating from different secretariats. A framework to achieve the above points should be put in place in the medium term. The impact of such actions would be, over time, to reduce the cost of doing business for

Mexican entrepreneurs, especially compared with other Latin American countries, with an emphasis on entry, licensing, and tax and labor regulations.

- **Increasing cooperation with subnational jurisdictions and the private sector to keep improving regulations at all levels is important.** The aim is to improve local competitiveness conditions by (1) benchmarking the cost of doing business in at least 12 states in 2006; (2) facilitating the creation of competitiveness action plans at the subnational level; and (3) building an inventory of existing state and municipal regulatory improvement mechanisms. In turn, these activities will increase the quality of the systems used by the municipalities (percentage reduction in proceedings and procedures, improvement of administrative processes, response times, etc.) and reduce the time and costs of business operations pertaining to entry regulation, property registry, contract enforcement, access to credit, and others.

Lessons from Mexico and Implications for Latin America

Latin American countries, such as Mexico, need to undertake important regulatory reforms to boost their competitiveness. In Mexico, specific sectors, especially in the manufacturing industry, are losing exports and even domestic market share to China and other Latin American countries such as Honduras. While Mexico's labor wages cannot be reduced to compete with its competitors' low labor costs, the government needs to undertake actions to reduce the indirect costs of doing business. Other governments in Latin America also need to consider these important points. Specifically, these are as follows.

1) Procedures that impose large burdens on entrepreneurs need to be eliminated, replaced, or improved (starting a business, licensing, employment regulation, tax regulation).
2) Business interactions with government need to be streamlined so as to reduce uncertainty and implementation efficiency issues.
3) Industry sectors that are key to Mexican competitiveness and under specific competition threat from foreign markets could benefit from a thorough review of administrative barriers in order to identify where action can be taken to reduce cost. Such sectors and issues could include foreign trade, manufacturing, property, finance, norms and standards, transport and telecommunications, energy, and labor.
4) Latin American countries ought to create COFEMER-type of institutions with similar mandate, jurisdiction, and convening powers and authority to implement far-reaching programs of regulatory reforms and investment climate improvements, the latter in close coordination with municipalities.

* The findings, interpretations, and conclusions expressed in this paper are entirely those of the authors. They do not necessarily represent the view of the World Bank, its executive directors, or the countries they represent.

References

Castelar Pinheiro, Armando, Indermit S. Gill, Luis Serven, and Mark R. Thomas. 2001. "Brazilian Economic Growth, 1900–2000: Lessons and Policy Implications." Paper presented at the GDN Conference, Rio de Janeiro, December 9.

Christainsen, Gregory B. and Robert H. Haveman. 1981. "Public Regulations and the Slowdown in Productivity Growth." *American Economic Review* 71 (May): 320–325.

Dollar, David, Mary Hallward-Driemeier, and Taye Mengistae. 2003a. "Investment Climate and Firm Performance in Developing Countries." Washington, D.C.: World Bank.

_____. 2003b. "Investment Climate, Infrastructure and Trade: A Comparison of Latin America and Asia." Washington, D.C.: World Bank.

Fundación de Investigaciones Económicas Latinoamericanas. 1991. *Regulatory Costs in Argentina.* Buenos Aires: ALIANZA.

Guasch, J. Luis, and Pablo Spiller. 2004. *Managing the Regulatory Process: Design, Concepts, Issues and the Latin America and Caribbean Story.* Directions in Development Series. Washington, D.C.: World Bank.

Guasch, J. Luis, and Robert W. Hahn. 1999. "The Costs and Benefits of Regulation: Implications for Developing Countries." *World Bank Research Observer* 14 (1): 137–158.

Hahn, Robert W. 1996. "Regulatory Reform: What do the Government's Numbers Tell Us?" *Risks, Costs, and Lives Saved: Getting Better Results from Regulation.* New York: Oxford University Press, and AEI Press.

_____. 1998. "Government Analysis of the Benefits and Costs of Regulation." *Journal of Economic Perspectives* 12 (4): 201–210.

Hahn, Robert W., and John Hird. 1991. "The Costs and Benefits of Regulation: Review and Synthesis." *Yale Journal on Regulation* 8 (Winter): 233–278.

MacAvoy, Paul W. 1992. *Industry Regulation and the Performance of the American Economy.* New York: W. W. Norton .

Nigeria Manufacturers Association. 1996. "The Impact of Custom Processes in Nigeria." *The Nigeria Manufacturers Association Reports.* Lagos: Nigeria Manufacturers Association.

Organisation for Economic Co-operation and Development (OECD). 1997. "The Economy-wide Effects of Regulatory Reform." *The OECD Report on Regulatory Reform.* Vol. 2, *Thematic Studies.* Paris: Organisation for Economic Co-operation and Development. Ch. 1.

Secretaria De Comercio y Fomento Industrial (SECOFI). 1997. *Economic Deregulation in Mexico.* Mexico City: Secretaria De Comercio y Fomento Industrial.

Stigler, George. 1971. "The Theory of Economic Regulation." *Bell Journal of Economics* 2: 3–21.

World Bank. 2004. *World Development Report 2005: A Better Investment Climate for Everyone.* Washington, D.C.: World Bank Group.

_____. 2006. *Doing Business 2007: How to Reform.* Washington, D.C.: World Bank Group.

CHAPTER 14

Public Safety: The Cost of Living Dangerously

John Price

Public safety is rarely cited as a competitiveness issue but rather a quality of life indicator. Yet, if a nation's competitiveness hinges on its ability to attract and retain talented people and investment capital, then violence is a decisive factor. More than any other reason, it is the threat to family safety that has driven offshore the brightest minds and their capital from Latin America over the last two decades since violent crime began to escalate in the 1980s. Homicide rates in Latin America are the highest of any region in the world. From the early 1980s through the mid-1990s, intentional homicide rates in Latin America increased by 50 percent.[1] Two-thirds of homicide victims are teenage boys aged 15 to 19, a disturbing reality that robs the region of its future.

The World's Most Dangerous Place

Latin America has the dubious distinction as the world's most dangerous region, with a murder rate four times higher than the global average, seven times higher than Asia, twelve times higher than Eastern Europe, and 1.5 times higher than sub-Saharan Africa (see figure 14.1). Furthermore, studies have shown that in lower-income countries, crime, even homicide, often goes unreported. In middle-income nations, in which most Latin American countries are categorized, homicides were underreported by almost 20 percent in a comparison of WHO surveys versus nationally reported statistics.[3]

Within Latin America, there are vast differences of crime levels from country to country and between city and rural areas. Caribbean and Central American countries include some of the most dangerous nations on earth, while Costa Rica, Bermuda, and Aruba are some of the safest spots in the region.

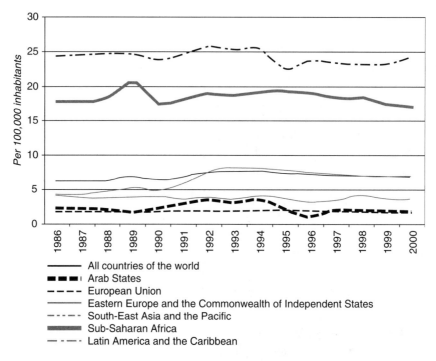

Figure 14.1 Rates of homicides, 1986–2000, selected regional trends[2]

On a regional basis, homicide rates in general are trending for the worse with big increases in murder and robbery rates in Jamaica, El Salvador, Guatemala, Argentina, Mexico, and Venezuela (see figure 14.2). Notable exceptions that have improved safety and security are led by Colombia and Peru. In 2000, Colombia had the highest murder rate in the world. By 2005, homicides in Colombia had fallen to half the number. Colombia offers some valuable lessons to the rest of the region in terms of combining political will with workable policies to lessen violence and cut its roots.

Beyond homicide, Latin America also leads the world in kidnapping. With 8 percent of the world's population, Latin America was home to 75 percent of the world's reported kidnappings in 2003.[5] Crime, violent or otherwise, is pervasive across the region, touching all walks of life. During the decade of the 1990s, 74 percent of Latin Americans (taken through a survey of urban populaces) were victims of some kind of criminal act.[6]

The exercise of measuring an emotionally charged issue such as public security in competitiveness terms is both challenging and controversial. But it is vital to translate what has become an epidemic across much of Latin America into hard, tangible economic figures. Perhaps only then will the political and economic elite, themselves somewhat isolated from the ravages of violence, grasp the importance of decaying public safety.

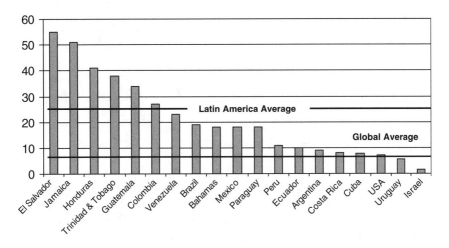

Figure 14.2 Regional annual homicide rates (per 100,000 people)[4]

Adding up the Bill

Most studies that link crime to the economy focus on the actual health and material costs of violence, plus security expenditure as well as the failure to capture foreign investment and tourism dollars. But such formulas, as dramatic as they are, capture only half the true cost of crime. Latin America's failure to capture foreign investment has several explanations, many of which are covered in preceding chapters. The true economic tragedy in Latin America is its failure to retain its own wealth and talent, both of which have emigrated en masse, particularly since the 1980s when crime rates began to escalate.

Measuring Hard Costs

The direct costs of crime in Latin America range from 3 to 13 percent across the region, a massive disparity that closely reflects income and development differences from country to country. Mexico is a useful proxy for analyzing costs for it tends to reflect a median average of crime in a region that includes countries such as El Salvador and Colombia where violence has crippled economic progress, and the vastly safer Chile, Costa Rica, and Uruguay. Mexico is also one of the better-documented nations regarding the direct and indirect costs of crime (see table 14.1).

The direct costs footed by government, corporations, and citizens alike in Mexico reach 8 percent of GDP or roughly U.S.$65 billion per year. That is equal to 75 percent of all income and sales taxes collected by government. It is two and a half times greater than the inflow of remittances, three and a half times greater than the inflow of foreign direct investment (FDI), and roughly twice as much as Mexico's oil exports. It is a massive drain on the country.

Table 14.1 Direct economic costs of crime[7]

	Source	Mexico	Notes
GDP (2006)	EIU	US$798.5 billion	
Health losses	ICESI (Instituto Ciudadano de Estudios sobre la Inseguridad)	1.9%	Actual money spent on medical expenses and burials
Material losses	ICESI (Instituto Ciudadano de Estudios sobre la Inseguridad)	0.8%	
Fighting crime	Violencia Americas, Lodoño y Guerrero	4.9%	Includes private and public expenditure on security personnzel, police, judicial and penal system
Security technology and installation expenditure	ALAS (Latin America Security Association), Reforma	0.1%	
Insurance	Reforma, InfoAmericas	0.2%	Personnel and business expenditure on theft, kidnapping, and fraud insurance
Ransoms	Reforma, InfoAmericas	0.011%	
Corruption (bribes paid to police and judicial authorities)	Transparency International	0.1%	Payments to police and judicial system = 39% of weighted average of household bribery payments
Total direct costs		8.0%	

By comparison, the U.S. military budget in 2006, while fighting two wars and maintaining a military presence in 130 countries around the world, accounts for approximately 4 percent of GDP. Mexican federal, state and municipal governments spend that amount fighting crime each year. In the United States, there are 2.3 active policemen per 1,000 residents.[8] In Venezuela, the number is 5.1, and in wealthier districts of Caracas, the number reaches 12.3.[9]

In Latin America, violence is now among the five main causes of death and is the principal cause of death in Brazil, Colombia, Venezuela, El Salvador, and Mexico. The emergency rooms of public hospitals are clogged by the mounting carnage of violent crime. Treating gunshot wounds is one of the most taxing medical emergencies that a hospital can handle. Gunshot trauma requires specialized, lengthy medical treatment. The average cost of a gunshot victim in the United States is $20,304, in South Africa U.S.$10,308,[10] and in Latin America, it is estimated to range from U.S.$5,000 to $10,000. In El Salvador, the medical costs of crime reach almost 4.5 percent of GDP, of which roughly half is paid for by the government.

Estimating the Indirect Costs of Crime

The more controversial part of the equation linking crime with competitiveness is the indirect cost of crime. Several attempts at a precise calculation have been made by economists, most of them erring on the conservative side in order to avoid question. Indirect costs combine the immediate opportunity costs of crime, that is, the productivity losses triggered by both the injury of people as well as the time and resource distraction of crime prevention, not to mention the loss of material wealth that would otherwise be invested in their businesses and homes. But crime also impacts other areas of wealth creation by keeping tourists and foreign investment away and driving offshore talented productive people and their savings.

Using Mexico again as a case study, the indirect costs of crime are estimated at approximately 11.5 percent of GDP, greater than all income and sales taxes levied in the country (see table 14.2). The lion's share of this loss is caused by Mexico's failure to attract its full potential in terms of tourists and foreign direct investment.

Table 14.2 Indirect economic costs of crime[11]

Loss of productivity	ICESI (Instituto Ciudadano de Estudios sobre la Inseguridad)	1.8%	Lost man hours plus lost personal investment capital
Loss of tourism dollars	ITO, InfoAmericas	3.1%	Mexico captures 43% of the tourism it could if it matched per capita receipts of equivalent destinations, i.e., middle income, semi-tropical, close to a large market (Jamaica, Turkey, Thailand, and Croatia)
Loss of foreign direct investment	EIU, InfoAmericas	4.1%	Mexico captures 55% of the FDI/GDP levels captured by its equivalent competitors (Poland, Hungary, China)
Emigration of people due to public safety issues	InfoAmericas	2.7%	Approximately 50% of college educated and 25% of low income emigrate for safety reasons. Emigrants accumulated since 1990 would earn this amount if working in Mexico.
Minus positive factor of remittances	InfoAmericas	−0.9%	30% of remittances (to match weight given to emigration due to crime)
Loss of investment capital due to crime considerations or due to emigration	InfoAmericas	0.8%	$300 bn in Mexican savings offshore earning 10% per year, of which 20% is driven offshore for personal safety considerations
Indirect total		11.5%	

Tourism—More Would Visit

Mexico is by all definitions a blessed tourism market, within proximity of the second largest outbound tourism market, laden with natural and cultural attractions, and relatively good infrastructure. And yet, Mexico attracts less than half the per capita receipts of comparable markets including Jamaica, Thailand, Croatia, and Turkey. Cancun, an isolated and relatively safe location, is by far Mexico's leading international tourism destination. By comparison, Mexico City, the country's largest city and a cultural gem, attracts paltry numbers of tourists who avoid the city out of fear.

Crime trumps all other factors in keeping tourists away. Despite South America's compelling natural and cultural tourist attractions, only the safest destinations have proven capable of developing an important hospitality sector. The region of Latin America and the Caribbean combines some of the best- and worst-performing nations in the area of inbound tourism (see table 14.3). In the

Table 14.3   Tourism receipts—safety matters[13]

Country	Tourism Receipts per Capita (2004)	Tourism Receipts as a % of the economy (2004)	Grouping
US Virgin Is.	$12,494.82	86.0%	Highly safe environs where tourism is
Aruba	$11,851.27	37.7%	the leading industry and governments
Bahamas	$6,202.06	30.9%	heavily promote and protect their
Bermuda	$5,382.15	7.9%	tourism image.
Barbados	$2,947.35	17.1%	
Guadeloupe	$923.19	11.9%	
Puerto Rico	$770.02	4.1%	Tourism is a leading industry but
Jamaica	$521.01	11.8%	competes with others for government
Dominican Republic	$346.25	4.7%	attention and funds. Tourism
Costa Rica	$333.23	3.0%	destinations are highly protected and
Trinidad & Tobago	$233.62	1.4%	safe to visitors even if other parts of the
Cuba	$168.24	4.8%	country are not safe.
Uruguay	$132.58	1.3%	
Mexico	$100.07	1.0%	
Chile	$80.02	0.7%	
Argentina	$64.20	0.5%	Tourism underperforms because of a
Guatemala	$62.63	1.4%	negative image problem associated with
El Salvador	$49.40	1.1%	crime.
Peru	$38.09	0.6%	
Nicaragua	$33.57	1.2%	
Ecuador	$27.09	0.6%	
Colombia	$23.67	0.3%	
Brazil	$17.13	0.2%	
Venezuela	$16.52	0.3%	
Bolivia	$14.68	0.5%	
Paraguay	$10.60	0.2%	

Table 14.4 FDI performance[14]

Country	FDI 2005 (USD millions)	GDP 2005 (USD millions)	FDI/GDP
Poland	$12,873	$235,000	5.5%
China	$60,000	$1,755,000	3.4%
Hungary	$4,000	$106,000	3.8%
Mexico	$17,805	$768,440	2.3%

Caribbean, where tourism is the leading export sector, public safety, both real and perceived, is a precious national asset. Even in countries with high crime rates such as Jamaica, designated tourism destinations within the country are protected as oases of safety. By contrast, tourism is a relatively unimportant industry in Brazil, Venezuela, and Central America (except Costa Rica). In those countries, the battle for scarce public sector funds is won out by other interests, and crime fighting and prevention are chronically underfunded and mismanaged.[12]

Foreign Direct Investment

Mexico prides itself on the fact that it is the leading Latin American recipient of foreign direct investment. Yet, Mexico fails to attract half the levels of foreign direct investment (FDI) as a percentage of GDP that its rivals China, Poland, and Hungary— nations struggling with many of the development issues facing Mexico in most areas except crime—are achieving (see table 14.4).

Successful foreign investment normally involves the transfer of dozens, if not hundreds, of foreign managers and technicians to the destination market for a number of years. Multinationals struggle to convince experienced managers to move with their families to Latin America and the leading reason for their resistance is public safety. It also helps explain why multinationals tend to buy companies in Latin America rather than launch a new greenfield. The downside to competitiveness of an acquisition is that it does less to raise competitive pressure on the market than would otherwise be achieved through the launch of a new competitor.

Is Mexico Really a Mecca for Foreign Direct Investment?

Scaring Away Talent

The greatest long-term threat to Latin America caused by intolerable crime rates is the exodus of talented people along with their ideas, their drive, and their capital. Brain drain is a global tragedy but one that is particularly taxing on the Caribbean and Latin America.

Wealth is created by capital, ideas, labor, and land. Latin America exports all but one of these and crime is one of the leading causes of this exodus. From 1990 to 2005, an estimated 1.5 million college-educated Latin Americans fled the region,[15] staying at least five years, if not permanently, abroad. A significant number of college-educated migrants leave to do postgraduate studies, only to remain abroad and work. Many others are entrepreneurs fleeing the targeting of kidnappers in places such as Mexico City or gang-led crime in São Paulo in search of a safer haven for their families. Though the United States has partially closed its doors by decreasing H1-B visa quotas by 80 percent, other countries such as Canada, Great Britain, Ireland, and Italy are aggressively wooing skilled immigrants from Latin America and other regions.

The cost to Latin America of its lack of competitiveness over the last 15 years, when measured only by net flight of capital and brain power is estimated at U.S.\$1.2 trillion[16] and continues to cost the region U.S.\$160 billion per year, equal to 7 percent of regional GDP. Latin America is forgoing U.S.\$35 billion per year[17] in tax revenue that is earned by those who fled abroad and the wealthy whose offshore income is near impossible to tax.

The Caribbean Brain Drain

With its respected British colonial legacy education system, the Caribbean educates some of the best and brightest in the Americas. However, the same educated classes in Jamaica, Bahamas, and Trinidad are also the targets of troubling violence levels and lack of opportunity and migrate in droves, chiefly to the United States, but also to Canada and the UK, to study and work (see figure 14.3).

The amount of monies sent home by educated islanders is substantial and along with tourism is the region's leading source of inbound dollars. However, when one combines the lost wages of émigrés with the huge investment by

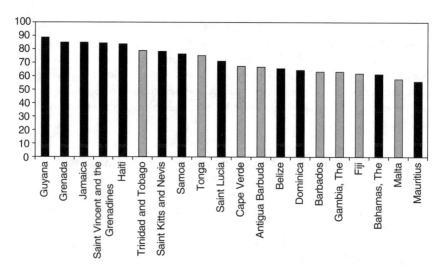

Figure 14.3 Top 20 countries in the world with the highest emigration rates 1970–2000 (percent of educated labor force that has migrated to neighboring OECD member countries)[18]

Note: Educated labor force is defined as having 12 or more years of completed schooling.

government in their education through the end of high school, one sees the true cost of the brain drain. While educated Caribbean émigrés contribute 5 percent to their country of origin's economy through remittances, their absence costs the same economy 10.3 percent of GDP in lost wages, taxes, and education costs not amortized.

Why Is Latin America Historically So Violent?

A long list of factors contributes to Latin America's status as the most dangerous continent on the planet. Economic stagnation and worsening income distribution are perhaps the most compelling.

Since 2003, Latin American per capita income has improved dramatically thanks to high global commodity prices that have lifted export incomes and currency values. However, only in Chile and Mexico has the per capita income steadily risen since the early 1990s. Argentina is more representative of the lack of upward mobility in the region over the years. It bears the infamous distinction of being the only country in modern history to have been relegated from first world to third world status. In the 1920s, Argentina was the world's fifth largest economy. By 2005, it had slipped to the 32nd place.

Income Inequality

For years, policymakers have debated over which is the worse of two evils— poverty or the polarization of wealth. In terms of how they influence crime levels, the pattern of wealth distribution is more important than average income levels. Intuitively, this makes sense. In a middle-income country such as Slovenia, wealth is relatively evenly distributed such that there is little incentive for the underclass to steal from the wealthier segments. Comparatively, the United States at three times the per capita income level but twice the GINI index reading as Slovenia, has commensurately four times the murder rate. The GINI index, considered the gold standard of measuring income distribution, is 70 percent correlated with homicide rates in a study of 48 countries (see figure 14.4).[19]

Countries that maintain very low GINI rates (less than 30), such as those in the northern half of Western and Eastern Europe as well as Japan, have the world's lowest crime rates. When a nation's GINI rate passes 40, then homicide rates (the most accurately measured violent crime index) begin to rise rapidly. Countries at the high extreme with GINI rates over 50 (Brazil, Mexico, Guatemala, El Salvador, Honduras, Colombia, South Africa) are the world's most dangerous countries.

Other nations defy the trend and stand out as anomalies that illustrate that income equality cannot explain all variances in crime levels. Chile is home to one of the world's worst income distribution levels but is a relatively safe country. Singapore and Kuwait are two nations with very low violent crime rates but worse than average wealth polarization. In all three countries, the rule of law is firmly enforced and the population has been traditionally tolerant of strong policing.

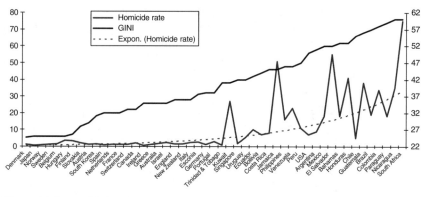

Figure 14.4 Wealth distribution as a driver of crime[20]

In the Caribbean, notably Jamaica and Trinidad and Tobago, income distribution is less polarized than the homicide rate reflects. In both countries, gang violence has proven more than a match for the police.

Income distribution reflects more than just a Robin Hood desire to steal from the rich. Poor income distribution leads to the arming of the wealthy and middle classes who fear for their safety. More guns in more homes inevitably leads to higher murder rates, usually caused by traditional sources of discontent between families, friends, and business partners. Income polarization leads to the maldistribution of policing funding, with wealthy neighborhoods policed in high numbers and better standards than the policing offered in poorer neighborhoods. Isolated from the ravages of crime, the governing elite quickly becomes numb to violence that occurs in districts of the city or country where they never visit or know anyone. This phenomenon is as prevalent in a middle-income country such as Russia or Brazil as it is in much poorer countries in Africa.

The Return of Subsidies and Stipends

The neoliberal reforms instituted across Latin America in the 1990s included the removal of several "economically inefficient" food, medicine, and transport subsidies that most dramatically impacted the poor. Cutting subsidies without completing reforms to the labor and tax codes and removing the stifling red tape meant that for subsidy beneficiaries (up to one half of the population), there was no upside compensatory opportunity to balance the loss of savings. Squeezing the underclasses further in Latin America served only to exacerbate the region's historic problem with wealth distribution and provided fertile ground for the expansion of organized crime as well as petty crime.

Some of the region's leaders now realize the danger of economic marginalization of the voting majority and are reintroducing stipends and subsidies that go directly to the underclass. Brazil's Bolsa Escola stipend program, though criticized for poor implementation, nonetheless brings U.S.$5 per child per month to families that keep those kids in school. The program proved instrumental in the reelection of Lula. In Peru, President Garcia, who narrowly defeated the radical nationalist, Humala Ollanta, is considering the creation of a similar stipend program along with the reenactment of different subsidies in underdeveloped regions.

Indeed, in a period of record tax collection in Latin America's natural resource–wealthy nations, the political need to subsidize the poor can once again be afforded by several governments. It is not a solution on its own to the region's crime issues but it does help keep kids in school and out of gangs.

Idle Teens and Gang Recruitment

The failure of many Latin American economies to generate employment for its youth has created masses of idle teens that are too easily recruited into organized crime, including gangs. Central America, which has not benefited from the commodity boom and increasingly loses factory jobs to Chinese competition, suffers today from massive youth unemployment and underemployment (see figure 14.5).

Worsening the situation in Central America is the mandatory return from the United States of Central American migrants who entered gangs and were imprisoned in the United States or joined the gangs while in prison. The end of their prison sentence in the United States brings automatic expulsion. Between 2000 and 2004, an estimated 20,000 criminals were deported to Central America from the United States, often left at the border without any official U.S. police documentation.

The arrival of hardened criminals to Honduras, Guatemala, El Salvador, and Nicaragua has turned those countries into breeding grounds for large and powerful gang networks, known as Maras, short for *marabunta,* a voracious

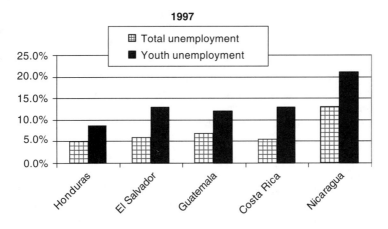

Figure 14.5 Central American unemployment[21]

plague of ants that destroys everything in its path. The often-fragmented Mareros number an estimated 100,000 members across Central America. In the United States, where many Mareros serve in prison, gang networks are found in most cities with significant Central American populations, notably Los Angeles and Washington, D.C. The gang linkages between Central America and the United States have proven the perfect conduit for northward drug trade. Two other partners play a role, the Mexican cartels that move product across the increasingly policed U.S.-Mexican border and Colombian cocaine producers who fly product to airstrips in Central America, principally Guatemala, to then be moved into Mexico. Guatemala appears to be making its piece of the smuggling pie bigger by expanding its Mara network into Mexico. Maras now smuggle cocaine all the way through Mexico, specifically up the Pacific coast highway. They finance their Mexican operations by preying upon Central American illegal immigrants in Mexico, either robbing them or extorting monies for safety.[22] They hand off the cocaine to the Tijuana cartel for the lucrative but highly risky U.S. border crossing but some speculate that it is only a matter of time before Maras build enough strength to take on the U.S. border crossing themselves, thus tapping into the most profitable segment of the entire cocaine supply chain that sees product marked up more than 18,000 percent[23] from its production in the Andes to its consumption in the United States.

The underpopulated lowland jungle region of Peten in eastern Guatemala is an ideal transit point for Colombian cocaine. Planes can approach and take off under radar in the flat topography. In and around the Laguna de Tigre national park, some 15 kilometers from the Mexican border, Guatemalan and U.S. units destroyed 80 clandestine landing strips and found a graveyard of small airplanes, destroyed and burned. The operation lasted for 142 days, ending on April 27, 2006.[24] Drug enforcement officials connect the Peten air-shipment operation to the Maras.

Guatemala is the only Central American country that is both a transit point and point of origin for regional drug trafficking. In the province of San Marcos in north-western Guatemala, more than 1,800 hectares of poppy are harvested to make opium, the prime ingredient of heroin. According to the U.S. embassy in Guatemala, the country ranks sixth amongst the world's poppy producers. Farmers in the San Marcos providence normally earn some U.S.$350 a month. Once they begin to grow poppy, this number jumps to U.S.$6,000 a month, according to Guatemalan antinarcotics officials.[25]

Central American governments have tried to combat the gang violence, launching zero tolerance programs such as Mano Dura in El Salvador, Libertad Azul in Honduras, and Plan Escoba in Guatemala. However the emphasis on enforcement without sufficient recognition of the underlying problems of unemployment and broken families has proved a losing formula. The enforcement plans have only succeeded in forcing gang activity to move around the region but has failed to reverse the growth in gang membership, its violence, or the negative economic impact.

Central America loses approximately 300,000 migrants each year,[26] disproportionately men, often young fathers and older brothers to youngsters left behind. Over 40 percent of families in Honduras today live without their father, victims of emigration, violence, or separation.[27] Such a high level of broken families also contributes to an environment that spawns the recruitment of teenage boys into the world of crime, be it through gangs or other elements.

Central American murder rates and violent crime rates are now the highest in Latin America and some of the highest in the world. A survey taken in El Salvador in 2006 revealed that 36.3 percent of people believe it is "very likely" their homes will be assaulted, while 40 percent of families say they have been victims of some form of crime-related physical violence.[28] Not surprisingly, the economic impact of crime is higher in Central America than in other regions.

Drugs Are No Longer Just an Export Issue

The cultivation and transport of Andean cocaine and Mexican/Guatemalan heroin to U.S. and European markets is a well-documented problem in Latin America. But drugs are no longer purely an export issue for Latin American governments—domestic consumption is rising quickly.

The redirection of Andean cocaine southward through Brazil flooded that market with cheap product and helped to kick-start demand, distributed principally through Brazilian gangs. Interpol reports that up to 60 percent of the cocaine that enters Brazil stays in Brazil, while the rest lands in Europe, Africa, and in some cases the Middle East and Asia. Established links now exist between Colombia's Fuerza Armada Revolucionaria de Colombia (FARC) and Brazilian gangs in Rio de Janeiro. The Colombians export cocaine and the Brazilians pay in cash or in guns.

A similar phenomenon is taking shape in Mexico. Improved policing at the Mexican-U.S. border helps detain product within Mexico, which has found a market amongst its increasingly affluent urban consumers. Per capita income levels in Mexico City, now over U.S.$10,000, are high enough to support demand for cocaine that sells there for one-fourth or less the street price in Los Angeles.

Governments are scrambling to launch new prevention and law enforcement programs as drug use takes a toll on public health and depletes public coffers. One report from Brazil estimates the cost of medical care for drug addiction soared from U.S.$902 million 1993 to U.S.$2.9 billion in 1997. At the same time, the percentage of AIDS cases from intravenous drug use rose from 2.5 percent of needle users in 1985 to 25 percent in 1998.[29]

In Buenos Aires, a city of 12 million, the first official government poll on drug use showed consumption at 4.1 percent of the population, similar to levels in Washington, D.C., and New York.[30] In the same report, the number of people in Mexico City who said they have tried drugs at least once increased to 7.3 percent, up from 4 percent in 1993.

In Chile, an official 1998 national survey showed 5.3 percent of the population between the ages of 12 and 62 had used marijuana, cocaine base, or refined cocaine during the past year, up from 4.3 percent in 1996, with rates higher than the national average in the capital, Santiago. In Peru—mainly in Lima and other major urban centers—the number of people between 12 and 50 saying they had used cocaine at least once rose to 3.2 percent in 1998, compared with 1.3 percent in 1988. Those saying they had used marijuana jumped to 8 percent from 5.3 percent during the same period, according to the Lima-based Center for Information on Prevention and Drug Abuse.

The illegal status of drug consumption in Latin American countries means that drugs reach consumers through illegal channels, often heavily armed gangs. The resulting violence drives up the demand for guns and the toll of homicides.

The Proliferation of Guns

Latin America is responsible for over 40 percent of the homicides by firearms worldwide. Close to 70 percent of all homicides in Latin America are committed with firearms, one of the highest rates in the world. In Brazil, close to 35,000 people die from gunshot wounds each year, more than any country in the world. According to the Viva Rio researcher Luke Dowdney, between December 1987 and November 2001, violent death claimed 3,937 of Rio de Janeiro's adolescents under the age of 18. In comparison, 467 minors died violently during the same four-year period in the West Bank, a region considered a war zone by the United Nations (UN).

Guns enter the region largely through illegal channels, often countertraded for drugs. The same Mexican and Colombian cartels that export cocaine to the United States also import U.S. small arms. With over 220 million firearms in the United States (one-third of the global total), small arms are a leading U.S. illicit export. Other important suppliers of guns to Latin America include Spain, Belgium, Thailand, Germany, Canada, Venezuela, and the Philippines.

Many guns remained in Central America following the end of civil conflict that resulted in the heavy arming of militaries, guerrillas, counterinsurgents, and private militias. Today, there are more than 1.6 million small arms in Central America, of which more than 1 million are unregistered.[31] With the exception of the Costa Rican government, Central American governments have failed to get a handle on controlling gun ownership. Even where black market guns are relatively insignificant as a percentage of total gun ownership, illicit arms play a disproportionate role in the violence currently plaguing Latin America since they constitute the principal weaponry of insurgents, warlords, drug traffickers, and criminal organizations.

Sadly and ironically, guns are prolific in Latin America in spite of the claim that "Latin America is a world leader when it comes to implementing arms control measures, both domestically and regionally," as was articulated at the 2006 United Nations Review Conference on Small Arms. The same conference went on to point out that Brazil's Disarmament Statute and Chile's Gun Control Law limiting the access to guns in the civilian population are significant examples along with similar laws adopted by other nations such as Argentina, Venezuela, the Dominican Republic, and Costa Rica.

The conference did illustrate some positive results of recent gun control methods, specifically, the Brazilian Disarmament Statute, which came into force in December 2003 and restricted the civilian right to carry weapons, among other measures. Brazil's national disarmament campaign removed approximately 500,000 firearms from its streets and homes. A UNESCO report issued in September 2005 based on data from Brazil's Ministry of Health showed that there was a drop of 5,563 deaths by firearms in 2004, the year of the disarmament campaign. It was the first recorded drop in the death rate in 13 years.

The 2003 roundup of guns was particularly effective at reducing accidental gun deaths and suicides that are best prevented by disarmament efforts. However, the growing violence in Brazilian Favelas, led by growing legions of gang members, was not halted by the gun buyback program. That fact led to a popular revolt amongst voters in Brazil in 2006 when they rejected a plebiscite effort to ban all guns. Indeed, any future efforts to buy back or illegalize gun ownership will continue to be hampered by a widespread disaffection and distrust by the public of their police and security forces.

End of Military Rule

The end of military rule in Latin America and the rise in power of politicians who themselves were victims of imprisonment or political asylum served to radically lessen the appetite for violence as a tool of governance in times of crisis and public dissent. In the 1960s and 1970s, the present crime levels would have been met with a strong hand by presidents who regularly exercised their powers to unleash the military on its own people to fight crime. Many contemporary leaders prefer to turn a blind eye to the dissent and violence.

Vicente Fox, Mexico's president from 2000 to 2006, never followed through on his election promises to fight crime, particularly in Mexico City, one of the most dangerous cities in the world. Upon seizing power and addressing the issue, he realized the political cost of the heavy-handed policing that would be needed to break the hold on the city of organized crime. At the end of his term, President Fox's inaction on public security proved to be a catalyst of the generally negative opinion of his administration by most Mexicans.

Presidents Lula and Kirchner were both vocal opponents of military rule in their respective countries, Brazil and Argentina. Perhaps out of fear of hypocrisy, both leaders have been reluctant to use force when confronting public dissent or rampant crime.

In Brazil, the lack of effective policing became painfully evident during the week of May 12–19, 2006, when 100 prison riots erupted simultaneously, leading to 150 murders. During Mother's Day weekend in Brazil, it is customary to release "non-dangerous" prisoners on short-term leave to visit their mothers. Those released were used as marksmen for vendetta killings, orchestrated from within prison by the First Capital Command, known in Portuguese by its acronym PCC. The PCC, an organized gang of an estimated 640,000[32] members and supporters, sought vendetta against two officers of the Department of Investigation of Organized Crime who had testified against the group.

The riots served to enlighten the media and the public of the extent to which PCC had been allowed to expand. With an estimated annual operating budget ranging from U.S.$500 million to U.S.$1 billion,[33] the PCC is larger than some of Brazil's state governments. It is responsible for an estimated 70 percent of Sao Paulo's kidnappings, much of the illegal traffic in arms, and bankrolls most of the city's bank robberies. A team of 18 lawyers provide legal counsel and support to PCC's sprawling membership.[34] Its tentacles run deep into the legal system, enabling the PCC to obtain judicial and police intelligence and thus evade capture. The PCC moved its riots forward two days to May 12 to avoid having its leaders moved to a more secure prison, a tip it got through its network.

The PCC has effectively positioned itself as a defender of the imprisoned, lobbying for better prison conditions, and providing legal support for arrested members and friends of members. For an important segment of the urban poor, the PCC is perceived to better defend their rights than the federal or local governments. This may help explain President Lula's reluctance to come down on the group. Lula draws his political base from the nation's poor and while maintaining conservative financial policies, has kept loyal to his base on social and judicial policies in order to preserve his antiestablishment credentials.

Public tolerance for violence can only be stretched so far. Eventually, voters will seek political leadership that can deliver on fighting crime. President Uribe of Colombia won his first round with the promise of a tougher approach to stemming violence. His administration's impressive track record of reducing homicide and kidnapping levels from 2002 to 2006 earned him a second mandate, even if the Colombian government's collusion with paramilitaries damages U.S. relations. Likewise, one of the key messages in Felipe Calderon's presidential run was a promise to get tough on crime. He went so far as to separate himself from his fellow party leader, former President Fox, on the issue of crime. The political gamble paid off and helped explain his sudden surge in polls prior to the election of July 2006. As the legacy of military rule becomes muted by time, the electorate and political leaders will gain the courage to confront the issue of crime with tough measures.

Ineffective Police

Latin America disproves the notion that more policing lowers the crime rate. The ineptitude and corruption of most of the region's police forces is so grave that political leaders are left without the very tool they need to combat crime.

In the 1990s, a UN study revealed that only 1 out of 17 recorded crimes resulted in a conviction in Latin America. Latin Americans are lax to report crime precisely because they have so little faith in the integrity of their police forces. In many parts of Latin America, in order to convince the police to take action on one's behalf, bribes must be paid. In other cases, people avoid contacting the police for fear that the police may turn and prey on them, the victims. Kidnap units within police forces are infamous for being in cahoots with kidnappers, stealing ransom monies, and botching rescue attempts. Interviewed on the subject in the late 1990s, Kroll Associates Deputy Chairman Brian Jenkins stated,

"Seventy-nine percent of all hostages are killed during rescue attempts in Latin America." As a result, fewer than one-third of kidnappings in Mexico, for instance, are reported to the police.

The respected Latinobarómetro survey published in 2003 revealed that only one in three Latin American citizens expressed any confidence in the police. In Mexico, 75 percent said they had no confidence in police or judicial authorities. Chile proved to be an exception where 60 percent of those in the same survey expressed high confidence in their police force. In 2003, close to half of the province of Buenos Aires police force, almost 23,000 individuals, were investigated for corruption or abuse of authority. More than 4,000 of them were convicted.[35]

Without a competent legal and policing system, in most Latin American countries bribery is rampant as a means of avoiding both the legitimate and unscrupulous attention of authorities. In Mexico City, a police officer is provided with a turf to patrol, as small as a street corner, which is his to "protect." In reality, the policeman is under contract to collect bribes from those who break the law as well as to collect protection funds from legitimate businesses.

Each turf carries a price, a daily fee, that the policeman must pay to his superior in exchange for the right to patrol that area. The policeman's superior similarly pays a daily fee to his boss for the right to supervise a neighborhood, made up of a few dozen patrolmen. And the chain of corruption moves upward from there like a very efficient pyramid scheme. It is impossible to measure how much money is extracted through police corruption. But if 60,000 patrolling police each collect 300 pesos (about U.S.$32) per day except on Sundays, the total comes to U.S.$520 million annually in Mexico City alone. That's more than half a billion dollars stolen from the public every year by the very authorities who are paid to fight crime. Mexico City, by virtue of its size, is an extreme example, but the same pattern can be seen across hundreds of Latin American cities.

Raising the standards of policing and judicial bodies is a lengthy process that requires years of reform, technical assistance, and above all political support from the highest ranks. Yet, without progress on such reform, crime will not be combated as it ought to be.

Reforming police forces combines the expulsion of bad apples, the incarceration of the most criminal senior officials, and retraining and reincentivizing the rest. Incarcerating senior police officials can be difficult in judicial systems that are compromised by corrupt judges who may be reluctant to act against senior police officials. The sudden expulsion of hundreds, if not thousands, of corrupt low-level police can create in short order a new army of criminals, self-organized or working for larger gangs. Retraining those who remain in the force is a process that can take years. Police forces are often woefully undereducated, even functionally illiterate in some municipalities, recruited for their loyalty, not their wits. Retraining must be combined with new investments in technologies that help provide the checks and balances to policing. For instance, if there is not adequate computerized tracking of drivers' licenses and vehicle registrations, there is no way of collecting fines legally from drivers who have broken the law and been issued a fine. Without such a system, it only behooves the police force to collect traffic fines the old-fashioned way, cash paid to the policeman's pocket.

Where Progress Is Found—Medellín, Colombia

In 2000, Medellín was the world's most dangerous city, where 211 out of 100,000 residents were murdered each year, or 20 per day, in a city of only 3.5 million.[36] The average young man living in the city stood a one in six chance of being murdered. The drug-running street gangs of the 1980s gave way to control by guerrilla militias in the 1990s who roamed Medellín's hillside slums donning ski masks and armed with machine guns. They spray painted political slogans, and carried out social cleansing, killing with impunity.

Starting in 2000, the Autodefensas Unidas de Colombia (AUC) paramilitaries, armed by drug money and at war across the country with guerillas, began an offensive in Medellín's slums. The murder rate soared as a bloody, two-year civil war ensued in neighborhoods where the police or military did not dare to enter. The paramilitaries won the battle of Medellín, and rule of the *barrio* (streets) consolidated under the rule of two men, Diego Fernando Murillo, or Don Berna, head of Cacique Nutibara Bloc (BCN), and Rodrigo 00, commander of the Metro Bloc. Sniffing out the lingering presence of the FARC took until 2002, and then the paramilitary factions turned upon one another—resulting in one warrior-king, Don Berna.

In 2002, Alvaro Uribe, the former governor of Antioquia, of which Medellín is the capital, was quick to act upon his promise to get tough on guerillas. He ordered operation Orión, which helped finish the paramilitary's mission of eradicating the guerillas in Medellín, After Orión, however, soldiers and police remained inside Medellín's slums, setting up outposts there, and continued to patrol roughly half of the troubled areas, ostensibly leaving the paramilitaries in control of remainder of Medellín's ghettos.[37]

Defeating the guerillas was part one of Uribe's security offensive. Having secured Medellín and other hot spots in the country, negotiations began with the paramilitaries to disarm their thousands. In November 2003, 868 members of the BCN turned in weapons. To date, over 17,000 assault weapons have been handed over by paramilitaries to the government.[38]

Don Berna, known colloquially as the "Pacifier of Medellín," is now in jail but has avoided extradition to the United States thanks to a conditional immunity written into the justice and peace law. A democratic congress in the United States may apply new pressures to uncover evidence that could nullify his immunity and make him eligible for extradition. That action, however well intentioned, would send the hundreds of paramilitaries in Medellín who presently keep the peace into wartime mode against the government's still-underresourced police and army units.[39]

Cognizant of the frailty of peace today in Medellín, the local government, led by Mayor Sergio Fajardo, has done what few local governments in Latin America have even attempted to do—to invest in changing the roots of violence. The government has spent millions on building parks, libraries, schools, and museums, several of them bold and splendid in design and budget, to change the external and internal image of the slums and create islands of safe haven, especially for the young.

Unlike other parts of Colombia that promised financial and training benefits to paramilitaries who turned in their weapons and renounced violence, Medellín has delivered. Over U.S.$10 million has gone to pay for retraining and to provide stipends to retiring paramilitaries. The success of the program has been a double-edged sword as paramilitaries outside of Medellín come to the city to hand over their weapons instead of participating in what should be similarly funded programs in other parts of the country. Even psychological attention is provided and former fighters participate in reconciliation exercises with victims to ask for their forgiveness. Other programs provide counseling to victims.

The additional costs of policing and now healing the city of its war wounds have been considerable. However, as the city and country prosper from declining levels of violence, tax revenues have jumped more than 20 percent in less than two years.[40] The "peace dividend" of a stable Medellín is practically immediate and positive. As of the end of 2006, Medellín's homicide rate is hovering at 30 murders per 100,000, 86 percent lower than its peak in 2000. Medellín's murder rate is now lower than that of Washington, D.C., Baltimore, or Detroit. Using the same benchmark, Medellín, in 2006, was safer than Mexico City, Sao Paulo, Caracas, or Rio de Janeiro.

What Could Happen if Crime Is Not Controlled?

Intolerable levels of violence have always been the calling card of a return to authoritarian rule in Latin America. Since the region became politically independent in the early nineteenth century, democracy and authoritarianism have traded places over time as the region's economy and public safety levels rose and fell together. Latin Americans, like most governed people, have demonstrated their preference for democratic governments, so long as they deliver economic growth and public safety to all and limit their levels of corruption. Failure to deliver on at least two of these three factors usually results in regime change and can invite the rule of dictators.

Latin America's latest wave of democratization (at least the fourth in its history), began in the 1980s when the region's citizens became fed up with the economic malaise of collapsed commodity prices, escalating debt, and devaluations, along with increased evidence of corruption. The conclusion of the cold war also helped by ending the flow of politically motivated military aid monies from Washington and Moscow that propped up some pretty unremarkable puppets across the region.

The region's contemporary democracy experiment stood a challenging test in 2006 when 12 presidential elections were held. The region squeaked by with the narrow victory in Mexico and Peru of pro-market democrats ahead of more authoritarian-populist candidates. Where other centrists won, such as Lula in Brazil, Bachelet in Chile, and Arias in Costa Rica, a ring of populism was heard as leaders embraced the notion that free markets were not delivering wealth to the vast majority of the working poor.

Violence and the promise to quell it played a role in most elections. In Colombia, Uribe's tangible success in his first term (2002–2006) at lowering crime was key to his reelection. Felipe Caderón, who trailed through most of the campaign, may well have won the election thanks to his promise to make the country safer, a resonating message to middle and working-class voters. Rising crime in Mexico City helped limit the support for losing Presidential candidate, Andres-Manuel Lopez Obrador, who had previously served as mayor in the world's new kidnapping capital.

Between 1996 and 2001, Latinobarómetro, the most respected annual poll of Latin American attitudes toward government, found that average support for democracy, "as the best system of government" dropped from 64 percent to 48 percent on average across the region.[41] Democracy, as practiced in Latin America, was criticized en masse as a system that benefited only the elite and perpetuated social inequality. This time period overlaps with much of "the lost half-decade" (1997–2002) when the economies of Brazil, Argentina, Ecuador, and the Dominican Republic all collapsed and when Chile, Colombia, and Venezuela suffered major devaluations. It also coincides with the greatest growth in crime levels that the region has ever witnessed.

A more recent Latinobarómetro poll published in the *Economist* magazine on December 9, 2006, showed a rebound for democracy, with 58 percent responding positively to the statement: "Democracy is preferable to any other kind of government." The positive results follow four years of consecutive positive economic growth for Latin America, some of its highest growth in a generation, thanks to booming commodity prices. The last three years have also seen some notable successes in lowering crime rates in Colombia, Brazil, and Panama, all of which saw big gains in their preference for democracy. The successful completion of 12 elections in 2006, often in contentious campaigns and decided on several occasions by second rounds of balloting, proved to Latin Americans that their vote counts.

The ups and downs of the last decade illustrate that Latin American faith in democracy is neither waning nor is it be taken for granted. When crime, corruption, and economic malaise converge, voters will opt for a Caudillo, Hugo Chavez providing a shining example. He replaced two incumbent parties that were rife with corruption and whose lack of leadership had turned Caracas into one of the world's most dangerous cities. Those factors combined with historically low oil prices at the end of the 1990s enabled Chavez to win 70 percent of the vote in 1999.

In spite of tremendous progress at managing its economies, Latin America is the world's most globalized regional economy and is highly vulnerable to external economic pressure. A collapse of commodity prices, rising interest rates, or a major slowdown in the U.S. or Chinese economies could trigger currency depreciation, capital flight, and negative growth in Latin America. With high crime levels and corruption still rampant in Latin America, democracy remains vulnerable come the region's next economic crisis.

Now Is the Time to Invest in Safety

Violence works as a vicious cycle economically. It requires money to tackle the job of fighting, preventing and ultimately reversing the drivers of crime. Without safe streets, investment remains weak and productivity underperforms. Wealth cannot be created without safety, nor safety without wealth.

Fighting crime, like all of society's ills, requires a concerted effort, combining both leadership and popular support. Ending the bloodshed is only part one of the solution. Until the breeding ground of crime is changed, violence will soon return after the political will has lost its focus. For instance, Colombia has made wonderful progress in making its principal cities much safer. However, what will happen when President Uribe, *el hombre indispensable* (the indispensable man), or Mayor Fajardo in Medellin leave office?

Long-term economic growth and stability in Latin America is simply not achievable without continued advancement with public safety. No one wants to take long-term bets on a region that is not safe. It is one of the great differentiating qualities when comparing Latin America to Asia. Though Asia has suffered more contemporary wars than Latin America, it is largely seen as a physically safe place to invest.

In the 1960s, as Korea emerged from a war that split the country in two, per capita income in South Korea was slightly less than that of Honduras. Today, it is 15 times greater.[42] Certainly other factors such as education and the system of law differentiate these two countries. However, from the 1980s onward, Koreans and Korean capital no longer emigrated in large numbers from the country, because Korea was a safe nation again with opportunities at home. By contrast, Honduranean emigration to neighboring countries as well as to the United States has grown steadily since the 1980s as the country has become increasingly dangerous, investment has dried up, and unemployment rates have risen.

When targeted as a leading political issue, crime can be quelled, as Medellin has shown the world. Ultimately, crime is a local issue. No amount of national leadership and resources can stop crime at the local level without local political, judiciary, and police support. Policing works but a strong hand alone is ineffective without the support of the softer hand of development. Criminals need more than incarceration; they need training and education to be converted into productive citizens. Poor, crime-riddled neighborhoods need investment to change their economies from illicit to legal, investment first by government and other public sources but soon after by the private sector, lured by incentives and less red tape.

For the first time in a generation, Latin American economies and their governments are flush with cash, thanks to a commodity-led export boom and the repatriation of billions of dollars residing offshore. The laundry list of catch-up items from infrastructure to education will keep legislators busy for a while. As Latin American politicians ponder where to spend political and fiscal surpluses, they would be wise to not forsake their most basic promise as public servants—to keep their citizens safe.

Notes

1. Mark Shaw and Jan van Dijk, "Determining Trends in Global Crime and Justice," *Forum on Crime and Society* 3, no. 1 (December 2003).
2. Ibid., figure 1.
3. Ibid.
4. Ibid., figure 2.
5. Luis Esteban Manrique *A Parallel Power: Organized Crime in Latin America* (Washington, D.C.: ARI, 2006).
6. Ibid.
7. Andrew Morrison, *Violencia en las Americas: Hacia una respuesta basada en la ciencia* (Washington, D.C.: World Bank, September 2004).
8. James T. Quinlivan, *Burden of Victory* (Santa Monica, California: Rand Corporation, 2003).
9. Mongabay.com, Venezuela Profile (2006).
10. Phillip Cook, MD, "Should Gun Manufacturers Be Required to Compensate States for Hand Gun Violence?" *The Future of Children* 12, no. 2 (Summer/Fall 2002): various pages.
11. Morrison, *Violencia en las Americas.*
12. John Price, "What Drives Tourism in Latin America?" *Tendencias,* December 10, 2000.
13. John Price, "The Cost of Living Dangerously," *Tendencias* 31 (November 2001).
14. EIU Country Indicators, April 2007.
15. Çaglar Özden, "Educated Migrants: Is There Brain Waste?" *in International Migration, Remittances and the Brain Drain* (Washington, D.C.: World Bank, October 24, 2005).
16. The $200 billion of capital flight over the last 15 years has a present value of $389 billion, given 10 percent annual returns. The estimated 1.3 million college-educated Latin Americans who fled the region earned $682 billion abroad over 15 years and would have earned one-third that level or $227 billion if they had stayed home. The 12 million less-than-college-educated Latin Americans living abroad earned $1.8 trillion abroad over 15 years and would have earned $616 billion, if they stayed home. $389 billion + $227 billion + $616 billion = c. $1.2 trillion.
17. The present value of capital flight measures $389 billion and generates capital gains of $38.9 billion per year (10 percent return). Average top-end tax brackets in Latin America are 35 percent. Since offshore tax revenue is almost never collected in Latin America, this represents $13.6 billion in untaxed income. Highly educated migrants' untaxed income that would have been taxed locally = $32.5 billion income x 25 percent tax bracket = $8.1billion. Less-educated migrants' untaxed income that would have been taxed locally = $88 billion x 15 percent tax bracket = $13.2 billion. $13.6 billion + 8.1 billion + $13.2 billion = c. $35 billion.
18. Prachi Mishra, *Emigration and Brain Drain: Evidence from the Caribbean* (Washington, D.C.: IMF, January 2006).
19. InfoAmericas, 2006.

20. Shaw and van Dijk, "Determining Trends in Global Crime and Justice."
21. Caroline Fawcett, *Latin American Youth in Transition* (Washington, D.C.: American University, November 2005).
22. Sam Logan, *Illegal Migration, Crime and Mexic's Maras* (Rio de Janeiro: Self published, 2006).
23. US Drug Enforcement Agency, *Prices of Cocaine through the Distribution System* (Washington, D.C.: US Drug Enforcement Agency, 1997).
24. Sam Logan, *Guatemala: Possible "Colombianization,"* (Zurich: International Relations and Security Network, 2006).
25. Ibid.
26. Sarah J. Mahler and Dusan Ugrina, *Central America: Cross Road of the Americas* (Miami: Florida International University, April).
27. Dr. Susan Purcell, *Competitiveness Task Force* (Miami: Center for Hemispheric Policy, University of Miami, 2006).
28. Manrique, *A Parallel Power.*
29. Anthony Faiola, "Use of Illicit Drugs Soars in Latin America," *Washington Post,* Wednesday, September 15, 1999.
30. *US Drug Czar Report* (Washington, D.C.: The White House, 1998).
31. International Action Network on Small Arms, *Small Arms Survey: Americas* (London: International Action Network on Small Arms, 2006).
32. Samuel Logan, "Brazil's P.C.C.: True Power Behind the Violence," *Power and Interest News Report,* May 24, 2006.
33. Ibid.
34. Ibid.
35. Manrique, *A Parallel Power.*
36. Secretaria de Gobierno Distrital, Colombia, 2001.
37. Adam Isacson, *Notes from Medellin, Plan Colombia and Beyond* (Washington, D.C.: Self-published, 2006).
38. Derechos Humanos, www.derechoshumanos.gov.co, 2006.
39. Isacson, *Notes from Medellin.*
40. Sergio Fajardo, *Letter from the Mayor of Medellin to National Geographic* Magazine, 2005.
41. Alvaro Garcia, *Latin America 1980–2005: Institutions, Growth and Poverty* (Washington, D.C.: World Bank, June 2005).
42. EIU Country Data.

Conclusion: Lessons Learned and Looking Forward

Jerry Haar and John Price

As the speed, scope, and depth of globalization intensify, all regions of the world are faced with daunting challenges. Latin America is no exception. Interdependence through technology, communications, human capital migration (particularly skilled labor), transportation, and cross-national commercial relations, whether by choice or necessity, is a dominant feature of the international landscape. Given the greater mobility of capital, technology, and human capital, the competition among developing regions in particular has become much greater in recent times.

During the last decade, the rise of Asia—especially China and India—has generated remarkable interest, hope, and financial commitment in emerging markets among multinational corporations, their suppliers, and financial institutions the world over. However, this has come at the expense, to some extent, of Latin America. Foreign direct and portfolio investment destined to emerging markets was once dominated by Latin America but this is no longer so. Though foreign direct investment to Latin America has increased since 2003, the region's share of emerging market investment has dwindled steadily since 1999 as Asia and Eastern Europe have gained greater favor. While commodity-producing sectors in countries such as Chile, Peru, Brazil, and Argentina have benefited from Asia's insatiable demand for these inputs, other countries such as Mexico, where over half a million manufacturing jobs have been lost to China, have felt the brunt of this change.

Simultaneous with the relentless expansion of globalization, internal changes have been reshaping Latin America's internal political economy. For the last quarter of a century, the twin currents of democratization and economic liberalization have made impressive gains and experienced dramatic setbacks as well. Chile stands as a benchmark for the former, Venezuela for the latter. In some cases, nations in the region have made steady progress to reform their political and economic systems and institutions, thereby enabling them to compete more effectively in the global economy while improving political participation, governance, and opportunity for its citizens. In many other cases, countries have paid mere lip service to reform, providing rhetoric rather than action or have instituted change partly or incompetently. Most distressing is the return to failed policies of the past in countries such as Venezuela, Bolivia, Ecuador, and even Argentina—actions that will retard competitiveness for years to come.

The contributors to this volume have surveyed and analyzed key factors that impact and shape a nation's competitiveness. They have also presented viable courses of action that Latin America can take to increase its ability to compete in the global economy. The topics addressed by the writers may be classified under one of the following rubrics: *infrastructure, institutions,* and *human capital.*

Before highlighting some of the major recommendations within each of these three categories, it is vitally important to emphasize the importance of *macroeconomics* as a prerequisite for success. As Claudio M. Loser compellingly presents in the first chapter, prudent fiscal and monetary policies underpin the development framework that requires stability, predictability, and consistency. Through a combination of hard work, favorable world conditions, and luck, Latin America has made remarkable progress in macroeconomic policy—progress that contributes positively and significantly to the region's competitiveness. However, Loser cautions that sound fiscal, monetary, and exchange rate policies are necessary but not enough to guarantee competitiveness. His admonition segues into the chapters that follow.

Infrastructure

The future potential growth impact of infrastructure investment is large in Latin America, in part because the region is not competitive at present. Total investment in infrastructure in Latin America over the last 20 years equals 2 percent of GDP, while in Asian countries it is three times higher. Drawing on the example of water, Lee M. Tablewski zeroes in on the region's critical deficiencies, caused by a lack of political commitment, public skepticism of private utilities, inadequate regulatory power and frameworks, and widespread corruption. He argues that the region must focus on maintaining affordability of utilities through competitive markets, proper legal frameworks, and improving the use of subsidies where used. Policy reform is also necessary, including the improvement of regulatory frameworks and institutions; tariff subsidy schemes; transparency initiatives; incentives to expand investment; local financial markets; municipal government transparency and fiscal responsibility; and regulation to align the cost of capital and rate of return for investors.

Underinvestment in modern logistics and transportation infrastructure adds enormous costs to business in Latin America and inhibits the region's ability to capitalize on commodity price increases. John Price highlights Colombia as a successful case due to support at the federal and state level, its stronger fiscal position, its ability to attract private investment, and its efficient regulation and management of projects. He notes that barriers exist in the region in reforming the logistics and transportation services because of a lack of trust (especially corruption in legal system and cultural differences), currency risk, trucking regulations, and inefficient customs administration. Price proposes a logistics remodeling solution that includes the input of 3PL operators who bring objectivity and a focus on efficiency to the task.

Institutions

The critical importance of institutions to economic and political development has been well established. Perhaps no scholar has delved more thoroughly or more insightfully into the subject than Nobel Laureate Douglass C. North.[1] In discussing why some economies develop institutions that produce growth and development while others develop institutions that produce stagnation, North argues that once institutions create the incentive structure in an economy, then organizations will be created to take advantage of the opportunities provided within a given institutional framework.[2] The chapter writers in this book tackle eight institutions or institution-related phenomena that directly impact competitiveness. John H. Welch examines *capital markets,* noting that over the last 40 years, Latin American countries have attempted to reform their capital and financial markets as a critical aspect of their economic growth strategies. This route has proved longer than originally thought, and different countries have taken different approaches to deepen their financial systems. Using Brazil as a case example, he lauds that nation as one of the first to undertake reform while recognizing that the country still has much to do to achieve meaningful results. While Brazil has made improvements to decrease inflation, maintain a better fiscal stance, and make improvements in bankruptcy procedures and corporate governance, wealth is still concentrated in government bonds and the financial market is shallow compared to others in the region. In the credit market, the government has done much to improve the state banking system but still needs to unify the credit markets to help strengthen liquidity and lower the cost of capital. Welch calls for policy action to facilitate the development of private pension funds and, above all, to remedy the deficit in the social security system, which costs Brazil the equivalent of 8 percent of its GDP.

A modern *banking* system is a prerequisite of competitive economies. Higher growth and income equality are associated with financial systems that provide not only intermediation for large firms and government entities but consumer and small business credit as well. Mexico is one nation that recognizes this, and the country's recent forays into mortgage lending for small borrowers have proved to be highly successful and beneficial to both lenders and borrowers. Jan Smith, Tricia Juhn, and Christopher Humphrey assert that Latin America is at the end of radical structural reforms and has come to a stage for promoting growth via the banking system. While banks are now using ATMs, cards and terminals, and mobile banking, more than 70 percent of Latin Americans remain unbanked, versus an OECD (Organisation for Economic Co-operation and Development) average of 10 percent. The region's competitiveness on the global market depends in large part on the *participation,* rather than the exclusion, of middle and lower incomes in the formal economy.

In the area of *technology,* expenditures on research and development, laboratories, and science parks, by both the public and local private sectors, are a paltry sum compared to that of industrial nations, Asia, and Central Europe. No Latin American country has made significant progress to close the technology gap in the last decade. Chile and Brazil are the most technologically competitive countries but still lag behind many Asian countries including China and South Korea. Peter T. Knight and Rosane A. Marques recommend that Latin American countries study the experiences of China and Korea in order to close the technology gap that exists between Latin America and the developed world, as well as the ICT gap between large and small cities in Latin America. Specifically, they recommend that governments increase R&D, strengthen ICT firm competitiveness, create political and public support, and develop the necessary infrastructure to compete.

Linked to technology is *innovation.* Scott Tiffin and Isabel Bortagaray argue that Latin America lacks the interest in innovation, the knowledge of how to manage it, and the public support for it. Overall, Latin America is steadily losing ground relative to other regions in the world. Tiffin and Bortagaray, in examining innovation clusters in various cities in the Americas, call for universities, government, industry, and philanthropic organizations to work in concert to strengthen, broaden, and expand innovation tied to competitiveness.

In the domain of *legal reform,* Linn Hammergren points out that the legal and judicial system is another area that drags on Latin American competitiveness. Outdated laws, flawed judiciaries, and their combined impacts on juridical and citizen security, as well as on political and policy stability, raise the costs of economic transactions, constrain credit availability, and discourage long-term investment. She recommends reform measures that focus on the need to track quantity and quality of outputs, the responsible and transparent use of resources, internal discipline, and providing explanations of policies and decisions. Reform should be led by the courts but with the input of all stakeholders and should be proactive and permanent.

Property rights, addressed brilliantly in Hernando de Soto's seminal work *The Other Path,*[3] is an area that Peter F. Schaefer and P. Clayton Schaefer deem critical to competitiveness. They assert that without property law, entrepreneurship, commerce, and growth are stifled. Formalization by providing property right systems is the only way to create the elusive "rising economic tide" in Latin America. The Schaefers argue that every group will benefit profoundly from formalizing the extralegal economy. Moreover, connecting the most basic interests of the voters to the political system will create a greater sense of responsibility of citizenship and, thus, a greater interest in good government.

Mauricio Carrizosa argues that *tax reform* is essential, since there is a clear relationship between the quality of tax policies and economic performance in Latin America. As demonstrated in the experience of select Latin American countries, an increase in the tax burden has led to an increase in expenditures rather than a resolution to fiscal imbalances, and the higher taxes may have led to decreased growth and decrease in the rate of poverty reduction. The recommended policy approach is to control government expenditures, improve the effectiveness of expenditures and let competitive tax provisions encourage the private sector to invest, employ, and generate growth.

José Luis Guasch and Benjamin Herzberg call for Latin American countries to undertake much more *regulatory reform* to boost their competitiveness. The heavy paperwork burden of federal regulations hinder competitiveness by affecting the time, cost, and overall productivity of doing business. Using Mexico as an example, they note that the Federal Regulatory Improvement Commission has set a precedent for other Latin American economies as a best-practice model for improving competitiveness through regulatory streamlining. Guasch and Herzberg recommend a number of steps that Latin American countries should consider in reforming regulations. These include removing procedures burdening entrepreneurs, streamlining business interaction with the government, revising product regulations, and creating supervisory institutions to implement programs of regulatory reform.

Finally, *public safety* and the institutions charged with law enforcement are often overlooked in discussions of competitiveness. As John Price points out, if a nation's competitiveness centers on its ability to attract and retain talented people and investment capital, then violence plays a role. Long-term economic growth and stability in Latin America is simply not achievable without public safety. Price recommends that local political, judicial, and police support be mobilized and committed with sufficient resources to stop crime. He concludes that public safety should be designated a high priority for the allocation of any budget surpluses.

Human Capital

The linchpin to any nation's ability to compete in the global economy is human capital. Most nations in natural resource-rich continents such as Africa or South America cannot compete nearly as effectively as countries in natural resource-poor nations such as the Netherlands, Taiwan, Israel, and Singapore. However, competitiveness is not just a question of budgetary allocations to education and technology but the quality and appropriateness of each within countries. To illustrate, the tuition-free public higher education systems in Latin America turn out huge numbers of graduates, overwhelmingly in fields where supply continues to far outstrip demand (for example, law, sociology, psychology, communications) while failing to produce the science and technology graduates the region sorely needs to compete in the global economy.

Jeffrey Puryear and Tamara Ortega Goodspeed argue convincingly that the quality of the labor force in Latin America depends on the quality and relevance of education. While Latin America has definitely seen improvements in education, it still lags behind other regions. They point out that the region faces four major barriers: quality, equity, science and technology, and teachers. They recognize that revamping education in ways to enhance competitiveness will take time and call for urgent changes in two broad categories: (1) making learning the main measure of education success and (2) making schools accountable to citizens for achieving educational standards. As for the labor markets in the region, Christopher Sabatini's examination of what he calls the "dysfunctional labor situation" and lack of reforms that characterize the region lead him to call for changes to law and policy that will grant workers (formal and informal) better protection for core labor rights and access to social services in exchange for reductions in hiring and firing costs. In his opinion, updating outmoded labor codes will generate more formal jobs. With flexibility in work rules, an upgrading of the quality of labor, and decreasing costs, Latin America will witness increases in labor productivity, investment, and competitiveness overall.

A Postscript on the Role of Economic Freedom

Many of the analyses and recommendations of the chapter writers fall within the rubric of economic freedom. According to the *2007 Index of Economic Freedom*[4] that measures and ranks 161 countries across 10 specific freedoms,[5] the Americas region presents a mixed picture. Only Chile ranks among the top 20 (#11) of the top 50 nations in the world in economic freedom.[6] Compared with 2006, 18 countries in the Americas saw their scores decline, while 11 improved. Studies in previous editions of the index confirm the tangible benefits of living in freer societies. Not only is a higher level of economic freedom clearly associated with a higher level of per capita gross domestic product (GDP), but GDP growth rates also increase as a country's economic freedom score improves. The lesson here, therefore, is that the greater the economic freedom, the greater the likelihood that a nation will be able to compete.

A Word about Culture

The historical development of regions and nation-states and the political, social, economic, and legal institutions that societies fashion are all shaped by culture. Although "culture" is not treated as a separate chapter in the book, one may infer from reading the chapters that this societal feature is a strong current that impacts the environment of competitiveness. In fact, the precursor to any analysis and discussion of competitiveness—the backdrop—would begin with three prime questions: Which cultural values, beliefs, and attitudes best promote competitiveness? Which ones retard the process? What can be done to *change* the culture (since sociopolitical and socioeconomic cultures can be changed)?

A number of scholars and writers have shunned "political correctness" and tackled head-on the issue of culture in political and economic development.[7] Latin America has received "case study" attention, as well,[8] with scholars such as William Ratliff who concludes, in comparing cultural and competitive factors between Latin America and Asia, that

> [i]nstitutions and paternalistic thinking that go back for centuries persist in adapted forms and today are not only not producing for the majority but dragging Latin America farther and farther behind more successfully reforming countries, particularly in Asia. Latins have it in their power to change things, if they will.[9]

His case studies of Chile, Argentina, Peru, Mexico, and Venezuela lead him to conclude that Latin American reform efforts will not produce results unless, as in the case of Asia, they stress competent and honest governance, shared growth, and basic education and health.[10]

With the Doha Round of the World Trade Organization stalled, the Free Trade Area of the Americas comatose, and the U.S. Congress divided over further free trade agreements with developing nations, the prospects for wider trade liberalization are grim. On the other hand, a free trade agreement in and of itself is not a panacea for a nation to grow, develop, and compete in a globalizing world.

It is *competitiveness* that will shape a nation's economic destiny. Although individual sectors, industries, and companies may be able to compete successfully, entire nations can do so only by planning and implementing policies, programs, and actions that transform institutions, infrastructure, and human capital.

Can Latin America compete? To transform what has been a rhetorical question to one with a bona fide answer is up to the region and its stakeholders. Almost all the problems of infrastructure, institutions, and human resources are ones that have plagued the region for a century or more. Some have been exacerbated in recent times, such as public safety, and others have been magnified in importance due to globalization and the competitive challenge from other regions. The competitive ball is in Latin America's court, and the need to return the serve is more urgent than ever.

Notes

1. Douglass C. North, *Institutional Change and Economic Performance* (Cambridge and New York: Cambridge University Press, 1990).
2. North asserts that the mix of skills and knowledge facilitated by the structure of an economy will determine the direction of change and incrementally reshape the institutional framework. For direct relevance to the Americas, see Shahid Javed Burki and Guillermo E. Perry, *Beyond the Washington Consensus: Institutions Matter* (Washington, D.C.: World Bank, 1998).
3. Hernando de Soto, *The Other Path* (New York: HarperCollins, 1989).
4. Tim Kane, Kim R. Holmes, and Mary Anastasia O'Grady, eds. *2007 Index of Economic Freedom* (Washington, D.C.: Heritage Foundation, 2007).
5. Business freedom, trade freedom, fiscal freedom, freedom from government, monetary freedom, investment freedom, financial freedom, property rights, freedom from corruption, and labor freedom.
6. Chile, Trinidad and Tobago, the Bahamas, Barbados, El Salvador, Uruguay, Jamaica, Panama, Mexico.
7. Among the most notable books on the subject are Lawrence E. Harrison, *The Central Liberal Truth: How Politics Can Change a Culture and Save It from Itself* (New York: Oxford University Press, 2006); Ronald Inglehart and Christian Welzel, *Modernization, Cultural Change, and Democracy: The Human Development Sequence* (Cambridge and New York: Cambridge University Press, 2005); Lawrence E. Harrison and Samuel P. Huntington, eds., *Culture Matters: How Values Shape Human Progress* (New York: Basic Books, 2001); David S. Landes, *The Wealth and Poverty of Nations: Why Some Are So Rich and Some So Poor* (New York: W. W. Norton, 1999); and Lawrence E. Harrison,

Who Prospers? How Cultural Values Shape Economic and Political Success (New York: Basic Books 1993).

8. Mariano Grondona, *Las Condiciones Culturales del Desarrollo* (Buenos Aires: Planeta, 1999); Enrique Krause, *Las amenazas a la democracia en América Latina* (Rosario: Fundación Internacional para la Libertad, 2003); Lawrence E. Harrison, *Underdevelopment Is a State of Mind* (Lanham, MD: Madison Books, 2000); Alvaro Vargas Llosa, *Liberty for Latin America: How to Undo Five Hundred Years of State Oppression* (New York: Farrar, Straus and Giroux, 2005); Plinio Apuleyo Mendoza, Carlos Alberto Montaner, and Álvaro Vargas Llosa, *Manual del perfecto idiota latinoamericano* (Barcelona: Plaza y Janés, 1996).

9. William Ratliff, "Latin America's Fledgling, Fumbling Democracies," *Review of Policy Research* 23, no. 2 (March 2006): 295–310.

10. William Ratliff, "Development and Civil Society in Latin America and Asia," *Annals of the American Academy of Political and Social Science* 565, no. 1 (September 1999): 91–112. Also see William Ratliff, "Get Serious, Amigos," *Hoover Digest,* 1, 2006.

Index